LEGENDS

LEGENDS

Georgians Who Lived Impossible Dreams

Gene Asher

Mercer University Press | Macon, Georgia | 2005

ISBN 0-86554-977-X | MUP/H696

© 2005 by Mercer University Press
1400 Coleman Avenue
Macon, Georgia 31207
All rights reserved

FIRST EDITION

The paper used in this publication meets the minimum
requirements of American National Standard for Information
Sciences—Permanence of Paper for Printed Library Materials,
ANSI Z39.48-1992.

Layout design by Burt and Burt Studio

Library of Congress Cataloging-in-Publication Data

CIP data are available from the Library of Congress

This book is dedicated to James A. "Jim" Hale, Zelma Turner, and Genie Certain. Without Hale's constant prodding, cajoling, and encouragement for more than three years and without Zelma's and Genie's expertise and enthusiasm in getting these columns on and off the computer *Legends* never would have been written.

Laurie, Susan and David Asher, my three children, mere tots at the time, accompanied me to many of the sporting events I covered for the *Atlanta Journal.* They not only saw some of these legends in action but their presence made my working assignments sheer joy.

ACKNOWLEDGMENTS

This book would not have been possible without the help of the University of Georgia and Georgia Tech Sports Information offices, who provided photos and clips for each article, or without the consent of *Georgia Trend Magazine,* on whose pages these articles were originally printed.

My heartfelt thanks go out to Neely Young, the publisher and editor; Susan Percy, the executive editor; Penny Alligood, art director; Millard Grimes, the publisher emeritus; and long time friend Bill Shipp whose strong recommendation got me a Trend tryout in the first place. Shipp has been a dear friend for more than fifty years. He is my daughter Susan's hero. He also is mine.

Gene Asher

CONTENTS

PREFACE

One of the first things I did when I checked into Atlanta in 1950 was write a column. That was only one of the reasons I had been imported from Charlotte. The other was to run a sports department that was in serious disarray, and I didn't get a lot done to improve it right away. Soon thereafter, I did make a move that made a difference.

I hired a student correspondent to cover athletics at the University of Georgia. That was way before the day of bureaus, which have since popped up like mushrooms around the state. Gene Asher was a one-man bureau. A boxer. A Marine. A faithful reporter. A promoter. Not all at the same time, but I will venture to say, speaking of legends, Gene Asher was a legend before his time.

As our prep editor, for years he staged the *Atlanta Journal* High School All-Star football game, as professionally done as if his name were P. T. Barnum. He had connections around this town. He knew where to go to find missing links, or whatever else might be missing. He had his heroes—Larry Lafkowitz comes to mind here—and he had his mindset.

It wasn't easy to turn him down, even when he told me one day he had a story: that an amateur boxer Olympic heavyweight champion, Pete Rademacher of Columbus, was going to fight Floyd Patterson for the championship of the world. *An amateur was going to turn pro fighting the world heavyweight champion.*

Preposterous. Except that it was Asher, and even though an old fight referee had told him, "Write that story and they'll run you out of town," I bought it.

He wrote it. They didn't run him out of town. Rademacher did fight Patterson in Seattle. He didn't win, but there has never been a title fight like it.

One day Gene came in to say he was leaving to go into the insurance business. "You are going to miss it," I said. "All those late-night hours, the overtime you don't get paid for, the thrill of writing 1-D headlines at 6:30 in the morning, the ecstasy of being all-star promoter Gene Asher."

None of my persuasion moved him, and he was on his way. But he never gave up his motivating urge to write, and he's still at it, glorifying legends of our athletics past in his flowing style. See, Ash, I told you you'd never be able to get away from it.

Furman Bisher

1996

LEE BURGE
An Horatio Alger Story

William Lee Burge could put Horatio Alger to shame. As a teenager starting in the mailroom at the old Retail Credit Company (now Equifax), Burge climbed every step in a fifty-two-year career that culminated in his selection as chairman of the board. He was named one of the "Shapers of Atlanta" back in 1976; twenty years later, at age seventy-eight, Burge continues to shape Atlanta. He is spearheading for his church (Second Ponce de Leon Baptist) the Summerhill project, solving neighborhood economic and housing problems that have existed since the construction of Atlanta-Fulton County Stadium back in 1965.

In 1936, while a student at Georgia Evening College (now Georgia State University), Burge went to work at Retail Credit and never left. He started as a mail sorter and advanced to field investigator, branch manager, regional vice president, senior vice president for marketing and sales, and president and chief executive officer before being named chairman of the board. Under Burge's twenty-one-year stint as CEO, Equifax increased its revenues 471% to $671,000,000 and its branches from 307 to 1100—worldwide. At his retirement eight years ago, he was named Board Chairman Emeritus.

While climbing the corporate ladder, Burge was out front in every civic and educational activity. He was president of the Fernbank Museum of Natural History and Chairman of the Fernbank Board of Trustees. He was campaign chairman of United Way, chairman of the United Negro College/Atlanta

University campaigns, a director of the American Red Cross, a founder of the Central Atlanta Progress, a trustee of Mercer University, a member of the state university system Board of Regents, and president of the Atlanta Kiwanis Club. Burge chaired the seventy-fifth anniversary celebration of Georgia State University and was a prime mover in the establishment of the Georgia State University Law School. He was 1988 recipient of the GSU Distinguished Alumni Award.

When he is not working on the Summerhill project or traveling with his son, Roger, daughter, Judith Lynn, and his four grandchildren, he travels the globe on educational projects for the University System of Georgia. Burge heads educational caravans to eastern and central Europe to exchange ideas with professors and administrators in higher education. "We have a lot to learn from our neighbors," Burge says. "In some places in eastern and central Europe, there is nowhere near the illiteracy we have here. Nor the discipline problem." Burge also travels the world for the university system through its Council of International Education, focusing on economic development and adult education.

At an age when most people have long retired, Lee Burge, an old World War II infantryman, is nowhere near ready to take off his pack.

JAMES H. FINCH
A Marine's Marine

In the red and gold reference book entitled Heroes of The US Marine Corps, you can find the name of Atlanta's James H. Finch, Colonel, USMCR, Retired.

In World War II, it was Finch's company that raised the flag atop Mount Suribachi on Iwo Jima, after which he was awarded the Bronze Star. In Korea, it was Finch's battalion that, under withering fire, retook Reno, Vegas, and Carson, three North Korean strong points, in one of the bloodiest battles of the war. Finch was awarded the Legion of Merit.

If there ever was a Marine's Marine, it was James H. "Bill" Finch. But his Marine Corps life was no more distinguished than his architectural life, from which he retired sixteen years ago. Finch designed Atlanta-Fulton County Stadium (he sheds no tears over its demise) and twenty-nine other professional and college sports stadiums around the country. Four years ago he received the Philip Shutze Distinguished Alumnus Award from the Georgia Tech College of Architecture.

Today, at age eighty-two, Finch is physically fit. He works out every morning with weights and walks a rapid five miles. The rest of his day is spent working on his fifteen-acre farm in Alpharetta, shoveling manure, mowing, pruning, chipping, shredding, and feeding more than 100 animals, which do not include his four house cats. "Actually," he says, "I am doing nothing constructive and loving every minute of it."

1996

Finch never was one to brag. When he was president of FABRAP (Finch, Alexander, Barnes, Rothschild and Paschal), one of the most prestigious architectural firms in the country, the only award hanging from the cream-colored walls of his modest (8' by 10') office was his diploma from the old Atlanta James L. Key Elementary School. His twenty-odd national architectural awards were kept out of sight.

Paraphrasing Will Rogers, Finch's former partner Cecil Alexander said, "Finch never met a client he liked. He was a brilliant architect but he would have been much happier in the Marine Corps."

About the dismantling of the Atlanta-Fulton County Stadium, the first stadium he designed, Finch said, "I have no regrets. There is no need to treasure it. It served its purpose, a dual stadium for football and baseball." He added, "The city got a tremendous bargain...$14,000,000. Compare that with $250,000,000...the cost of a stadium today."

Finch says the dual-stadium concept is long gone. "No two teams want to share a stadium. Each teams wants to run it. There are too many conflicts: who has concession rights? who makes management decisions? Football and baseball overlap and that guarantees conflict."

Finch was born in Atlanta in 1914. He was a baseball star at old Atlanta Tech High School, graduated with honors from Georgia Tech, and promptly left for the US Marine Corps and World War II. "I should have stayed in the Corps", he said. "I loved every minute of it. My Marines were the most unselfish people I ever knew."

After World War II, Finch came home and together with Cecil Alexander, also a Marine and native Atlantan, formed FABRAP. In 1951, he left for two years to be with the Marines in Korea. In 1967 he volunteered for duty in Vietnam but there was no demand for fifty-two-year-old Marine Reserves.

Finch stayed with FABRAP. He spent his time designing stadiums and office buildings (Coca-Cola, Southern Bell) and teaching architecture at Georgia Tech. "When I was teaching, I should have been at the office. When I was at the office, I should have been teaching."

Finch and his wife Bess, a respected ballet and water aerobics instructor, have been married for forty-five years. They have two children, Lewellyn and Anne. Anne has the lead in the Milwaukee Ballet. "I used to wonder," Finch quips, "why Bess and Anne always pranced around the house on their toes." Of Lewellyn's husband, Finch says, "He is the perfect son-in-law. He is in the whiskey business." About the only function Finch attends is the annual Marine Corps Birthday Ball. He still fits into his World War II dress uniform.

"I wear it not to boast how trim I have stayed," he said. "I am too damn cheap to buy a new uniform."

ELLIOTT H. LEVITAS
A Bundle of Perpetual Motion

As is the case with a few dedicated men, Elliott H. Levitas was at his office desk on Saturday afternoon. It was 3:30 p.m. He had been there since early morning finishing preparations for a case to be presented in Washington, DC, on Monday. Levitas, who represented Georgia's Fourth Congressional District in the US House of Representatives from 1975 to 1985, is a senior partner in the Atlanta law firm of Kilpatrick & Cody. He splits his work time between Atlanta and Washington where he specializes in cases involving the US government.

Levitas gets more accomplished than most people because he puts in more hours than most people. That is the way it has been for the venerable public servant ever since he attended old Atlanta Boys' High School.

He was Phi Beta Kappa at Emory University where he earned B.A. and J.D. degrees. He was first in his class at the Emory University Law School. A Rhodes scholar, he received an M.A. degree from Oxford University.

At age sixty-five, Levitas thinks not of retirement but of his next project. He and former US Marine Corps Commandant General P.X. Kelley are planning a victory celebration for the men and women who helped the US win the Cold War against communism and what was the Soviet Union.

Levitas is a lot like the old featherweight world boxing champion Willie Pep—a bundle of perpetual motion. Besides his law practice, he serves on the Board of Trustees of the Georgia Conservancy and the National Building

1996

Museum. He is on the National Commission on Savings and Loan to Mongolia. He serves on the Emory University Law School Council. He teaches, writes, speaks, plays tennis, and serves his state whenever called upon.

Governor Zell Miller picked Levitas to head the Georgia Hazardous Waste Management Authority to correct a serious pollution problem in Taylor County. Levitas got the job done and then abolished the Authority. It was Levitas' idea to establish the present state pollution prevention program.

Elected to the Georgia House in 1965, Levitas spent five consecutive two-year terms in the General Assembly. At the end of each term, he was named by his colleagues one of the "Ten Most Effective Members" of the state House. A six-hour video segment of Levitas' political career is being prepared for the Georgia State Archives.

As a US Congressman, Levitas was chairman of the oversight committee that served as a watchdog of the Federal Aviation Administration. Fifteen years ago, he introduced a bill which would have removed the "promotion" responsibility from the FAA and left it with only one job—insuring safety. Long before the ValuJet crash, Levitas made a statement that the FAA took drastic action "only over the corpses of the people who had been killed in the last air accident."

"ValuJet was an airline which was bringing tremendous opportunity to the traveling public. There is no reason why you cannot have low fares and high safety if the persons who are responsible are doing their jobs."

In his twenty years of public service, Levitas is most proud of what he did to protect the environment and the natural resources of the country. It was Levitas who proposed legislation that created the Chattahoochee River National Park and it was his investigative committee that blocked an attempt to roll back progress made in environmental protection and led to the resignation of thirteen top officials of the EPA.

He was narrowly defeated for election to a sixth House term in 1984 by Republican Pat Swindall, on the same day President Ronald Reagan swept the state and the district by a wide margin over Democrat Walter Mondale. But Levitas has never stopped serving the public as a private citizen.

In 1991, Levitas was chosen by *Georgia Trend* as one of Georgia's "100 most influential" people.

1997

ARCHITECT ALEXANDER
Citizen Deluxe

At age seventy-eight and "retired" three times, Cecil Alexander, listed in the World "Who's Who," and winner of every conceivable architectural and civic award, is at it again. He is the principal in the Atlanta office of the prestigious Leo A. Daly firm, one of the largest and oldest design and management firms in the United States.

Alexander's name is indelibly stamped on the Atlanta architectural scene: the forty-story First National Bank Tower, Georgia Power Company Headquarters, Phipps Plaza, Coca-Cola Company Headquarters, Southern Bell Headquarters, Atlanta Fulton County Stadium, the MARTA Five Points Station, to name only a few. He did the design work for the Georgia Medical College at Augusta and for the dormitories at West Georgia College in Carrollton.

Outside Georgia, he designed the US Pavilion at the 1982 Knoxville, Tennessee, World's Fair, the Carrier Dome at the University of Syracuse, Cincinnati Riverfront Stadium, and the Saudi Naval Headquarters in Saudi Arabia, to name only a few. So what fields are left to conquer?

"It is not a question of conquering," Alexander said. "I want to make a contribution with the years I have left. I have accumulated a great deal of experience. It would be a shame not to use it."

Alexander organized and chaired the first Citizens Advisory Committee for Urban Renewal in Atlanta. He organized and chaired the Atlanta Housing

Resources Committee, which put together 22,000 low-income housing units. He helped launch MARTA.

He was on the Board of the Atlanta Chamber of Commerce and co-chairman of the Atlanta Metropolitan Planning Committee. A contribution? Alexander founded and was first president of Resurgens Atlanta, a biracial civic club. He founded and served as president of the Georgia Foreign Trade Zone. He was vice president of the Atlanta Symphony Orchestra. He was advisor to Ivan Allen in his successful run for mayor of Atlanta. He was a campaign chairman in John Lewis' successful run for Congress and spearheaded several committees for former governors Jimmy Carter and Joe Frank Harris.

None of his volunteer work touched his heart like the day he founded and organized the Atlanta Committee to Combat Drugged and Drunken Driving. Twelve years ago last October, the Alexanders were hosting a fundraiser at their Mount Paran Road home for his alma mater, Yale University. After dinner, he was planning to drive some of his guests back to their downtown hotel. His wife, Hermi, wanted to accompany him. The drive downtown was uneventful, but on the way home, only seventy feet from his driveway, a sixteen-year-old drunken driver, flying at an estimated speed of 100 miles per hour, hit the Alexander car head-on. Hermi was killed instantly. Cecil, lucky to be alive, suffered head, leg, and arm injuries. He was hospitalized for two months and in a wheel chair for one year. The accident was used in a documentary by Gannett and shown on national television.

"Losing Hermi was the low spot in my life," Alexander said. For years afterwards, I kept telling myself what Winston Churchill said—never, never, never give up."

Two years after the accident, Cecil married an old friend, Helen Mantler. "Hermi told me once if any thing ever happens to me, marry Helen." Helen had been an actress on Broadway and a national "Junior Miss." She toured the country in Moss Hart's World War I play, "Winged Victory." In the cast were Lee J. Cobb, Red Buttons, and Mario Lanza. When the show was in Atlanta, Helen met and married Arthur Harris, founder and board chairman of Atlanta Paper Company, and later board chairman of Mead Paper and Packaging. The Harrises had two sons: Art, who covered the O. J. Simpson trial and the Centennial Park bombing for CNN, and Alex, head of Duke University's documentary studies department. While Cecil was battling in the civic arena, so was Helen. She helped form "Partners in Progress," a group working to integrate public facilities, and was the driving force behind organizing a speech school for blacks. The school is now operated by the Atlanta public school system. She is a former president of the American Jewish Committee.

On the Alexander side, Cecil's son, Doug Alexander, last year was elected to the Atlanta City Council. Cecil has two other children, Terri Milkey and Judith Augustine.

An Atlanta native, Cecil grew up in the Virginia-Highlands area on St. Charles Place. He attended Marist School where the late Marist principal and president, Rev. Vincent P. Brennan, called him and the late Bert (Jacobson) Parks "Marist's two most famous graduates."

Alexander attended Georgia Tech and M.I.T. before earning his bachelor's degree at Yale University and his master's degree in architecture at the Harvard Graduate School of Design. He joined the US Marine Corps at the start of World War II and flew sixty missions as a dive bomber pilot in the war against Japan. For gallantry against the enemy, he was awarded two Distinguished Flying Crosses.

After returning from the war, he and his Marine Corps friend, James H. "Bill" Finch, started what became one of the nation's leading architectural firms, Finch, Alexander, Barnes, Rothschild and Paschal. The firm merged with Rosser and White in 1985 and Alexander retired. One year later he unretired and spent three years as a design instructor and coordinator for continuing education at the college of architecture at Georgia Tech. He retired again before joining Portman Architects as vice president. Two years later he retired from Portman. He lasted one year before unretiring to become head of the Leo A. Daly Atlanta office. Explains Cecil, "Old architects never die, they keep designing."

Alexander will not say how long he will stay with Daly but "long enough to give them a major presence in Atlanta." The Atlanta office employs thirty people. Alexander sees trouble ahead for Atlanta. "In fifty years, there will be ten million people in the area and I don't want to be here when that happens. Traffic is a terrible problem now. Unless we get a regional method of governing, a federation of municipalities, this city will choke."

If he had it to do over again, what would he change? "I wouldn't be an architect, that's for sure. It may be an interesting profession, but it is a lousy business. Your career is in the hands of thousands of small parts.

"[Charles] Lindbergh was my hero. When he flew across the ocean, I was nine years old. All I wanted to do was build model airplanes and become an aviator. After flying for the Marine Corps, I got my commercial pilot's license. Maybe I should have flown for one of the airlines."

Luckily for the citizens of Atlanta, he didn't. Lucky then and now. His current civic project is designing a new flag for the state of Georgia.

RAYMOND G. DAVIS
Georgia's Four Star Leatherneck

LEGENDS GENE ASHER

1997

The Medal of Honor citation, presented by President Harry S. Truman to then–Lt. Col. Raymond G. Davis in a 1952 White House ceremony, reads in part:

> For conspicuous gallantry and intrepidity at the risk of his life above and beyond the call of duty as Commanding Officer of the First Battalion, Seventh Marines, First Marine Division, in action against the enemy aggressor forces in Korea, December 14, 1950.
>
> Always in the thick of combat, Lieutenant Colonel Davis led his battalion over three successive ridges in deep snow against a numerically superior enemy. Constantly inspiring and encouraging his men throughout the night, he brought his unit within 1,500 yards of a trapped and surrounded Marine Corps rifle company.
>
> Although knocked to the ground when a shell fragment struck his helmet and two bullets pierced his clothing, he arose and under withering enemy fire, fought his way forward at the head of his men until he reached the isolated Marines…He bravely led his battalion in securing the vital mountain pass from a strongly entrenched and numerically superior hostile force, carrying all his wounded with him, including 22 litter cases…Despite repeated, savage assaults by the enemy, he held the vital terrain. By his superb leadership, outstanding courage and brilliant tactical ability, Lt. Col. Davis was directly instrumental in saving the beleaguered rifle company

from complete annihilation and enabling two Marine Corps regiments to escape possible destruction…His valiant devotion to duty and unyielding fighting spirit in the face of insurmountable odds enhanced and sustained the highest traditions of the US Naval Service.

Ray Davis, a native of Fitzgerald, Georgia, rose to the rank of four-star general and served as assistant commandant of the Marine Corps. No other Marine holds as many impressive personal decorations. To list them all would require more space than allotted. They include the Navy Cross, two Distinguished Service Medals, two Silver Stars, two Legions of Merit, five Bronze Stars, and the Purple Heart.

In addition to his unsurpassed combat record in three wars—World War II, Korea, and Vietnam—he filled every one of the possible staff and command assignments over three-plus decades: G-1 (Personnel), G-2 (Intelligence), G-3 (Plans, Operations and Training), G-4 (Supply and Logistics).

General Creighton W. Abrams Jr., a career Army officer who commanded the US Military Assistance Command in Vietnam from 1968 to 1972 said, "Of the fifty or so division commanders I knew in Vietnam, General Davis had no equal. He was the best."

General Davis, now eighty-two years old and looking twenty years younger, is the only Georgian ever to become a US Marine Corps four-star general. He retired twenty-five years ago. His retirement lasted four hours—long enough for him to leave his retirement ceremony at Marine Corps Barracks, Washington, DC, board a plane at Washington National Airport for Atlanta, and report for duty as executive vice president of the Georgia Chamber of Commerce. The job lasted three years.

"It got to be too much," General Davis said. "We had 159 counties and each of them wanted a piece of my time. There were not enough hours in the day." So he resigned and formed a land development company, RGMW, in Stockbridge, Georgia, where he lives with Knox Davis, his wife of fifty years.

In the living room of General Davis' home, you feel the magnitude of his life. There are military history books, framed sayings like "Time Waits For No Man," wartime cigarette lighters encased in glass, and photographs of him with people like Billy Graham and Presidents Truman and Lyndon Johnson. A short distance away, in western Rockdale County, Davis' firm bought 300 acres of raw land. Now there is a well-kept residential community there with fifty-five houses, an eighteen-hole golf course, and eight lakes.

Like his Marine Corps days, General Davis' day begins early at 7 A.M. One day last week he was organizing a Korean American Friendship Society in the Southeast and recruiting Emory University's president William Chase, US Ambassador to Korea James T. Laney, and Korean businessman Sunny Park to assist him. That was daytime activity. The same night he met with Korean Marine Corps veterans and US Marine Corps veterans who fought in Korea to organize a show commemorating the US Marines landing at Inchon, Korea, forty-seven years ago. General Davis put together a club of Korean Marines and former US Marines. There are 300 members.

The next morning he was introducing Rockdale County's war hero, Tommy Clack, at a Republican get-together. "A day does not go by," General Davis said, "that I am not offered one or two challenges. I do not like to turn them down."

General Davis' biggest civilian challenge came when he served as chairman of the Korean War Memorial Advisory Board, which selected the sight of the Korean War Memorial (in Washington, DC, near the Lincoln Memorial, south of the Reflecting Pool, across from the Vietnam Veterans Memorial), picked the memorial design team, and raised the required funds of $23.5 million. "It was one of the few things I have spearheaded that everyone likes—even the Washington Post." Despite a near record ninety-nine-degree temperature, more than 500,000 veterans from all over America and other United Nations countries attended the July 1995 dedication, and there was not a dry eye in the crowd. The Korean War would no longer be known as the "Forgotten War" "The war never really ended," General Davis said. "We are still over there, face to face with the North Koreans. All we have is an armistice.

"When our troops came home after three years of combat, there were no parades, no celebrations. They just came home. The Memorial is a fitting tribute to all who served. In defending South Korea, US veterans of the Korean War saved a free republic which had risen from ashes to become a great nation, a world power and nation of free, enterprising people."

General Davis grew up in Atlanta, attending old Bass Junior High School and old Tech High School. His military career started at Tech High where he was named "best-drilled cadet" in the ROTC unit. At Georgia Tech, he was in the Army ROTC program, earning a commission as a second lieutenant upon graduation. He was able to swap it for a commission in the Marine Corps and the rest is history.

What's good about the Marine Corps today? "We are turning out well-rounded Marines. The Commandant has added one week to recruit training (boot camp) and that week is devoted to teaching 'values.' We don't want Marines who lie, cheat, or use drugs. We are building character. The week on 'values' is as important as the week on the rifle range."

On today's sex scandals in the military, General Davis says, "The women are as guilty as the men. It takes two to make a baby. I do not believe a boy and a girl should share the same foxhole. Male and female Marines sleeping and bathing together will not work."

General Davis' favorite subject is not the Marine Corps or his development business. It is his wife, Willa Knox Heafner Davis. "She has stood by me for fifty years, through three children and three wars. Of our first twelve years of marriage, I was overseas six years. My prime time is family time with Knox, my three children, Miles, Gil, and Willa, and my seven grandchildren."

When General Davis was division commander in Vietnam, one of his platoon leaders was son Miles. Miles was twice wounded and twice General Davis presented him with the Purple Heart.

The General has no plans to take off his pack. He hopes to continue to give birth to veterans memorials, write letters to lawmakers, and speak to Marines, civic clubs, and veterans groups all over America on the need for self-discipline and leadership. "Ray Davis is a man of action," says retired Marine Corps Lieutenant General John N. McLaughlin of Savannah, Georgia. "And he is the best combat leader the Marine Corps ever produced." Whoever said "The Marines have landed and have the situation well in hand" must have thought Ray Davis was in command.

The state of Georgia paid tribute to General Davis six years ago when Governor Zell Miller, himself a former Marine, dedicated a stretch of Georgia Highway 42 which runs from Stockbridge to Locust Grove. Governor Miller spoke of honor and of duty above and beyond the call, and with great pride proclaimed the new road the "General Ray Davis Medal of Honor Highway."

TEARIN' UP PEACHTREE AGAIN

When Sherman's Blue troops were a-marching this way;
They got to the edge of the city one day.

The men and artillery just couldn't get in
They were tearin' up Peachtree again, again.
They were tearin' up Peachtree again.

Music by Carleton Palmer, lyrics by Jack Kaplan and made famous by Phil and Nancy Erickson and their Wit's End Players

"Tearin' up Peachtree" was on the lips of most everyone who saw the Wit's End Players during their thirty-plus-year run of poking fun at Atlanta and Atlantans. The Ericksons opened their first Wit's End Cabaret in 1953 on Third Street, moved to West Peachtree Street, then Fifth Street, the Empire Suite at the old Biltmore Hotel, Peachtree Center, the old Gene and Gabe's, and finally Underground Atlanta.

"Nobody closed more places than we did," quips Phil. And nobody entertained more Atlantans and conventioneers than Phil and Nancy did with their rare brand of satire and humor. Atlantans did not just appreciate the Ericksons; they loved them.

In 1986, almost two years after closing their last club, Phil and Nancy Erickson planned a twenty-fifth anniversary show to be held at the Fox Theatre.

"Don't do it," warned Theatre of The Stars impresario Chris Manos. "The Fox is too large; the house will be half empty."

But more than 4,500 Erickson fans attended, taking every seat in the house. Phil brought in 100 of his old performers, including Dick Van Dyke, Dick's brother Jerry Van Dyke, and noted New York cabaret pianist Bobby Short. The show lasted three hours. Dick Van Dyke was M.C., Jerry played the banjo, and, of course, Short sang and played the piano.

The critics raved. Banner headlines read, "Wit's End Show Socko!"

"It was the highlight of my career," Phil said.

Today, Phil and Nancy Erickson, at age seventy-five, are retired and living in a Sandy Springs condominium. Phil suffered a stroke one year ago and neither he nor his wife Nancy has performed since. Phil's speech is normal but his balance is impaired. He has difficulty walking. Nancy is his fulltime nurse. Phil spends most days with his vast stamp collection and reminiscing with his theater memorabilia from the past forty-five years.

Phil's career surfaced in Atlanta in 1949 when he and Dick Van Dyke formed a dynamic comedy duo called the "Merry Mutes." They played the Paradise Room of the old Henry Grady Hotel (where the Peachtree Plaza stands today), a see-and-be-seen place frequented by out-of-towners and Atlantans alike. Their production equipment consisted of a record player that played the old 78s of Bing Crosby, Mary Martin's "Wait 'Till the Sun Shines, Nelly," and Mozart's "Figaro." The comedians did lip-sync and pantomime.

The "Merry Mutes" were so successful that they were on the wanted list of every television station in Atlanta. It was not long before they would be seen on WSB-TV, WAGA-TV and old WCON-TV. The TV run lasted until 1954 when the duo split. Van Dyke got a role in the Broadway musical "Bye Bye Birdie" and went to New York, and Phil stayed in Atlanta and organized the Wit's End Players.

"It was a great break for Dick," Phil said, "one I viewed with mixed emotions. On the one hand, I hated to lose him and our act but on the other hand, I was overjoyed. You don't get many chances in this business and when a Broadway opportunity comes along, you grab it. Dick had enormous talent as a comedian and an actor."

In a recent telephone conversation from his Malibu, California, home, Van Dyke said, "Phil Erickson put me in show business. I was working at a Danville, [Illinois,] radio station. He convinced me to quit and go to Atlanta with him. We had a five-year run at the old Henry Grady and I enjoyed every minute of it. Phil taught me everything. I never worked with a better partner or a more caring human being."

Of Phil's wife, Van Dyke said, "Nancy was a star in her own right. She not only had talent; she had the most sparkling personality of anyone I have ever known." Phil and Nancy's acting career started in the drama class at Danville High School in Illinois. Two of their classmates were Van Dyke and Short.

At the Wit's End, Phil was the producer, performer and creator of his five-person satirical shows. Two of his writers were Jack Kaplan, now a Hollywood producer, and Terry Kay, now an Atlanta novelist.

Erickson was the first to integrate the Atlanta stage. At the Wit's End, he had a black dishwasher, Sally Street, who was so good at her job that he promoted her to hat check girl. "She charmed our customers," Phil recalls, "so I thought, why not put her in the show? She had never been on stage before but once she got up there she stayed for fifteen years."

In one of the shows, "Cleopatra or Nobody Likes a Smart Asp," there was a take-off on the TV show "To Tell the Truth." It was during the year Lester Maddox was giving out axe handles at his old Pickrick restaurant to protest integration. When the show opened, the spotlight identified the first two women, who said, "My name is Mrs. Fester Maddox." When the spotlight shined on Sally Street, her line, "I pass," brought down the house.

"We were the first nightclub in the South to integrate," Erickson recalled. "I was not a crusader. Sally had talent. We gradually gave her bigger parts in the show. She could sing and she was funny."

Erickson's Wit's End Players, whether at the Fifth Street location or the ornate Empire Suite, drew blacks as well as whites, tuxedo-clad clients and customers in jeans. Putting together a cabaret show is a grinding, stressful business but to Phil and Nancy, it was fun and a labor of love. Everyone seemed to be pulling together. Even the audience was congenial, although some were in mink and some in polyester.

"If I had life to live over again," Phil said," I would not change a thing. If I die tomorrow it will be with a smile on my face. I have had fifty-four years of marital bliss. I have four wonderful children. I have friends in every social and economic strata. I am truly blessed.

"Happiness is not what happens to you; it is your attitude about what happens to you."

If Phil had life to live over again maybe there would be one thing he would change. He always said he would like to pop in on one of those lavish Christmas parties on West Paces Ferry Road where the Caddies, Lincolns, and Mercedeses were parked out front. "We would tell the host one of his guests hired us. Then we would do our act. Wouldn't that have been wild? The host would spend the rest of the year trying to find out which one of his guests hired us."

The love Atlantans feel for Phil and Nancy was demonstrated four years ago when more that 100 persons attended their fiftieth wedding anniversary party, given by sons James and Steve and daughters Kristen and Shari. Van Dyke sent a video and Short made a special song audiocassette.

The Wit's End Players may be gone but the name, with a slight variation, lives. Phil's sons founded Wit's End Productions, a corporate audiovisual firm in Atlanta. Like their parents, their business is "Socko!" Revenues are in the millions.

A COACH WITH
NO CHANCE TO WIN

Whether or not Johnny Leonard Griffith could have been a top-notch, major college football coach, no one will ever know. In his three years at the University of Georgia, he never had a chance. What is crystal clear is that he is and always has been a gentleman, a straight shooter, a class act.

In 1961, when he became Georgia's head coach, he was saddled with a staff he inherited from his predecessor, James Wallace Butts who had been fired, for which he was extremely bitter. It was common knowledge on the University of Georgia gridiron and among certain alumni that the loyalty Griffith had from some of his assistants was something less than desirable.

Then there was the "Story of a College Football Fix" in which *The Saturday Evening Post* alleged that Butts, who was allowed to remain on the scene as Athletic Director, gave team secrets to Alabama coach Paul "Bear" Bryant before the Georgia-Alabama football game in 1963. Alabama won the game 35-0, and Butts and Bryant won a libel suit from *Post* in a dramatic eleven-day trial in the US District Court of Georgia, seated in the old Post Office building in Atlanta.

About the game, Terry Scott, who played first-string guard for the Bulldogs, said, "Alabama backs knew where to run and where not to run. They knew who our weakest defensive backs were and that is where they threw passes. Whether Butts gave information to Bryant or not, I certainly do not know. But if information was not given, Alabama would have won anyway. Alabama had the best team and was superbly prepared."

In three seasons at Georgia (1961–63), Griffith won ten games. He was replaced at the end of the 1963 season by coach Vince Dooley.

Concludes, Scott, "There was no way Griffith could have won at Georgia. There were too many Butts people on the coaching staff and few of them were pulling for Griffith. Dissension was out in the open and all the players knew it."

Says Larry Rakestraw, Griffith's record-setting quarterback for three years, "No one could have been successful in that atmosphere. Some of the players were more loyal to Butts than to Griffith. They were not 100 percent dedicated."

Highly respected assistant coach, Bill Hartman, (not on Griffith's staff,) a longtime friend of Coach Butts, said "Griffith did not have a fair chance. He coached under the poorest of circumstances. Some of his assistant coaches thought they knew more about football than Griffith did and they shared that feeling with other staff members as well as alumni. I never would have taken a head coaching job without the right to pick my own staff. Johnny stepped into a bad situation at best.

"If Griffith was evaluated on his record, you would have to rate him low. But you also would have to consider the circumstances. And I will tell you this: I never have seen a more conscientious worker," Hartman said.

If his previous coaching experience could be a criterion, with a level playing field, Griffith may well have succeeded. In four years as head coach at South Georgia College, his team won four Georgia Junior College championships and went to four Bowl games. When he left Georgia, Griffith went into the insurance business for nine months. But he missed coaching and was delighted when he was offered a job on the staff of Coach Bobby Dodd at Georgia Tech. Griffith graduated from Georgia in 1950, and some Bulldog diehards considered Griffith a traitor when he accepted Dodd's offer but what they did not know was that Griffith took the job on the condition he would not recruit, or coach when Tech played Georgia.

After two years at Tech, Griffith left coaching permanently. He went into the construction and crushed stone business and took a company that was doing $2,000,000 in sales to $40,000,000. He headed Davidson Mineral, a division of Koppers International. Griffith sees a great similarity between coaching a football team and heading a business enterprise.

"They are both competitive. You have to know what your opponents are doing and how they are doing it. And you have to constantly motivate sales people and staff just as you have to consistently motivate players and assistant coaches."

Today Griffith is retired. He and his wife of fifty years, the former Dorothy Cowart, split their time between Duluth and Saint Simons where they have homes. There is little spare time for Johnny, who is constantly involved in organizing, promoting, and playing in charitable golf tournaments, as well as chairing the Georgia Sports Hall of Fame.

Johnny is age seventy-three, Dot seventy. They have five children: Susan, forty-six, who works at the University of Georgia alumni office; Buzzy, forty-four, and Robert, thirty-two, who like their dad went into the crushed stone business in Marietta; Ginger, thirty-nine, an elementary school teacher; and Georgia, thirty-six, who has gone into business for herself.

In the evenings, Johnny and Dot Griffith reminisce: how they met on the University of Georgia campus…their fiftieth wedding anniversary last January…Johnny as a University of Georgia freshman player, touching the football for the first time in 1946 and promptly setting two school records…as a coach in 1963 when his Bulldogs shocked a heavily favored University of Miami, 31-14. That night at Miami, his quarterback, Rakestraw, completed twenty-five passes for Orange Bowl, University of Georgia, and NCAA records.

True freshmen are expected to break into the Bulldog lineup this season but if Griffith was on the NCAA rules committee, it would not happen. "I don't think freshmen are ready for major college football, either physically or mentally. The coaches are on the hot seat to win and that pressure filters down to the players. Freshmen are not ready for that. They need time to adjust academically as well as athletically."

Griffith was born May 27, 1924 in Crawfordville, Georgia. He grew up in Atlanta where he was a standout halfback on coach R. L. "Shorty" Doyal's Boys' High football team in 1942. He served his country in the US Navy during World War II, after which he entered the University of Georgia. As a freshman and third-string halfback in 1946, he ran only one play. It went for eighty-nine yards and a touchdown against Furman University. It stands in the UGA records as the longest touchdown run from scrimmage and gives Griffith the highest single game rushing average in UGA football history. Griffith transferred to South Georgia College in 1947, scored twelve touchdowns, and won "Little All-America" honors. He went back to Georgia to earn his four-year degree.

When he landed the University of Georgia head coaching job in 1961, Douglas, Georgia, home of South Georgia College, held a "Johnny Griffith Night." South Georgia College president Will Smith said, "Johnny gave South Georgia College its best football as a player and as a coach. He was the finest coach this college ever had."

When Dooley arrived at Georgia to replace Griffith, Johnny met with his successor and went over the recruiting list and varsity squad, giving Dooley the strengths and weaknesses of each player. He showed great love and concern for Georgia's football future, even though he would no longer be a part of it.

Griffith has a lot of love for his alma mater, his family, friends, and particularly his late parents, Fred and Eloise Griffith, the biggest supporters and best role models he ever had.

THE BROTHERS GROSS
A Miracle

Some people give until it hurts; Alex and Ben Gross, Holocaust survivors, give until it feels good.

It is not the millions of dollars they have donated to charities during the past thirty-five years. It is their personal involvement in community life, their decision to enter the arena of public service and make a better life for mankind.

More than 40,000 families annually use their lake at Fieldstone for picnics, swimming, boating, or just digging in the sand. The lake has served Masonic lodges, civic clubs, Rockdale County employees, police auxiliaries, weddings, and bar mitzvahs. Gross Lake has been the site of charitable fundraisers. It has hosted the Shakespearean Festival, rodeos, and barbecues.

Give until it feels good. In between building 4,000 homes in Conyers and some 40,000 more along with golf courses, lakes, and shopping centers elsewhere in Georgia and the southeastern United States, the brothers Gross have made time to speak to Kiwanians, Rotarians, veterans' organizations, and students in middle school, high schools, and universities. The subjects are the same— "Surviving the Holocaust" and "What It Means to Live in a Land of Freedom."

Give until it feels good. Ben worked his way through the chairs of the Georgia Home Builders Association; Alex chaired the Israel Bonds Committee for Greater Atlanta. Ben brought soccer into the lives of most everyone in Rockdale County, organizing leagues for men, women, and children. Thanks to the generosity of the Grosses, there are sixteen soccer fields in Rockdale County with seventy or more teams practicing or playing league games every day.

Until last year, when Ben suffered a stroke and Alex a heart attack, one-third of their fourteen-hour workday was spent serving their fellow man. Today, seventy-six-year old Ben and sixty-eight-year old Alex still get to their Atlanta Suburbia Estates office in Conyers at 8 A.M. But they rarely work past 8 P.M. And sometimes they are home in time for dinner.

Gross real estate developments turned the one-horse town of Conyers (6,000 residents) into a thriving community of 50,000. And when you consider where these native Czechoslovakians started, it is nothing short of a miracle.

At age thirteen, Alex was in the Nazi concentration camp at Auschwitz—headed for the gas chamber. When he was liberated by the US Army, he was skin and bones, scarcely weighing fifty pounds. Once liberated, Alex was sent to Russian-held territory. Friends smuggled him on a boat bound for Great Britain where he found a home in a Jewish orphanage. There he was fed and clothed.

Ben had a third-grade education. The Nazis incarcerated him in another death camp, where he was liberated by the Soviets in 1944. Ben fled the Russians in 1944 and with the help of an uncle made his way to the United States. The uncle brought Ben to his home in Pittsburgh, Pennsylvania.

Their parents were not as fortunate. Their mother died in a gas chamber and their father suffocated on a train of boxcars headed for Auschwitz. Recalls Ben, "Our brothers and sisters lived. The Nazis killed our cousins, nieces and nephews."

Emaciated at Auschwitz, Alex soon looked like a human being again. He learned to play soccer at the orphanage and four years later was the British Isle's soccer sensation. In the Edinburgh Games, he received the famed Scotland Blue Ribbon award.

Meanwhile, Ben, who had been working in a Pittsburgh butcher shop, saved enough money to bring Alex to his Pittsburgh home. From butchering, Ben went into home building, first in Pittsburgh, then in Ohio.

Alex was working when the Korean War started. "It was payback time," Alex said. "I enlisted in the US Army and served in the intelligence corps. In one way," Alex recalled, "the Army was like Auschwitz. They gave me a serial number. Only this time it was on a dog tag, not tattooed on my arm."

When the Korean War ended, Alex used his G.I. bill to attend Ohio State University, where he took courses in building and the development of communities. One of his professors advised him to go to the southeast to develop new communities, so after completing his studies, Alex moved to Atlanta and Ben went with him.

Their first projects were in Conyers. First there was Fieldstone, where there are now 2000 Gross-built homes, gardens, lakes, and a golf course. Next came Salem Village, Salem Lake, and Surrey Trails.

The Grosses manage property in Rockdale, Newton, Houston, Spalding, and DeKalb Counties. They put together sixty lakes in Rockdale County, eighteen subdivisions in Conyers and Houston County, plus shopping centers, golf courses, and office parks. This year the brothers sold 316 residential units to the Flornoy Company in Columbus and they sold John Wieland enough land to build 500 more homes in Rockdale County.

"We are cutting back," Alex said. By the end of the year the twelve-hour workdays will be history. I will continue to get up at 5:30 A.M. for my workouts at the Atlanta Sporting Club but I am going to take more vacations and have more fun."

It has been an incredible journey, and no one is more aware of it than Ben and Alex.

At Auschwitz, thirteen-year-old Alex was standing in a line headed for the gas chamber. An old man nearby walked up to him and whispered in his ear in Yiddish, "Tell him you are eighteen years old."

Moments later, a bull-necked Nazi guard looked down at Alex and growled, "How old are you?"

"I am eighteen," Alex replied.

The guard looked at him closely and then snapped, "Then get out of this line and take the line to the left." Instead of being gassed and dying, Alex became a slave laborer and lived.

If strength comes from adversity, Alex Gross may be the strongest man alive. While at Auschwitz, he learned of his parents' deaths.

After he moved to Atlanta, tragedy struck twice. First, his wife Linda (they had just celebrated their twentieth wedding anniversary) became a victim of a rape-murder. Then his only son was killed in a farming accident at age fourteen.

Faith has kept Alex going.

What has given him the most satisfaction?

"Finding my wife Daisy [his wife of one year] and the love I have for her and my daughters Etta [thirty-eight], Stephanie [thirty-three], and Robin [thirty-two]."

Ben and his wife, Sylvia, have been married for forty-six years. They have four children: Cindy (forty-three), Howard (forty-one), Marcy (forty), and Michael (thirty-eight). Howard and Michael have their own building businesses.

You want the right to burn the American flag? You had better stay clear of the Gross brothers. "We have more freedom than any people in the world", says Ben, "and many of us take it for granted. In America, you are free to go as you please, say what you want. In America, you push a button and you get ice. You push another button and your garage door opens. You can attend the church or synagogue of your choice. You can walk the streets, day or night without fear of being arrested. Burn the American flag? For people who want to do that, I would hang them. I thank God every day that I am an American. The flag is our precious jewel and no one should forget it."

Next to God, America, and his family, Ben's favorite love is soccer. He started playing at age six and never stopped until he suffered a stroke. In 1958, he brought the Manchester, England, soccer team to Conyers for an exhibition. He developed eleven youth soccer fields complete with sprinkler systems. He provided uniforms, shoes, and balls for all the teams, plus uniforms for coaches and referees. He is one of thirteen members of the Georgia Soccer Hall of Fame.

Besides being a past president of the Georgia State Home Builders Association, Ben has been president of the Metropolitan Atlanta Home Builders and the Rockdale Home Builders, and an eight-time director of the National Home Builders.

Alex has lectured at Emory University, Mercer, Vanderbilt, and the Universities of Miami and Alabama. He holds an honorary law degree from Emory. He has served on the Board of the Atlanta Jewish Federation. He is a past president of the Association of Holocaust Survivors and has been honored for extraordinary service to B'nai B'rith, Rotary, and Kiwanis.

Although the stroke has curtailed Ben's speaking engagements, Alex plans to continue speaking to middle schools, high schools, and colleges whenever he is invited.

Like brother Ben, Alex gives until it feels good.

THE FABULOUS PHANTOM
OF FITZGERALD

In 1948, James Lauren Hargrove was the most sought-after prep football player in America. His name was on the lips of every college coach from Maine to California and every fan from Rabun Gap to Tybee Light. At 6'1", 190 pounds, and gifted with balance, quickness, and world-class speed (9.7 seconds for 100 yards), Hargrove scored 450 points in three seasons, a national record. He was elusive and versatile. He ran inside and outside, kicked off, kicked extra points, caught passes, returned punts, and played defense.

He carried Fitzgerald High School to the Georgia State Class A championship—its first—and in the state title game against favored Decatur High School, he scored two touchdowns and kicked the game-winning extra point. Hargrove was the first Georgian named to the All-America High School team. To the southeast Georgia town of Fitzgerald, and more specifically to the home of Mr. and Mrs. A. J. Hargrove, coaches came calling—in droves. There was Frank Leahy of perennial national collegiate champion Notre Dame. There were representatives of the University of Michigan, Southern California, Texas, Georgia Tech, and, of course, the University of Georgia, to name only a few. "Lauren Hargrove is the best prospect I have ever seen," Georgia coach Wallace Butts told Victor Smith of the *Fitzgerald Herald-Leader*. "If we cannot make an All-American out of him, they better get a new set of coaches at Georgia."

Hargrove signed with Georgia, a decision he soon came to regret. Not only did he not make All-American, he did not make the All-Southeastern Conference team. At best he shared a starting role and in his senior year did not get in the game against Georgia Tech. This is not to say he did not have his moments. In 1950, as a sophomore right halfback, he scored a touchdown against Texas A & M in the Presidential Cup Bowl game, and in 1951 he raced seventy-nine yards for a touchdown against Auburn. In the Auburn game, in the first half, he gained 167 yards. But in the second half, he was a permanent fixture on the team bench. He did not get back into the game.

To say the "Fabulous Phantom of Fitzgerald," so named by University of Georgia publicist Dan Magill, did not live up to advance billing, would be a masterpiece of understatement. The $64,000 question is why.

Some football practice observers say it was because Hargrove was constantly browbeaten by Coach Butts, so much so that he lost confidence in himself. In what may have been a shot at pushing Hargrove, Coach Butts blatantly questioned his desire to compete when the going got tough.

Others, like longtime coach Bill Hartman, said, "It was either a lack of coaching or a lack of attitude, I do not know which. I do know Hargrove was given every opportunity to excel." Edwin Pope, sports editor of the Miami Herald who covered Georgia football practices for the old United Press in the 1950s, said, "Hargrove was the best running prospect I ever saw at Georgia. And that includes [Charley] Trippi and [Frankie] Sinkwich."

Comments Dan Magill, the University of Georgia sports publicity director in the 1950s, "Hargrove was hurt a lot. When he did play, he did not get the ball much because of Coach Butts' system. He was a right halfback and most of the ball carrying was done by the left halfback. We threw a lot of passes in those days and most of them went to our ends, not our backs." Today, at age sixty-seven (he looks much younger), Hargrove is retired from the Ford Steel Company where he was a salesman and sales manager for twenty-seven years. He lives in Dunwoody, Georgia. He is the father of three children: John, thirty-three, a student at Life College; Lauren, thirty, a student at the University of Georgia dental school; and Ashley, twenty-eight, a Wofford College graduate who is studying for the CPA exam. Hargrove is not reluctant to reminisce about his Georgia football career:

> I chose Georgia because my brother Billy was there. Some people said I would do better at Georgia Tech playing for a father figure like Bobby Dodd. But Coach Dodd did not have enough money in his budget to pay for all the tutoring I would have needed.
>
> Playing football for Coach Butts at Georgia was like going through Marine Corps boot camp, probably worse. We did not do well in those years [1950–52] because we left our game on the practice field. We stayed physically beat up. It seemed like we scrimmaged every day, sometimes on Sundays. Game day was a relief.
>
> I was hurt much of the time because of the heavy scrimmaging. I separated my shoulder once, fractured my leg, had several teeth knocked out, and my nose broken several times—all in scrimmages.

It was a frustrating four years. I never got the ball enough. It was like the Auburn game when I gained all those yards in the first half and did not play in the second half. I am convinced that if I could have run the ball twenty or thirty times a game, I would have scored two or three touchdowns a game.

In my senior year, I suffered an ankle injury. After that, Coach Butts would start people in my place, people that I could outrun going backwards.

The fact that Hargrove did not get the ball often angered fans not just from Fitzgerald but from every nook and cranny in the state. Letters to the athletic office poured in, asking for an explanation. The Fabulous Phantom became so discouraged that once he left school and headed to the University of Miami where he planned to enroll. He was intercepted en route by Magill who, Hargrove said, "told me that Coach Butts promised things would be different for me if I would come back to Georgia." Hargrove returned to Athens, which he views as another mistake.

The first day I got back, we had a scrimmage. I finally got the ball. In fact, I got it almost every down. And each time I did the defense knew exactly where I was going. It was like putting your head into a meat grinder. But the biggest blow of all was the final game of my career against Georgia Tech. I never got off the bench. At Fitzgerald, playing for Coach [Earl] Wheby, I loved football. At Georgia, I came to hate it.

Explains Hartman, who was Georgia's backfield coach then and is today's kicking coach, "A lot of players are superstars in high school. In college, they are competing with players just as fast and quick at they are. All the college players have impressive credentials or they would not have been offered a scholarship."

Says Hargrove, "If I had my life to live over, I would go to Harvard University, play football and try to get the best education possible.

"I would never smoke the first cigarette or take the first drink."

Although he may never be considered a Bulldog immortal, Hargrove will forever live in the hearts and memories of South Georgia prep football fans.

Last October, at the Fitzgerald (Georgia) Centennial, among the natives honored were Medal of Honor winner General Raymond G. Davis, USMC (Ret.), former Brandeis University president Morris Abram and Valdosta football coaching immortal Wright Bazemore. As they were introduced, each honoree received a standing ovation. No one received more applause that the Fabulous Phantom of Fitzgerald, honoree James Lauren Hargrove.

LIPSHUTZ
Presidential Advisor

It was Christmas Eve in 1974. I had stopped by the Atlanta law offices of Robert J. "Bob" Lipshutz to wish him a happy holiday season. I was not prepared for what followed.

"Sit down," Bob said, "I have something to tell you. Jimmy Carter is going to run for president."

"President of what," I asked.

"President of the United States," Bob replied, matter-of-factly. And, of course, he is going to win!"

What is happening, I thought incredulously. Has Bob Lipshutz, one-time Cadet Colonel and Commanding Officer of the University of Georgia ROTC (cavalry), past president of the Temple, Atlanta's largest and oldest Reform Jewish Congregation and former president of the Atlanta B'Nai B'rith Lodge, gone absolutely mad? He is telling me our governor is going to be president of the United States? He is not only telling me, he is practically assuring me! So it is with Bob Lipshutz, who went on to become campaign treasurer and President Carter's Counsel and one of his most trusted advisors. Lipshutz rarely speaks without knowing what he is talking about. Maybe that is why President Carter said, "In picking a campaign treasurer and legal advisor, I needed someone whose reputation was absolutely pure and whose track record was flawless."

Today, Lipshutz, who was President Carter's personal and legal counsel for three years, is senior partner of the prestigious Atlanta law firm of Lipshutz, Frankel, Grenblatt & King. When he is not practicing law or spending time with Betty, his wife of twenty-four years, he is heavily involved at the Carter Center where he is on the Board of Trustees, performs legal services, and serves on the advisory committee of the Jimmy Carter Library. He is also a Trustee of Inner Harbour Hospital in Douglas County.

Lipshutz, whose grandparents fled repression in Czarist Russia, is a native Atlantan. He attended old Atlanta Boys' High School and the University of Georgia, where he obtained his undergraduate and law degrees. After serving three years as an officer in the US Army during World War II, Lipshutz came home and opened his first law office. As an office-opening gift, his father, the late Alex Lipshutz, gave him a framed photograph of Bernard Baruch, advisor to Presidents Roosevelt and Truman. His father's gift was a harbinger of his future.

Lipshutz was a major player in the Camp David Accords and Israeli-Egyptian Peace Treaty. He also spent many nights at his White House desk helping to implement "affirmative action," which he says "made us a nation with equal opportunity for everyone, regardless of race, sex, religion, or national origin."

At a B'nai B'rith dinner at which Lipshutz was presented the coveted Distinguished Service Award, then Governor Carter said, "Bob, you helped guide and shape my life for the better. As a close and intimate friend, you have been a conscience and inspiration for my administration as governor and my campaign for president. I love you and Betty."

Along with God, duty, and country, family has been foremost in Lipshutz's life. When his first wife, Barbara, died twenty-six years ago, Lipshutz had a son in his freshman year at college, two daughters in high school and one in middle school.

Now, his son, Randy, is a partner in the Lipshutz law firm. His daughter Judy is an administrator as the Communicable Disease Center in Atlanta; daughter Wendy is a social worker in domestic violence at Atlanta Jewish Family Services, daughter Debbie is a family therapist in Philadelphia; stepson Bobby Rosenberg is a successful attorney in Washington, DC; and stepdaughter Nance Rosenberg, Ph.D., is a professor at Fordham University. Lipshutz has five grandchildren.

Lipshutz is seventy-four years old. His pace has not slowed. He is at his law desk five days a week and continues to involve himself in religious, political and civic endeavors. Explaining that involvement, he says,

> My interest in public affairs is based upon a deep-felt historical per-spective and appreciation for America and all that our system of government means. Only in America have we enjoyed religious freedom, freedom to choose our own vocation or profession, freedom to choose the place where we might live, freedom to fully educate our children, an equal right to simple justice and the ultimate right to life itself.
>
> No one of us alone can assure the success of our society, or that our democratic system of government will survive and flourish. But it must not fail because as individuals we did not make the effort.

DAN MAGILL
My Bulldog

Quick now, who convinced the starting pitchers in Game Two of the 1941 world series to manage opposing teams in a Georgia high school All-Star baseball game? Who brought in Andy Griffith to do his famous "What It Was Was Football" at halftime of a University of Georgia home football game? Who is the winningest tennis coach in NCAA Division I history?

If you answered Daniel Hamilton "Dan" Magill Jr. to all of the above you are 100 percent correct.

It is the same Dan Magill who holds the only record known to man for playing the longest time (one hour and fifty-eight minutes) for a single point in a state championship table tennis match and the same Dan Magill who won eight southern championship tennis matches in age brackets thirty-five to seventy-five.

And that is not all. It is also the same Dan Magill who tagged former Bulldog football players Lauren Hargrove "The Fabulous Phantom of Fitzgerald," Ronnie Jenkins "The Ebullin Embalmer," and Peter Rajecki, a place kicker from Germany, "The Bootin' Teuton." Known as "Mr. Versatility" and "Mr. Bulldog," Magill has done it all. He has been batboy, player, coach, recruiter, Bulldog Club organizer, assistant athletic director, writer, promoter, and, yes, even gardener. He received a commendation from the Garden Club of America for his contribution to horticulture. Magill, who retired two years ago after a fifty-nine-year association with University of Georgia athletics, continues to live in Athens and serve his

1997

alma mater. Last month he hosted a Bulldog alumni tour of England, and when he is not at his Athens home, where he has raised 800 azaleas, he is speaking to Bulldog groups in nearby areas or working as curator of his NCAA Tennis Hall of Fame. He plays tennis three times a week at the university's Dan Magill Tennis Complex and walks briskly two miles every morning in his neighborhood. Magill is seventy-six years old but you would never know it. His durability on the tennis courts usually exceeds his opponents, many of whom are half his age. If Bernard McFadden were alive, Magill would put him to shame. His youthful looks belie his age. The only connection he has with seventy-six is his spirit. "I enjoy what I do," he says. "If I get involved with something that gets me down, I get away from it. There are many pleasant activities and careers in life. You have to find them and not get bogged down in something you do not enjoy. I think I have led a charmed life."

Charmed life, indeed. Since his days as a seven-year-old at the Athens YMCA, Magill, an Athens native, has done what he wanted. He played tennis, ping-pong, baseball, and basketball, and he swam. While in high school, he was batboy for the University of Georgia baseball team and manager of the UGA tennis courts. As a student at Georgia, he was on the varsity swimming and tennis teams and was a jack-of-all-trades assistant to coach Harry Mehre's football teams.

He joined the US Marine Corps in World War II and attained the rank of captain.

At the *Atlanta Journal,* where he served as prep sports editor and sports promotion director, he helped put Georgia high school sports on the map. He covered the state, writing feature stories about star athletes from Rabun Gap to Tybee Light, from Rossville to Omega and Fort Oglethorpe to Nashville, Georgia.

He promoted prep All-Star football and baseball games. His build up of "The Fabulous Phantom from Fitzgerald," Hargrove, in the 1948 high school All-Star Game helped draw a football crowd of 25,000. To get his baseball All-Star game off the ground, he enticed the late Spud Chandler to manage one team and Whitlow Wyatt to manage the other. Chandler, a former Bulldog and ace of the New York Yankees pitching staff, had dueled with Wyatt, a native of Buchanan, Georgia, and ace of the old Brooklyn Dodgers pitching staff, in the World Series. (Memo to Dodger fans: Wyatt won 2-1).

Of all his innovations and promotions, none compares with his founding of the Georgia Bulldog Club and turning a nondescript University of Georgia tennis program into a veritable giant. In the early 1950s, Georgia football was at its lowest ebb. Victories were few and far between and fan enthusiasm went down faster than the 1929 stock market.

Enter Superman Magill. He traveled the state from one end to the other, rallying alumni and organizing Bulldog Clubs in almost half of Georgia's 159 counties. For a mere pittance, you could attend your own Bulldog Club meeting and shake hands and personally converse with head coach Wally Butts and players like All-Americans Harry Babcock and John Carson, and future NFL stars Dick Yelvington, Marion Campbell, Claude Hipps, Bobby Walston, and Art DeCarlo.

In 1950, at some games, you could have fired a howitzer in Sanford Stadium and not hit a soul. With the advent of the Bulldog Clubs, most home games became sellouts. Thank you, Mr. Magill. When Magill took command of the Georgia tennis team in 1954, it was a nonentity. During the next thirty-four years, his teams won a record thirteen SEC outdoor championships, eight SEC indoor titles and two NCAA national crowns.

His players won five national collegiate individual championships. He brought the NCAA tournament to Athens eighteen times, including thirteen consecutively from 1977–89. He built a new tennis complex, considered the finest on-campus tennis facility in the country. There are twelve outdoor courts, four indoor courts, a grandstand, and private boxes. The complex will seat 5,000, and is sold out for most collegiate matches.

It was Magill who convinced country music legend Kenny Rogers, who lives near Athens, to build a Collegiate Tennis Hall of Fame on the University of Georgia campus. For Magill's efforts, the entire tennis facility was officially named "The Dan Magill Tennis Complex."

Says University of Georgia Athletic Director Vince Dooley, "I do not know of anyone who has contributed more to our sports program. Dan Magill has given us his time, his commitment, his life. He is truly the greatest Bulldog of all." In his three decades as Georgia's tennis coach, Magill posted a 706–183 won-lost record, making him the winningest coach ever in NCAA Division I.

Says Bulldog immortal Bill Hartman, an assistant football coach for more than fifty years, "Some coaches understand the game but are not able to teach or communicate. Dan did both, injecting humor when needed and the needle when needed. He had a heart for the game. His players were inspired by his love and commitment, his caring and his concern. Dan was a winner, not only as a coach but more importantly as a human being. He gave his players all the credit."

When Magill was simultaneously serving as assistant athletic director in charge of sports information, tennis coach, Bulldog club chieftain, and assistant to the coach of the swimming team, he was introduced at one Southeastern Conference meeting by former Bulldog assistant football coach and Alabama athletic director Hootie Ingram, as "a one-man athletic department."

Says Magill, "I loved it all. If I had been a wealthy man, I would have worked for nothing. I had something money cannot buy—happiness." Magill did not work for "nothing" but he did work for $100 weekly when he was hired in 1949 as Director of Sports Information. When he retired two years ago, he was being paid $50,000 annually, a mere pittance considering the variety of jobs he was handling and the glory he was bringing to the university and its alumni.

Where today directors of sports information have assistants for every sport, Magill was indeed a one-man show. He wrote news releases, interviewed coaches and players, set up radio and television shows, managed the press boxes, kept statistics for all sports, edited the media guide, and attended football practice daily both in the fall and in the spring.

During the years of Coach Butts, the football practices were long and grueling. They started in mid-afternoon and often did not stop until it was pitch-black dark. Coach Butts was a perfectionist. He wanted it done right and he would run plays in scrimmages again and again until they were executed with precision. He would rant, rave, yell, and scream at his players if the plays did not go according to plans. Most of the players would have chosen combat rather than face Coach Butts' wrath.

One of Magill's fondest memories came during practice in the fall of 1950. Coach Butts was trying to spring his ace halfback, Zippy Morocco, loose on an off-tackle play. But some defender would sneak across the line of scrimmage and throw Morocco for a loss. "Run it again!" Butts bellowed. Again some defender would find a way to get across the scrimmage line and dump Morocco for a loss.

Coach Butts could not figure out where they were getting through. "Damn it!" Coach Butts hollered, "We are going to get it right or we will stay here all night."

On the next down a redshirt freshman named Ed Worley came from nowhere to smear Morocco for another loss. Coach Butts exploded. He checked off the assignments and figured there was no way Worley could have gotten through to make the tackle. Angered beyond description, Coach Butts charged across the field, met Worley eyeball to eyeball and bellowed, "All right, Worley, where did you come from?" Worley looked Coach Butts squarely in the eye and said in his soft, southern drawl, "ELLIJAY."

Among the many honors Magill has won is his induction last year with the inaugural class into the University of Georgia's "Circle of Honor." It is the highest recognition a former athlete or coach can attain. Magill was inducted along with Frankie Sinkwich, Charley Trippi, Bob McWhorter, and Teresa Edwards. Magill also received another signal honor when the nation's most famous mascot, Uga V, was christened Daniel Hamilton Magill IV.

Magill is married to the former Rosemary Reynaud of New Orleans. They have three children: Ham, a 1966 graduate of Princeton and a 1970 graduate of Emory Medical School, Sharon Brown, and Mollie Sloan, both of whom are University of Georgia graduates.

When is Magill the happiest? "When I lie down at the end of the day, put my head on my pillow and think of the successes of my children." What does Magill consider the most important things in life? "Looking after one's family and living by the Ten Commandments." Magill lives his creed of "If you first do not succeed, try until you do."

"From 1966 to 1970, our tennis team was runner-up for the SEC title. In 1971, we won it and that was the biggest thrill I ever had in my life."

WADE MITCHELL
Renaissance Man

In the past year, Wade Treutlen Mitchell has been inducted into more Halls of Fame than most heroes would see in a lifetime.

Last April, along with Supreme Court Justice Byron "Whizzer" White, he was chosen to the Academic All-America Sports Hall of Fame. In November, Mitchell was selected to the Georgia Tech Engineering Hall of Fame, and last December the former Georgia Tech All-American quarterback was placed into the Gator Bowl Hall of Fame. Mitchell played in the Gator Bowl and Sugar Bowl the same year and was a standout in both games.

Mitchell, who went on to a distinguished career at the old Trust Company of Georgia (now SunTrust Bank) and an equally distinguished career as a civic-minded Atlanta citizen, is in his third year of retirement, but you can scarcely tell it. He continues to serve on the boards of the American Red Cross, USO, Canterbury Court, and Downtown Development Authority. He recently completed a tour as a director of MARTA. And he continues to raise funds for United Way, Georgia Tech, Atlanta Arts Alliance, and the Boy Scouts of America.

Mitchell lives with his wife Mary Lu Wright Mitchell in their spacious Atlanta Buckhead home on Arden at Argonne. Their son, Wade Wright Mitchell, a former quarterback himself at the University of South Carolina, practices law in Atlanta, and their daughter, Catherine, a track and cross country runner of note, is a junior at Wake Forest.

If you think the fictional Jack Armstrong was the "all-American boy," to paraphrase the late Al Jolson, "You ain't heard nothin' yet." At Georgia Tech, 6'4" quarterback (safety on defense) Mitchell directed Coach Bobby Dodd's Yellow Jackets to four consecutive winning seasons (1953–56), four consecutive victories over the University of Georgia, and four consecutive bowl wins. All the while, Mitchell was maintaining a 3.9 scholastic average. His name was a fixture on the Dean's List. When he was not playing football or studying, he was serving as commanding officer of the Naval ROTC.

"I have never seen anyone like him," says Mitchell's longtime friend, Atlanta insurance executive John M. DeBorde. "He would practice football or basketball Monday through Friday, play a football game on Saturday or a basketball game on Saturday night and while his teammates were out on the town Sunday afternoons and evenings, Wade would hole himself up in his room and study."

In 1956, Mitchell scored all the points in a 7-0 win over Pittsburgh on January 1 in the Sugar Bowl, and the next season on December 30 he led the Jackets to a 21-14 victory over Pittsburgh in the Gator Bowl. Despite the fact that his 1952 team was co-national champions, Coach Dodd called his 1956 Mitchell-led Jackets the best group he ever had.

A native Atlantan, Mitchell grew up in Brookwood Hills. He attended old North Fulton High School where he was a perennial honor roll student and a two-time selection on the Georgia high school All-State football and basketball teams. In 1953, his double-digit scoring, dominant rebounding, and flawless defense enabled the North Fulton Bulldogs to win the State Class AA basketball tournament championship. Mitchell was named most valuable player in the tournament.

After Georgia Tech, Mitchell served two years in the US Navy as a Communications Officer on a destroyer. He went to Harvard University where he received his MBA and met his wife-to-be, Mary Lu Wright. After Harvard, it was on to West Point, Georgia, and the old West Point-Pepperell Manufacturing Company. Recalls Mitchell, "There was not a lot doing in West Point on Saturday nights. I went back north to marry Mary Lu. We moved to Atlanta and I joined the Trust Company's management training program."

For Mitchell, the training program was short-lived. He advanced rapidly to the national accounts division, became manager of the Buckhead office, and was brought downtown to head the personnel department. He became chief of the administrative services division, which had responsibility for charitable giving, institutional banking, security, training, food service, and human resources.

Just like at Georgia Tech, Mitchell was doing everything. And not just for the Trust Company. He served on the Atlanta City Council, Advisory Board of the Atlanta University Graduate School of Business, Shepherd Spinal Center, and chaired the Governor's Advisory Council on Employment and Job Training. Marathon man? With all his Trust Company and civic activity, he made time to coach basketball and soccer at the Peachtree Road United Methodist Church and baseball in the Buckhead Little Leagues.

During his son's four years of football for the South Carolina Gamecocks, Mitchell never missed a game. Nor did he miss many of Catherine's track and cross country meets at Lovett and Wake Forest. He and Wright fish and play golf and he and Mary Lu travel most every year.

Mitchell's first love is his family. His second is college football, which he finds to be in deep trouble:

> For the coaches and players, it is no fun. In the old days, once the college season started, Coach Dodd maintained a relaxed atmosphere. We played volleyball, had foot races and ran signal drills without pads. There was little physical contact.
>
> When we traveled to a game, Coach Dodd always built into the schedule enough flexibility so that we could see whatever city we were visiting. We not only had time to see the campus, we had time to see the town and countryside.
>
> It is totally different today. Coaches are too focused on the game. They get the players on the airplane, get them on a bus, get them to the motel, get them to the stadium, and after the game, get them back on the airplane. The kids don't know where they have been.
>
> For most of today's players, college football is simply a chance to spring to a professional career.
>
> The pressure for the coaches to win in unbearable. Look how many head coaches resigned last year—about eight. Colleges keep enlarging the stadiums and that means more seats to fill. And the coaches know that only a winning team fills seats. College football is no longer fun; it is big business.

1997

ARTHUR LOWNDES MONTGOMERY

The Man Who Brought Big Leagues to Atlanta

If you think former mayor Ivan Allen was the person who brought major league sports to Atlanta, think again. Although Allen was captain of the team, it was Arthur Lowndes Montgomery, then president of the Atlanta Coca-Cola Bottling Company and chairman of the Atlanta-Fulton County Recreation Authority, who did the steering and ultimately made Atlanta home of the Braves and the Falcons.

Today, Montgomery, age seventy-five, and his wife of twenty-two years, Julie Purvis Montgomery, spend their time at their three homes in Atlanta, Bartow County in Georgia, and Wellington, Florida. Montgomery has a few business and real estate interests but is about "90 percent retired."

About the Braves and Falcons, former Atlanta Constitution sports editor Jesse Outlar remembers, "Arthur never got the credit he deserved and he never really cared. Mayor Allen and Mills Lane [former chairman of the old C&S National Bank] were in the news a lot but the truth is Montgomery was constantly in the fore, making telephone calls to team owners, flying all over the country for meetings and ultimately getting a National Football League franchise when it looked as if Atlanta was headed for the American Football League."

Since the AFL and NFL eventually merged, it made little difference in which league Atlanta would compete. But at the time, in 1964, it made a sizeable difference. Half the AFL teams were bordering on bankruptcy and the league had no TV contract as did the NFL. Recalls Montgomery:

> Allen had commissioned J. Leonard Reinsch, president of WSB, to get a major league football team here—any team. So Reinsch went to Denver and was close to a deal for the Broncos.
>
> I did not want an AFL team here because of the league's shaky financial condition. I wanted the best for Atlanta so I zeroed in on the NFL and its commissioner, Pete Rozelle. Rozelle and I became fast friends. He visualized the TV market here and he promptly went to the NFL owners and pleaded Atlanta's case for an expansion team.
>
> Rozelle got me in front of the league owners but it was futile. George Halas, owner of the Chicago Bears and papa Bear of the whole NFL, wasn't buying. And neither was Dan Reeves, another giant in the league and owner of the Los Angeles Rams.
>
> When I got back to Atlanta, there was a call from the mayor. He told me Reinsch was nearly locked into having a pro football team—the Atlanta [Denver] Broncos.
>
> I got off the phone as quickly as I could and telephoned Rozelle. 'If you want an NFL team in Atlanta,' I said, 'you better move now. Otherwise, it will be too late.'

Whatever Rozelle was doing at the time, he put aside and flew to L.A. and Chicago. He convinced Halas and Reeves to give Atlanta an expansion team. Then he flew to Atlanta where Montgomery held an emergency session of the Recreation Authority. "We voted to accept the NFL expansion team. It made the mayor furious because he thought we were already in the AFL. But he got over it and Reinsch, who had lured the AFL, never really cared."

Montgomery could have owned the Falcons instead of Rankin Smith. When the NFL deal was official, commissioner Rozelle said, "We want you to own the team"

Montgomery said, "Pete, I cannot own this team. It would be a direct conflict of interest. I am Chairman of the Stadium Authority. I cannot negotiate with myself for a contract. And besides, everyone in Atlanta would think I had done all this for myself."

"Well," Rozelle said, "we have to have a majority owner. The league will not work with committee ownership."

"So," Montgomery said, "we thought of Rankin Smith. He was a good friend of mine and an avid sports fan. We telephoned Governor Sanders and got an appointment at the old Governor's Mansion. When we got there, we told Governor Sanders that we wanted Rankin Smith. So, Sanders got on the phone and told Rankin to get over to the mansion immediately. It was business that could not wait."

"When Smith walked in," Montgomery said. "Sanders greeted him thusly, "How would you like to own an NFL football team?"

Rankin said, "I would love it". And that was that.

The landing of the Braves was a different story.

Charlie Finley, owner of the Kansas City Athletics, wanted to move to Atlanta but the American League said no. Meanwhile, Montgomery and his stadium authority had started construction of the Atlanta-Fulton County Stadium but had no team to play in it. Enter, again, Arthur Montgomery. He received a telephone call from a good friend of his, Delbert Coleman, chairman of the Seaburg Corp., maker of jukeboxes and vending machines. Coleman was part owner of the Milwaukee Braves.

"I understand you have a stadium going up in Atlanta with no team to play in it." Coleman said. "How would you like to have the Atlanta Braves?"

It was one of those win-win situations. The Milwaukee Braves were having problems negotiating a new stadium deal with the city of Milwaukee and the stockholders could see a vast television and radio market in Atlanta that they never would have in Milwaukee. Atlanta would have major league baseball for its brand new empty stadium.

So, with Montgomery, mayor Allen, Mills Lane, architects James H. "Bill" Finch and George Heery and Stadium Manager Sidney Scarborough pushing full speed ahead, Atlanta erected a stadium in fifty-one weeks in 1965.

The Braves were ready and eager to move to their new home. But there was one hang-up. The city of Milwaukee got an injunction to stop the Braves' move. So, in 1965, the old minor league team, the Atlanta Crackers, opened Atlanta-Fulton County Stadium. After shelling out $800,000 in legal fees in 1966, Atlanta finally became the home of the Braves.

Although many Georgians recall Montgomery's involvement with the Falcons and Braves, few knew that he also played key roles in building the Omni and helping Tom Cousins acquire the Atlanta Hawks.

Although the major league sports coups were highlights for Montgomery, they were only a portion of the vital part he played in enriching the quality of life for all Atlantans and many citizens throughout America.

For instance, he received the national award for "Distinguished Service in Cancer Control" from the American Cancer Society for 1958, won the Radio Free Europe award for "meritorious Service" for 1967, received the Atlanta Rotary Club's "Armin Maier" award for the member contributing "the most outstanding service" for 1964–65, received the 1965 National Athletic Hall of Fame award for "special service to sports," won the University of Georgia Business School 1973 "Award of Merit" for outstanding service as an alumnus, received the "Distinguished Service Award" from the Atlanta Business League for 1988, and the "Exceptional Service Award" from the Christian Council of Atlanta in 1988.

A list of all the leadership roles he has played in the growth of Atlanta would fill this magazine issue and many more. But to name a few, they are: chairman of the Board and CEO of the Atlanta Coca-Cola Bottling Company; director of Sun Trust Banks; executive vice president of the Atlanta Landmarks, which "saved the

Fox Theatre" and had it designated as a national historic landmark; emeritus trustee of the University of Georgia Foundation; trustee of the Georgia Student Education Fund; national associate director of the Boys' Clubs of America; director of the Atlanta Arts Alliance; trustee of Georgia Baptist Hospital; director of the Atlanta Art Association; member of the Advisory Board for the Atlanta Juvenile Court; director of the Atlanta Traffic and Safety Council; director of the Atlanta Better Business Bureau; director of the Atlanta Fair and Exposition Association; director of Central Atlanta Progress; director of the Tech-Georgia Development Fund; etc.

Where and how did Arthur Montgomery find time to do all this civic work? "I sometimes wonder myself," he said. "I do know that Atlanta made my Coca-Cola business successful and I felt a tremendous urge to pay back what the city did for me. I was young. I was full of energy. I was motivated to serve. But there is no way I could have been involved in all those projects without an outstanding team in my business office. The fine job my associates did at the bottling company sprung me loose for civic endeavors."

Montgomery was born in Atlanta in 1923. One of the "Buckhead Boys," he attended old Atlanta North Fulton High School. He graduated from the University of Georgia with a Business Administration degree. After serving in the US Signal Corps during World War II, he went full-time with the Atlanta Coca-Cola Bottling Company where he had worked part time as a preteen and as a teenager. His dad, the late LaFayette Montgomery, was president and CEO.

"I never considered any other career," Montgomery said. "I adored my father and could not imagine passing up an opportunity to be in business with him." In 1961, after having served in several managerial jobs, he succeeded his father as president and CEO. He took the company to new sales levels in each of the next twenty-seven years. Then he sold the company to the Coca-Cola Company and "retired."

Next to his achievements with the Atlanta Coca-Cola Bottling Company, Braves, and Falcons, his most satisfying experience was his twenty-year volunteer work with the American Cancer Society. He started with the Fulton County unit, headed the Georgia division, and spent fifteen years as a member of the national board of directors. As chief fundraiser, he took the Cancer Society to unparalleled heights.

One of his favorite hobbies has been sports car racing. Like every thing he has done, he has been a leader in the field. He grew up listening on the radio to the old Indianapolis 500 races. In the 1950s, he owned exotic sports cars himself. In the early 1960s, when word spread of his interest in sports car racing, a group of car buffs came to him about building a racetrack. Before you could say, "Arthur," Road Atlanta, one of the finest road racing tracks in America, came into being. The track, located off Georgia Highway 53 in Braselton, hosts many sports car and NASCAR races and in 1999 will host an International Grand Prix. The person who is former president and board chairman is also the former president of the US Auto Club. His name is Arthur Montgomery.

1997

What advice does Montgomery have for the new college graduate or aspiring businessman? "Do not overlook technology but the main emphasis should be on liberal arts—music, art, literature. This country needs people who can get along with others and talk knowledgeably on many subjects."

Arthur has two children from his first wife, Eleanor Morgan of Savannah. Arthur Montgomery Jr. is a forty-four-year-old movie producer in Hollywood, California, and Jeannette Montgomery Barron, his forty-one-year-old daughter, is a professional photographer in New York.

To paraphrase the slogan of a famous soft drink beverage, for much of what has been accomplished in Atlanta, it has been "Always Arthur."

AUBREY MORRIS
The First Newsman

Aubrey Richard Morris would feel at home anywhere—from the White House to the Federal Penitentiary. He would be comfortable with presidents, kings and riffraff. He has mingled with all.

B.M. (Before Morris), Atlanta radio had "announcers," not "newsmen." But Aubrey changed all that by getting interviews with people when no one else could. It was Aubrey and Aubrey alone who tracked down King Gustav of Sweden on Atlanta's East Lake golf course, placed his microphone between him and the king, and asked in his gravelly voice, "Tell me king, how did you do on the last hole?" It was Aubrey and Aubrey alone who traced Emperor Haile Selassie of Ethiopia to the Dr. Martin Luther King gravesite and got into the emperor's limousine to do a live interview.

On April 12, 1961, Aubrey was in France and was the first radio newsman in America to get on the air and report that Russia had put an astronaut, Youri Garin, in space. And it was Aubrey Morris who was the lone Atlanta journalist who went to the scene of the tragic Orly Airport crash in Paris to report back live on the death of more than 100 prominent Atlantans in 1962.

Make no mistake about it, Morris was Atlanta's first bona fide radio newsman. He was emulated by many but in gathering and broadcasting the news as it happened, he was in a class by himself. "He could do it all," said his former associate at WSB, Frank R. Stiteler.

1997

"Aubrey had more news sources than anyone in town. If there was a fire, he would immediately get called by one of the city's firemen, and if there was a homicide, one of Atlanta's finest made sure Aubrey knew about it first."

Morris learned the news gathering business at the *Atlanta Journal* where he served as special assignment and police reporter for thirteen years. He covered the big stories and almost always was the first reporter on the scene, such as in December 1946 when he got word first of the tragic Atlanta Winecoff Hotel fire which claimed the lives of 119 people. In those days, the *Atlanta Journal* and the *Atlanta Constitution* were under separate ownership and Morris took delight in whipping the opposition with scoop after scoop.

But his lifelong ambition was to do live news on radio, and Elmo Ellis, then program director for WSB, made him an offer he could not refuse—broadcasting news events as they happened. Indeed, Morris' "live" newscasts made "remote" broadcasting a thing of the past.

As he was in the newspaper business where he earned the respect and admiration of his peers, he was held in the same high esteem by broadcasters of radio stations throughout the South. There was only one Aubrey Morris and there has been nothing like him since. Morris served more than thirty years as news and editorial director of WSB and he was as competitive at the end of his career as he was the start. He retired in 1987.

Aubrey is age seventy-five. He lives with his wife, Tera, in north Fulton County, several miles above Alpharetta. His layout, about an acre and one-half, is called "Perkins Place," because it is the ancestral home of his mother's family. The Perkinses were among Roswell's first settlers.

Aubrey, in retirement, works in his vegetable garden and sits on his porch watching butterflies. But he scarcely misses a beat. He still gets excited when he hears a fire engine. In an upstairs room in his home, there is a "writing corner" with computer and memorabilia from his long career as a journalist. There he writes a column for the Alpharetta-Roswell Revue & News, a weekly newspaper. He recently wrote and published a family history. Morris is active in the Roswell Historical Society and a lay leader in Saint Aidan's Episcopal Church and, until recently, continued to write editorials for WSB Radio.

For his countless hours of volunteer work in the Roswell library and archives, the Roswell Historical Society honored him in October 1997 with an "Aubrey Morris Night" at the Capital City Club in Brookhaven. Elmo Ellis, retired vice president of WSB radio and, of course, the man who took Morris from the newspaper business to radio, was honorary chairman, and Bobby Harper, Aubrey's old WSB colleague, was master of ceremonies at the black tie event.

Ellis said, "Aubrey is one of my best friends. Like everyone else who knows him, I have the utmost admiration for him. Not only was he always dependable but he was always lovable. Before I hired him, I got a reference from his city editor at the *Journal*, Don Carter. Carter told me, "He is a great reporter but he has a terrible nasal voice."

Said Ellis, "That voice became the best known voice in Georgia broadcasting."

Morris was born in Roswell in 1922. While a teenager, he was the Roswell correspondent both for the *Atlanta Journal* and its archrival, the *Atlanta Constitution*. At the University of Georgia, he edited the student newspaper, the *Red and Black*, and the school's annual, the *Pandora*. He also made time to free-lance for the local newspaper, the *Athens Banner-Herald*.

It was Ralph McGill, editor of the *Constitution* and eventual Pulitzer Prize winner, who encouraged Morris to attend Georgia and get his degree from the Henry W. Grady School of Journalism. Morris had met McGill while he was working summers as a copy carrier for the *Constitution*.

The same day Morris graduated from journalism school he began work as a fulltime employee of the *Atlanta Journal*. One year later he covered the Winecoff hotel fire, one of the biggest news stories in Atlanta's history.

Morris says, "It was not the fires or the interviews with kings that made my reputation. It was the peculiar sound and unique character of my gravelly voice."

Whatever it was, Morris has received his accolades. At the University of Georgia, his portrait hangs in the Demosthenian Literary Society's "Wall of Fame." He received the John F. Drewry Award (named for the late, legendary University of Georgia Journalism School dean) for Distinguished Achievement in journalism. He also is a member of the Georgia Broadcasters Hall of Fame.

Aubrey says none of his honors has given him as much thrill as his discovery, more that forty years after his graduation, that one of his ancestral grandfathers had been elected sheriff of Clarke County in 1817 and marched at the head of the University of Georgia graduation procession.

Today, when is Aubrey the happiest? "Discovering new things from the Fulton County record offices." He said the happiest day of his life was when he married his wife, Tera, who was a nurse at Atlanta's Grady Hospital.

"Today my biggest pleasure is my family. Tera and I have been married forty-nine wonderful years. We have three lovely daughters and six beautiful grandchildren. Who could be blessed more?"

Commenting on some of today's less-than-refined talk show hosts, Morris says "when talk radio becomes unacceptable, people will get rid of it. Trash flows down the river."

His fondest memories of his newspaper days was "knowing the greats. People like McGill, Margaret Mitchell, *Constitution* associate editor and brilliant writer for magazines Harold Martin, the late publisher of the *Atlanta Journal* George Biggers, and director of *Atlanta Journal* promotions Pat LaHatte.

Morris' advice to aspiring journalist: "Be curious about every thing in the world."

"Belief in God," Aubrey says, "and good friends are the most important things in life."

He said that God and friends were with him last March when he began thirty-eight radiation treatments for prostate cancer. He is doing fine, thank you.

One reason why Aubrey was such a good newsman was that he would not take "no" for an answer. For instance, when Carl Sanders was governor of

Georgia, Aubrey interviewed him about taxes. "Tell me, Governor Sanders, what are you going to do about taxes?"

"Aubrey, I am not going to comment on that."

"But what about your PLANS for taxes?"

"Aubrey, I said I was not going to comment on that."

"Governor, I know you are not going to comment on taxes but if you were, what would you say?"

And Aubrey got his story.

When Aubrey was on the air, whatever he said, the people believed. And back in the late 1950s and early 1960s, 90 percent of radio listeners were tuned in to WSB and Aubrey Morris.

One morning, arising at his normal wake-up time of 5 A.M. Aubrey looked out his bedroom window and saw blankets of snow covering his neighborhood. He quickly dressed, rushed outside, and got in his automobile to check on the streets. But the snow was so thick that he could not get out of the driveway.

In those days, malls were few and far between. Shopping was done downtown. The office and restaurant boom northward had not begun. If you did anything in Atlanta, you did it downtown. A concerned Aubrey got on the air about 6 A.M. and stayed there until 9 A.M. warning all Atlanta citizens to "stay home. Do not attempt to go downtown. It is too dangerous."

Shortly after Aubrey went off the air, not only did it stop snowing, but sun broke through the clouds and temperatures began to rise. Snow melted. There was no ice on the roads and no people downtown. It was an event Atlantans would remember as the day Aubrey Morris paralyzed the city.

JESSE LAMAR OUTLAR
From the Bushes to the Majors

When Jesse Lamar Outlar retired as sports editor of the *Atlanta Constitution* ten years ago, he did not retire "to" anything else, he flat out retired. No more writing, no more speaking engagements, no more golf, no nothing.

"I don't do," he said, "I just be."

"I had been working since I was five years old. I worked fifty-nine years. That was enough. I was not only retired at age sixty-four, I was just plain tired."

Outlar was a *Constitution* sports staff member for forty-one years, and sports editor and sports columnist the last thirty of those years. He lives with his wife, Johanna Kristjans Outlar, in a lake-view home in Peachtree City, Georgia. During the week, Outlar, seventy-four, has no trouble doing nothing. But on football weekends, he has three television sets going at one time and he is in front of all of them.

"A few Saturdays ago," he said, "I was watching TV football from noon until midnight. When the last game on the west coast was finished, I had seen part of fourteen games."

During his writing years, success came but did not spoil Jesse Outlar. Named by his colleagues "National Sports Writer of the Year" three times, Associated Press' "Sports Writer of the Year" five times, and one of the first recipients of the University of Georgia's "Dan Magill" award for long and lasting contributions to sports, Outlar's personality never changed. He was, and is, the same genuine, unpretentious person that he was when he came out of Omega (yes, Omega) Georgia in 1946. He was loved and admired by his peers, superiors and employees.

Recalls Hal Hayes, who was one of Outlar's staff members, "If I have met any great people in my life, Jesse Outlar would be one of them. When he hired me, he said he treated every staff member alike. In the twenty years I was with him, he did exactly that." When Furman Bisher came to Atlanta in 1950 to become sports editor of the *Constitution*, Outlar was on the staff covering high school sports. "The first move I made," remembers Bisher, "was to put Outlar on the old Atlanta Crackers. He was the star of the sports staff and he became as good a baseball writer as there was anywhere." When the award-winning Bisher became sports editor of the *Atlanta Journal* in 1957, Outlar was chosen to replace him at the *Constitution*. For the next thirty years, he wrote five to seven columns a week.

Whatever went on in the sports world, Outlar covered it: high school, college and professional football, basketball and baseball; the Kentucky Derby, the World Series, the Super Bowl, the Masters Golf Tournament, the Butts-Bryant Saturday Evening Post libel suit, world championship boxing, Hank Aaron's record-tying and record-breaking home runs, Georgia winning the national collegiate football championship, and Outlar's all-time favorite—Georgia's breaking of the eight-year drought against Georgia Tech.

"I had the world's greatest job," he said. "I got paid to watch (and write about) ball games." But the job almost cost him his life.

It was October 7, 1973, on a gray Sunday afternoon. Outlar had been watching the Falcons lose another one. After the game he wrote his column and stayed on in the press box to chat with Rex Edmondson, an old pal and former *Constitution* sports staffer who had moved on to become sports editor of the *Jacksonville* (Florida) *Journal*. Outlar gathered up his notes for another column and placed them in his new, leather briefcase given to him by then Georgia Tech Sports Information Director Ned West. Then he and Edmondson walked to the stadium parking lot as darkness was beginning to set in. They walked to Edmondson's car and then Edmondson drove Outlar to his car—about 100 yards away. Outlar got out and Edmondson drove away.

What happened next is indelibly printed in Outlar's mind. A teenager came out of nowhere, walked up to Outlar and said, "Where are you going?"

Good Samaritan Outlar replied, "I will be glad to take you wherever you want to go."

The teenager replied firmly, "You ain't goin' nowhere. I want that briefcase!"
Outlar said "No."

The youngster reached into a paper bag, pulled out a pistol, and fired at point-blank range. The bullet ripped into Outlar's abdomen. The teenager ran and Outlar fell to the pavement bleeding with a hole in his stomach.

A passerby heard the gunshot and telephoned for help, and after what seemed like eternity to Outlar, an ambulance arrived and rushed him to the Grady Hospital emergency ward.

Frank Wall, then president of the Falcons, heard the news on the radio and arranged for Outlar to be transferred to Piedmont Hospital. He was met at Piedmont by Falcons physicians Charlie Harrison and Frank Wilson. Later, Dr. Wilson removed the .38 caliber bullet that had been lodged, no more than one-half an inch, between Outlar's aorta and spine. He was lucky to be alive and lucky he was not paralyzed.

"I came close to following in the footsteps of my father," Outlar said. "A deputy sheriff in Pulaski County, Georgia. He was shot by a robber. He died from the wound. I was three years old."

Outlar spent two weeks recovering at Piedmont Hospital and then another two weeks recuperating at home. Then he was back at his desk as the *Constitution*, turning out his daily column. A sixteen-year-old Decatur man eventually was charged with Outlar's shooting but Outlar could not make a positive identification. "I would rather let a suspect go free than send an innocent man to jail," Outlar said. The case went to trial and ended in a hung jury. The suspect was released and no one else ever was charged.

Outlar may be the only person born in a town of less than 100 people (Finleyson, Georgia), raised in a town of less than 200 people (Omega, Georgia) and went on to become sports editor of a major, metropolitan daily newspaper. Omega is in Tift County and as the late *Atlanta Journal* columnist Ernie Rogers said, "It is about 12 miles from Tifton and a helluva long way from Alpha."

Outlar literally went from delivery boy to sports editor. He had an exclusive in Omega where as a third grader, he delivered to homes the *Atlanta Journal*, the *Atlanta Constitution*, and the *Jacksonville* (Florida) *Times-Union*.

He began his writing career in Omega, where he founded and edited the high school newspaper. At the University of Georgia, he was sports editor of the *Red and Black*, and in the US Marine Corps he was managing editor of the *Camp Lejeune* (North Carolina) *Globe*.

After getting out of the Marine Corps in 1945, he went to Waycross, Georgia, where he was a one-man show. He was not only sports editor of the *Waycross Journal-Herald*, but during baseball season, he also covered the Waycross professional team (in the old Georgia-Florida League), broadcast the games over the local radio station, ran the public address system, filed game stories for the *Savannah Morning-News*, and was home game official scorer.

With all his jobs in Waycross, he took a pay cut when Johnny Bradberry called him to join the *Constitution* sports staff in 1946 with a starting salary of $50 weekly.

His favorite *Constitution* assignment was when Bisher put him on the Atlanta Crackers.

"I got to see Eddie Mathews when he was a nineteen-year-old in his rookie season," Outlar said. "He hit thirty-two home runs. You did not need to be a baseball expert to know that if he stayed healthy, he was headed for the Hall of Fame."

1997

Outlar's favorite Crackers manager was Whitlow Wyatt, the former Brooklyn Dodgers pitching great who is alive at age eighty-seven and living in his native Buchanan (Georgia).

"What I remember mostly about Whit," Outlar said, "was when the Crackers were in the Dixie Series championship game against Houston [Texas]. We had the bases loaded with two outs in the last of the ninth. We were trailing by one run but Bob Montag, our great home run hitter, was due up next. Wyatt had the intuition and courage to pull his slugger for a pinch-hitter, second-string catcher Jim Solt. Solt hit the first pitch out of the park."

"The best athletes" Outlar ever saw were the University of Georgia's football immortal, Charley Trippi, the Braves' Henry Aaron and Eddie Mathews, and the Giants' Willie Mays.

His most memorable sports event was seeing Aaron's 714th and 715th home runs to tie and break Ruth's record. "No one," Outlar predicts, "ever will break Aaron's hone run record."

Outlar's biggest scoop was writing that Atlanta would be home of a new National Football League team (the Falcons) in 1966 when the day before the *Atlanta Journal* had predicted Atlanta would be the home of an American Football League team.

The best writers he ever knew? "Without doubt," he replied, "Furman Bisher would be in the top two or three."

Outlar loved to write about people, and in a positive way. He never put the knock on anyone. "He had as many friends among the readers and the people he wrote about as anyone I ever knew," said retired *Atlanta Journal-Constitution* executive editor Jim Minter. Quips Outlar, "I think most of my admirers were those readers who read my football picks. They would see who I would pick and then they would bet the other way."

Outlar has two children by a previous marriage to Florence Beaton, a daughter, Jan Edwards, who is director of an advertising firm in Fresno, California, and a son, Barry Outlar, who lives in Lilburn, Georgia, and is employed by Delta Air Lines. Outlar has five grandchildren.

Outlar has written two books: *Between the Hedges*, highlights of University of Georgia football, and *Caught Short*, about the life and times of the late Atlanta Braves traveling secretary and vice president, four-foot Donald Davidson. In 1993, Outlar was inducted into the Georgia Sports Hall of Fame.

What advice would he give to an aspiring sports writer? "Get a degree in communications, English or history. Write for your college newspaper and in your summer, college years, intern at some daily or weekly newspaper."

If he had it to do over again, what would Outlar change? "A lot," he said, "but I would still choose to be a sports writer. As the late *New York Times* columnist Red Smith used to say, 'It beats lifting boxes.'"

JAMES P. "JIM" WESBERRY JR.
I Won't Sell My Soul

In 1965, James P. "Jim" Wesberry Jr., son of the then renowned pastor of the Morningside Baptist Church, was on a political shooting star.

A member of the Georgia State Senate, he was chairman of the Fulton County Senate Delegation, a vital part of leadership Atlanta and respected by people like Carl Sanders, Ivan Allen, George Berry, and the late Dan Sweat.

He was the principal plaintiff in *Wesberry v. Sanders*, which laid down for the first time in writing the maxim that congressional districts had to be apportioned according to the ideal of "one man, one vote." In this landmark decision, the US Supreme Court mandated the reapportionment of the US House of Representatives.

Said Bill Shipp, then political editor of the *Atlanta Constitution*, "Wesberry was on his way to becoming mayor of Atlanta or governor of the state of Georgia."

One year later, at the age of thirty-two, Wesberry quit the Senate and left the state of Georgia, decisions he never has regretted.

"I decided to be honest. That is why I quit. My brilliant decisions so far have been quitting politics and marrying my second wife. I would have become corrupt had I stayed and run for higher office. There was no choice. I was not prepared to sell my soul."

Today, Wesberry lives in northern Virginia and works for the World Bank in the Caribbean as the principal adviser in Accounting and Auditing for Latin America and the Caribbean. In plain, simple language, Wesberry's job is to

1997

uncover fraud and corruption, which he says there is plenty of both, and to pinpoint government accountability. "This work is a calling from God," he said. "Eliminating corruption is my mission in life."

It was following his second re-election to the Georgia State Senate that Wesberry realized that he would have to "give up my principles to stay in politics. You cannot raise money without compromising yourself. I did not want to sell my integrity. I hated humbling myself before friends and strangers. If someone gave me fifty dollars, I felt indebted to him. It was a compromising position. The guy who gave me money would come back to see me when he had a bill he wanted passed. Nobody gives you money because they believe in you. They give it to you because they want to own you. I couldn't stomach it."

To stay free of promised favors, Wesberry said he tried to pay political campaign bills himself. "They cost me enough to send three children through college twice. My Senate career cost me $15,000 per year in lost potential income I could have earned as an accountant. Meanwhile, my personal net worth nose-dived. I was unable to pay creditors, people were threatening to sue me. I concluded that if I was going to stay honest and solvent, I would have to get out of politics."

And what advice would Wesberry give today's political aspirants?

"Stay out of politics. It is rotten. Political parties are rotten. Someone needs to come up with a better system. No matter how you look at it, votes are bought. There is no free lunch. One day the bottom will fall out. We are the most financially irresponsible country in the world. Miami looks like the forerunner of a series of bankrupt cities. Atlanta could well be next."

For the state of Georgia, Wesberry predicts disaster due to the lottery.

The lottery is the greatest tragedy in Georgia's history. It is run by criminals so the state is in bed with criminals. The lottery is a corrupt system which corrupts human beings. People embezzle from employers to pay off lottery losses. The lottery is nothing but a tax on the stupid. Only foolish people play the lottery. The state is supposed to protect the foolish and widows and orphans. Instead, with a lottery, it fools the foolish into paying a tax they cannot afford. The lottery is an addiction, just like alcohol, tobacco and drugs. I cannot think of a worse idea for Georgia than a state lottery.

Wesberry fears no one but God. In his Georgia Senate days, he was called "the most controversial politician since Gene Talmadge." Critics said he gave up effectiveness as a legislator for the luxury of saying what he thought. He often was called a "maverick, an independent and an original thinker." When Senator Wesberry resigned, an *Atlanta Journal-Constitution* editorial commented, "The state will miss him. We shall think of him whenever the public needs a champion at the Capitol and nobody volunteers for the job."

James Pickett Wesberry Jr. was born in Columbia, South Carolina, in 1934. At the age of ten, he moved to Atlanta where his father became pastor of the Morningside Baptist Church. He attended old Bass Junior High School in Little

Five Points, and Grady High School in midtown, before moving to Washington DC and spending three years in the Capitol as a House of Representatives page. Returning to Atlanta, he spent three years at Georgia Tech before transferring to Georgia State University where he earned his accounting degree. At the age of twenty-one, he earned his CPA designation.

His first marriage, which lasted twenty-three years and produced four children, ended in divorce. "The lowest part of my life was telling my father of the breakup, " he said, "but I would not have survived had it not been for his understanding along with a good psychiatrist and an anti-depressant. My dad looked me in the eyes and said, 'You can't let this end your life. Why, if I looked at my congregants, 50 percent of them would be divorced. Now, get on with your life.'"

He joined the World Bank and moved to Peru where he met his present wife, Lea Esdras Castenada. "We have been on a honeymoon for twenty-two years. Lea is the most wonderful, compassionate person I have known. The Lord placed an angel with me. We are like one person. Marrying Lea was the best thing that ever happened to me."

Jim and Lea have three children: Jonathan, nineteen, a student at Northern Virginia Junior College; Perry, fourteen, who is deaf and a football player in his northern Virginia high school; and twelve-year-old Ruby Lea, who attends middle school in northern Virginia.

Jim's four children by his first marriage are, James III, forty-seven, a stock broker; Elisa, forty-seven, a home health care nurse in Atlanta; Suzie, thirty-nine, the wife of a musician in Atlanta; and Paul, twenty-eight, in the computer business in Las Vegas. There are five grandchildren.

Financially, Wesberry has come a long way since his early days in the State Senate where he made $2,000 annually. "I won't say how much I earn but it is at least eighty times more than what I was earning when I left the State Senate."

Four years ago, Wesberry received the US Agency for International Development's coveted "Career Achievement Award" for "invaluable and lifetime contributions to the improvements of financial management systems and the fight against corruption in Latin America." He has been listed in Who's Who in America since 1990 and Who's Who in the World since 1976.

About his work, uncovering fraud and corruption, Wesberry says that white-collar crime is the fastest growing economic phenomenon on the planet. Prosecutors must divide resources between drug cartels, the Mafia, street crime, and business fraud.

"The shortages of jail cells has become the number one problem in American public administration," he said.

"A Brazilian congressman is alleged to have processed $51 million through his personal bank accounts in less than five years. Cocaine-financed bribes give public officials in South and North America a choice between receiving more money than they could earn in 100 years or tortuous death for themselves or their loved ones. That is what we are up against."

1997

1998

BARON HENRY "BUD" ASHER
Asher Made Dreams Come True

Compared to the life of Baron Henry "Bud" Asher, the life of James Thurber's Walter Mitty would be a monumental bore. Where Mitty only dreamed, Asher made his dreams come true. World War II hero, All-Star football player, municipal judge, head football coach of high school, college and professional teams, and dancer with Betty Grable. You name it. Asher has done it.

A native Atlantan and undergraduate and law school graduate from the University of Georgia, Asher moved to Daytona Beach, Florida, forty-six years ago. The Florida east coast city had never seen any thing like him and most likely never will again. He is one of a kind. I know. I am his brother.

This fall he will be running for his third term as Mayor of Daytona Beach and it is unlikely anyone will have the chutzpah to run against him. Someone tried it in his first re-election campaign and was buried by a landslide.

Asher has been an achiever since his days as a student at old Atlanta Tech High School, where he punched typewriter keys for the *Rainbow*, the school's weekly newspaper, and noses for the Tech High boxing team. He never has been content to sit on the sidelines. And at age seventy-three, he is still in the arena, competing with everything he has got.

"He is a bundle of energy," says Daytona Beach City Manager Carey Smith. "When his staff is exhausted with tongues hanging out, he continues to move full speed ahead."

1998

What is a typical day for Mayor Asher? After a forty-five-minute, morning workout with calisthenics and exercise machines, he scans the *Daytona Beach Morning Journal*, shoves down a bowl of cereal and heads to his office. About 9:15 A.M., he bounces into City Hall with a gleam in his eye and more spring to his step than a bantam rooster.

Without Groucho's big, black mustache, long black coat, heavy black eyebrows, and black-rimmed glasses, he comes in singing "Hello, I must be going; hello, I must be going; I would really like to stay but I must be going!"

He distributes smiles and handshakes like campaign fliers to everyone in the office and then heads to City Manager Smith's desk, leans over and whispers, "I have only five minutes to talk about your project." The five minutes stretches into fifteen and then he sings again," I would really like to stay but I must be going!" And then, like a bolt of lightning, he is off to a ribbon-cutting ceremony, reading a proclamation, or standing at the speaker's rostrum at the Daytona Beach Kiwanis Club meeting.

"It is amazing," Smith adds, " how a man so short of time, finds enough of it to accommodate everyone. He is a favorite guest on the luncheon circuit at Volusia County's civic and business group meetings. As a licensed notary, he performs weddings for anyone willing to meet his fee of a $100 donation to a local charity."

Most evenings he and his beautiful blonde wife of ten years, Dawn, are out knocking on doors on both sides of the Halifax River. His work philosophy always has been, with work comes the reward.

Asher and his wife live in a Halifax River front ranch house with their two Alaskan huskies, Wolf and Fang. He has been a dog lover since childhood. Asher has two children from an earlier marriage: Baron W. "Ron" Asher, a Naval aviator who commands a squadron at North Island Naval Station in Coronado, California; and Marybeth Lawson, a Presbyterian minister in Pennsylvania. He also has a stepson, Louis, and a stepdaughter, Wendy.

Asher is immensely popular with the white and black leadership of Daytona Beach and even more so with the average citizen. He was elected city commissioner in 1983 and won re-election five consecutive times. He is vice chairman of the Volusia County Metropolitan Planning Council and a director of the Florida League of Cities. On the national level, he is on the steering committee on crime prevention for the National League of Cities.

One of the reasons he is so popular is that most of the male voters—black and white—played for him when he was either a Pop Warner, high school, college, or professional football coach. Says Wes Chandler, who played for Asher at New Smyrna Beach High School and went on to winning All-America honors at the University of Florida and All-Pro honors for the New Orleans Saints and San Diego Chargers, "Everyone did not love him but everyone respected him. He was a well-organized disciplinarian. He gave 100 percent effort and he expected his assistant coaches and players to do the same. He said if we physically and mentally stretched ourselves to the limit, we not only would win championships but we would prepare ourselves for adversity later in life. He was right on both counts."

Asher grew up in northeast Atlanta, sold *Liberty* magazines door to door and scorecards and ice cream at old Ponce de Leon Park when the Atlanta Crackers were dominating the Southern Association.

He spent a year at Georgia Tech, where he was freshman manager of the 1942 Georgia Tech football team. At the end of the season, he enlisted in the US Navy and saw combat in the Pacific, where he was rear gunner on a torpedo bomber, flying off the USS Bunker Hill with Torpedo Squadron 8.

He played football with the Kaneohe Clippers at Kaneohe Bay. When the war ended he returned to the states with two Air Medals and a desire to resume his education. On the way home, he stopped in Hollywood, California, where he entered a USO dance contest and was declared winner. His prize: a dancing partner for the evening—film star and pinup girl Betty Grable.

Asher never has been one to take "No" for an answer. When he decided to enter the University of Georgia as an undergraduate student, he also decided to play football. He weighed 140 pounds, soaking wet. He told Coach Wallace Butts he wanted to go out for the Georgia football team. Butts told him, "Those big linemen will knock you into the nickel seats."

Asher and Butts became friends. And if Asher couldn't play for Butts, by gosh, he would start his own football team. So, instead of playing for the Bulldogs, Asher formed a semi-pro football team comprised mainly of former Georgia stars who had played out their eligibility but were still on campus—people like Gene Chandler, Billy Henderson, Joe Jackura, and Al Bodine. Asher did not need a quarterback. He played that position himself when he was at Kaneohe. When he was not serving as an instructor at naval gunnery school, he was quarterbacking the Kaneohe Clippers to an unbeaten season. And if he could do it for Kaneohe, why not the Georgia All-Stars?

He placed an advertisement in the *Red and Black*, the University of Georgia's student newspaper: "Wanted—former college and high school football players to try out for the traveling squad of Georgia's newest football team: THE GEORGIA ALL-STARS! Contact the coach, Bud Asher, Milledge Hall dormitory." Coach Butts was so impressed with Asher's determination that he lent his team pads, red jerseys, silver headgears, and silver britches worn by his own Bulldog team. Asher had not only a team but a fully equipped and uniformed team. He was not only the team organizer and promoter but he was also the coach, quarterback, and extra point kicker.

The Georgia All-Stars, with Asher serving as booking agent, played and defeated semi-pro teams around the South. In 1950, Asher took his All-Stars to Charlotte, North Carolina, where they upset the highly touted and previously unbeaten Charlotte Clippers. After all five of his team's touchdowns, his placements split the uprights for five extra points.

Douglas Clyde "Peahead" Walker, head football coach at Wake Forest, was sitting in the stands that late, fall Sunday afternoon. He had just been named head coach of the South for the annual North-South college All-Star game. He

1998

was in dire need of a place-kicker, and when he saw Asher deliver five extra points he knew he had his man. What he did not know was that Asher never played a minute of college football. Asher thus became the only non-college player ever named to a college All-Star team.

It was Asher who forever changed one of the rules in NCAA football. For years, each team had been responsible for providing one man to hold one end of the yardstick chain to measure first down yardage. Asher wanted that job for the Bulldogs and Coach Butts gave it to him. It was the season of 1950. Georgia was playing Auburn in jam-packed Columbus Memorial Stadium. It was a typical Georgia-Auburn game, hotly contested. Emotions were sky-high on both sides. Late in the fourth quarter, with Auburn leading, 10-6, Georgia was driving toward the Auburn goal line. It was fourth and three and the Bulldogs desperately needed a first down. Time was ticking off the clock. It was now or never. The Bulldogs ran Lauren Hargrove on a sweep, and despite being hit at the line of scrimmage, a second Hargrove effort looked like he might have netted a first down. But it was close and the referee called for a measurement.

Asher and the Auburn chain holder brought in their chains from the side-lines. When they placed their chains down, the Auburn rep pulled heavily on his end of the chain to move it past the forward point of the football and deny Georgia the first down. When he did, Asher, the old Tech High boxer, came out of his fistic retirement. He promptly threw down his end of the chain to the ground, sprinted the ten yards to the Auburn chain holder, and unloaded a right cross to the jaw. The Auburn rep's knees buckled and then he sagged to the ground—out cold. The referee decided the Auburn rep pulled the chain excessively and awarded Georgia the first down. The Bulldogs went on to score and won the game 12-10. But the next year there was a new rule in the Southeastern Conference. First-down markers would be held by SEC officials.

After graduating from law school in 1951, Asher returned to Atlanta to practice law with Paul Ginsberg, a former Fulton County Solicitor. But the action was too slow for Asher so he quit his practice, borrowed $25,000, and with the help of a Daytona Bank, moved to Daytona Beach and became the owner of the Nassau Villas Motel.

To say Asher was, at age twenty-seven, a young man in a hurry, would be a masterpiece of understatement. He was a bundle of perpetual motion. How else, in one decade, could he simultaneously have been an ocean-front motel operator, CEO of the Bowman Nursing Home, and night club operator, as well as scout college games on weekends for the San Diego Chargers, coach Father Lopez High School football, and serve on the Daytona Beach City Commission?

When Asher arrived in Daytona Beach, aside from the well-established Daytona Plaza, there was not an inn or hotel on the ocean front that could show a profit for the months of March, April, and May. The retail establishments in town were suffering as well. The snowbirds who had come down to spend the winter had by then gone home where the temperatures were slowly rising. The summer vacation crowd with its families would not arrive until school was out so it looked like another bleak spring for Daytona Beach. That is, until Asher took charge.

"Why," he asked me, "does the college spring break crowd go to Fort Lauderdale when they could be coming to Daytona Beach? Why should those students drive another 200 miles when they could get as much fun and sun here?" The Asher dream became an obsession. He would show Fort Lauderdale a thing or two.

While construction was beginning on his new, fifty-seven-unit Safari Beach Motel, Asher packed his bags, gassed up his 1957 yellow Chevy convertible, and headed for the Midwest. Like Paul Revere, he carried a message from Athens, Georgia, to Ann Arbor, Michigan. "In Daytona Beach," he announced at fraternity and sorority houses, "we are catering to college students in March, April, and May. Not only are we offering reduced room rates but every night we give you free barbecues and free dances with live bands."

The call to Daytona Beach worked. Not only did the students come in 1958 but they came in droves. Asher's new motel was booked solidly and his overflow filled most of the hotels south of the boardwalk.

In 1969, while he was building winning football teams at Father Lopez High School, the neighboring all-black Bethune-Cookman College was in the midst of a drought. "It is going to be a long, rough season," Coach Cy McClairen warned his president, Dr Richard Moore. "We simply do not have the talent."

"Then get Asher, that high school coach on the beach," Dr. Moore replied. "He has done everything else around here. Maybe he can get us football talent."

Coach McClairen telephoned Asher. "There is no way we can compete next season," he said, "unless we have a recruiter who can get us some football players in a hurry. The season opens in three months."

A white recruiter at a black college? Intriguing, Asher thought. He accepted the challenge.

Once more he gassed up his automobile, left his wife in charge of the motel, and headed for high school coaching clinics in Florida, Georgia, Alabama, and Tennessee. He came back with some of the finest white prep players in each state—all signed to Bethune-Cookman grants-in-aid. When the season opened, Bethune-Cookman shocked perennial power Florida A & M in more ways than one. Not only did it win the game, but six of its eleven players were white.

In 1973, the World Football League came into being and Jacksonville was awarded a franchise. Who would be named its head coach? Asher dreamed, This was it. Among his many different wants, one was to become head coach of a professional football team. As a Pop Warner League coach, if he could start Lenny Snow on his way to becoming an All-American at Georgia Tech, and if he could win region championships as coach of Daytona Beach Father Lopez and New Smyrna Beach High Schools, why couldn't he win championships in the World Football League? He was going to become head coach of the WFL Jacksonville Sharks and nothing, not even Fran Monaco and his twin poodles, would stop him.

Monaco, owner of the Jacksonville franchise, was considering several successful head college coaches to be his head man. Monaco, who owned a flourishing chemical laboratory, had not only never heard of Asher he was certainly not going to pick his coach from a high school, no matter how many championships he had won. Or so he thought.

One day after the announcement of the Jacksonville franchise was made, Asher drove to Deland, burst into Monaco's executive office, and announced, "You are going to be the owner of the first championship team in the World Football League. Now think about this: Monaco, champion of the World!"

He told Monaco, "Everywhere I have been, I have been a winner. My Pop Warner team won a national championship, my semi-pro team at the University of Georgia was undefeated, and my New Smyrna Beach team, which had not had a winning season in six years, won two region championships."

In a humid, July night in 1973, before a near-capacity crowd in the old Gator Bowl, the Jacksonville Sharks opened their WFL season against the New York Stars, coached by the sweet Kentucky babe, Vito "Babe" Parilli, Bear Bryant's first bona fide All-American and later a star with the New York Titans of the old American Football League.

Before the game, when the introduction was made over the Gator Bowl PA system, that Asher, the high school coach from Daytona Beach, would be coaching the Sharks, there was in unison, a deafening sound of "Booooooooooooo!" But when the game ended, the boos turned to cheers as the Sharks won and Asher bested Parilli.

For Asher, the victory was sweet but it was soured by the presence on the sidelines of Mrs. Monaco walking her twin poodles upfield and downfield, in front of the Sharks bench. Asher loved dogs, had five collies at one time himself, but he wanted no animals on his sidelines except the ones who played for him. He coached three more games, winning two, but the clash over the canines led to his dismissal. Before the season ended, attendance at Jacksonville and throughout the league dwindled and most of the franchises lost money. Asher never was paid but got an injunction and walked away with the Sharks game uniforms, pads, and footballs.

He returned to Daytona Beach disappointed but not defeated. He became coach of Spruce Creek High School's football team, won another championship, made his foray into politics, and resumed scouting duties with the Oakland Raiders.

In assessing his life, Asher said, I never have felt I did a day's work. As a kid, I loved to sell scorecards and ice cream at old Ponce de Leon Park in Atlanta, and I had fun as a door-to-door salesman for the old *Liberty* magazines when I was attending Atlanta's Highland Elementary School. I always loved what I did. It never was work."

Asher says he is the happiest when he is with his family and his dogs.

"If they gave the Heisman trophy to the outstanding wife in America, it would not be a contest. Dawn would win easily. She works for the Chamber of Commerce, campaigns for me all over town, has been a good-will ambassador for the city, a great mother, gourmet cook, and loving mate. What more could anyone want?"

As a twelve-year-old selling magazines, he earned enough money to pay his way to Washington, DC for the World Boy Scout Jamboree. He helped his brother (me) get off to a good start in the life insurance business and he has been a caring brother to his seventy-four-year-old sister, Hope Everett.

If he had his life to live over what would Asher change?

"Nothing," he answered. "I have been blessed doing things I enjoyed. I feel at peace. I have no more worlds to conquer."

Take it from his brother: don't bet on it.

1950 BULLDOGS
MISSED BILLY GRANT

How would you like to coach a college football team that was so talented that ten of its players would go on to professional football careers? How would you like to coach a college football team that didn't simply upset the nation's No. 1 ranked team but annihilated it? Such a team was the 1950 University of Georgia Bulldogs who in their opening game destroyed a star-studded University of Maryland squad, touted as the greatest college football machine since the unbeaten World War II Army team, which featured Felix "Doc" Blanchard and Glenn Davis.

The mighty Maryland Terrapins, ranked No. 1 by the Associated Press, United Press, International News Service, and Street and Smith's in preseason polls, came into Sanford Stadium on a sizzling, humid mid-September Saturday afternoon and were soundly thrashed 27-7.

Led by a sophomore quarterback out of Valdosta, Georgia, named Billy Grant, and a staunch defense anchored by Marion Campbell, Art DeCarlo, and Derwent Langley, this Georgia team coached by Wally Butts looked unbeatable.

On his way to the Athens (Georgia) Airport, where his humiliated Terps were going to board an exceptionally long flight back to College Park, Maryland, veteran coach Jim Tatum said flatly, "Georgia is the most underrated football team I have ever seen." The Bulldogs were the talk of the football world, but the pride and glory did not last long.

The following Saturday they traveled to San Francisco, California, where they were criticized by the media for scheduling such an "unworthy opponent," little Saint Mary's College. One Atlanta scribe said Atlanta's Marist School would be a tougher foe. For the second successive weekend, Georgia shocked the football world. Only this time the conqueror of the nation's top-ranked team became the victim of the nondescript Gaels of Saint Mary's. The Bulldogs barely escaped with their lives, getting battered and bruised in a 7-7 deadlock.

The Saint Mary's game was an omen of things to come, for what had promised to be a spectacular season after the opener turned into a mediocre year of six wins, three losses, and three ties. What happened? How could a team loaded with future National Football League players miss? Count 'em, no less than ten...Bobby Walston, John Carson, Marion Campbell, Harry Babcock, Dick Yelvington, Nick Feher, Art DeCarlo, Claude Hipps, Hamp Turner, and Billy Mixon would earn starting jobs in the NFL, and three of these, Walston, Carson, and Campbell would earn All-Star status.

Walston, six-foot-three and 185 pounds, a Georgia state Golden Gloves heavyweight boxing champion and a holder of the three-year pass receiving record at Georgia, went on to become the leading scorer in the NFL catching passes and kicking field goals and extra points for the Philadelphia Eagles.

Carson, six-foot-three and 194 pounds, also became a leading scorer in the NFL and a perennial team leading scorer catching passes for the Washington Redskins. He holds the record for the most pass receptions (forty-five) at Georgia for one season.

Campbell, twice coach of the Atlanta Falcons, was an All-SEC tackle at Georgia and an All-Star selectee in the NFL while playing for the Philadelphia Eagles.

Yelvington, six-foot-two, 225, played six seasons as a starting offensive tackle for the New York Giants. He never missed a game. It was his pass blocking that gave Y. A. Tittle time to throw, and his quickness and devastating blocks that opened holes for the inside running of Frank Gifford as the Giants won the 1956 NFL championship.

The Pittsburgh Steelers were the one team that stopped the Giants during regular season play and two of Yelvington's former Bulldog teammates, Hipps and DeCarlo, were the reason why. Each intercepted two passes, killing Giants TD drives. Babcock sprang from Georgia to the old New York Titans where he led his team in pass receiving. Ever since the 1950 season, the question has been haunting me. Why didn't a team so richly endowed win more that six games? To get the answer, I contacted one of the two assistant coaches still alive, the captain and alternate captain of the team, and seven of the starting players.

Here is where they are now and what they had to say.

Captain Michael Eugene "Mike" Merola, 6'0", 210 pounds, offensive and defensive end. Merola is seventy-one years old, retired, and living in Athens, Georgia. He has been married to Nell Veal Merola for forty-five years. They have four daughters. Merola was a public school administrator in Parsippany, New Jersey, the post from which he retired. Earlier, he coached football at Washington County High School in Georgia. Merola was a walk-on football player at Georgia. He was the son of immigrant parents from Italy who could not speak the English language. He was discovered by Howell Hollis, then assistant athletic director. Hollis was watching a pickup, touch football game one day when he spotted Merola making one-hand pass receptions. He told Coach Butts about it and soon thereafter Merola had a scholarship. Today he is in good health. He plays golf five times a week. He had tremendous respect for Coach Butts. If he had his life to live over again, he would do the same things but would do them better. His proudest moment came when he earned his master's degree from the University of Georgia.

What does Merola say about what happened to the 1950 Georgia Bulldogs? "When we lost Grant (who broke his leg in the final quarter of the Maryland game and was lost for the season), we lost our magic. We had two other quarterbacks (Mal Cook and Ray Prosperi) but neither could ignite us like Grant did. We had a great defense, shutting out four opponents and allowing only one touchdown to three others. But once Grant was gone, on offense, it was three downs and punt."

Alternate Captain Richard Joseph "Dick" Yelvington, 6'2", 225 pounds, offensive tackle. Yelvington is seventy years old and living in Lake Charles, Louisiana. At the age of sixty-five, he married for the first time his high school sweetheart from Daytona Beach, Florida, Peggy Sembler Quirk. He has a forty-nine-year-old stepson. After playing professional football for the Giants for six years, he became an agent for the Federal Bureau of Narcotics, forerunner of the Drug Enforcement Agency. Due to a cerebral hemorrhage in 1970, he took medical retirement. At the age of eighteen, he went to the University of Georgia on a football scholarship. He had no idea what he was going to face. It was head-knocking in full pads the first week. Yelvington would line up facing one blocker who was to protect the ball carrier. When Yelvington upended his head-on blocker and made the tackle, it was just the beginning. Then he had to get through two defenders to get to the ball carrier. Then he was matched against three defenders. These were not rookies like Yelvington; they were seasoned lettermen. This was followed by game-type scrimmages followed by wind sprints. Yelvington quit and joined the US Army. This was like going from the fire to the frying pan. At the end of an eighteen-month Army tour, he felt ready to handle any thing Coach Butts could ask of him so he returned to Georgia and convinced Coach Butts to restore his scholarship. This time he was ready. He became a two-year starter and the most devastating blocker of the 1950 team. He was an honorable mention All Southeastern Conference choice. Of all his accomplishments, he says he is most proud of going through spring practice, summer practice, and fall drills five years in a row and never crying "uncle." Occasionally, he will watch the Bulldogs on TV but he does not attend any games. He says his generation is gone. He has no interest in living in the past. He says he would swap TV football for a good movie any day. The toughest college player and the toughest professional player he ever played against were one and the same: Bob Gain of the University of Kentucky and the Cleveland Browns.

Here is what Yelvington has to say on what happened to the 1950 Bulldogs.

We were stereotyped. Our offense had no diversity. We had good running backs in [Billy] Mixon, [Lukie] Brunson, [Zippy] Morocco, and [Lauren] Hargrove but we had little cross-blocking and few trap plays...

We missed Grant. After he got hurt, we would have done better if Coach Butts had gone from the straight-T formation to the split-T. Mal Cook would have been an ideal split-T quarterback. He was big (6'4", 220), fast and a good runner. But he was not a drop-back passer...

I played much better in practice and during game scrimmages than I ever did in a regular game. By Saturday, I was worn out...Some of the coaches belittled us. If you hear how sorry you are often enough, you get to believing it. We got too much criticism and too little praise.

Bill Hartman, backfield coach. At the age of eighty-three, Bill Hartman married Mary Brazell Williams, a lady he met in military intelligence in the US Army during World War II. They will celebrate their first anniversary December 29. They honeymooned at the Outback Bowl last December in Tampa and recently returned from a trip to Europe, where they cruised the Danube River. They also have had trips to the beaches in North Carolina and New Jersey. Mary is seventy-six years old. Bill's first wife, Ruth, died two years ago. Hartman was picked as a member of the Silver Anniversary All-America football team. He played four years of football at Georgia during the mid and late 1930s and coached at Georgia from 1939 to 1972, first as backfield coach under Butts and later as kicking coach under Vince Dooley. During his coaching career, he also was a legendary life insurance salesman, becoming a life and qualifying member of the Million Dollar Round Table and a perennial sales leader nationwide for the National Life of Vermont. Hartman also headed the Tech-Georgia Development Fund.

Here's what Coach Hartman says on what happened to the 1950 Bulldogs.

When Grant broke his leg, we were left with no leader. [Mal] Cook was the finest physical specimen in a football uniform that I ever saw. We thought he was going to be a sensational quarterback but neither he nor [Ray] Prosperi was able to get the job done...I disagree that our intense practice sessions and the type of offense we used had anything to do with our record. The conduct of our practices and our motivational schemes were no different than they were in 1942 when we went to the Rose Bowl, in 1946 when we went to the Sugar Bowl, and 1948 when we went to the Orange Bowl. Talk to all the players who ever played for Coach Butts and you will find that 96 percent of them appreciated him and respected him. Coach Butts was doing more than getting players ready for a game. He was getting them ready for life...

Why didn't we play redshirt [Zeke] Bratkowski when neither Cook nor Prosperi produced? Well, we thought about it. We even had him dressed out

1998

and standing by Coach Butts' side. But when we started doing that, half the season was over and we decided it wasn't worth losing a year's eligibility for a half a season.

Arthur Anthony "Art" DeCarlo, 6'2", 195 pounds, linebacker. Art DeCarlo is sixty-eight years old, retired from the copier industry, and living in Endicott, Maryland, a suburb of Baltimore. Before his twenty-year copier career, he worked for the National Security Agency as a recruiter. He played professional football for seven seasons, first with the Pittsburgh Steelers and then with the Baltimore Colts. He has been married to Mary Kerr DeCarlo for forty-two years and they have five children. DeCarlo had no scholarship to the University of Georgia, but a friend of former Bulldog fullback Al Bodine sent him a train ticket to Athens where he "tried out." The "tryout" consisted of the coaches lining up the biggest backs they had and running then straight at DeCarlo, one at a time. Everyone was in full gear. DeCarlo, in one session, must have had fifteen running backs trying to go over him, one at a time. DeCarlo stopped them all and was awarded a scholarship. He not only made All-SEC at Georgia but also honorable mention All-America. Today DeCarlo plays golf four times a week. He does 100 sit-ups and 100 leg raises every day and is down to 215, twenty pounds above his playing weight at the University of Georgia. He is most proud of the fact that all five of his children graduated from college and that one has a master's degree from the University of Georgia. His biggest disappointment was when Coach Don Shula said he was one of two people he was considering as assistant head coach of the Baltimore Colts and Shula picked the other candidate, Chuck Knoll. Knoll later took the Steelers to the Super Bowl Championship. DeCarlo says that when he played for the Colts, the best player in the NFL was the highest paid. That person was quarterback Johnny Unitas, whose top salary was $30,000. Today DeCarlo says a Unitas would be worth the whole franchise. DeCarlo attends one Georgia home game a year and follows the 'Dogs when they are on TV.

Says DeCarlo on what happened to the 1950 Bulldogs:

> Without Grant, our offense did not work. We needed a leader. In practice, we spent too much time on fundamentals and had too much emphasis on hitting. We were expected to beat down the guy in front of us, not outsmart him. We tried to overpower teams we couldn't but we could have out-finessed those same teams. The practices were brutal, much more so at Georgia than with the Colts or Steelers.
>
> I felt like at Georgia there was more emphasis on beating up the other team than winning the game...The coaches misused [Lauren] Hargrove. He had everything...size, speed, agility. He needed to run outside but the coaches wanted him to run inside. Had he gone to Georgia Tech, I think he would have won the Heisman trophy.

Claude Marion Hipps, 6'1", 185 pounds, defensive halfback. Hipps is sixty-nine years old and living in Columbus, Georgia. He is married to his University of Georgia sweetheart, Betty Eaves. With Coach Butts' approval, they got married during the 1950 season forty-eight years ago. Hipps retired from Frito-Lay as national sales manager of its vending company in 1987. He plays golf twice weekly, takes meals to shut-in patients, and serves as a deacon of the Wynnbrook Baptist Church in Columbus. He rarely goes to a Bulldogs game but watches them on TV, as he does his old pro team, the Steelers. He weighs 175 pounds, ten below his playing weight at Georgia. He jogs 3–4 miles every day. He was an All-SEC defensive back at Georgia and a member of the All-Service team while serving in the Marines 1944–49. His favorite professional memory is stealing three passes when his Steelers upset the New York Giants, 63-7. The Hippses have three children .Hipps has long been considered one of the finest defensive backs the University of Georgia ever had.

What does Hipps say on what happened to the 1950 Bulldogs?

> We missed a take-charge guy. Our defense was super but every time we gave the offense the ball, they either fumbled it away or threw interceptions…The practices were much tougher at Georgia than they were in the pro ranks. Once the season started in the pros, you simply polished up your plays. There was little hitting. It was different at Georgia. Hitting was the name of the game. Coach Butts had a dual personality…He would be a taskmaster on the field but he was your best friend off it. He was a good man. When I finished my senior season and I knew I was headed for the Steelers, Coach Butts told me that I would make it professionally if I hustled and always went the extra mile. Later, one of the Steelers coaches, Gus Dorais, told me, "We never had a problem with a Butts-coached player."

William Raymond "Billy" Mixon, five-foot-eleven, 180 pounds, offensive halfback. Mixon is sixty-nine years old and living in Jackson, Mississippi. He retired from the insurance business at age sixty-two and has been suffering from Alzheimer's disease for the past five years. This interview was conducted with Patricia Thompson Mixon, his wife of forty-seven years. The Mixons have two sons, ages forty-three and forty-five . Before Alzheimer's set in, Mixon played golf regularly and was an avid hunter. Since stricken with Alzheimer's, he has confined his activities to walking, riding with Pat to the store, and watching TV. After the 1950 Georgia season, Mixon joined the Marine Corps and played two seasons for the Parris Island (South Carolina) Marines. He led them to the All-Marine Corps championship. He played two seasons for the San Francisco 49ers along with two of his Bulldog teammates, Nick Feher, now deceased, and Campbell. The 49ers drafted him in the third round after his senior season at Georgia where he was the leading ground gainer and an All-SEC choice. He played in two college All-Star games, the Senior Bowl at Mobile and the Blue-Gray game at Montgomery, Alabama. Wife Pat said she never has seen Billy unhappy.

Pat said Billy never would say anything bad about anyone. But she recalls him telling her how tough the practices were and how they had no quarterback after Grant got hurt.

Anthony Joseph "Zippy" Morocco, 5'10", 170 pounds, offensive halfback. Morocco is retired and living in Athens. He has been retired from a tremendously

1998

successful real estate business since 1985. He has been married to the former Fran Matonis, a registered nurse, for thirty-eight years. As a junior in 1950, Morocco averaged 9.9 yards each time he touched the football. Running from scrimmage, he averaged 4.1 yards per carry. He gained 217 yards rushing, 206 yards pass receiving, 143 on kickoff returns, and 244 on punt returns for a total of 810 yards. Morocco has lived in Athens since 1948. A native of Youngstown, Ohio, the same town from which came Fireball Frankie Sinkwich, Georgia's first Heisman trophy winner, Morocco came to Georgia because of Sinkwich and encouragement from Charley Trippi, another Georgia legend. He had met Trippi when Trippi played in the College All-Star football game. Morocco, Georgia's first basketball All-American, came close to missing all the glory. During his sophomore season, Coach Butts chastised him at one practice for "not hustling" and ordered Morocco to leave the field. Morocco not only left the field, but left the university, went home, and enrolled at the University of Cincinnati. One week later he got homesick for Athens, telephoned Bulldog assistant coach Quentin Lumpkin and asked if he might come back. Coach Lumpkin talked to Coach Butts and got the okay. The rest, as they say, is history, more so in basketball where he was All-America and led the Southeastern Conference in scoring. Although he was a starting halfback at Georgia he never was a starter in high school where his main emphasis was basketball. After graduating from Georgia, Morocco reported for Army duty at Fort Jackson, South Carolina. He played football at Fort Jackson and was named to the All-Service team. Morocco says his most satisfying moment in life was when his son Chris, not given a scholarship to Georgia, accepted a scholarship to Clemson and led the Tigers to a victory in the Gator Bowl. His happiest moment came when Chris was named the most outstanding athlete in the state of South Carolina.

Morocco says of the 1950 Bulldogs, "After the Maryland game, we had no quarterback. If Grant had stayed healthy, we would have gone unbeaten. I don't think I was utilized well. I had the deception and speed to go outside but the coaches always had me running inside. But I think the biggest trouble was that we had nothing left to give on Saturday. We had given it all Monday through Friday with lots of scrimmaging and lots of wind sprints. We had no legs by game time. They were on the practice field."

Elijah Hampton "Hamp" Tanner, 6'2", 255 pounds, tackle. Hamp Tanner is seventy years old and living in Athens, Georgia. He is married to the former Carolyn Ogletree and they have three children. The Tanners have had their share of tragedy. Daughter Susan, age forty, was recently released from the hospital after a bout of seizures. Daughter Lisa Louise, age thirty-five, has had both breasts removed because of cancer. For the past five years, Tanner has worked as a clerk and grocery bagger at Kroger's. Last month he missed two weeks of work because of pneumonia but he is feeling fine now, thank you. He played one season of football with the San Francisco 49ers and another season with the old Dallas Texans who later became the Baltimore Colts.

After being released by the Colts, he coached at Calhoun (Georgia) High School and worked in the building business before joining Kroger's. Tanner was born in Waycross. When he was two years old, his father died. His mother remarried and the family moved to Macon, where he attended Lanier High School. He played only one season at Lanier High and that was on the second team. He weighed 264 pounds and, at 6'2", that was good enough to interest Georgia and Clemson.

His highest paid professional year was when he played for the 49ers. There was no signing bonus. His salary for the season was $5,500. Fifteen years ago his weight zoomed to 315 pounds but today he is down to 240. When he was at Georgia and weighing 265, a close Bulldog friend promised to buy him a tailor-made suit at Athens' finest men's store if he got down to 235. A tailor-made suit? That was something Tanner had always dreamed of but never could imagine owning. But he went to work on a strict diet, ran extra wind sprints after practice and then walked in the evening.

Sure enough, he got down to 235. His friend figured with the tailor-made suit Tanner could not afford to put the weight back on and that he would remain at 235 and be a much faster and quicker lineman. And maybe it would have worked that way except that when Tanner met the tailor, he got him to put extra material in the waist so that when he got off the much-hated diet, he could let the trousers out two or three inches.

Tanner says, "No one stepped forward as a leader after Grant went down. And then we spent an awful lot of time scrimmaging. But that should have come as no surprise. Before the season started, Coach Butts told everyone what to expect. No one should have been looking for a picnic."

During that 1950 season, I covered football practice every day for the *Atlanta Constitution*. I remember the hitting, the scrimmaging, the one-on-one and two-on-two head-knocking drills. But what I remember most happened during a game-type scrimmage. The first offensive team was playing against the scrubs. Coach Butts had installed a new play that he was sure would work. But this day, every time he ran it, the ball carrier would be nailed for a loss. Coach Butts was furious, screaming, shaking his fists. "We will run that play again and again," he shouted, "until we get it right."

This time Coach Butts personally went up to the line of scrimmage to make sure each lineman knew whom he was going to block. There would be no way any defender could get through. On the next play, Lauren Hargrove got the ball and just as he got it, a nondescript guard named Ed Worley somehow slipped through and threw Hargrove for a loss. Coach Butts was livid. He ran to the line of scrimmage, made his checkoffs, and could not figure out how anyone could have gotten through.

In desperation, he ran up to Worley and screamed, "All right Worley, where did you come from?" Worley, kind of dumbfounded at the question, smiled, and said politely, "Ellijay."

THE 1950 SEASON

27 Maryland 7
19 Boston College 7
0 Georgia Tech 7
7 Saint Mary's 7
7 Alabama 14
20 Texas A & M 40*
0 North Carolina 0
6 Florida 0
27 Mississippi State 0
12 Auburn 10
13 LSU 13
40 Furman 0

Presidential Cup Bowl

SAN JOSE CITY COLLEGE

WILLIAM DAPRANO
Chasing the Gold

William Lewis Daprano has been chasing the gold for sixteen years, ever since he retired as one of Atlanta's most successful homebuilders. Never mind that he has won more than 100 Masters Track awards. Never mind that he helped establish world records as a member of the United States' 2 x 400 and 4 x 400 relay teams. Never mind that he has won three national titles in the 200- and 400-meters, a national pentathlon (five events) and raced on two 4 x 400 national championship relay teams. What matters mostly to the seventy-one-years-young Daprano is winning one of the biggest prizes of his life…the heart of svelte Suzanne Magrogan.

At a regional Masters meet last June at Charleston, West Virginia, Daprano was winning the 100 meters, long jump, discus, and javelin while Magrogan was capturing the women's 100 meters and long jump. At a dinner dance that evening, the two met and have since been inseparable.

"We danced the night away," Daprano fondly recalls. "I liked every thing about her: her competitiveness, her sense of humor, her brains, and her body. I thought to myself: why is she out here running? With that figure of hers, she could be modeling." The next day Daprano flew home to Atlanta and Magrogan headed home to Baltimore.

They have talked on the telephone every night for hours at a time. Last August they drove to Maine together where she won medals in the long jump and triple jump and he won medals in the pentathlon, triple jump, and javelin. Whenever there is a Masters Championship meet, whether it is in Dover, Delaware, or Dover, England, they are a steady twosome. Before the year ends, they will be competing in Barbados and at Disney World. Next March they will be in Sweden for the European championships and in Boston for the US Nationals.

Competition is new for Magrogan, a former schoolteacher, psychologist, and accountant, but competition, and more specifically winning, has always been a part of Daprano's life. For instance, he was a champion in running the sprints and hurdles at old Atlanta Tech High School. As a University of Georgia freshman in 1948, he was a mild sensation when he ran a 9.9 100-yard dash. His true love, however, was football, but at 140 pounds he saw little chance of playing for the Bulldogs. So he transferred to Livingston State College in Alabama, where he not only lettered in football but led the old Southern Intercollegiate Athletic Association in yards rushing.

Daprano pushed himself to the hilt as a player, coach, and businessman. As head coach at Atlanta's old Saint Joseph's High School in the 1960s, he kept his team on the practice field until dark. But the dedication paid dividends. His Saint Joseph's teams won three region football championships, posted a 25-game winning streak and a ten-year record of fifty-nine wins, thirty-one losses, and four ties. Daprano was selected as a coach in the state's annual High School All-Star football game.

"I have always wanted to be No. 1," Daprano said. "I adhere to the late coach [Vince] Lombardi's philosophy: 'Winning is not every thing; it is the only thing.'"

Today, Daprano lives in a three-story house he built in Riverdale, Georgia. He is an early riser (7:30 A.M.) and a healthy eater (granola muffins, oatmeal, and fresh fruit for breakfast and fish or pasta for dinner). By 10 A.M. he is on the track at either Atlanta's Lakewood Stadium or Landmark Christian School. His punishing workout six days a week consists of the following: jogging for thirty minutes (a warm up), running 100 meters, 200 meters, and 300 meters five times each, followed by two hours of throwing the javelin, discus, and shot put. Daprano will be seventy-two in February. How long will he continue this pace? He said,

> As long as I can. I am having fun and that is what life is all about. Can you imagine me being around people my age who are always complaining

about their aches and pains? As it says in the Good Book, this is the day the Lord hath made, rejoice and be glad in it.

As long as there is a place in competitive sports for people my age, I am going to be there. I do not ever want to become just one of the million joggers. It would be terribly monotonous to run every day and not know I was the best in my class. I want the thrill of crossing the finish line first.

Finishing first has rarely been a problem for Daprano. He has brought home the gold in every Masters age category. In the age fifty-five to fifty-nine division he set an American Pentathlon (long jump, javelin, 200 meters, 1500 meters, and discus) record. And in so doing, he beat his old hero, former US Olympic champion Bob Richards, the man whose photograph used to be on the Wheaties boxes.

In the sixty to sixty-four age category, he was a member of the 4 x 100 relay team that won the world championship in Myasaki, Japan. In the age sixty-five to sixty-nine age bracket, he was a member of the 4 x 400 relay team that set a world record. This year, in the seventy to seventy-four age division, he was a member of the world record–setting 4 x 200 relay team. To quote Atlanta journalist Hal Hayes, "Age must pick up speed if it hopes to overtake Daprano."

Competing in the Master Track program may have saved Daprano's life. At age fifty-four, he was a huge success in homebuilding and real estate development but the pressure he put on himself to be No. 1 in business almost cost him his life.

I could not build houses fast enough. I was on the job site every day, encouraging the supervisors, giving a compliment here and a kick in the rear there. Time was of the essence. I pushed so hard and so often that by midafternoon I was a bundle of nerves. The tension was terrific.

I began to think about how soon I could get to the nearest bar. I thought that two or three drinks would relieve the heat. And it did but it was the same thing again the next day. So, working full speed all day and drinking after work became my standard operating procedure.

One day we were working on a home for a physician. He happened to be there and he overheard me explode at one of my crew. He took me aside, led me to his automobile where he pulled out a blood pressure machine and put the cup on my arm. The blood pressure was out of sight. He knew I was a drinker.

CDC says if you take fifty-six drinks a month you are an excessive drinker. I was drinking that many in one week.

The doctor told me I could give up alcohol and the torrid pace I was on or I could die. It was my choice. Of course, I wanted to live.

Daprano not only gave up drinking but he gave up the home building and construction business. "I vowed to take care of myself. I started running road races, including the annual Peachtree Road Race. And then I heard my old hero, Richards, was coming to town to run a race for people fifty-five and over. It was the first I had heard about the Masters Track program. This was for the US National championships and when I saw some of those old geezers out their running, I thought, shoot, I can beat some of those guys. But I never thought I would beat Richards."

Daprano changed his diet and began a rigid training program. One year later, at age fifty-five, he entered and won the 200 and 400 meters at the National Masters Sports Festival and followed that up by winning the National Masters Pentathlon. He felt like a man reborn. "Working out did more for getting me relaxed than alcohol ever did. Booze relaxed me for a few hours but exercise put me at ease all day."

Daprano was born on the Atlanta southside near Grant Park. His first race came when he was seven years old. The nuns at his school lined up all the boys from ages six to twelve for an all-school race, with the winner getting a chocolate cake. Daprano won the cake but his biggest thrill was the exhilaration he felt crossing the finish line first. "Ever since I won that race, I wanted to be first in every thing I did."

It is no wonder Daprano excelled in athletics. As a preteen his Grant park neighbors included Joe Salome, George Maloof, Gene Chandler, Morris Harrison, and the Jones boys, Billy and Johnny. Salome went on to become the greatest passer in the history of Atlanta's Marist school and a starting quarterback at Georgia Tech. Maloof, also a star football player at Marist, played fullback at Georgia Tech as did Harrison. Maloof is the only player in Tech's football history to score five touchdowns in one game against archrival Georgia. Chandler was an All-Southeastern Conference end at Georgia and the Jones boys were two of old Atlanta Tech High's all-time great linemen.

"I had to excel, Daprano recalls, "just to hold my head up in the neighborhood."

Daprano did more than excel. Not just at old Tech High and the University of Georgia, as Livingston State's coach and a coach at Saint Joseph's (he was named Georgia State "Coach of the Year" in track and football) but also in business. He started a property and casualty insurance agency and built it into one of the largest agencies in Greater Atlanta. Then he began a real estate development and home building business and in ten years he earned enough money to retire at age fifty-four.

Life has not always been a bowl of cherries for Daprano. His late father, an Italian immigrant, scratched out a living as an electrician, but when the Depression came his business went down the drain. Daprano was three years old. Less than one year later the Daprano home caught fire. No one was injured but the house burned to the ground.

When Bill was financially able to retire, tragedy struck again. His childhood sweetheart and wife of twenty-nine years, Judy, a chain smoker, developed lung cancer and a malignant brain tumor. She died at age fifty-one.

"It was the low point in my life," Daprano said. "Thank goodness for the National Masters program. It helped me get over my loss."

Conditioning-wise, Daprano is nothing short of amazing. When he started the Masters program sixteen years ago, his weight was 167 pounds. Today he weighs 165. Five years ago, when he won in the intermediate hurdles at the Nationals, his time was fifty-three seconds. When he won the hurdles again this year, he had lost only three seconds.

"I haven't slowed down much because I train just as hard now as I did five years ago. I not only wanted to win again. I wanted to make darn sure I wasn't going to become a seventy-one-year-old with a pot belly. I can get into the same clothes I did five years ago. When I brag about this to my friends, they say it is not because I have remained trim, but because I am too cheap to buy new clothes." Whatever the case, at seventy-one, Daprano could pass for a man age fifty. There is no fat around his waist and there is a clear sparkle in his eye.

If Daprano has any regrets, it is that financial circumstances forced him out of his first love, coaching:

> After fifteen years as a teacher and high school coach, my annual earnings were $9,800. And I was putting in something like sixty-five hours a week, sometimes seven days a week. In addition to football practice four days a week, we had team meetings, coaches meetings, and film meetings to review last week's game and next week's opponent. And, of course, if we played a game on Friday night, I was usually scouting on Thursday and Saturday nights.
>
> When I retired from coaching, I had three children in high school. They needed clothes, food, a roof over their heads, doctors and dentists. My $9,800 income just did not cut it. I figured if I put in as many hours selling as I did coaching I would make more money. In my first year in the insurance and real estate business, I tripled my income.
>
> Coaching gave me a good work ethic. I learned how to get up after I had been knocked down. My second year in the home building business, interest rates zoomed to 20 percent. I was a million dollars in debt. I had thirty-seven houses sitting on the ground unsold. I had to let employees go. I went to the job site and worked just like one of the hired hands. I also worked with the bankers and we figured out a way to hold on. When interest rates went down, our business took off like a rocket. We sold all thirty-seven houses.
>
> I would love to coach young people again, but I know the game has passed me by. So much has changed. When I coached back in the sixties, you had one or two assistant coaches. Today some colleges have fifteen. We had one offensive formation. Today one team may use six or seven. We would have one wideout on a passing formation. Today coaches spread players all over the field.
>
> I had my day coaching football and I would not swap it for all the money in the world. And if I could have made ends meet, I would never have left.

Despite his heavy emphasis on competition, Daprano is no one-dimensional man. He snow skis in Colorado every winter, plans to learn hang gliding, writes articles for a bimonthly newspaper, and spends holidays with his three children, Christy, twenty-four, Judy, thirty-one, and Bill Jr., forty.

Christy and Bill Jr. inherited some of their dad's genes. Christy, a special education teacher in Greenville, South Carolina, has a roomful of trophies she won in the Greenville Track Club. Bill Jr., who took over the building business when his dad retired, was a four-letterman at North Clayton High School and a varsity tennis player at Oglethorpe University. He officiates basketball in the Southeastern Conference. Judy is a fourth grade teacher at a Morrow, Georgia, elementary school.

What's next for Daprano? "We will be competing in the world games next year in England."

The "we" means Bill and his lovely lady, Suzanne Magrogan. Who knows? By then Bill and Suzanne may be the first husband-wife team ever to bring home the gold.

STAN "THE MAN" GANN

When I left the *Atlanta Journal* in 1962 after serving six years as prep sports editor, I was asked to select the twenty-two finest high school football players I ever saw. Heading my list was Stanley Vickers Gann, the prep All-American quarterback at Atlanta Northside High School. Gann was appropriately nicknamed "Stan the Man," for if there had been a better man than Gann I have yet to meet him.

Today, Gann is fifty-eight years old. He lives in a two-story, colonial home fronting the Houston Lake Country Club Golf Course. His official residence is Kathleen, Georgia, about ten feet from the Perry city limits. His occupation: retired.

If strength comes from adversity, Gann may be the strongest man alive. He has survived three heart attacks and the loss of two children at birth.

At Georgia Tech, in his sophomore and junior seasons in 1960 and 1961, he was not just the starting quarterback but the offensive leader of the Yellow Jackets' football team. In his senior season, he lost his starting quarterback job and was relegated to holding the ball on placements (extra points, field goals, and kick-offs) for the player who took his job. Men of lesser ilk might have quit. Not Gann. He accepted his new assignment with pride and enthusiasm and handled the ball as expertly on placements as he did when he was carrying or pitching out as a quarterback.

1998

Coping with setbacks and disappointments was nothing new to Gann. During the week preceding the Georgia High School All-Star Football Classic in 1958, Gann was billed as "one of the most talented prep football players ever to come out of Atlanta." The Atlanta newspapers had his name blazoned in big, bold headlines on the lead sports page daily while such an affair as Mickey Mantle and Roger Maris being engaged in a torrid home run race for Babe Ruth's record, was pushed to the inside pages.

First, headlines roared, "GANN BEST SINCE CASTLEBERRY" (Clint Castleberry, killed in World War II, had been an immortal at old Atlanta Boys' High School and had been selected on one All-America team in his freshman and only season at Georgia Tech). By game day Atlanta media referred to Gann as "maybe the best Atlanta prep player of all time." During All-Star practice sessions, Gann dazzled the media, spectators, teammates, and coaches with his slick running of the option, booming punts, and long, accurate passes. Gann, who led his Northside High team to the State Class AAA championship, looked prime for a stellar performance in the All-Star game.

On the eve of the game, however, Gann was stricken with mononucleosis. He should have stayed in his sickbed. He had chills, fever, and swollen glands. Yet somehow he made his way to a jam-packed Grant Field and by game time was sitting on the bench in his street clothes, shivering and cheering on his teammates on every play. Such is the character of Stan Gann.

At Northside, Gann was in a class by himself. In his junior season, he guided Coach Wayman Creel's Tigers to a berth in the state finals. As a senior quarterback, he turned what were supposed to have been three highly competitive games into complete routs. It was Gann's running, passing, faking, and punting that did in Coach Frank Jernigan's North Fulton Bulldogs, 26-0; Coach Erk Russell's Grady Gray Knights, 20-0, for the Atlanta city championship; and Coach Ralph Pyburn's Columbus Blue Devils, 20-0, for the state AAA crown.

Said the late Sid Scarborough, then Athletics Director of Atlanta City Schools, formerly head coach at old Atlanta Tech High School and a onetime starting halfback at Auburn University, "Gann can do more things on a football field than anyone I have ever seen. And that goes back to the early 1930s." Punter, passer, runner, and master of the quarterback keep, in directing Northside to the state title, Gann ran for seven touchdowns, passed for seven more touchdowns, kicked twenty-six extra points, punted for a 39.7 yard average, and posted a pass completion record of 65 percent.

Gann was the *Atlanta Journal-Constitution* "Back of the Year," the Associated Press "Back of the Year," the Atlanta Touchdown Club "Back of the Year," and a bona fide selection on two All-America prep teams. He was the most sought after prep football played in Georgia, receiving twenty-three college scholarship offers, including one from Notre Dame. He chose Georgia Tech and never regretted it.

At Georgia Tech, Gann continued to roll, first as the No. 1 freshman team quarterback and then as the No. 1 varsity quarterback. In 1960, as a sophomore, he completed forty-three of ninety-six passes, five for touchdowns, and gained 679 yards.

In his junior season in 1961, he completed forty-three of seventy-nine passes for 577 yards, leading his team in total offense for the second successive year. But toward the end of the season, another superstar blossomed and he just happened to be a quarterback.

At 6'2", 190 pounds, Billy Lothridge, out of Gainesville, Georgia, was bigger, taller, and stronger than the 5'8", 165-pound Gann. Like Gann, he could run, pass, and punt, and he could also kick field goals from forty yards out. Like Gann, he had been a prep All-America, and with his ability to spot and hit receivers in the open field he gave every indication that he would become a college All-American. Before the season ended, Lothridge was sharing the starting quarterback role.

When the 1962 season opened, Lothridge was in command. Gann became the holder for placements and a backup quarterback while Lothridge went on to become runner-up to Roger Staubach for the Heisman Trophy, the award emblematic of the most outstanding college football player in America. "Lothridge was the complete football player," Gann said. "He was superb at every phase of the game."

Gann says today:

> Holding for Lothridge never bothered me. I was happy to be in a Georgia Tech uniform and blessed to play for a coach like Bobby Dodd.
>
> Coach Dodd was like a second father to me. Whenever I would see him on campus on in the athletic office, he would inquire about my studies. He always stressed the importance of a college education. He not only wanted to know how well I was doing but how much I liked the subject matter.
>
> He had a major influence on my life. So did two of his assistants, Coach [Ray] Graves and Coach [Jack] Griffin. And of course, I never respected anyone more than my high school coach, Wayman Creel.

It was because of the admiration he had for his coaches that Gann went into coaching himself. He received his degree in industrial management from Georgia Tech and then went for a master's degree in education at Mercer University.

Gann's first coaching job was working with his old coach, Creel, at Atlanta Northside. When Creel left to go to Lakeside High School in DeKalb County, Georgia, Gann moved to Middle Georgia and Warner Robins High School, and became offensive coordinator, a job he held for seventeen years. During two of those years, his team won national championships.

He became head coach at Warner Robins Northside and once again his ability to handle adversity was tested. He suffered a series of three heart attacks over a four-year period. But like a determined prizefighter, out on his feet, bleeding badly, knees wobbling, and hitting the canvas time and time again, Gann kept getting up and coming back. After the first attack, he underwent a triple by-pass in the middle of his first season and was back on the field when the next season started. Two years later the second attack floored Gann again, and once more he rose up and resumed his duties. The third attack, less than one year later, did not take him out but his physicians did. "If you don't get out of all this stress," his cardiologist told him, "you may not survive the next attack. There is only so much punishment even Stan Gann can take."

So, after playing four years of Gray-Y football when he was the star of the Buckhead Red Devils, four great years at Northside High School, four years at Georgia Tech, and twenty years of coaching, one for which he was named "Middle Georgia Coach of the Year," Gann retired.

What few people ever knew about Gann was that he could have gone to college on a baseball scholarship rather than a football grant.

In high school, three times he made the All-City team. In the *Atlanta Journal's* annual City vs. Greater Atlanta All-Star game held at old Ponce de Leon Park, in front of a bevy of professional scouts, he belted a towering home run over the third tier of signs. It was no fluke. He had done it before during the regular prep season. His Northside batting average was .386. As a catcher, he may have been the best since Pierce McWhorter came out of old Atlanta Tech High School and went on to make it professionally with the Atlanta Crackers in Class AA and Denver in Class AAA.

Today, Gann lives with his wife of thirty-three years, Sissi Smith Gann, his son, twenty-one-year old Stan Gann Jr., and his ninety-year-old mother, Jane Gann. Although his athletic days are gone, those of his wife and son are not. Sissi is captain of the Georgia State Golf Association team, which does battle annually with a like team from Florida. Stan Jr. won the Georgia State High School Championship, firing a remarkable 67, the lowest score ever posted in a state tournament. Stan Jr. also has won a PGA State Junior title. He was named by the *Macon Telegraph* "Middle Georgia Player of the Year."

Stan Sr. plays practical nurse to his mother, does volunteer work for the Georgia and Houston County Heart Associations, organizes golf tournaments for the local Parent Teachers Associations, and helps promote charitable tournaments for the Professional Golf Association.

As a player and coach, what changes would Gann like to see in high school and college football? "They ought to give the game back to the players. The quarterbacks should be out calling signals, not the coaches. Calling plays would be a great opportunity for the quarterbacks to build self-confidence. The important thing is not whether the quarterbacks make the right call or not, the important thing is that these kids would learn to make decisions. What better way to prepare for the real world. And if they call a few bad plays, so what? Is the world going to end? Tell me what executive doesn't make a bad decision now and then?"

Recalls Georgia Tech coach Griffin, "Gann was a prince of a guy. And I think he proved at Tech that he was a champion, not just as an athlete but as a human being."

THEY BELONG
IN THE HALL OF FAME

LEGENDS GENE ASHER

The name of this column has been "Where are They Now?" For this issue, it will be named "Where They Aren't Now?" Specifically, it applies to the late Erskine Mayer and Ron Blomberg and "where they aren't" is in the state of Georgia Sports Hall of Fame where they should be. A strong case for admittance to the Georgia Hall also could be made for Erskine Mayer's brother Sammy Mayer, Dr. Noah Langdale Jr., Natalie Cohen, the late Jake Abel and Leman L. "Buzzy" Rosenberg. Now I am optimistic enough to believe that someday these highly qualified candidates will be accepted for membership but wouldn't it be nice if those living would be inducted while they can smell the roses? No such luck for the Mayer brothers. For three years, I have been recommending the Mayer brothers and for three years I have been receiving that old Dodgers' war cry, "Wait 'til next year." Next year never seems to come.

What is going on here? It took Jackie Robinson, a longtime member of Baseball's Hall of Fame, thirty-two years to get into the Georgia Hall. How do you justify, pray tell, inducting a former sporting goods store owner and a golfer who played the PGA tour but never won an event into the Georgia Hall and omit Erskine Mayer, who had eight seasons in the major leagues and twenty-one back-to-back game winning seasons, and pitched the old Philadelphia Phillies into the 1915 World Series? I requested the "criterion for membership" in the Georgia Hall three months ago. As yet, I have not received it.

1998

Now, I have many dear friends in the Georgia Hall, including All-American Pete Brown, and all are deserving to be there, but come on, fellas, leaving out the man who pitched Philadelphia into its first World Series and shunning Blomberg, baseball's first designated hitter and the finest high school baseball-basketball player ever, and I do mean "ever," to come out of the state of Georgia is absolutely ridiculous.

Now you may say being baseball's first designated hitter is no big deal and maybe you are right. But being selected to the American League All-Star team is a big deal and so is playing in three World Series whether you hate the New York Yankees or not. All this Mr. Blomberg did. He spent eight seasons with the Yankees, playing commendably in the outfield posting a career batting average of .296. It was Blomberg who replaced Mickey Mantle in centerfield. At Atlanta Druid Hill High School, Blomberg was a Parade All-America football player, a two-time All-American basketball player, and the No. 1 baseball pick in America. He passed up 100 college football scholarships and almost 200 college basketball scholarships to sign a baseball contract with the New York Yankees. Blomberg lives in Roswell, Georgia, where he is president of a career-counseling and marketing firm. He is forty-nine years old.

Erskine Mayer's brother Sammy Mayer never made it big in the major leagues although he did have a cup of coffee with the old Washington Senators. What he did was write his name indelibly into Atlanta Crackers baseball history, playing centerfield and serving as team captain, team manager, and part owner. Samuel Franklin Mayer was born in Atlanta in 1893. He died in 1962. In between, he played professional baseball for twenty-two years, helped the Crackers win a league championship and was selected to the old Southern Association All-Star team.

During a game in Memphis, while he was playing with the Crackers, Mayer climbed the flagpole eight feet, held on with one hand, and caught a long fly ball to end an inning and clinch a victory. According to old newspaper clippings and senior citizens who saw him play, Mayer often took would-be base hits on the first bounce in short centerfield and threw out runners at first base.

Mayer attended the old Georgia Military Academy (originally Woodward Academy) and graduated from Georgia Tech. He played for the late Clark Griffith when Griffith owned the old Washington Senators in the American League. In 1959, three years before his death, he won the hearts of Atlanta's youth when he managed a high school All-Star team in the *Atlanta Journal's* old City vs. Greater Atlanta baseball classic. Mayer's team lost but he won the love of his players, constantly shouting words of encouragement and praise at the weeklong practice sessions and during the game.

Noah H. Langdale Jr., whose name is synonymous with Georgia State University, is retired now and living with his lovely wife, Wiggy, and his son, Michael, in a ranch-style home on Blanton Road, near Chastain Park in Atlanta. If ever there was a miscarriage of justice, it might be in the case of Langdale. He was selected on *Sports Illustrated's* Silver Anniversary Football Team and served as state chairman of the National Football Hall of Fame. He was on the first

President's Commission of the National Collegiate Athletic Association, composed of twenty-two university presidents. He served for ten years. He has spoken at high school and college football banquets all over the country as well as at the nation's top Touchdown Clubs.

What is ironic is that Langdale was asked to serve as chairman of the Georgia Sports Hall of Fame in its second year of existence, which he did but has never been tapped for membership. Talk about chutzpah.

At 6'1", 235 pounds, Langdale was a starting tackle on Alabama's 1941 football team that defeated Texas A & M and the mighty John Kimbrough, 29-21, in the Cotton Bowl. He was line coach of the 1942 Alabama team that defeated Boston College, 37-21, in the Orange Bowl. After the 1942 season, Langdale joined the Navy and played football for the University of North Carolina Preflight and later for the University of Georgia Preflight. Following the 1944 season, he went to war in the Pacific. When the war ended, he returned to his home in Valdosta, Georgia, and officiated high school football for six years with the Georgia State High School Football Officials Association.

Langdale came to Georgia State College as president in 1957 and promptly turned what was a parking garage, a.k.a. the Atlanta Division, University of Georgia, into one of the top educational institutions in America. Under Langdale's leadership, Georgia State College became Georgia State University with a thriving campus and 30,000-plus students.

Langdale is seventy-eight years old and not in the best of health. With all his exuberance and loquaciousness, deep down, he is a modest, caring, sensitive person who would never suggest that he be recognized for any achievement. He was vehemently opposed to being included in this article.

If selected for the Hall, Langdale would be the only member of that august body who is as familiar with Dr. Hugo Z. Hackenbush and Rufus J. Flywheel, Groucho Marx aliases, as he is with Chaucer and Shakespeare.

Natalie Cohen's nomination for Hall membership was submitted five years ago but somehow it must have been lost in the shuffle. What never will be lost or forgotten is her incredible record on the tennis courts. She won thirteen consecutive Georgia State Women's Open Doubles championships, thirteen consecutive Atlanta City Women's Open Doubles championships, two Atlanta City Women's Open Singles championships, one Georgia State Women's Open Singles championship, one Atlanta City Open Mixed Doubles championship, and one Georgia State Women's Doubles championship. She is listed in "International Who's Who in Tennis." She is a recipient of the Marlborough Award from World Tennis awarded for "long and meritorious service" to tennis and was recognized by the Southern Lawn Tennis Association for "outstanding sportsmanship." A native of Atlanta and a graduate of old Atlanta Girls' High School and the University of California, Cohen began playing tennis at age eight. At age forty-two, she won the "Grand Slam" of Georgia tennis, capturing singles and doubles titles in the Atlanta City and Georgia State tournaments.

Natalie Cohen is single and lives alone in Buckhead on Peachtree Street in Atlanta. She is eighty-five years old. Cohen has been a certified tennis official for more than fifty years, serving as linesman, umpire, and referee for city, state, southeastern regional NCAA and professional tournaments, both men's and women's. If the Hall of Fame is ever going to admit Cohen, if not now, when?

Buzzy Rosenberg, at 5'7", was called by his old Atlanta Northside High School coach, the late Wayman Creel, "inch for inch, the finest football player I ever saw." At the University of Georgia, Rosenberg was called "The Frog" because he could leap up in the air and intercept passes intended for six-foot-plus enemy receivers. As a quarterback, Rosenberg was "all everything" at Northside High. He was named "Most Valuable Football Player" in the city of Atlanta. At the University of Georgia, he played safety and twice was selected to the All-Southeastern Conference team. Rosenberg is listed in the University of Georgia media guide ten times for holding or being close to holding individual Bulldog records. Among them are first for average punt returns for one game and first for most punt return yardage for one game.

At age forty, out of 1100 contestants, he was one of four picked from the South to participate in the nationally televised "American Gladiators," a sort of gymnastics decathlon. He competed against athletes twelve to twenty years his junior. Rosenberg is now forty-seven years old. He lives in Jacksonville, Florida, where he is sales manager for a beverage company.

Born Jacob Abelson in Russia, Jake Abel grew up in Chattanooga, Tennessee, and then Atlanta. At the old Atlanta City Auditorium, he fought and went the distance with Benny Leonard, considered the greatest world lightweight boxing champion who ever lived. Jake died in 1963 at age seventy. That is where they are now and what they did. It is also where they are not now but where they ought to be: in the Georgia Sports Hall of Fame.

CHARLES HARRIS
A Wonderful Life

Yes, mama, there really is a George Bailey (the lead character in the movie *It's A Wonderful Life*). And he lives right here in Georgia—Ocilla, to be exact, the county seat of Irwin County. His real name is Charles Harris, and about the only difference between him and that Bailey fellow is that Harris went off to war in World War II as a combat leader in the US Marines. Thanks to George Bailey, people had a wonderful life in Bedford Falls, New York, and thanks to Charles Harris, it has been a wonderful life for people in Ocilla and for many others throughout the state of Georgia.

This is the same Charles Harris who, with his lovely wife, Esther Stein Harris, owns and operates the A. S. Harris Department Store on the corner of Cherry and Fourth streets in Ocilla; the same Charles Harris who has been adviser to presidents, governors, senators, school children, and janitors; the same Charles Harris who served on the University Board of Regents eight years and as chairman an unprecedented three years.

For the most part, people have been conditioned to expect so little of themselves. But not Charles Harris. "Doing for others is what it is all about," Harris says. "It is your dues for just being around." If anyone has paid his dues, it is Charles Harris. He has helped the sick, the critically injured, the young, the unskilled, the illiterate, and the mentally retarded. He has helped his neighbors

1998

build homes, start businesses, and enter professional careers such as law and medicine. He has put clothes on people's backs and food on their table.

If I had waited for Charles Harris to tell me these facts, I never would have learned them. All I could get out of him in a long distance telephone call was that he was "just a country Jewish merchant." So, after I had talked with Charles Harris, I wanted to talk with the people who knew him best—his neighbors. Here is what they had to say:

Emory Walters:

> I have known Charles more than fifty years. Charitably, he has done more for this county than anyone I know or ever knew. No poor person ever went to his department store and was turned away for lack of money. I do not know of one charitable drive he has not headed. Heart, cancer, kidney, whatever, Charles was the leader, more times than not. I am not going to name names because I do not want to embarrass anyone. But whenever there has been a sick child in this community and the parents were unable to pay for medical bills, Charles Harris took care of them. To my knowledge, he never asked to be repaid. He never said no to anyone.

Harry Mixon:

> Before the interstate highway was built, Highway 129 was a main artery from New York to Miami. We had traffic accidents almost every week, and if it was a serious one and the injured were rushed to the hospital badly in need of blood, Charles Harris would hear about it. When the ambulances arrived at the hospital, Charles would already be there, lying on a table in the emergency room, ready to give blood for a transfusion. He must have given blood 100 or more times in those days.
>
> At one time or another, you will see license plates from almost every county in Georgia parked outside Charles' store. They all seek his help, be it for their children to get into some college or for a job recommendation for themselves. A good word in the right place from Charles is as good as it gets.
>
> When Herman Talmadge was governor of Georgia and needed to get away from it all, Charles and Esther would put him up until he was ready to go home.

Kermit Elliott: "I came here as football coach in 1963. I had come from Fitzgerald High, a bigger school than Ocilla. I had to take a salary cut. I never could have made it financially without help from Charles. He believes in serving his community and his fellow man."

So it goes. From one end of Ocilla to the other—they all love Charles Harris. How else could Harris' small town department store survive with discount malls up and down the interstate highway and a Wal-Mart just twelve miles down the road? Customers may get lower prices elsewhere, but they can't get Charles Harris.

From Ocilla, drive to Fitzgerald, twelve miles to the east, and you will find Diane Harper, president of East Central Technical Institute and the Charles Harris Learning Center. Ms. Harper says:

> Let me tell you, I have known Charles Harris since I started elementary school. I was five or six years old. Like all the other children who grew up in this county, I loved him. He helped us with school clothes. He knew each of us by our first name. He was a role model in good citizenship. He was in the forefront of every civic activity and every worthwhile cause. He was our adviser. I often wondered, what more can one man do?
>
> I remember him once telling me that there were two things that could change a person's life for the better—reading good books and associating with good people. Following that advice helped me get where I am today.

If you go to Fitzgerald, have lunch at Tony's Restaurant and hope that Charles Harris is dining there, as he frequently does. I had lunch with Charles and Esther Harris at Tony's. There must have been sixty or seventy people eating there. One by one they got up from their tables and came over to speak to him. Then came the chefs, then the owners, then the waiters and waitresses. The restaurant incident reminded me of something that Ken Breeden, commissioner of the Georgia Department of Technical and Adult Education, had told me earlier. "Everywhere Harris goes, he draws a crowd," Breeden says. "Last year, he underwent knee surgery. We were having our annual Legislative Appreciation Day and because of his surgery, we were not expecting him. It was a barbecue at Fitzgerald's Paulk Park. There were about 250 guests. We were all eating our stew and chicken when Charles came hobbling in on his walking cane. Everyone put down their food and began to cheer. And then everyone surged forward to hug him or shake his hand."

How can one man have so many friends? The answer is service to mankind, God, country, city, state. Service to citizens, from schoolchildren to governors to presidents.

For more than fifty years, Harris has been the driving force behind the Fitzgerald Hebrew Congregation. He has been a director of the State Bank of Ocilla for forty years. He was chairman and founder of the Ben Hill-Irwin Vocational Technical and Trade School, now the Charles Harris Learning Center. He was chairman of Ocilla's first hospital authority.

He was commander of American Legion Post 100 and Veterans of Foreign Wars Post 6048. He was Irwin County chairman of Jimmy Carter's campaign for governor and was in on the Egyptian-Israeli peace treaty signing when Carter was president. He was a member of the executive committee and treasurer of the Georgia Democratic Party when Joe Frank Harris ran and was elected governor. He is a member of the Georgia State Judicial Qualifications Commission, a disciplinary board for judges in Georgia.

He financed the building of the Irwin County Hospital. He has been a director of the Mercer University Hospital. He was a member of the Ocilla City

1998

Council for six years and twice served as mayor pro tem. He has been a member of the Mercer University Medical School Board of Governors for twenty-five years. He serves on the Georgia State Board of Technical and Adult Education. He has been a member of the board of directors of the University of Georgia Research Foundation. He is partly responsible for better teacher pay in Georgia, since that was his pet project when he served on the state Board of Education to study and improve the state teacher salary structure.

To name all the worthy causes for which Harris has worked would fill this magazine. Harris' daughter, Joan Harris Kent of Macon, sums it up best: "He radiates warmth and human kindness. He takes time to listen to the student or the new person in town as well as the governor and the president. All people are equal in his eyes."

The esteem in which Harris is held was evident in 1996, when he was chosen to carry the Olympic Torch from the A. S. Harris Department Store to City Hall. Harris may describe himself as "just a Jewish country merchant," but Robert Lipshutz, counsel to Jimmy Carter when he was president, describes Harris as "a giant in the human race."

Charles A. Harris was born in Ocilla in 1922. He had no middle name until he joined the US Marine Corps during World War II. The Marine Corps recruiter asked him for his middle initial and Harris quickly responded, "A, sir, and that stood for Abe."

The late Abe Harris, Charles' father, came to America from Russia at age thirteen. With a peddler's pack on his back, he found his way to Ocilla, where he opened the A. S. Harris Dry Goods Store in 1906. For as long as he can remember, Charles worked in his father's store, first sweeping the floor, then making sure the overalls were stacked neatly on the tables. By the time he was a teenager, he was waiting on customers, selling everything from ladies' hose to men's suits.

He graduated with honors from Ocilla High School and Emory University, where he was editor of the yearbook. In 1942, Harris took his Emory diploma to the Marine Corps Recruiting Station, underwent a physical examination and was soon on his way to Quantico, Virginia, and USMC Officers Candidate School.

He wanted to fight the Germans, but his marine unit was sent to the Pacific to fight the Japanese. Newly commissioned 2nd Lt. Charles A. Harris commanded a rifle platoon during amphibious landings in the Japanese-held Marshall Islands. The Marines took the islands, and Harris took an enemy sniper's bullet in the stomach.

"The average life span of a Marine platoon leader in combat was about five minutes," Harris recalls. "I was happy to be alive."

He later took command of a communication battalion, composed of 2,000 Navaho Indians. The Navahos, using their native language, established a radio communications code, and the Japanese were never able to break it. When the war ended, Harris, with the rank of major, retired and returned to Ocilla to take over the family store. He upgraded the inventory and put in complete lines of men's, women's, and children's clothing.

He and Esther still live in a four-bedroom home about ten blocks from the Harris store. They raised four children—Lee, Raye, Joan, and Anita—and have eleven grandchildren. Lee, their thirty-nine-year-old son, died last year of cancer. "There is no way to tell of the deep sorrow we felt," Charles said. "I cannot imagine anything more devastating than a parent losing a child." The Harrises' faith in God and the sympathy shown by friends (more than 600 people attended Lee's funeral) brought them solace.

With all his contacts, in business and in politics, Harris has had opportunities to move to larger cities. But he never wanted to be anywhere else. "I wouldn't trade my rural life in Ocilla for anywhere in the world," he said. "Being here and serving other folks has been great. It is like one big family." An important part of "the family" are his employees—Mary Ellen Murray, Juanita Ketchum, and Virgil Mixon. Murray and Mixon have been with the department store more than fifty years. They could have retired years ago, so why do they keep working?

"Because of Esther and Charles," explains Murray. "Their smiles, their concern for us and our families. A day without them is like a day without sunshine. Charles is such a generous man, not only with his money but with his time. I was here when his parents were alive and running the store. They were just as giving as he is."

The Harris department store opens at 8 A.M. and closes at 6 P.M. Charles is there from opening to closing unless he is attending some board meeting, as he did last week when he was in Atlanta attending the regular meeting of the State Judicial Qualifications Commission. Harris, appointed by Governor Zell Miller, is one of only two lay members of the board. The rest of the board is composed of attorneys and judges.

Harris says he never will retire "as long as my mind is good and I am ambulatory." To his friends this will come as no surprise. They know that when he was a member of the State Board of Regents he traveled to every school in the state university system at least once a year, many twice. He was present when Jimmy Carter announced his intention to run for the presidency, and he was the first to support Carter financially by giving him a series of post-dated checks to start that campaign. Later, as a member of the Peanut Brigade, he traveled to thirty states to campaign for his friend. Says former President Carter, "Charles Harris was my first and one of my strongest supporters. And that goes back to the first time I ran for governor and lost. He never gave up on me. I never had a more loyal friend."

Harris served on the National Finance Committee for Carter's 1980 presidential re-election campaign, and was an early supporter of former Governors Joe Frank Harris and Zell Miller.

Where does Harris find time to do all he does?

"We can find time to do what we want to do," he says. "The world would be a disaster if everyone said, 'I'd like to help but I don't have the time.'"

Two years ago, upon receiving the Emory University Medal for his service to community, state, country, and humankind, Harris said, "You don't do anything alone. You need God's blessing and the help of your fellow man. I've had both."

WHACK HYDER
Winning Is Not Everything

LEGENDS GENE ASHER

They used to call it "practice what you preach." Today it is called "walk the talk."

Whichever you prefer, John Carl "Whack" Hyder, the former Georgia Tech basketball coach, did it from the day he started coaching in 1946 until his retirement in 1973.

Hyder, now eighty-six and looking twenty years younger, lives with his bedridden wife, Vera, in a modest Buckhead bungalow in Atlanta on Darlington Circle, just off Piedmont Road. The Hyders have lived in the same house for thirty years. You can't miss the house from the mailbox, which is emblazoned in gold with the initials "G.T." and with an unmistakable gold and black Yellow Jacket.

Hyder's "talk" was peace, tranquility, love, education, and treating your fellow human being as you want to be treated. Then came basketball. He cared more about the moral character of his players than he did their ability to dunk with either hand. He cared more about producing good students and good citizens than he did good ball-handlers and good long-range shooters.

Hyder's priorities were unique in the world of basketball coaching and he never compromised them. And yet he produced winning teams, some of which defeated the unbeatable foe, the University of Kentucky, with consistency. Indeed, when no one else could do it, Hyder's teams brought high-riding

Kentucky down to earth, whipping the Baron of the Bluegrass, the late Adolph Rupp, and his Wildcats six times in their last nine meetings.

Hyder is proud of his dominance of Rupp's Wildcats but he is more proud of the fact that of the hundreds of his Yellow Jackets who completed their eligibility only one failed to graduate. "I hope," he says today, "that every player who played for me left a better man spiritually and with a feeling of joy that he graduated from Georgia Tech."

When recruiting became vicious in his latter years at Tech, Hyder never lowered his value system. His high moral standard did not win any championships but that never was his primary goal. The spiritual, social, and educational development of his players always came first.

Said Rich Yunkus, one of Hyder's two All-Americans, "He was a fine coach, a good tactician but what I remember mostly about him was that he was a true gentleman. In my four years at Tech, I never heard him use one word of profanity. When he was angry, his face sometimes would turn red but all he would shout would be 'CONFOUND IT, CHEESE AND CRACKERS!'"

Said Roger Kaiser, Hyder's first All-American, "He was my father away from home. I always respected him. He neither smoked nor drank. I wanted to give him 100 percent effort, 100 percent of the time. He made me feel I was wanted and needed. He got his message across to the players and he did it without hollering or belittling anyone."

Kaiser, who won a national championship as coach at Life University in Marietta, Georgia, two years ago, added, "My goal in life is to become the caring and concerned human being Coach Hyder is." Kaiser, hotly sought-after as a Dale, Indiana, prep star, was headed for Vanderbilt or the University of Indiana when he met Hyder. Then his plans changed abruptly.

"He was warm, empathetic. He made me feel like a member of the family. He talked more about the importance of a good education than he did about basketball. I saw him as a role model. I felt like playing for Coach Hyder was going to be a positive influence on my life. And it was."

Hyder's emphasis on caring for his players did not diminish his desire to put a winning team on the court. It was just not his top priority. His twenty-two-year head-coaching record of 292 wins and 271 losses does not look impressive, but his first six teams had to play in an old Naval Armory that seated only 2,200. Once he moved into the new Alexander Memorial Coliseum, his record was 251-189. Although he never won a conference championship, three of his teams were runners-up in Southeastern Conference races and one finished second in the once prestigious National Invitational Tournament. His 1958 team won the Detroit Classic and his 1960 team won the Gator Bowl Tournament. All during his coaching years, he taught three physical training classes every week.

Hyder was twice named SEC "Coach of the Year." He is a member of the Georgia Tech Basketball Hall of Fame as a player and as a coach. He is a founder and life member of the National Basketball Hall of Fame. He is a member of the Georgia Tech Hall of Fame and the Georgia Sports Hall of Fame. He was the first and only non-faculty member selected to ANAK, Tech's highest honor society.

"I had a love affair with Georgia Tech," Hyder said. "There never was any pressure on me to win, either from Coach [Bobby] Dodd or the student body." In his first two seasons his teams finished 7-15 and 5-17. In his third year as head coach, he won only two of twenty-four games. There was no heat from the top and the student body, and faculty responded with a "Hyder Appreciation Day," at which they presented him with a gold watch. One year later, Hyder's Jackets fired a shot heard around the basketball world. It emanated from Lexington, Kentucky, where Rupp's Wildcats were defending a 129-game home winning streak, claiming an SEC championship seven of the previous eight seasons, and not losing a game anywhere in four years.

Hyder's Jackets, who had lost more games than they had won, refused to be intimidated by the brash 'Cats and pulled off a startling 59-58 upset. There were twelve seconds on the clock when Tech's Joe Helms, the shortest man on the court at 5'9", fired a one-hand jump shot to clinch the impossible dream. Kentucky fans were so startled they sat in their seats long after the game ended, many of them in tears.

"It was the first time," Hyder recalled, "I ever saw grown men cry." The next week Kentucky came to Atlanta for the rematch in front of an overflow crowd of 7,000-plus. Before the tipoff, Rupp chided Hyder thusly, "You can't emphasize education at the expense of building winning basketball teams, at least not in the SEC."

The two teams took the court and Tech whipped Kentucky again, this time by six points.

Three seasons later the Tech-Kentucky drama was staged again. Kentucky came to Atlanta not only on top of the SEC but ranked No. 1 in America. The week before Tech had lost to the University of Wisconsin by thirty points. Kentucky had routed the same Wisconsin team by thirty points. But Hyder's Jackets shocked Kentucky and the basketball world again, winning by twenty-one points. Hyder received another watch from grateful fans and it is on display in his living room showcase with some twenty other watches he received during his career.

In all, Hyder teams beat Rupp teams eight times, all upsets. "I had no magic touch on Coach Rupp," Hyder said, "It was a case of our guys wanting to prove something and being willing to work hard in preparation for the challenge."

Hyder was born in Lula, Georgia, on the edge of Banks County. He was one of six boys and two girls. At the age of four his family moved to Clermont, Georgia, where the family lived on a farm. Hyder attended Clermont High School but before he left for classes, he milked cows, plowed fields, and helped clean the house.

Basketball was the only sport at Clermont and Hyder wanted to compete in all sports. So after his graduation, he went to prep school at Monroe A & M, where he excelled in football, baseball, basketball, track, and cross-country. Tech football coach William A. Alexander saw Hyder play basketball at Monroe A & M and watched him lead his team to a surprising win over Alexander's Tech freshman team. Alexander was so impressed he offered Hyder a football scholar-

1998

ship to Tech to play basketball, as there were no basketball scholarships in those days. At Georgia Tech, Hyder played in the first Tech-Georgia freshman football game (1933), which was played for the benefit of the Scottish Rite Children's Hospital. Those were the days when everyone paid to get into Grant Field for this charity classic—the fans, players, coaches, sports writers, and game officials. The first game drew 6,000 but by 1960 attendance was up to 48,000. At Tech, Hyder became one of only two Tech athletes, the other being Doug Wycoff, to letter in five sports. He earned freshmen numerals in football and varsity letters in basketball, baseball, track and cross-country.

He graduated from Tech in 1937 and then played three years of baseball in the New York Yankees farm system. Feeling he never was going to make it big in baseball and mostly wanting to work with young men, he accepted a coaching job at Monroe A & M where he stayed until the Japanese bombed Pearl Harbor. Hyder beat a path to the US Navy Recruiting Station and served in the Navy until the war ended.

He headed back to Tech where Coach Alexander, also Athletic Director, made him assistant basketball coach to Roy McArthur. When McArthur resigned in 1951, new Athletic Director Bobby Dodd was considering Hyder and another assistant, Dwight Keith. A number of the varsity players went to Dodd and told him they wanted Hyder as their coach. That was the start of Hyder's head coaching career. For his dual role as varsity basketball coach and physical training instructor, Hyder was paid the grand sum of $19,000—$10,000 for coaching and $9,000 for PT instructing. When he retired, his combined salary was $24,000. Today, coaches in the Southeastern Conference and Atlantic Coast Conference, of which Tech is now a member, are paid as much as $750,000. In one season, some of them make more money than Hyder did in twenty years.

But Hyder harbors no bitterness about his pay or anything else. "I love Georgia Tech," he said. "It was a comfortable place for me. The administration and I agreed on what the mission was—to see that our players earned a degree…I remember coaching in a college All-Star game one year and one of my players told me he rarely went to class. I told him he was lucky he did not go to Georgia Tech."

Today Hyder thinks college sports are out of control and he puts the blame squarely on college presidents. "Most of the players today are looking for a meal ticket, not an education. I don't have the figures to support this but I would estimate at least one-third of today's players are in college because they know it is a stepping stone to the professional game. Most colleges are minor leagues for professional sports, not just for basketball and football but baseball, too. College presidents are remiss in their duties when they allow kids to play inter-collegiate sports when they have no intention of earning a degree."

At age sixty, Hyder retired as Tech head coach following two losing seasons in 1971–72 (6-20) and 1972–73 (7-18). Tech's home attendance sagged dramatically. His final home game against archrival Georgia was designated "Whack Hyder Day" and then Governor Jimmy Carter issued a proclamation making it official. A near-capacity crowd gave Hyder a standing ovation. He received a plaque from his former players. Then his team went out on the court and battered the Bulldogs, 77-67. As the final seconds began to tick off the clock, Tech fans began yelling, "We love you Whack; we love you!"

Announcing his retirement in a letter to Coach Dodd he wrote, in part:

> As an alumnus of Georgia Tech, I suggest we retire our basketball coach at the end of the fiscal year, June 30, 1973...I told you in the beginning that when I felt the time had come for me to step aside, I would. I feel the time is now...I made this decision with the knowledge of my family. I feel our young players have progressed enough during the past season for a new coach to stop in and get off to a good start...I feel badly the way our attendance has dropped and I hope this change will restore the attendance we had during most of my career.
>
> The students have been wonderful to me and my teams. With their enthusiasm they helped us win many games. The faculty always was behind us 100 percent.
>
> Thank God for schools like Georgia Tech. I pledge my support to my alma mater for the rest of my life.

When he resigned, there never were any second thoughts. "I was ready to get out," he said. "I was just plain tired. And mentally, I no longer was with the game. Recruiting was what winning was all about and recruiting became so vicious I detested it." Hyder wanted players who wanted an education, not athletes looking for big bucks. He shared the philosophy of "The Wizard of Westwood," former UCLA coach John Wooden. They both preached to their players that "the final score is not the final score; that there was nothing wrong with the other person being better than you so long as you did everything possible to prepare for the challenge. The score never can make you a loser if you have done your best. Knowledge and fairness is what counts in life."

At a "Whack Hyder Night" given by friends, family, and former players in 1973, Hyder said, "I am not the greatest coach in the world, not by any stretch of the imagination. But I am grateful and humble. You all know me as Whack but my real first name is John. Tonight you made me feel like my last name is Wooden [who won ten NCAA championships at UCLA]."

Hyder calls Kaiser, whose twenty-three-point per-game average led Tech to a 22-6 record in the 1959–60 season, "the best basketball player I ever coached. He could hit the basket consistently from anywhere on the court and he was as good a ball handler as I ever saw." Hyder ranks Rich Yunkus, who led the Jackets to back-to-back appearances in the National Invitational Tournament in 1970 and 1971, "the best inside shooter I ever had." Yunkus scored forty-seven points in one game and averaged thirty points per game in his junior season. Hyder calls Pres Judy of the 1965–67 squads the most knowledgeable of all his players. "He was like a coach on the court," Hyder said. "He knew the game and he knew how to handle players." Judy was the captain of the 1966 and 1967 teams and joined Hyder as an assistant coach after he graduated.

Since his wife suffered a stroke two years ago, Hyder has stayed close to home. But he manages to get out to a basketball game occasionally. "It is a lot different being a spectator," he said. "I can't talk to the players or diagram plays but I find myself pulling, twisting, wincing, and wanting to holler. But the only time I miss coaching is when we play Georgia." Hyder has two children, Tommy, age forty-eight and a former player for his dad at Tech, and Julia, age fifty-two. The Hyders have four grandchildren.

At the Alexander Memorial Coliseum, there is a "Hyder Room," filled with memorabilia from his twenty-two-year head coaching career. As a player and a coach, Hyder personified the prayer of a ball player, which reads, in part,

Dear Lord, in the battle that goes on through life
I ask but a field that is fair,
A chance that is equal with all in the strife
A courage to strive and to dare;
And if I should win, let it be by the code
With my faith and my honor held high;
And if I should lose let me stand by the road
And cheer as the winners go by…

MARY DOROTHY "DOT" KIRBY
A Nice Girl Finished First

Mary Dorothy "Dot" Kirby is an international golf legend who proved nice girls finish first.

With a placid temperament and a winning smile, during her years of competition she was known across the land as the sweetest athlete of them all. After finishing second in the US Women's National Amateur tournament in 1946 and 1947, some of the nation's top golf writers wrote that she never would become a champion. They said she was "too nice." They said she lacked the "killer instinct."

Wrong.

In 1951, at the age of thirty-one, she won the National Amateur, shaking off the loss of a three-stroke lead and coming back to beat Claire Doran, 2 and 1 for the title.

"I always figured," she said, "that golf was only a game. There was no place for bitterness in an effort to gain victory. I tried to play my shots the best I could and I treated my opponents as friends, not foes."

In the Curtis Cup matches, where the finest amateurs in the United States meet the best amateurs of Great Britain, her four appearances in 1948, 1949, 1951, and 1952 are the most ever by a member of the US team. In the 1952 matches, she staged one of the greatest comebacks in Curtis Cup history. Five down with eleven holes to play, she rallied to tie her match on the thirty-fifth hole and went on to win, 1-up, on the thirty-sixth.

She twice won the National Women's Titleholders and was a one-time winner in the Southern Amateur and North and South Championships. In "Who's Who in Golf", Dot is referred to as a "model of persistence."

Today, she is still a "model of persistence". A sales agent with Harry Norman Realty, she qualifies for the Million Dollar Club regularly, although she already is a life member. Before entering real estate sales, Dot spent thirty years with WSB-TV and WSB Radio, first as a sportscaster, then as a sales representative. She will be seventy-nine on the fifteenth of this month. For the past seventeen years, she has lived in the same brick ranch house in Atlanta's Sherwood Forest where she shares her domain with her two German Shepherds, Murphy and Cates.

Dot was born on January 15, 1920 in West Point, Georgia. She is the only child of William Jackson Kirby, who was a cotton mill supply salesman, and Mary Scott Kirby, who was a homemaker. Both parents are deceased. Neither played golf.

When Dot was ten years old, her family moved to Atlanta at 1055 Piedmont Road, about a hundred yards from a miniature golf course where she learned to use a putter. As a sixth grader, she wandered off to the nearby Piedmont Park course for her first taste of "big golf." She liked it so much she began playing nine holes every morning, then grabbing her books and rushing off to classes at Tenth Street School. When the bell rang, signaling the end of the school day, once again she would gather her books, hurry home, and then head to the Piedmont golf course to play eighteen more holes.

She was directed to Howard "Pop" Beckett, then the professional at the old Brookhaven Golf Club, originally Capital City Country Club, and under Beckett's guidance her game took serious form. When Dot was twelve and weighed less than ninety pounds, she entered and won the Ansley Golf Club tournament. She also entered the state women's championship at age twelve and became the youngest golfer ever to qualify for the championship flight. She reached the semi-finals.

When she was thirteen and still a mere mite of a youth, she entered and won the first of five Georgia State Women's Championships before stepping aside to give others a chance. She was the youngest golfer ever to win a state women's championship. Her victory prompted the late Jimmy Burns, former sports editor of the old *Atlanta Georgian* to write, "Veteran women golfers in Georgia one day will boast of having been beaten by a thirteen-year-old child."

At age seventeen, Dot won the Southern Women's championship. At age twenty-one, she won the first of two back-to-back National Women's Titleholders, after which she was besieged by national companies to turn professional.

She said "no" to "pro" because "I did not like the idea of making money off a game I played for fun. I used to watch the men pros," she said, "and it always looked to me as if golf was not fun to anybody who had to work at it for a living."

"When I won the Titleholders Tournament, I was working at WSB Radio learning to be a sportscaster. It was like having my cake and eating it, too. I arranged a national broadcast with National Women's Open Cup Champion

1998

Babe Zaharias. It was a thrill for Babe because it was the first time she was on a national broadcast and it was a thrill for me because it was the first national hook-up I ever directed," After her second successive Titleholders win, she began a long period of coming in second: twice in the National Amateur, once in the Western Women's Open, and once in the Southern Amateur. "It was discouraging, to say the least," she said. "I used to wonder what I was doing wrong. But I knew I was going to keep going. Something inside me said, You are not going to give up."

Dot had an intense rivalry with former Atlantan Louise Suggs, now living in Sea Island, Georgia. She lost to Louise in the finals of the National Amateur, Western Open, and Southern Amateur. But she came back to whip Louise in the 1949 Georgia State Women's championships.

Even in defeat, Dot was brilliant. For example, when she lost to Suggs in the finals of the 1947 National Amateur, she shot a final round of seventy-two, as good a golf game as ever was played by a female finalist. But a near miraculous shot by Suggs was good for a seventy-one and victory on the final hole.

Win or lose, Dot was always the same, sweet, good-natured player.

She stopped her tournament play in 1974. She is a charter member of the Georgia Golf Hall of Fame and the Georgia Sports Hall of Fame. A color portrait of her, presented by Bobby Jones, hangs in the Capital City Club. In 1971, the Atlanta Country Club inaugurated a tournament in her honor, "The Dorothy Kirby Invitational." Dot no longer plays golf, not even an occasional round with friends. But she does have her memories.

Winning the national amateur at Saint Paul in 1951 and the welcome home parade are unforgettable events. I had a 3-up advantage after twenty-seven holes, "but [Claire] Doran squared the match at thirty-one. On the next hole, I sank a twenty-five-foot putt, which had to curve to the right before dropping in the hole for a birdie deuce. Claire parred.

The thirty-third and thirty-fourth holes were halved. On the five-par thirty-fifth, Claire took a six. I sank an eight-foot putt after it momentarily hung on the lip of the cup for a par five and the crown. Before the ball fell into the cup, it seemed to hang for five minutes. It was probably there only a second. But it was the longest second of my life.

The victory came at age thirty-one, twenty-one years after Dot picked up her first golf club and nineteen years after she won her first amateur tournament.

The welcome home was equally memorable. She was greeted by a clamorous motorcade at the Chattahoochee River on the last lap of her automobile trip from Saint Paul. She was first greeted by her parents and the legendary Bobby Jones. Then she was whisked through mid-morning traffic behind screaming sirens to the Atlanta City Hall and there accorded an official greeting by Governor Herman Talmadge and Mayor, William B. Hartsfield. City Hall steps were lined with hundreds of cheering Atlantans. Mayor Hartsfield issued an official procla-mation declaring it "Dorothy Kirby Day."

Another lasting memory:

Early in my career, Bobby Jones telephoned me after watching me win the Georgia State Women's title. He invited me to his club [Peachtree], took me out on the course and got me to straighten out my hands in my backswing. And then he would take me into the clubhouse and talk about the mental side of the game. I remember him stressing concentration…not letting my mind wander…staying focused, one shot at a time. He got me on the right track.

Dot never married, but threatened on three occasions. "Each time I talked about it, there always was an objection and it was always the same…my traveling to play golf. My boyfriends wanted me to stay home and I wasn't willing to do it. One of those three gentleman remains a good friend."

Her biggest disappointment: "Losing to someone I should have beaten. Specifically, Louise Suggs. I should have beaten her in the National Amateur in 1947 but I didn't. And I had just beaten her in a state tournament."

If she could live her life over again, what would Dot change? "Nothing. I have done the things I wanted to do. I have had a career in golf and a successful career in business. I have had an enjoyable life." What would Dot like to be remembered for: "For being a decent person."

Dot Kirby not only will be remembered as being a "decent person," but as a golfing child prodigy and "the sweetest athlete of them all."

THE MAHAFFEYS
Family Dominance

In the history of Georgia high school basketball, there never has been a band of brothers like the Mahaffeys of LaGrange. The Castleberrys...Clint and Jimmy were great in the 1940s. So were the Edelsteins, Asher and Ben. Then in the 1950s there were Clyde Mynatt and his younger twin brothers, James and John, and the Casey twins, Pat and Gene.

But the Mahaffeys...Tommy, Donnie, Randy, and Richie were something else. They dominated the court like no family before them and established feats that no other family is likely to equal, much less exceed in the future.

At 6'7" each, Tommy, Randy, and Donnie owned the Georgia prep backboards in the late 1950s and early 1960s, as 6'8" Richie did in the early and mid-1960s. Randy may be the only Georgian ever to twice win the most valuable player award in the State Class AAA tournament, which he did in 1962 and 1963. From 1958 to 1963 the Grangers, with at least one Mahaffey in the staring lineup, made it to the state tournament every year and twice won the championship. Tommy, Randy, Donnie, and Richie were all named to the All-Tournament teams.

The Mahaffeys had their choice of any college in the country that had a basketball team but, like their dad before them, they all chose Clemson. And what a legacy they left. They rank in the top ten career rebounders. A Mahaffey led Clemson in rebounding nine consecutive seasons and ten out of eleven years.

Today, the Mahaffeys are together again, dominating the business scene almost as much as they did the basketball court. They are owners of Ply Mart, the second leading building materials company in the Southeast with sales of $140,000,000.

The same dedication, drive, and desire the Mahaffeys exhibited on the basketball court got them through the homebuilding crunch in the mid-1970s. The Mahaffey brothers started Ply Mart in 1968. When Ply Mart was scarcely five years old, it was on the verge of bankruptcy. Owners' equity, once valued at $1,000,000 and growing rapidly, had shrunk to less that $100,000. The company's bankers were getting nervous and there was a question about calling in loans. But those who knew about the twenty-plus consecutive winning seasons the Mahaffeys put together at LaGrange and Clemson did not have the slightest concern.

"We were committed to survive," President Randy Mahaffey remembers. "We had to reduce operating expenses and all of us had to tighten our belts. We were hit as badly as any other homebuilding company. We rode it out because everyone in the company gave a little extra effort." Ply Mart not only "survived" but, when the real estate slump ended, it took off again—like a rocket. Owners' equity has zoomed to $138,000,000 and Randy expects sales to reach the one-billion mark in five years. Ply Mart has nineteen lumber/specialty branches throughout metropolitan Atlanta and offices in northern and western Georgia, North Carolina, and Florida. They now have more than 600 employees and a home product line that will match any in the industry. Corporate headquarters is in Norcross.

What began as a pre-finished plywood paneling company now features hardboard sidings, a complete line of home exterior trim, a door and window fabrication plant, interior and exterior doors, an insulated glass shop, framing materials, an architectural millwork shop, custom stairs, and vinyl siding. Ply Mart sells directly to the homebuilders and delivers and installs products directly to the home sites.

The Mahaffeys pioneered the use of ventilated steel shelving in the late 1970s and have become the largest dealer of that product in America. In the 1980s they installed a specialty division that offers tub and shower enclosures, custom mirrors, and a complete line of bath hardware.

"We grew because we picked good people," Randy says. "People who were unselfish, willing to put personal goals behind team goals. As President, I see my role as chief cheerleader. I help our people elevate their sights and establish sales and service goals they may never have dreamed of previously. Our major quest is to build a deeply loyal clientele. We are not looking for one-time customers. We are looking for customers who are so satisfied with the service they receive that they would not think of going anywhere else for our products."

As a youngster, Randy had no idea of becoming a business executive. "Whenever I got into trouble, I wanted to be a minister. That would get me back into good graces with my mother. But I really wanted to be a medical doctor. I studied pre-med at Clemson and was accepted at the University of Georgia and

Emory Medical Schools." Basketball got in the way of medical school. With a flaming, competitive spirit, a deadly eye for the basket, and a jumping ability that enabled him to clear offensive and defensive boards, Randy was not only elected to the Atlantic Coast Conference All-Star team at Clemson, but he was high on the professional basketball draft list. He joined the Kentucky Colonels in the American Basketball Association and in his rookie season was a starter in the first ABA All-Star game.

While Randy was playing professionally, Donnie, who had graduated from Clemson and was selling fiberglass, settled in Decatur and opened the Ply Mart doors in 1967 to sell paneling. His first executive decision was to make brother Tom, who also had graduated from Clemson and was selling textiles for West Point-Pepperell, an offer he could not refuse—a partnership. Randy played two more seasons, one with the Carolina Cougars and one with the New York Nets. Although he excelled for both teams, he had a burning desire to help other people, which he visualized doing as a working member of the Ply Mart team. The next year Richie graduated from Clemson and the brothers were reunited. Although still a partner, Donnie moved to Ellijay, Georgia, to open a new company, Fireside Log Homes. Donnie is age fifty-seven. He is married to the former Robin Belcher of Anderson, South Carolina.

Ply Mart is in its thirtieth year, with two generations of Mahaffeys involved. Tom's two sons, Tom Jr. and Danny, are on the management team, as are Richie's older son, Chris, and Randy's oldest son, Matthew. The Mahaffey brothers and their sons regularly put in a sixty-hour workweek. "Business is like most things," Randy says. "According to the effort is the reward."

Richie Mahaffey, at age fifty, the baby of the family, manages five stores: Ellijay, Marietta, Cartersville, Douglasville, and Newnan. Like brother Randy, he, too, was a star at Clemson and high on the pro draft list. But he turned down a pro offer to join his brothers. He is vice president of sales.

Richie is married to the former Beth Moon of Liberty, South Carolina. His son Chris, twenty-five, works in the Ply Mart headquarters in inventory control. He has three other children: Lindsey, a junior at the College of Charleston, Mary Bess, a senior at Paideia High School in Atlanta, and John, a freshman at Woodward Academy in College Park, Georgia. Mary Bess plays basketball and soccer and young John, fourteen, runs track and plays on the varsity football and basketball teams at Woodward Academy. Richie looks forward to the day he can spend only forty hours at his business and spend the rest of the time with his family.

Tom is age fifty-eight. He was the first link of a string where there was a Mahaffey brother playing for Clemson for twelve consecutive years (1959–70). Although he graduated with a bachelor's. degree from Clemson, Tom holds a master's degree in textile engineering from Georgia Tech. He is secretary-treasurer of Ply Mart. Like his brothers, he starts his day at 6 A.M. and usually finished it at 6 or 7 P.M. He and his wife Nancy walk one to two miles nightly before dinner. They have been married thirty-four years. "Our parents taught us hard work," Tom said. "When we were starting the business, our dad [H. T. Mahaffey] told us to design a business plan showing where we wanted to go and how we were going to get there." Both H. T. Mahaffey, who was a plant manager at Callaway Mills in LaGrange, and his wife are deceased but they both lived to see their sons succeed in business as well as in sports.

Tom's advice to anyone starting a new business? "Have plenty of capital, seek advice from those who have gone before and succeeded, be patient, and do not expand too quickly."

Tom and Randy married sisters. Tom is married to the former Nancy Lee Daniel and Randy is married to the former Diane Daniel. The sisters, like the Mahaffeys, are from LaGrange.

Big basketball thrills were numerous for the Mahaffeys but for Tom and Donnie it was being starters on a Clemson team, which reached the ACC finals. For Richie and Randy, it was playing on a Clemson team that in seven days demolished Duke, UNC, N.C. State and Wake Forest, all ranked teams.

For the Mahaffeys, it has been brains as well as brawn. Randy and Richie were "Academic All Americans." All the brothers went through the Boy Scouts, and became scoutmasters and committee chairmen.

If Ply Mart expands as projected, the basketball legend Mahaffeys may write their own sequel to a former best seller. It would be called, "How to Succeed in Business by Really Trying."

EDWARD JOHN NEGRI
Save the Fox

Edward John Negri will leave three legacies, not one. He played the key role in the smooth integration of Atlanta's restaurants in 1963. He organized the Atlanta Landmarks, the driving force behind "Save the Fox Theatre." Now, he is releasing—exclusively to *Georgia Trend* magazine—the coveted recipe for his shrimp arnaud, the *piece de resistance* at old Herrens Restaurant which Negri operated for more than forty years. In the old days, the restaurant was known far and wide as Atlanta's finest.

Today, Negri and his wife of fifty-four years, "Beautiful Jane," live in a two-story home in East Ellijay, Georgia, with a panoramic view of the northwest Georgia mountains. In the daytime, Negri is running full speed at Mountain-Aire Realty, Inc., showing property and taking real estate listings for mountain homes. In the evening, he is at his own home playing the organ, reading, or simply just being with "Beautiful Jane."

It is a dramatic lifestyle change for Negri who used to spend daytime and nighttime checking recipes, supervising employees, and welcoming his lunch crowd of 600 diners. The Herrens patrons included the "Who's Who" of Atlanta, who preferred Negri's culinary delights rather than those served at their private clubs.

The restaurant, located on Luckie Street, just off Forsyth, was done in a Williamsburg motif. It would seat 300 people on two levels, the lower of which was decorated with European paintings. Make no mistake about it, Negri's Herrens was the place to see and be seen. Many business deals was closed there, and often times the terms of the deal were written on Negri's white linen tablecloths.

Good food, particularly the seafood platter and the much adored shrimp arnaud, and good service attracted citizens from all walks of life. But the guest list was heavy with lawyers, judges, journalists, educators, and chief executive officers of the city's leading business establishments. Food was on a first-come, first-served basis, and if you were not inside the restaurant by noon you could prepare for a wait. It made no difference who you were—Dick Rich, Noah Langdale, or Ralph McGill. Everyone was treated alike.

Before 1966, when the only game in town was Georgia Tech football on Saturday afternoon, out-of-town fans of the visiting teams flocked to Herrens. And somehow, Negri got them in and out in time to make the 2 P.M. kickoff. Herrens was not only the favorite dining spot for the fans, it was the favorite selling location for hustlers of college colors: banners, badges, and mums. These were the days before Munson Steed and anyone who could pay for a three-dollar city license could stand on the city streets and peddle their wares. From 11:00 A.M. to 1:30 P.M., the top hustlers always stood by the Herrens entrance.

Negri spent hours operating Atlanta's premiere restaurant, but he made time to involve himself in most every civic endeavor. He started the "Save the Fox" campaign, headed the restoration of the Wren's Nest, old home of Joel Chandler Harris, author of the Uncle Remus tales, and was the dinner host and key planner in the plan to integrate Atlanta's restaurants. He served as a director of the Atlanta Chamber of Commerce, Atlanta Convention Bureau, and Georgia Hospitality and Travel Association, and was on the Board of United Appeal, Red Cross, Boy Scouts, and Campfire Girls. He founded the Atlanta Boys' High School Alumni Association and served as its first president.

He was president of the Atlanta Restaurant Association and Georgia Restaurant Association and a director of the National Restaurant Association. He was named "Man of the Year" by the Atlanta Kiwanis Club and "National Restauranteur of the Year" by the Hotel and Management School of Florida State University.

Negri is a man of courage and action, not reaction. He desegregated his restaurant voluntarily, prior to the enactment of the civil rights law. The June 25, 1963 "integration date" was decided at a dinner meeting hosted by Negri of fifty restaurant owners, who were not all in agreement. "Some of them walked out," Negri recalls, "but most stayed. After discussing the racial unrest in our sister city, Birmingham, where violent confrontations were occurring every day between police and civil rights demonstrators, and where blood was running in the streets, we agreed to obey what was soon to become the law of the land." After the dinner meeting, Negri held a meeting of his restaurant employees and told them what was going to happen. "I explained that we would be serving our first black guests. Employee reaction was favorable. Only one waitress left."

When word leaked out about the integration plan and Negri's hosting the meeting, he was deluged with threatening letters and a few bomb threats. Says Negri:

> Beautiful Jane and I stayed up most of the nights after the bomb threats, but thank God nothing ever happened. On June 25th, I arrived at the restaurant early. I stationed myself at the front door, looking for any sign of trouble. All we had were pickets—members of the Ku Klux Klan and one well known restaurant owner.
>
> One of our most loyal customers came up to me when we opened for lunch and said, 'I have eaten with Negroes all over the world but I will not eat with them in your restaurant.' He never did.
>
> We had maybe a dozen well-dressed Negroes to dine but none of the white customers seemed to mind. When the day ended, I told my mama we did a great service for Atlanta. We put an end to this segregation foolishness.
>
> She replied, "What took you so long?"

With the integration of restaurants, the city had to pass a new ordinance for city licenses. The old restaurant licenses were stamped indelibly with "White Only."

Integration did nothing to dampen the Herrens business. About twenty regulars stopped eating there but most of them soon returned. What did start the Herrens downfall was the move by professionals and business owners from downtown northward. Lawyers discovered they did not need to be downtown to get to the courthouse, so they headed to Buckhead and points north. New office buildings were rising from midtown to Dunwoody, and many downtown businesses soon followed. All this happened in the 1970s. "Our business was going down steadily. With the professionals and entrepreneurs moving out, a seedy element began to move in. And downtown security no longer was as tight as it once was."

For Herrens and most downtown restaurants, the slide downhill intensified in the 1980s. We held on as long as we could," Negri said, "but we eventually decided we were getting too old to go bankrupt. We shut the doors in 1987 and followed, rather belatedly, the crowd north." In the silk stocking district of Buckhead, Negri opened "E. J.'s," a full service restaurant and lounge serving a mixed continental and American menu and featuring internationally known jazz musicians. The business was a colossal flop.

"Nothing was right at E. J.'s," Negri said. "The food was good and so was the service. But the rent was exorbitant and fiscal control was nonexistent. Employees were stealing us blind. Our shtick was to profit from serving a midnight jazz breakfast. People loved it. The problem was they loved it so much they did not come for dinner." In less than seven years, the restaurant was gone. Next came a Cobb County Herrens on Powers Ferry Road. It lasted less than one year. Ed Negri became a mountain man.

Of all Negri's adventures, including a 33,000-mile trip around the world to help select the US Air Force's finest mess hall, he is most proud of his role in saving the Fox Theatre. In the mid-1970s, when the once grand and glorious Fox was drawing less than a hundred people to its movies, Southern Bell was looking for a new home. It cast its eye upon the Fox property and negotiations for its purchase were well underway. Enter Ed Negri who was, by gosh, not going to let any telephone company or anyone else take a wrecking ball to this historic landmark, the place where he spent most of his childhood—following the bouncing ball, singing along with Bob Van Camp at the organ, and watching his favorite movies.

Negri organized, hosted, and promoted a "Save the Fox" dinner and invited fifty of Atlanta's most influential citizens to attend. No one declined, not even Atlanta mayor Maynard Jackson, vice mayor Sam Massell, publisher of the *Atlanta Journal-Constitution* Jack Tarver, general manager of WSB Radio Elmo Ellis, the Coca-Cola Bottling Company CEO Arthur Montgomery, super salesman Joe Patten, or executive vice president of the Woodruff Arts Center Beauchamp Carr.

Many of those movers and shakers formed a group called "The Atlanta Landmarks" and quickly raised $3,500,000. The Southern Bell purchase had gone through, but the Landmarks purchased an adjoining piece of property, which they traded to Southern Bell for the Fox property. Negri served on the Landmarks Board of Directors. Spearheading another fundraising drive, Negri and his friends insured that the grand old showplace on Peachtree Street would be restored to its original elegance and be around for generations to come.

Some people will insist that "Saving the Fox" was Negri's greatest achievement; others will point to his role in the smooth integration of Atlanta's restaurants and still others his volunteer work for the Red Cross. Negri headed the Red Cross disaster committee and more than once came up with food to feed searchers for lost children and hundreds of policemen when they were out to preserve order in what could have been a major riot at old Atlanta Stadium.

For the culinary artist, however, Negri's greatest legacy is his shrimp arnaud, the recipe for which has been more guarded than the formula for the hydrogen bomb. At Herrens, the dish was served either hot or cold, and either way, it was the diner's delight. No one outside Negri's immediate family ever had access to the recipe, even though thousands of Herrens customers sought it. You will not find the dish in New Orleans, not at Antoine's, Galatoire's, or K-Paul's. Not even at Arnaud's. Now you can find it in this issue of *Georgia Trend.*

Ed Negri was born in New York City in 1923. At the age of two, his family moved to Atlanta where his father, Guido Negri, became food manager at the old Atlanta Biltmore Hotel. He was lured away to the Piedmont Driving Club, where he spent thirteen years as food director before he purchased Herrens restaurant in 1939. Ed Negri took over Herrens when his father died in 1947.

Ed went to Sacred Heart Elementary School, O'Keefe Junior High School, and Atlanta Boys' High School. He graduated from Georgia Tech in 1947 with a mechanical engineering degree. He is married to the former Jane Fuller of Atlanta and they have three children: Steve, fifty-three, Paul, fifty-two, and Ellen, forty-five. They have five grandchildren and one great grandchild.

At age seventy-five, what is next for Ed Negri? "You can only read and play the organ so much. What I would really like to do is promote and raise money for a giant playground in the mountains for children of all ages." With Negri's track record, they will probably be filling the sand boxes any day now.

Negri's Top-Secret Shrimp Arnaud Recipe
1/4 large onion
1 stalk celery
1 garlic clove
2 tablespoons olive oil
1 pint Kraft brand French dressing
1/2 cup Zatarain brand Creole mustard
1/2 cup sweet relish
1 teaspoon paprika

Chop the first three ingredients and sauté in olive oil. Mix French dressing, Creole mustard, sweet relish, and paprika. Add onion mixture to dressing mixture. Refrigerate until used. May be served hot or cold. Pour sauce over raw shrimp and bake until bubbly.

GEORGE RAMEY PENDLEY
Faith in God Kept Him Alive

As I write these words, I wonder if George Ramey Pendley will be alive to read them.

Pendley, one of Georgia's all-time great senior, amateur tennis players, is dying of bone cancer. According to his radiation oncologist, Dr. Fred Schwaibold, he should have been dead five years ago. "Only his moral strength to persevere, his indomitable spirit, and his faith in God have kept him alive," Dr. Schwaibold said. Until six months ago, Pendley was not only surviving, he was excelling.

Despite blood clots in his chest, a pulmonary embolism, prostate cancer, and bone cancer, he was dominant in doubles tournament after doubles tournament, being on the winning team six times in the past six years. He has been nominated for the Georgia Tennis Hall of Fame, an honor he should have received years ago. Now the least that can be done is for the Hall of Fame to call a special meeting to vote on his selection while he can still smell the roses.

Pendley is a medical miracle. Sometimes playing with excruciating pain from the bone cancer, he has consistently defeated people ten to twenty years his junior. "I consider him one of the most remarkable human beings I have ever known," Dr. Schwaibold said. "When most people would have been home resting, he was out on the tennis courts playing competitively. He was determined to achieve his goal. He was able to do it because of his faith, his relentless persistence, and his unwillingness to surrender."

"I see 700–800 patients a year," Dr. Schwaibold added, "but none like George. I never heard him complain. He is courage personified. That is the legacy he will leave."

As I conduct this interview, George continues to be upbeat, despite the fact that he has had blood transfusions every week for the past five months. Six months ago he was playing tennis, weighing 165 pounds. Today he scarcely weighs 130.

"God is with me," he said, " and I am doing fine. Optimism is easy with God and a loving wife like my Barbara looking after me. "Although I can dress and feed myself, Barbara does the driving—to the doctor, to the hospital, and occasionally to the tennis courts. I am just a spectator now but it is fun to watch." George and his wife, the former Barbara Miserocchi, live in a two-story home in Roswell in Martins Landing.

Although empathetic and saddened by his condition, George's one-time ALTA foes are glad to see him in the stands rather than across the net. He won six consecutive ALTA matches with six different partners in the A-5 through A-7 levels before his confinement this past summer. At age seventy-three, he was always the oldest player on the court. Over a thirty-year period, in state, regional, and national competition, Pendley won 200 tournaments with thirty different partners in age groups from forty-five to seventy. He also won fifty singles titles.

His dominance on the doubles scene is reflected in the record. He won seven Crackerlands, twelve state tournaments, six Atlanta city meets, five Southern meets, and invitational tournaments in Florida, South Carolina, and North Carolina.

The coup de grace came in 1980 when he and Gustavo Palafox won the US Tennis Association's National 55 Clay Court championships. From ages forty-five to sixty-five, he has been ranked No. 1 in every age division in singles and doubles.

George is a native Atlantan. He grew up on Penn Avenue in midtown, living next door to the legendary Georgia Tech football coach, Bobby Dodd. He attended O'Keefe Junior High School and old Atlanta Boys' High School. He learned to play tennis during the summers on the old, red clay courts at Piedmont Park. By the time he got to Boys' High School, he was good enough to earn a berth on the varsity.

When it came time to attend college, despite the presence of the No. 1 Yellow Jacket next door, Pendley picked the University of Georgia. He planned to major in journalism and hoped to become a radio announcer. Pendley enrolled at Georgia in 1942. All the tennis players had gone to war but there were enough athletes to field a baseball team. So George put his tennis career on hold and became a starting pitcher on the Bulldog baseball squad.

"I lasted two years," George recalled, " and then the urge to serve my country became the most important thing in my life." He quit Georgia and joined the US Navy.

He volunteered for submarine duty and saw duty in the Pacific on the USS Nautilus. When the Nautilus was decommissioned, his two years of journalism school at Georgia helped him land an assignment with Armed Forces Radio. He put together his own jazz and sports show and his live interviews with people like Lefty O'Doul, Harry James, Stan Kenton, and Kitty Kallen were heard by servicemen throughout the Armed Forces Network.

When the war ended, Pendley returned to the University of Georgia, which had resumed its intercollegiate tennis program. He earned three varsity letters while earning a degree from journalism school. His first job was with radio station WGGA in Gainesville, Georgia, and then with WSB in Atlanta. In Atlanta, he met Barbara and that changed everything.

Radio stations back in the 1940s were not known for high-paying announcer jobs or normal working hours. George wanted to marry Barbara, raise a family, and have time to play tennis. He left WSB, went to work for a trade association, married Barbara, and began his meteoric rise to tennis prominence.

His first big doubles victory came at age thirty-six when he won the Crackerland tournament. He won it again at age fifty-five and again at age fifty-nine. By age sixty-two, the cancer had developed but George kept on playing and winning. He won back-to-back singles and doubles championships in the Georgia Hardcourts tournament in 1987 and 1988, and with the cancer spreading from his prostate to his bones, went on to win the Georgia State Senior championship in sixty-five-and-over doubles.

He umpired professional matches at the old Atlanta City Auditorium when Atlanta tennis brought in world champions like Pancho Gonzales, Jack Kramer, Bobby Riggs, Lew Hoad, and Pancho Segura.

He co-founded the Senior Tennis Players of Georgia, an organization that grew from two players to 150 and annually brought in the top senior players in America. He has been honored by his peers for "outstanding tennis sportsmanship" and for "long and meritorious service" to senior tennis in Georgia.

The memories have been many for George Pendley. His favorite is from the year 1980 when he and his partner did not lose a set in winning the National Clay Courts doubles for age fifty-five and over. Although it did not compare with the determination he would need to play with cancer, ten years after he started playing competitively, he suffered a serious knee injury. He underwent surgery. His orthopedic surgeon assured him he "would be okay" but added, "of course, you will never be able to play competitive tennis again." Pendley was forty-five years old.

He stayed on the sidelines for one year before his burning desire put him back on the circuit. He won forty-five more tournaments, despite an aching knee that sometimes buckled.

Says Dan Magill, University of Georgia tennis legend and curator of the Georgia Tennis Hall of Fame, "George is not only one of the most courageous athletes I ever saw but he was one of the best senior doubles players we have ever had in the state of Georgia. He could get to the net quicker than any player I have ever seen."

Pendley is no one-dimensional human being. He is an expert fisherman, gourmet cook, avid collector of fine wines, former newspaper columnist (*Forsyth*

County News), and lover of jazz. He not only served on the Board of Directors of "Theatre Atlanta" for eight years but he also played in several of the productions himself. Until last season, when he began the blood transfusions, he rarely missed a University of Georgia football game, dating back to 1967.

Of all his achievements, what is Pendley most proud of? "A loving wife. God blessed me by giving me Barbara." What advice does Pendley have for cancer patients? "Have faith in God. Pray. Go to support groups. Talk to people at church or synagogue and ask them to pray for you." If he had his life to live over again, what would he do differently? "Despite the low pay and long hours, I would have found a way to stay in broadcasting. Radio was never work. It was always a joy."

What does Pendley consider the most important thing in life? "To love and be loved. I have that with Barbara and my children." Pendley has one daughter, Karin Koser, thirty-eight, of Decatur, Georgia, and one granddaughter, Carson, four. Karin is Public Relations Director of Egleston Hospital in Atlanta. He has two stepdaughters, Diana Kirbo of Bainbridge, Georgia, and Pam Miserocchi of Duluth, Georgia. Diana has twins, Barret and Amelia Kirbo, age eight.

Considering Pendley's refusal to quit in the face of insurmountable odds, one wants to paraphrase the late, great sports writer Grantland Rice: It matters not whether you won or lost, but in spite of your handicaps, you played the game.

JOHN ROUSAKIS
"Mr. Savannah"

John Paul Rousakis is a legend in his own town.

Mayor of Savannah, Georgia, for a record twenty-one years (1970–91), former president of the National League of Cities, representing some 15,000 American cities, past president of the Georgia Municipal Association, movie actor, prep basketball phenom, a vital cog on the Atlanta Olympic Committee, and so forth.

A survivor of triple by-pass heart surgery and bladder cancer, today Hizzoner is doing well, thank you. He is sixty-nine years old. He lives with his second wife (his first wife died of cancer), the former Elizabeth Lattimore, in a 2,000-square-foot, split-level home at the Landings on Skidaway Island.

Savannah is the charming, well-manicured, exciting city it is today, thanks mainly to Rousakis. Maybe that is why there is a "Rousakis Riverfront Plaza," beautifully decorated with flowers and shrubs directly across from the riverwalk shops. It is a fitting tribute to the man who brought this once racially divided city together.

Exhibiting the same courage and determination he did when he played basketball for Savannah High School in the mid-1940s, Rousakis, during his tenure, made history when he appointed blacks to every commission on which he had the power to appoint. Thanks to Rousakis, blacks and women from all economic levels served on the airport commission, the housing authority, and the arts committee. Rousakis, while mayor, strongly supported Bowles Ford for the Savannah City Council and most Savannahans will tell you it was Rousakis' support that made Bowles the first black ever elected to the Savannah City Council.

One of the wisest moves the Atlanta Committee for the Olympic Games ever made was when it invited Rousakis and his wife to Tokyo to participate in the presentation bid to the Olympic Committee. As the late Lewis Grizzard once wrote, "Nobody can woo like Johnny Rou." Rousakis also hosted foreign Olympic delegates in Savannah, and when Atlanta got the games, Rousakis got the yachting events for Savannah.

Credit Rousakis for turning Savannah into a near "second Hollywood." When Jimmy Carter was Governor of Georgia, he appointed Rousakis to the first state movie board. Since then, Savannah has been the scene of some fifty movies, including "Forrest Gump," "Midnight in the Garden of Good and Evil," and the upcoming "The General's Daughter" with John Travolta.

Rousakis himself played in four movies filmed in Savannah: "Gator" with Burt Reynolds; "Pals" with George C. Scott, Don Ameche, and Sylvia Sydney; "The Lincoln Conspiracy"; and "Odyssey." "They were all fun," Rousakis recalls, "but I do not think any of my performances sparked a drive to get me an Oscar."

Maybe his acting was not of Academy Award caliber, but his devotion and dedication to his city earned him all kinds of awards. For instance, in 1962, he was recognized as the "Outstanding Young Man in Savannah" by the Savannah Junior Chamber of Commerce. In 1977, the Georgia Municipal Association named him the "Outstanding City Official of the Year" and in 1979, the *Savannah Morning News–Evening Press* selected him "Savannahan of the Year." Other awards heaped upon Rousakis include the University of Georgia's "Distinguished Alumni Award" and the Jewish National Fund's "Tree of Life Award," emblematic of outstanding service to one's community. The Atlanta Olympic Committee presented him with a special Olympic medal for wooing members of the Olympic Site Selection Committee.

Rousakis, the son of Greek immigrant parents, was born in Savannah on January 14, 1929. He went to work in his father's soda shop, Paul's, at the age of six, first sweeping the floors, then delivering orders and providing curbside service to customers who wanted to be served in their automobiles. He also washed dishes and claimed to be "the best soda jerk in Savannah."

His leadership was first evident on the basketball court at Savannah High School where he led his Blue Jackets in 1946 and 1947 to consecutive championships in the old Georgia Interscholastic Athletic Conference. He was captain of both championship teams, twice selected on the All-GIAA squad twice and picked for the All-Southern team. At 6'2", and with his complete dominance of the backboards and an unerring eye for the basket, he attracted the attention of almost every college scout in Dixie. The most persuasive of these was the late Harry Lancaster, who also was assistant head varsity coach for the University of Kentucky Wildcats. Lancaster was so impressed that he told his boss, Adolph Rupp, Baron of the Bluegrass, that Kentucky had to have Rousakis. Rupp extended the scholarship himself and in those days no one said "no" to Coach Rupp.

But the year was 1948, the year perhaps of Kentucky's greatest team. There were Alex Groza, Ralph Beard, and Kenny Rollins, three All-Southeastern Conference first team choices; and Wallace "Wah Wah" Jones and Jim Line, All-SEC second team choices; and Dale Barnstable and Cliff Barker, All-SEC honorable mentions. Even a phenom like Rousakis could not crack that group. Kentucky won both the National Collegiate Athletic Association and National Invitational championships and Rousakis always had the best seat in the house. He watched from the bench.

With most of the squad returning and the second Kentucky team almost as good as the first, Rousakis saw no chance of getting off the bench. So, he transferred to the University of South Carolina, then to Armstrong College and finally the University of Georgia where he did not play basketball but graduated with a degree in Business Administration. After Georgia came the US Army where he served three years in the counter-intelligence corps.

Back in Savannah in 1956, he began his meteoric climb to the top, not only in politics but also in the insurance business where he regularly qualified for the million-dollar club. He became president of the Savannah Jaycees and president of Saint Paul's Greek Orthodox Church. He was elected vice chairman of the Chatham County Commission, and by 1970 he was serving the first of five terms as mayor of the city of Savannah.

As a leader of the National League of Cities, he worked with four US presidents—Richard Nixon, Gerald Ford, Carter and Ronald Reagan. He was honored for playing a key role in the development of federal policies dealing with urban renewal and revenue sharing with the cities.

While Rousakis was mayor, Savannah began its urban redevelopment program and enjoyed unprecedented growth. The St. Patrick's Day celebration brought in tons of visitors, making it one of the largest Saint Patrick's Day events in America. The city population more than doubled with 350,000-plus revelers. Businesses like Gulfstream and Dixie Crystal flourished, military bases like Hunter Air Force Base and Fort Stewart expanded, tourism increased as people from all over the country came to see the sights they saw in movies, and the seaport became one of the largest on the South Atlantic. Rousakis contracted with the Savannah Symphony and the Savannah Ballet to perform free, not just in the civic center but in places all over the city four times a year. The new suspension bridge linking Savannah to South Carolina went up. So did the civic center with a seating capacity of 10,000 and the Johnny Mercer Theatre with seating for 2,400. Once dormant, Savannah became a hotbed for state conventions.

So, with all he got going in Savannah, why did he lose in his bid for a sixth term as mayor—to Susan Weiner, a Republican in a predominantly Democratic city, and a female Republican from New York at that? Rousakis simply says, "It was time for a change. Twenty-one years is a long time for one person to serve as mayor." Missing the excitement of being in the arena, Rousakis, like boxing champions who lost their crowns, tried for a comeback four years later. But like most fistic champions in their comeback bids, he went down in defeat, losing in the primary to Floyd Adams who became Savannah's first black mayor. Rousakis supported Adams in the General Election and again in his successful reelection bid in 1995.

On the one hand, Rousakis says he has no more political aspirations. On the other hand, he says he would like to be a part of a campaign to bring horse racing to Savannah:

> If our people had an opportunity to vote on it, they would be strongly in favor of it. Allen Paulson [of Gulfstream] has racehorses here. So did Bill Grainger [of Grainger Motors] and Richard Bowan [president of the Savannah College of Arts and Design]. The state legislature would have to approve it but I think it should be each community's right to decide if it wants gambling or not. We have a state lottery. Why shouldn't we have horse racing with parimutuel betting? The state ought to authorize a referendum for each community.

On the one hand, Rousakis says he is content. "I am happiest when I am with my wife, my children [Rhonda, Paul, Thea, and Tina], my stepchildren [Robert, Bill, and Ashley] and my five grandchildren. I like to play a round of golf occasionally. Three times a week I swim and walk in the neighborhood. I enjoy serving on the Boards of Directors of the American Cancer Society and the Union Mission. I am really quite satisfied with my life."

He quickly adds:

On the other hand, it is not like being mayor. I cannot think of anything more challenging than being mayor of a beautiful city like Savannah unless it is being president of the United States.

I did not enjoy being mayor. I loved it. I loved welcoming conventions. I loved the recognition when people saw me at a movie or in a restaurant and I loved it when these same people would bring me their problems. Helping people solve problems made me feel like a better person. It made the many hours I spent going to Atlanta and politicking at the state capitol and going to Washington and doing the same at the nation's capitol all worthwhile. Maybe it sounds corny but I treasure getting things done that will benefit my fellow citizens.

I never was meant to sit on the sidelines. This is something new to me. I don't like it. Never have. Not when I was on the bench at the University of Kentucky and not now."

So if Rousakis misses the political battlefield so much, misses serving his fellow human beings, and does not want to run against his friend, the incumbent Savannah mayor, why doesn't he run for higher office? He is a workhorse. He makes things happen. He has a grin from ear to ear. He makes a stranger feel like he is the most important person in the world. Asked why he never considered running for Governor, Rousakis replied, "What, and leave Savannah? Not in fifty years, not in 100 years, not ever."

1999

THE WRIGHT STUFF

Quick now, how many fathers coached their sons in Georgia high school sports? To name only a few, there were R. L. "Shorty" Doyal and his sons, Buck and Larry, at old Atlanta Boys High School; Chick Shiver and his son, Chick Jr., at Savannah High School; and Oliver Hunnicutt and his son, Pat, at LaGrange High School. They were all football coaches and players.

In basketball, one father-son combination stands out above the others—that of coach Emmett W. Wright Jr. and his son James H. "Jimmy" Wright.

In 1967, with the Wright stuff, Westminster's Wildcats of Atlanta, after losing to Commerce High in the region tournament, captured the state Class A championship in one of the most dramatic finishes in Georgia prep basketball history.

Following the region tournament, fate would have it that Westminster and Commerce would clash again, this time in the state tournament for the championship. The two schools were in opposite tournament brackets and both came through unscathed. Thus the rematch was set, with the top-seeded Commerce Tigers a slight favorite to win again. All they had to do was stop the coach's son, Jimmy Wright, who had been averaging eighteen points per game.

The Commerce defensive plan was simple enough: double-team Wright. And it worked so effectively that with six seconds left in the game, Wright had scored only four points. Commerce was holding a one-point lead. Westminster called time-out.

Coach Wright assembled his troops and said, "Get the ball to Jimmy. He will win it for us." Enough said.

With a screaming crowd of 3,000 hanging from the rafters of the old Macon City Auditorium and the clock running out, Randy Brunner put the ball back in play for Westminster, with a shovel pass to Wright. With four enemy hands in his face, Wright bounced the ball once, leaped high into the air and fired a thirty-five-footer that swished the net as the final buzzer sounded. Westminster had won its first and only state basketball crown.

Today Coach Emmett Wright is retired and living in Orange, Virginia. Jimmy Wright is director of the Jefferson Scholars program at the University of Virginia in Charlottesville, a stone's throw from his dad's home.

Regarding the championship victory, Wright's assistant coach, Kenneth O. "Ken" Kiesler, recalls, "I would never have believed Jimmy could have made that shot. First of all, he was thirty-five feet away, out of range for him or most anyone else. And then there were those two defenders almost smothering him. Somehow he protected the ball, leaped off the floor and with one hand fired. It was a perfect shot; the ball never touching the rim or the backboard. All it hit was net."

If good teachers make the best coaches (their teams once had a twenty-one-game winning streak), it is no wonder that coaches Wright and Kiesler were immensely successful. At Westminster, Wright was chairman of the history department and Kiesler was head of the math department. Both were honored for their classroom professionalism.

Wright was eventually named principal of the Westminster Boys School, a post he held for three years before accepting the headmaster's job at Metarie Park Country Day School in Louisiana. When he left for Metarie Park, he took Kiesler with him and made him assistant headmaster.

Wright was one of the most sought-after headmasters in America. His ability to inspire both faculty and students alike was known far and wide. After only four years at Metarie Park, he was chosen headmaster of the prestigious Woodberry Forest College Prep School in Orange, Virginia. He held that coveted post for seventeen years, before retiring seven years ago.

Meanwhile, Kiesler left Metarie Park to become headmaster of the Heritage School in Newnan. Like Wright, he also was much sought after, and after four years at Heritage, he was named assistant headmaster and principal of the Upper School at Atlanta's prestigious Lovett School. He left Lovett twelve years ago to open his own academic counseling and tutoring service. For the past ten years, he has been on the faculty at Kennesaw State University. He plans to retire after the 1999 school year.

Wright recently selected his all-time basketball team during his sixteen years as Westminster head coach. It included son Jimmy (1968), who had been named Most Valuable Player in the 1967 state tournament and to the Georgia State Class A All-Star Team in 1967 and 1968.

Others on Wright's all-time team are Jim Bostick (1965), now associate director of computer services at Commonwealth University in Richmond, Virginia; Bob Nast (1958), an independent businessman in Lithonia, Georgia; Brunner (1969), vice president of the Haas Publishing Company in Atlanta; Jack Wagner (1969), a manufacturers representative in Austin, Texas; Jimmy Fluker (1959), one of Atlanta's leading real estate developers; and Tommy Bates (1955), an Atlanta life insurance agent and a lifetime member of the Million Dollar Round Table.

Also included are Pat Hodgson (1962), an All-American end at the University of Georgia and now the tight ends coach for the New York Jets of the National Football League; Robert Blackwood (1961), an attorney in Richmond, Virginia; Hicks Lanier (1958), chairman, president, and chief executive officer of Atlanta-based Oxford Industries; McKee Nunnally (1961), a retired Atlanta stockbroker; Bill Darby (1958), president of a software company with offices in Jasper, Georgia, and Stonington, Maine; and Matt Cole (1967), vice president and treasurer of the Norrell Corp. Wright named Frank Block (1968) his all-time statistician and Willie Harris (1955–69) his all-time equipment manager.

Now about Mr. Wright. At Westminster, besides coaching the basketball team, he was athletic director, college admissions counselor, and the leading voice of a program to challenge highly gifted students. He also served as an instructor of national defense education at seminars at the University of Illinois. At Woodberry Forest, his fundraising was so successful that the school's endowment program vaulted from $4,000 to $41 million.

Wright was born in Atlanta on May 24, 1926. He graduated from North Fulton High School, received his degree in history from Furman University and an M.A. in history from Emory University. He was a William Robertson Coe Fellow at Stanford University and Tulane University.

When his team won the state basketball championship, he was named Coach of the Year by the Georgia Athletic Coaches Association and the Atlanta Tipoff Club. He was chosen to coach the North team in the Georgia High School All-Star game.

Here is what some members of his all-time team say about Wright:

> BRUNNER—My first impression of him was that he was not very athletic looking. I thought of him as a great history teacher—period. But as I look back, the fact that he was a great teacher made him a great coach. He was a strict disciplinarian. I remember drills, drills and more drills. He taught me how to dribble, how to pass the ball, how to rebound and how to play defense. To get us in tip-top shape, he ran us constantly. I remember him telling us at the first practice that we may not have the best team in Georgia, but we were going to have the best-conditioned team in Georgia. He had the respect of every one of his players.

> COLE—Coach Wright was an inspiration to me. He told us that we were the finest student-athletes on earth and that no one on this team had better do anything to disprove it. He stressed fundamentals. He stressed moral superiority.

HODGSON—He brought out the best in us. He expected 100% from each of us and would accept nothing less. He convinced us that we were winners. And, by gosh, we were.

COACH KIESLER—He was the biggest influence on my life. He was a winner. I always wanted to be like him. He set high standards and expected you to live up to them.

Since his retirement, Wright has been playing golf six days a week. Every day he reads The Washington Post and Wall Street Journal from front to back.

"I always considered myself a teacher first," Wright says. "I never went into a classroom without first reading the daily newspaper and knowing verbatim the history lesson of the day. I felt I had to be prepared if I expected my students to be. Teaching gave me the most pleasure I have had in life."

What character traits did Wright try to instill in his students? "Honesty and ethical behavior. Without those traits, life is going to be a failure." Where does he see the future of education headed? "It is sad, but a person without training in computers is going to be lost, if he isn't already. We are turning out computer operators and programmers, but we are not turning out students who can read and write."

To Wright, the most important thing in life is "bringing sunshine into someone else's life." For the past seven years, Wright has not missed a day visiting the sick and disabled at a nearby nursing home. The concern for others rubbed off on son Jimmy. He has been a director of group homes for the disabled and coach of a youth basketball team.

Besides Jimmy, Wright has a son, Bobby, forty-four, who is a computer programmer in Richmond, Virginia.

Now about Coach Kiesler. At Westminster, he twice was chosen a STAR teacher and twice invited to teach in the Governor's Honors Program. He has been a consultant to Memphis (Tennessee) City Schools on advanced placement in calculus. At Lovett School, he was awarded the Marianne Kern Dennis plaque for exceptional contribution to the education of children. In his ten years at Kennesaw State University, he was nominated for the distinguished teaching award three times. As a track coach at Westminster, he was chosen Coach of the Year by the Georgia Athletic Coaches Association and the Atlanta Track Club. His Westminster track team won the state class AA championship.

What advice would Kiesler give high school and college graduates today? "Flexibility is the name of the game. The idea of pursuing one career for a lifetime is finished. People are going to have three or four different careers during their work life. I tell my students that if they want to get to the top, they are going to have to work harder than anyone else. But I remind them that there is more to life than making money. It is doing what gives you the most pleasure."

If he had his life to live over, what would he change? "I never would have taken that first drink of alcohol. I have not had a drink in twelve years, and life has been so much better."

When is Kiesler the happiest? "When I am teaching. When you are teaching, you are giving to other people. And that is what life is all about."

Kiesler and his wife of forty-two years, Cathy, live in a three-bedroom Victorian home in the Marietta Historical District. They have two children: a son, Rob, thirty-nine, and a daughter, Jennifer, thirty-three. They also have three grandchildren: Melanie, age ten, and Kenneth and Michael, twins, age eight.

WILLIAM AVNER
"BILL" PASCHAL
Pride of the NY Giants

1999 LEGENDS GENE ASHER

If you have the pleasure of meeting William Avner "Bill" Paschal this year, you'll never believe he's seventy-eight years old. He looks twenty years younger. And you will find it incredible—as I did—that this blond-gray haired, smooth-skinned senior citizen played only two minutes of college football, spent the next two years working on the railroad, and then resumed his football career, not as a collegian, but as a professional, starting at halfback for the New York Giants.

Talk about the impossible dream: this native Atlantan, who lives in Marietta with Carolyn, his lovely wife of fifty-six years, was not just a starter in his rookie season, he was the leading ground-gainer in the National Football League.

As if to prove this was no piece of Walter Mitty fiction, Paschal won the NFL rushing championship in his second season as well, gaining more yards (727 in ten games) than in his first season (575 yards in eight). This included nineteen touchdowns and a full day's work on defense. Paschal thus became the first player ever to win back-to-back rushing championships in the National Football League and the only Georgian and New York Giant ever to do it.

And what did all this net Mr. Paschal? In his rookie season of 1943, he was paid $150 per game. For winning his first rushing crown, he received a $2,500 bonus, thus giving him a gross income of $4,000.

When Paschal went to talk salary with owner Tim Mara in 1944, Mara said, "I'm giving you a raise to $4,000. That's a pretty good raise, even if you were the leading ground-gainer in the league."

Paschal said, "But I made $4,000 last year. I was hoping for an increase."

"No," Mara replied. "You made $1,500 and I gave you a $2,500 bonus. You get the $4,000 guaranteed this year."

With no agents on the scene in 1944, Paschal, wanting to play football, readily accepted the contract.

With multimillion-dollar contracts commonplace today, Paschal displays not one iota of bitterness. He accepts the fact that he came along at a different time—without the glitter of television and the big, fat paychecks that go with it.

"I count my blessings every day," Paschal says. "I have a wonderful wife and family. I may not be a multimillionaire in dollars, but I am in friends—friends that go back to my Atlanta Tech High School days. Who could want more than that?"

Paschal had auspicious debuts at old Tech High and with the New York Giants. At Tech High, the team practiced at Piedmont Park. Freshman running back Paschal was sitting on the sidelines watching the varsity scrimmage.

"One of the defensive backs walked off the field to get water," recalls Paschal. "I saw that as my chance. So I put on my leather headgear, lined up where the missing player had been, and was ready when the varsity quarterback called a pass play in my area. I intercepted the ball and ran it back ninety yards for a touchdown.

"The head varsity coach [the late Gabe Tolbert] ran over to my position, put his face in mine and said, 'Do you know the varsity plays? If you don't, learn them tonight.'"

For the next three years at Tech High, Paschal dazzled everyone with his speed, daring, and durability. At the end of his freshman, junior, and senior years, he was named to the All-City, All-State, and All-Southern teams.

The debut at old Tech High was a preview of what was to come with the Giants. In his first exhibition game (for which the players were not paid) against the Chicago Bears, the untested Paschal was sent in to receive the opening kickoff. He took it at the one-yard line, started up the middle, cut to his left, raced past two defenders, stiff-armed the safety, and completed a shocking ninety-nine-yard touchdown run before the first play had been run from scrimmage.

As five seasons went on in victory after victory for the Giants, it was Paschal getting the ball every time the Giants would get inside the ten-yard line. Said Giants coach Steve Owen, "Paschal was the best running back I ever saw. He was fast, powerful, elusive, a quick starter, and possessed an unmatched fighting spirit." With Paschal in the fore, the Giants earned their shot at two NFL titles, losing one to the Green Bay Packers and the other to the Chicago Bears. In each game, Paschal was the leading rusher.

After his old Tech High football days, Paschal had his pick of Southern colleges. He chose Georgia Tech because his wife-to-be was in Atlanta, and he wanted to be near her. Playing for the Yellow Jackets, though, was not in the

1999

cards. In his last season at Tech High, the team trained in Athens, where Paschal slept on the top of a double-decker bunk. He turned his 6'1", 195-pound frame too far to the right one night and landed on the deck—with a fractured knee.

Despite the injury, he played his final season for Tech High, breaking every state prep record on the books. On his first carry at Georgia Tech, his knee took a devastating hit and Paschal, everyone thought, was through. He dropped out of school and went to work for the Central of Georgia Railroad as a switchman, until one day he ran into Tech coach Bill Alexander.

"How's your knee?" Coach Alexander inquired.

"Coach, I'm ready to play," Paschal said.

Alexander backed off, but he ran into the immortal sportswriter Grantland Rice at a Sugar Bowl game and told him, "I've got a brilliant athlete in Atlanta, 6'1", 195 pounds. Maybe some pro team would give him a tryout. There would be nothing to lose. This guy could become one of the greatest running backs the game has ever known."

Rice called Coach Owen and told him the story. And the rest, as they say, is history.

Twenty years ago, Paschal was inducted into the Georgia Sports Hall of Fame. It was about that time he should have been inducted into the National Football League Hall of Fame. He once held twenty-two New York Giant offensive and defensive records. Today, a half-century after he retired, he still holds Giant records for touchdowns in most consecutive games in one season—seven in 1945; and the fourth-longest run from scrimmage—seventy-seven yards against Cleveland in 1945. And then there are those back-to-back NFL rushing titles in 1943 and 1944.

All of this, mind you, while playing with a leather headgear and no face mask, shoes that he purchased himself, and one tattered and torn game jersey that was repaired game after game.

When Paschal retired from professional football in 1949, he took over the family sheet metal business and ran it for forty years. Today he spends his time sleeping late, cutting grass, and working in his flower garden.

Bill and Carolyn live in a brick ranch home in Terrell Mill Estates. They have one son, Bill, fifty-seven, a graduate and former starting varsity tackle for Georgia Tech, and four daughters: Dianne, fifty-six; Pat, fifty-five; Jane, forty-five; and Ellen, forty-one. They have twelve grandchildren.

On the outside, Bill looks young and healthy. The inside is a different matter. His years of gridiron glory have left him with aching knees, ankles, and back. Asked what he would do differently if he had it to do all over again, Paschal replied, "I'd sure try to take a lot fewer hits."

RAY BECK
All-Pro in His Rookie Year

When Ray Beck was a freshman at Cedartown High School, if anyone had suggested that one day he would be in the National Football Foundation College Hall of Fame, that person would have been sent to the nearest psychiatrist. The scrawny Beck was 5'10" and weighed 125 pounds. He played end and guard— end of the bench and guard of the water bucket.

At the Friday night games, when Cedartown fans would chant, "We want Beck, we want Beck," Beck's coach would send him into the stands to sit with his admirers. The only time he got into a game was when it was a hopeless case for Cedartown and he could do no damage.

That freshman year of 1945, no one would have dared to predict that one day Beck would become an All-American guard at Georgia Tech, be named the Most Valuable Lineman in the Southeastern Conference, play in the college All-Star game and be selected on legendary coach Bobby Dodd's all-time Tech team.

Beck never should have become a guard in the first place. Whoever heard of a 125-pound guard? But at Cedartown's opening practice, when Coach Lloyd Gray assembled his players and instructed all line candidates to move left and backfield candidates to step right, Beck moved to the left. It was one of the best moves he ever made.

When that first season ended, Beck started his own season—twelve months of running wind sprints until his tongue hung out, hitting the blocking and tackling dummies until his bones ached, and undergoing punishing calisthenics. By the time he was a senior, he had earned a starting berth at guard and was one of the quickest, fastest, and most powerful players on the team. He was selected for All-State and chosen for the state high school All-Star game.

By then lean and mean at 6'2" and 195 pounds, Beck was ready for college football—but no one was ready for him. Not Tech or Georgia, and not even the University of Tennessee at Chattanooga or Furman. In the 1940s, colleges rarely looked for talent in small towns, but they did hold tryout sessions. After a tryout at Chattanooga, Beck was offered a half scholarship. At Furman, he wasn't even offered that, which suited him fine. He was intent on going to Georgia Tech.

It was 1947 and Tech was to enjoy a banner season and head for the Orange Bowl. Beck's tryout consisted of head-to-head combat against All-American guard Bill Healey and All-SEC guards Ewell Pope and Buck Doyal. When the bloody encounter ended, a bruised and battered Pope told Coach Dodd, "I don't know who that kid is, but you had better sign him." And Dodd did—to a full scholarship.

Recalls Dick Jones, a former Tech assistant football coach, "We knew after a game scrimmage we had a good one. Beck held his own against three of the finest college guards in America."

Beck started three seasons for the Tech varsity, playing offense and defense. In his All-America season of 1951, he seldom came out of a game. His blocking and tackling led the Yellow Jackets to an 11-0-1 season, a victory over Baylor in the Orange Bowl and a fifth place national ranking in the football polls.

Says George Morris, a Georgia Tech legend and All-America teammate of Beck's, "I think teammates know best who is doing what on the field. Playing with Ray for two seasons, I never saw him give less than 100 percent. He inspired the whole team."

Anthony Joseph "Zippy" Morocco, a Georgia Bulldog who played against Beck in college and with him at Fort Jackson, South Carolina, has this to say about Beck: "I had rather play with him than against him. I can still feel the hits he put on me in two Tech-Georgia games. And when we were teammates at Fort Jackson, when I got the call to run up the middle, I could count on Ray to open holes. I knew him off the field as well as on, and I can tell you I never met a finer gentleman."

After an Army tour in which he served in Korea, Beck played five seasons with the New York Giants in the NFL. Beck's National Football Foundation College Hall of Fame certificate reads, "For his outstanding playing ability as demonstrated in intercollegiate competition and for his sportsmanship and integrity, his name shall be forever honored."

At age twenty-eight, Beck retired from pro football and came home to Cedartown to run the family business—Cedartown and Atlanta Freight Lines. He expanded the company's operations to Florida, Alabama, and Tennessee.

Today, Beck lives in his hometown of Cedartown, where he is something of a folk hero. He is a member of the Georgia Tech Hall of Fame and the Georgia Sports Hall of Fame. He was named to the all-time Orange Bowl team, played offense and defense on the New York Giants 1956 NFL championship team, and was picked on the NFL All-Pro team in his rookie season.

Beck is not your ordinary guy. Indeed, he is a model citizen. Talk about giving to the community. He is chairman of the Cedartown Development Authority, president of the Northwest Georgia Development Company, and chairman of the First National Bank of Polk County. He is past chairman of the Polk County Hospital Board, the Cedartown Chamber of Commerce and the local recreation department. On the state level, he serves on the boards of directors of the Georgia Games Commission and Georgia Sports Hall of Fame Authority. No wonder the city of Cedartown held a Ray Beck Appreciation Day, with a downtown parade and dinner in his honor.

At age sixty-eight, except for his civic work, he is fully retired. He is fit, with no major illnesses and weighs no more than his playing weight for the Giants—225 pounds.

No one ever played for three greater coaches than Beck did. After Dodd at Tech, he played for Vince Lombardi and Tom Landry, then assistant coaches for the Giants.

"Dodd was the best game-day coach I ever had, and he was always a gentleman," says Beck. "Lombardi was a genius. Landry was the most brilliant coach I've ever seen. He designed defenses that took the opposition two years to figure out. And he could establish an offense that would penetrate the defense of any team we played."

A staunch supporter of his alma mater, Beck attends all Tech home football games and some road games. "I don't want to put Coach [George] O'Leary on the spot, but if Tech gets by Florida State in the opener, I look for an unbeaten, untied season and a national championship," he says. "Coach has the horses—lots of them. He has brought the football program back where it was under Coach Dodd. These are going to be good times at the Flats."

Beck has been married to the former Claire McKay for forty-nine years. They have three sons: Kyle, who runs a trucking business in Rome; Mike, a stockbroker in Cedartown; and Tom, a transportation consultant in Atlanta.

HARRY JOHNSON
Mr. America

Harry Lionel Johnson Jr., a two-time Mr. America, was decades ahead of his time. Back in the 1940s, when it was strictly taboo for an athlete to lift weights, Johnson was lifting 165 pounds daily. Not only did it not make him muscle-bound—as almost every high school and college coach in the nation then professed—it made him one of the strongest athletes in Georgia. And one of the best. At old Atlanta Tech High School, he twice won the state prep light heavyweight boxing championship and was an All-State guard on the Tech High football team.

Today, almost every college and high school in America has a weight room for their athletes, and they can thank Harry Johnson.

At age seventy-five, Johnson still pumps iron daily and looks as fit as he did at age thirty-six, when he became the oldest man ever to win the Mr. America contest. Known almost as much for his harmonica playing as for his strength and body build, Johnson leads a four-piece band that plays throughout the Metro Atlanta area at weddings, bar mitzvahs, and retirement homes. Twice a month, his band entertains at the Decatur Life Enrichment Center. "We usually get $100 per hour for playing, and $150 a hour for not playing," he jokes.

Johnson makes his home in the little town of Auburn, Georgia (population 5,600), about thirty-five miles north of Atlanta. He lives with his wife, the former Joyce Leonard of Atlanta, in a four-bedroom house on five acres. The Johnsons have six children and twelve grandchildren. The Johnsons are deliriously happy today, but it was not always that way.

Says Johnson:

> The trouble with being a champion athlete, especially a body-builder, is that young women throw themselves at you. They want to touch you, feel your muscles, and wrap their arms around you. I succumbed to the adulation and it was the biggest mistake of my life. It cost me my wife. She was the best friend I ever had. Talk about being down. When Joyce left, I was downright depressed.
>
> But I got close to my God and I have kept Him with me day and night. My faith in God helped me get my wife back. It took me thirty-seven years, but with God's help, I did it.
>
> Today, I never let an evil thought get in my head. We remarried two years ago, and I am the luckiest man alive. To me, Joyce is a rare, precious jewel.

Born in Atlanta, Johnson lived his early years in West End. By the time he was a teenager, he had moved to Inman Park and then to Durant Place NE, just around the corner from Tech High School.

At Tech High, Johnson was not only a bona fide two-sport star, he was one of the most popular students in the 1,200-plus student body. How so? Because he was happiness personified. He would offer words of encouragement to the despondent and sincere compliments to the achievers. At the end of each class, students would flock around him as he broke out his harmonica and serenaded his classmates with the Tech High Battle Song and the popular tunes of the day.

Warm and friendly as he was, he took no guff from students or teachers. The Tech High faculty was a class act, thanks to the principal, the late W. O. Cheney, a great educator, supervisor, and motivator. But there was one teacher on staff who was better fitted to be a guard on an old Georgia chain gang than to teach a group of bright teenagers. The teacher's favorite term was the longer version of "SOB." If a student was late to class, the teacher addressed him as a "tardy SOB." If a student missed class, when he returned, he was called a "delinquent SOB."

One day Johnson arose from his seat in class and searched for an ink bottle. He spotted one atop a steel storage cabinet. Johnson climbed on his desk, reached over for the ink bottle, and instead got his grip on the edge of the cabinet. It came crashing down over two wooden desks.

"All right, Johnson," the teacher barked, "what kind of an SOB do you want me to call you?"

Johnson walked over to the teacher's desk, looked him in the eye, smiled, and said calmly, "The same kind you are."

On the first play of the 1944 Tech High-Marist football game, the Marist guard playing opposite Johnson threw a wicked forearm into his face. There were no face protectors in 1944, so blood spewed from Johnson's nose. Johnson said nothing. But on the next play, with his left hand, Johnson grabbed the Marist guard by his jersey, and with his right hand delivered a crushing blow to the mouth. The Marist guard was carried off the field—minus two teeth. He never returned. No one else ever threw a forearm at Harry Johnson.

After five attempts, Harry won the Mr. America contest in 1959. Talk about self-discipline. He did his iron pumping at 6 A.M., before he started his daytime job as a dispatcher in tool control at Lockheed Aircraft, and again at 7 P.M., before he reported for duty as a bouncer at the old Hank and Jerry's Hideaway on Peachtree at 10th Street. When the Hank & Jerry's band would take a break, bouncer Johnson became the backup act and entertained the customers with his harmonica playing. He was as big a hit on stage as he was keeping order.

Recalls Byron Cohen, former owner of Hank and Jerry's, "Having Johnson as a bouncer was like having the fastest gun in the West. Seldom a night passed without some drunk or insecure bully wanting to prove he could whip Mr. America. But no one ever did."

Back in the 1950s, two Georgia Tech football players came in one night looking for trouble. They found it in Harry Johnson. One of the players, a 6'6", 240-pound tackle, shoved Harry against the bulkhead. Johnson politely asked him to return to his table. The player cocked his right arm but before he could deliver a punch Johnson unloaded a lethal right hook to the jaw that sent the Yellow Jacket into dreamland. At Tech High, they did not call Johnson "One Punch" for nothing.

"The ironic part of it," says Cohen, "is that Harry Johnson is the nicest, calmest, most unassuming guy I ever knew. He never looked for trouble, but he never ran from it."

Seven years after winning the Mr. America crown, Johnson won the Mr. America Over 40 title. If there were a Mr. America 75 and Over contest, Johnson would be the odds-on favorite.

At this writing, he is a trim 185 pounds, with these impressive statistics: neck—eighteen inches; waist—thirty-two inches; chest—fifty inches; biceps—seventeen inches; and thighs—twenty-five inches.

Johnson received his bodybuilding start under the tutelage of Jim Barfield, Karo Whitfield, and Bill Curry Sr., the father of the former Georgia Tech football coach. He was thirteen years old. He first entered competition in 1945, when he was named Best Developed Body in Atlanta. He went on to become Mr. South before taking the Mr. America crown.

"Every man over the age of forty can get himself in 80 percent better condition by doing some kind of exercise," advises Johnson. "What causes people to get fat is that they cut down on their physical activity and continue to eat the same amount of food. The reason I do deep knee bends with 200 pounds on my shoulder, two-hand curls with ten-pound weights and ten overhead presses three times a week is so I will feel good. I'm more alert and can accomplish more during the day. I plan to work out for the rest of my life."

Johnson's diet consists of two poached eggs, fresh fruit, and skim milk for breakfast; tossed salad (no dressing), cottage cheese, and skim milk for lunch; and meat, fresh vegetables, fresh fruit, and skim milk for dinner.

"Here is what bodybuilding and disciplined dieting have done for me," says Johnson. "I've never had a cold or headache. I've been in the hospital only to have my tonsils out and my hip replaced. I've never been sick a day in my life."

Johnson never made a bundle out of his two Mr. America crowns. He put on exhibitions around the country but all he ever got was a few hundred dollars, plus expenses. He always gave more that he received. For every paid exhibition, Johnson gave ten free exhibitions to school children, Boy Scouts and Boys Club members.

"Being Mr. America meant more to me than fame," he says. "It gave me the opportunity to help and inspire others. I wouldn't trade that for a million dollars."

A GOLDEN ERA OF SPORTS

A kaleidoscopic (and sports-intensive) look back at Georgia and our century: Atlanta hosting the Olympic Games...Whitlow Wyatt outpitching fellow Georgian Spud Chandler and the Brooklyn Dodgers beating the New York Yankees in the second game of the World Series...the University of Georgia defeating Notre Dame in the Sugar Bowl for the national title...Frank Sinkwich and Herschel Walker winning Heisman Trophies.

• Old Atlanta Boys High coach Shorty Doyal taking halfback Clint Castleberry out of games because he's scoring too many touchdowns and embarrassing the opposition...off a football team that wins only five games, Georgia sending eight players to the pros—Bobby Walston, Harry Babcock, John Carson, Dick Yelvington, Marion Campbell, Claude Hipps, Hamp Tanner, and Billy Mixon...John Heisman coaching at Georgia Tech.

• Atlanta Crackers reserve catcher Jim Solt pinch-hitting for home run king Bob Montag in the ninth inning and slamming a game-winning homer to beat Houston for the Dixie Series Championship...old Atlanta Tech High center Gene Chandler snapping the ball on punts, beating the ball downfield, and decking the returner as he takes his first steps...Lanier's Billy Henderson and Tech High's Pierce McWhorter staging the greatest shootout ever seen at Ponce de Leon Park and McWhorter winning, 26-19, before over 20,000 fans.

• Atlanta's Jake Abel fighting world lightweight champion Benny Leonard in the old Atlanta City Auditorium...Atlanta's Erskine Mayer posting back-to-back twenty-game seasons for the Philadelphia Phillies...his brother, Sammy Mayer, managing the Atlanta Crackers and once climbing the centerfield flagpole, holding on with one hand, and catching a fly ball with the other.

- Valiant Jim Minter, clad in a T-shirt in freezing weather, driving an open jeep to the North Georgia mountains to rescue Atlanta Constitution Editor Reg Murphy, held captive by an armed kidnapper...Bobby Jones completing his grand slam of golf and becoming a living legend...Georgia experiencing three governors simultaneously—Ellis Arnall, Melvin E. Thompson, and Herman Talmadge...Margaret Mitchell writing *Gone With the Wind*...Fitzgerald's Raymond G. Davis earning the Congressional Medal of Honor in Korea, becoming a four-star general, and serving as assistant commandant of the US Marine Corps.

- Paul Duke, a backup center in high school, making All-American at Georgia Tech...Marist graduates Kenny Adamson and Jim Carroll becoming near back-to-back football captains at Notre Dame...Atlanta producing two Mr. Americas—Harry Johnson and Harry Smith...Wally Moses hitting better than .300 for seven seasons with the Philadelphia Phillies...Noah Langdale turning a parking garage into thriving Georgia State University.

- The Falcons getting to the Super Bowl, the Braves winning a World Series, and Jimmy Carter becoming president. Who wouldda thunk? ...Pete Rademacher, an amateur prize fighter out of Fort Benning, making his professional debut in a world light heavyweight title match against champion and winner Floyd Patterson...Lee Burge working his way up from the mailroom to chair Equifax...Dr. Sid Williams, a chiropractor and former Georgia Tech football player, building Life University...Bryan M. "Bitsy" Grant ruling Southern amateur tennis...Natalie Cohen leading women netters.
- Dot Kirby and Louise Suggs dominating women's golf...Hank Aaron slugging 755 home runs...Tom Perry and Scottish Rite Hospital...Dr. Joe Patterson and Egleston Children's Hospital...Robert Woodruff, the pause that refreshes...Home Depot's Bernie Marcus and Arthur Blank...light heavyweight Young Stribling of Macon...referee Frankie Allen of Atlanta...The Varsity...Nipsey Russell...Flossie Mae.

- Year after year, Valdosta's Wright Bazemore turning out the two best football teams in Georgia: his first and second teams...Furman Bisher, Celestine Sibley, Ralph McGill, John Martin, and John Crown...The Atlanta Georgian pink edition and the *Atlanta Times*...Leo Frank, the pencil factory, the Ku Klux Klan, and Governor John Slaton...William L. "Bill" Rothschild, the first Jew admitted to the Westminster Schools faculty.

- Hall of Famers Eddie Mathews, Ty Cobb, and Luke Appling...Cecil Travis, Marty Marion, and Hugh Casey...Paul Anderson, the world's strongest man...linebacker Larry Morris, Papa Bear's favorite...the family rivalry out of Crabapple—Nap Rucker of the Brooklyn Dodgers and Johnny Rucker of the New York Giants...Beau Jack, from Augusta shoeshine boy to lightweight boxing champion of the world...Fran Tarkenton of the Minnesota Vikings and Forrest (Spec) Towns of the Olympics...FDR and Warm Springs...Elias Noor and Stone Mountain rescues.

- Eighty thousand Georgians, from every nook and cranny of Georgia, cheering on Herschel Walker...the sports greats of Cedartown: Doug Sanders, Ray Beck, Doc Ayers, and Edgar Chandler...Lee Walburn and *Atlanta* magazine...Bill Paschal, who played two minutes of college football at Georgia Tech, springing to the New York Giants and leading the NFL in rushing his first two seasons...Elmer Riddle of Columbus helping pitch the Cincinnati Reds to the World Series.

- Lou Silver, knocking out teeth in Atlanta's boxing rings and extracting them in his dental office...Lew Carpenter, working for the Bell bomber plant in the daytime and pitching for the Atlanta Crackers at night...Earl Mann, whose Crackers were known as the New York Yankees of the South...Benjamin Mays, president of Morehouse College and the first black president of Atlanta's school board.

- Taylor Branch, from the Westminster high school football team to the Pulitzer Prize...Erskine Caldwell, Pat Conroy, and James Dickey...Charlayne Hunter-Gault, the first black woman to graduate from the University of Georgia...Ray Charles of Albany and Johnny Mercer of Savannah...Jackie Robinson, playing at Ponce de Leon Park, KKK threats and all.

- Griffin Bell, attorney general under Carter...Judge Elbert Tuttle, whose court rulings led to the integration of public facilities throughout the South...Dean Rusk, secretary of state during the cold war and Vietnam...Maynard Jackson, Atlanta's first black mayor...Andrew Young, US ambassador to the United Nations.

- Don Adams, who never played anything but a trumpet, going out for football his senior season at Druid Hills High and leading his team in tackles...by mistake, Coach Oliver Hunnicutt sending in the wrong player to kick a last-minute field goal against Valdosta...Jerry Buttrum, bifocals and all, delivering as LaGrange wins the South Georgia football title and goes on to the state championship (with his first and only kick)...Bobby Hendley of Macon pitching a one-hitter for the Chicago Cubs, only to lose to Sandy Koufax, who hurls a perfect game for the Dodgers.

Yes, it was a great century.

2000

MOROCCO
A Two-Sport Star

Anthony Joseph "Zippy" Morocco, also known as No. 23 to longtime University of Georgia football fans, owns an office building and an Arby's restaurant, belongs to two country clubs, and owns homes in Athens and Saint Augustine, Florida.

Not bad for the son of an Italian immigrant steel worker who could scarcely speak a word of English. Indeed, not bad at all for a kid who shared a bed with his two brothers and, at age eight, helped his parents make ends meet by selling newspapers and shining shoes on the streets of his hometown of Youngstown, Ohio.

The matchbox-like, two-bedroom home in which Morocco lived was more crowded than the Marx Brothers' stateroom in the classic movie "A Night at the Opera." The Morocco brothers shared their eight-by-ten-foot bedroom with their two sisters, who slept in another bed. Their parents took the other bedroom.

"You had to have a reservation to get into the living room," says Zippy, "because we had two boarders living there. We had one bathroom downstairs in an unfinished basement. There was always a line to get in there. But nobody complained. We had a lot of love in our family."

With his dad's take-home pay from Republic Steel, rent from the boarders, and earnings from the children's after-school jobs, there never was a shortage of food on the dining room table. "We didn't eat fancy, but we ate plenty," says Morocco. "Financially, when I think of where I started and where I am now, it's unbelievable. I would not want to go through those old days of struggling again, but they taught me how to cope with adversity. And, believe it or not, I had fun."

Morocco holds out his hands. "You're looking at the hands that shined the shoes of old movie stars Bela Lugosi ["Dracula"] and song-and-dance man George Murphy, who later became a US senator from California."

These also are the hands that carried a football for the Georgia Bulldogs (averaging 9.9 yards per play) and shot a basketball (23.6 points per game). Morocco was Georgia's first All-American in basketball. Although he was brilliant on the gridiron—he still holds the Bulldog career record for punt return average (14.2 yards, set in 1949–51)—he never reached his full potential, because Georgia emphasized an inside running attack while Morocco's speed and deception were tailor-made for an outside attack.

Nevertheless, he thrilled Sanford Stadium fans in 1950 with a ninety-yard punt return for a touchdown against Furman University. Morocco had opposing tacklers diving hopelessly into space. That same year in the Presidential Cup bowl game, he broke tackle after tackle on a sixty-five-yard punt return for a touchdown against Texas A & M.

Playing halfback for Fort Jackson, South Carolina, in the US Army in 1953, Morocco finally could run with the wraps off. So he twisted, turned, and raced around the flanks, averaging a remarkable twelve yards per carry. Seemingly every time he touched the ball, it was "first down, Fort Jackson." Morocco was a unanimous choice for the All-Service, All-American team.

Today, forty-six years after his brilliant season for Fort Jackson, Morocco is long retired from contact sports and also retired from his incredibly successful real estate business. Nowadays, he spends part of his time in Athens, playing golf with former Bulldogs George Bulloch, Hokey Jackson, Charley Trippi, and Leroy Dukes, and part of the time in Saint Augustine, where he golfs with ex-Bulldog teammates Marion Campbell and Art DeCarlo.

Morocco looks much the same as he did the day he entered the University of Georgia in 1948. His height and weight are the same—5'10", 165 pounds. There are no wrinkles in his forehead and not a trace of gray in his full head of black hair. He looks fit enough to dress out on a Saturday afternoon and ignite the Bulldog offense.

In high school, Zippy was a basketball standout. In fact, he did not make the first team in football until his senior year. But what a season that was. He led his Ursaline Academy team in rushing, pass receiving, punt returns, and kickoff returns.

In Ohio's All-Star prep football classic, Morocco electrified the crowd of 30,000 by taking the first punt of the game and zigzagging fifty-six yards for a touchdown. By game's end, he had scored two more touchdowns and attracted the attention of college scouts from Ohio State and North Carolina.

But Morocco was headed to Georgia to follow in the footsteps of two earlier Youngstown prep stars—Frankie Sinkwich and George Poschner. Sinkwich was

Georgia's first Heisman Trophy winner (in 1942), and Poschner was one of Georgia's early All-Americans.

Those growing-up days in Youngstown, where his living quarters were something less than luxurious, were the Taj Mahal compared to what he had in his one basketball season at Georgia. Finished with his football eligibility as well as his football scholarship after the 1952 season, Morocco was forced out of Milledge Annex, then the football dormitory, and relegated to the basement of decrepit Memorial Hall. There he lived out of a footlocker and a metal clothing closet, hardly accommodations befitting Georgia's first All-American basketball player.

The king of the court may have lived like a pauper, but he never once complained. With Morocco's scholarship gone, basketball coach Harbin "Red" Lawson scrambled and found money for his winter-quarter tuition. It was the best investment anyone ever made. In that wonderful basketball season of 1953, in a game against Southeastern Conference power Tennessee, Morocco sank a last-second, forty-foot, two-handed set shot to upset the Vols, 87-86, on their home court. The two-point goal, which would have been three under today's rules, gave him a total of thirty-eight points, then Georgia's single-game record and still the standard for a Bulldog road contest.

People who saw the game still talk about the last-second shot. Tennessee coach Emmet Lowery called it "the most dramatic I have ever seen" and Zippy's performance "the finest I have ever seen."

For the season, Morocco tallied 590 points, a new Southeastern Conference record, breaking the mark set by Kentucky legend Cliff Hagan. He was voted Most Valuable Player in the Southeastern Conference. After the basketball season, Morocco went into the US Army and led the Fort Jackson football team to an 8-1-1 record.

When he completed his Army tour and returned to civilian life, Morocco was a lost soul. He had had enough of the Youngstown steel mills. He tried coaching high school football in Villa Rica. The hours were long and the salary small. He opened a drive-in restaurant and bar in Athens, and it soon fell by the wayside. He sold life insurance, then advertising specialties. He was a bust at both.

A friend put him in touch with the well-respected Athens real estate firm of Evans and Mitchell. It was a perfect fit. The newest member of the firm became No. 23, All-American Zippy Morocco.

Morocco took his share of rejection, but he figured if he got enough listings and called on enough prospects, the law of averages would work for him.

"It was like running the football," he says. "If you made enough runs, you'd score a touchdown." Morocco would take ten "no's" for every "yes," but he made sure he got in front of twenty prospects a week. When Evans and Mitchell went public, Morocco moved to the firm of Freeman and Messer. There he sold residential homes, so many in 1963 that he was able to go out on his own. For the next twenty-three years, Morocco was a fixture in the multi-million-dollar real estate sales club. He retired in 1986.

"God blessed me," he says. "I'm thankful for a standard of living I never thought possible for me, and, more importantly, I'm thankful for good health and a good family."

Zippy is married to the former Fran Matonis. They have two sons, Gregory, thirty-eight, and Chris, thirty-three; one daughter, Allison, thirty-seven; and four grandchildren. Chris was an All-State quarterback at Clarke Central High School in Athens. Like his dad, he wanted to play for the University of Georgia but was not offered a scholarship. So he went to Clemson, where he was an All-Atlantic Coast Conference selectee and passed the Tigers to a 27-7 victory over West Virginia in the 1989 Gator Bowl.

Good breeding tells.

HOWARD WHO?
DOC AYERS, THAT'S WHO

If you asked the man on the street who the heck Howard Edmonds Ayers is, the answer would probably be "Howard who?"

But ask most anyone who's been in Georgia twenty or more years who Doc Ayers is and the answer likely would be, "One of the most successful, best-loved coaches in the history of Georgia football."

Ayers, who coached high school and college football in Georgia for thirty-seven years, cared more about the health and welfare of his players than he did about winning. Yet he posted an enviable 147-66-6 won-lost-tied record as a head coach.

In his fourteen years as coach of Cedartown High School, Doc won one state championship, two region championships and seven subregion championships. In 1956, he was named head coach of the North Georgia All-Star football team. His many honors include being named Georgia State Class AAA Coach of the Year and membership in the Georgia Sports Hall of Fame.

Ayers never played an athlete—team leader or scrub—who was injured. Unlike some coaches, winning for Ayers was a priority but certainly not the top one. "I wanted my teams always to do their best, but I also told them I loved them, regardless of the score," he says.

Maybe that's why the Polk County Board of Education dedicated Doc Ayers Field last year at Cedartown High Stadium. At the dedication ceremony, Jerry Weaver, one of Ayers' former quarterbacks, told a crowd of Georgians from all over the state, "Everyone who played for Doc loved him. The wonderful thing about this night is that forever and ever, this will be known as Doc Ayers Field."

Ayers is as well known off the field for his concern for others as he was on the field. He has served the old Scottish Rite Children's Hospital (now Children's Healthcare of Atlanta) for thirty years, many of them as a board member. He's been a longtime promoter of an annual golf tournament that benefits the American Heart Association.

Ayers is one coach who says what he thinks, whether he agrees with his colleagues or not. For instance, for the safety of players, he advocates making college freshmen ineligible for varsity sports and eliminating red-shirting. He would like to see less coddling of recruits and less pressure put on game officials. Specifically, he calls the punishment of officials for a questionable call in the final moments of the Tech-Georgia football game last season "a disgrace."

The game referee ruled Georgia fumbled the football at the Tech goal line in the last minute of play. Georgia claimed it was no fumble, as TV instant replay indicated. The Southeastern Conference Football Officials Association reacted to the call and the ensuing red-hot controversy by barring the officiating crew from working post-season bowl games. All for a single missed call.

"Whether or not it was a fumble, the referee made the call the way he saw it," says Ayers, who coached at the University of Georgia for seventeen years. "If he missed the call, he would not have been the first official to miss one. When I was coaching, I always looked at the film right after the game. I'd say there were about twelve to fifteen missed calls in most games we played. Some of them cost us the game, but missed calls have a way of evening up for each team."

Ayers says, "Officiating is a tough job. You cannot expect perfection. No one does anything perfectly, whether it be in football, baseball, basketball, or running a business. Think about the home plate umpire in baseball. You'll see a number of balls and strikes in each game that could have gone the other way. It's all part of the game. It's all part of life."

In the best interest of players, Ayers recommends college freshmen be ineligible for varsity competition. "I don't think freshmen should even be allowed to scrimmage against the varsity," he says. "They're not ready physically or mentally to compete against players who have three and sometimes four years of varsity experience. I'd like to see the SEC have freshman teams like it did for many years. Then the players would compete against people their own size and maturity."

Ayers coached Georgia freshman teams for ten years, posting a 28-12 won-lost record, the best in Bulldog history. Ayers says:

Just think, if we had freshman teams again, we'd have two Tech-Georgia games—the Bullpups and Baby Jackets and the Bulldogs and Yellow Jackets. Back in the 1950s and 1960s, those Tech-Georgia freshman games would attract 45,000–50,000 fans every Thanksgiving. And all the proceeds went to the children's hospital. We raised hundreds of thousands of dollars. Today, we have to stage ten events a year to raise the kind of money we did back then with one Tech-Georgia freshman game.

Ayers is a member of the hospital board.

If Ayers had his way, red-shirting—holding a player out of competition for a year—would be eliminated. It's not fair to the players to keep them in college an extra year, just so they'll be bigger and more experienced football players," he says. "I always thought the purpose of college was to get an education. Five years of football is just too demanding. You knock heads and undergo strenuous weight programs almost twelve months a year. That doesn't leave much time or energy for studying."

As for recruiting, Ayers says:

There's an awful lot of pressure to get the best players because the coaches' livelihoods depend on it. But the number of visits a prospective player makes to a college should be reduced. So should the number of visits a coach makes to a player's home.

And instead of pitching the prospect on how soon he can play at a school or guarantee that he'll play quarterback or some other position, the pitch should be to his career interest. With a budding writer, the emphasis should be on the fine journalism school or the fine business school to a would-be entrepreneur. Kids should not pick a college because of its football team. They should choose a college because it will prepare them for a life-long career.

Doc Ayers was born in Toccoa, Georgia, the son of Clarence L. and Helen E. Ayers. His father was a medical doctor, hence the nickname. "Dad delivered half the children in Toccoa and probably treated the other half as well as their parents," he says.

Ayers attended Toccoa High School and Darlington School in Rome, where he played halfback on the football team and earned All Mid-South Conference honors and a scholarship to the University of Georgia. He participated in the longest spring practice (1946) in Georgia's history, during which be suffered a knee injury that ended his boyhood dream of playing for the Georgia Bulldogs.

Little did he know that eventually he would coach not one but four breeds of Bulldogs—in Lavonia, Winder, and Cedartown, and at the University of Georgia. At Lavonia High School (1948–51), he guided the Bulldogs to a 25-4-1 record and had a 3-7 mark in his one season with the Winder Bulldogs. His Cedartown Bulldogs were 91-43-5. In 1964, when Vince Dooley became head football coach at Georgia, the first assistant he hired was Doc Ayers. Ayers coached the Bullpups for ten years and spent the next seven years as administrative assistant to Dooley, recruiting, counseling players, and speaking to civic and Bulldog clubs all over Georgia.

Ayers and his wife, Glenda, live in Cedartown in a three-bedroom, two-bath home. At age seventy-seven, he's doing fine, thank you, and going full speed. He exercises daily, heads his own real estate company, and handles marketing and sales for the Dempsey Auction Company. He starts his day at 6 A.M. and doesn't stop until 6 P.M.

Some of Ayers' philosophy:

• No one knows it all and no one does it all.

• Rather than criticizing someone for his own good, praise him for his own good.

• No one is perfect, so forgive those who have hurt you, not for their sake but for yours.

• You can disagree without being disagreeable.

Doc and Glenda have three children: son Bucky, a former quarterback for his dad at Cedartown and later for the Auburn Tigers, and now a golf pro at the Auburn University Club; daughter Bunny, a flight attendant for Delta Air Lines; and daughter Buzzy, a physician's assistant in Athens.

LARRY MORRIS
The Brahma Bull

If you ever meet Larry Cleo Morris—better known at Decatur High School, Georgia Tech and in the NFL as the "Brahma Bull"—you'd never know he was the most highly praised football player ever to come out of the state of Georgia.

At age sixty-six, he is the same quiet, modest, unassuming man he was before he won every football accolade but the Heisman Trophy. You name it, Morris won it: All-American as a Decatur High Bulldog, twice All-American at Georgia Tech, All-Pro for the Los Angeles Rams and Chicago Bears, Most Valuable Player in the 1963 NFL championship game, etc.

Typical of his modesty is the comment he made after the 1954 Tech-Georgia game, in which his twenty-four individual tackles set a Tech record and kept the Bulldogs out of the end zone, preserving a 7-3 victory. Famed Tech coach Bobby Dodd called it "the finest individual performance I have ever seen." The late *Atlanta Journal* sports editor Ed Danforth wrote, "Morris hit a peak of brilliance. He played 60 minutes in the highest tradition of his craft." What did Morris say? "My tackles were made possible because our linemen wiped out the interference to give me a clear shot at the ball carriers."

The late Harry Mehre, former Ole Miss and University of Georgia head coach and the *Atlanta Journal* football analyst covering the game, wrote, "Morris was everywhere, rushing the passer, a human wrecking ball as a middle linebacker

2000

and sprinting to the flanks, where he personally stopped eight Bulldog scoring threats."

Two Georgia fans were overheard talking after the game. One said, "Why did we run all our plays at Morris?"

The other replied, "We didn't. He always was where our ball carriers ran."

Today Morris is still running, although not as fast. He is in the real estate development business, as he has been since he retired from professional football in 1967.

Morris builds apartments and shopping centers in Hall County and helps his son-in-law and daughter, Eddie and Kay Anne Staub, with their Eagle Boys' Ranch in Chestnut Mountain, about ten miles south of Gainesville. The ranch houses forty-two boys, all from dysfunctional homes. They were battered, neglected, or abandoned.

Morris works out of his two-story home in Flowery Branch, also near Gainesville, where he lives with his wife of forty-one years, the former Kay Wilder. He walks two miles daily. At 6'2", he maintains the same 220-pound weight he carried when he played at Tech and in the pros. When not at his office or at the ranch, he's off to job sites, visiting with subcontractors or his banker. In the fall, he coaches youth football. Last year his team was undefeated. One team stalwart was his 4'11", 90-pound grandson, Daniel.

Morris grew up an only child in Decatur. His father died when he was ten. His mother worked as a bookkeeper, and Larry kept busy after school doing chin-ups, pushups, running, and watching the Decatur High football and baseball teams.

As a high school freshman, he was a starting fullback on the varsity football team, and a starting centerfielder and .300 hitter on the varsity baseball team. In his junior and senior seasons, he led Decatur High to back-to-back state football championships. A fullback and linebacker, he led his team in rushing, scoring, and individual tackles. He scored three touchdowns in each of the state title games. His long-ball prowess on the baseball team earned him a contract with the old Class AA Atlanta Crackers, which he turned down to play football and baseball at Georgia Tech.

Said his Decatur High coach, Charlie Waller, who later coached the San Diego Chargers, "Larry was not only one of the greatest players I ever coached but one of the greatest I have ever seen—college or pro." When Morris fumbled early on in the second state title game, Waller thought, "We've got them now. Larry will be a raging bull the rest of the way."

At Georgia Tech, Morris was a four-year regular in football and baseball and was chosen All-Southeastern Conference in both sports. In 1953, playing center and linebacker, he was a consensus All-American, making every major team—Associated Press, United Press International, International News Service, Collier's magazine and the *Saturday Evening Post*. A junior, he was the only non-senior selected on the AP All-America team.

"I saw all the players we picked, and Larry Morris was the best," said the late Francis Wallace, who selected the Collier's squad. At age nineteen, Larry was the youngest player on that team.

As a senior in 1954, Morris became only the second Tech player ever to make All-American twice. (The first was end Bill Fincher in 1918 and 1920.) All told, Morris started in seventy-eight games at Decatur High and at Georgia Tech. In his four years as a Tech center and linebacker, the Jackets beat the Georgia Bulldogs every year, going to four consecutive bowl games and winning them all. "If my future depended on one game, I would rather have Larry Morris going for me than any other player I ever saw," Tech Coach Dodd once said.

In his senior season at Tech, Morris captained both the football and baseball teams. It was a familiar position for him. He had captained the football and baseball teams at Decatur High and later captained the Chicago Bears in their title run in 1963.

The Los Angeles Rams picked Morris in the first round of the NFL draft. In his rookie season in 1955, he played center, linebacker and fullback. "He could have played ten positions, everywhere but quarterback," said former Rams coach Sid Gillman. "He was the kind of player a coach dreams about. He had size, speed, and desire. And he only knew one speed—full. He didn't 'talk the talk,' as they say today. He was all action."

The late George Allen, who coached the Rams and later the Washington Redskins, called Morris "not only an outstanding football player but a role model for the whole Rams team."

Morris was respected and liked by his teammates as well as his coaches. "Larry was not only a devastating linebacker, he was like a steamroller blocking at fullback," said teammate Glen Davis, Army's legendary "Mr. Inside" in the 1940s. "It was easy for us to gain yardage when he was knocking down two and sometimes three players on every play."

Morris played twelve seasons in the pros—four with the Rams, seven with the Bears, and one with the Atlanta Falcons. In the 1963 title game, Morris did everything but carry the water bucket, making sixteen tackles and playing on special teams. As MVP, he was the toast of the Bears' victory over the New York Giants. Longtime Chicago coach George "Papa Bear" Halas—not known for lauding his players—grabbed Morris when the game ended, hugged his neck, and said, "You are the greatest Bear of all."

When the Falcons opened in Atlanta in 1966, Morris told Halas he wanted to finish his career in his hometown. But eleven years of head-knocking and bone-rattling in the NFL had taken its toll. Morris paid the price, undergoing four knee operations before the 1966 and 1967 seasons. He played one season and then retired in 1967. "Larry was not the type to sit on the bench," said Falcons coach Norb Hecker. "If he could not make a major contribution, he wanted no part of hanging on…He was a gentleman. In addition to his great athletic ability, he was one of the finest people I have ever known."

After hanging up the cleats, Morris went into real estate development, and he could not have picked a better time. Real estate was booming in Atlanta in the late 1960s and early 1970s. Morris built apartments in the Briarcliff-LaVista area, shopping centers in Glenwood and Tucker, upscale subdivisions in Dunwoody, condos in Saint Simons, and the Falcons complex in Suwanee.

In the mid-1970s, interest rates skyrocketed, and the banks began calling in loans. It was a low point for Morris, a time filled with anxiety. In the end, class won out. Morris negotiated with the banks, turned over developments to lenders and worked his way out of financial trouble without declaring bankruptcy.

The thought of doing so never entered his mind.

Morris entered politics briefly, becoming the first independent from DeKalb County to win a seat in the Georgia House of Representatives. He served one term and then returned to the real estate business. Morris also has been president of both the DeKalb and Fulton development associations.

If Morris played today, he would command big money. As a first-round draft pick, Morris signed with the Rams for $8,500. After he won the MVP Award in the 1963 title game, he received a career-high salary of $20,000. "If I were coming out of college today, I might get a bonus of $1 million and a minimum annual salary of $850,000," he said. "But I'm not bitter. I loved playing football. If I had it to do all over again, I would not change a thing."

Now you know the Larry Morris story. If you meet him, you won't have to pry it out, not that you could anyway. Morris is proud of his many feats on and off the gridiron, but what he cherishes most is the time he spends with his family. He'd rather talk about his wife, Kay, his four children, and eleven grandchildren. Some things never change.

RATCLIFFE 1,

Father Time 0

At an age when most people are in cemeteries or nursing homes, ninety-year-old Herman Lee "Bubba" Ratcliffe of Hapeville is playing competitive tennis—not only playing but winning. Not only winning, but winning more senior national championships (twenty-one) than any other Georgian in history.

This past April, Ratcliffe and former Atlantan Vince Connerat, who now lives in Charlotte, won the US Tennis Association's national hard courts title in the ninety-and-over age division. The next day, Ratcliffe reached the singles finals. The doubles crown was his twenty-first national title (fifteen doubles and six singles championships), and as this issue went to press, he was after Nos. 22 and 23 in the national indoor singles and doubles championships in Vancouver, Washington.

Not a bad record for someone who didn't pick up a tennis racquet until age seventy. Not bad for someone who drives his 1981 black Chevy van everywhere from Georgia to New England to California to play in national tournaments. Not bad for someone who sleeps in his van at tournaments, not in a luxury inn or even some budget motel. The light may be on and Tom Bodette may be waiting for him at Motel 6, but Ratcliffe needs to save every dime he can to put food on the table for himself and his eighty-seven-year-old wife, Nell. That's why he built a bed out of two-by-fours for his van and put in a hot plate and cooler.

Most of all, not bad for a man who grew up in poverty but is as cool as the ice in his cooler while thrashing foes from the country club set. Ratcliffe has won the grand slam of doubles three times and more national championships than the legendary Bryan M. "Bitsy" Grant. Needless to say, Ratcliffe is a shining light in the Georgia Tennis Hall of Fame, plus an inspiration to every senior citizen thinking of trading in the racquet for a seat in the gallery.

In 1990, Ratcliffe became the first Georgia native to win a USTA Senior Grand Slam. Playing with Gene Short of Miami, he captured the eighty-and-over doubles titles indoors and on clay, grass, and hard courts. As an eighty-five-and-over player, teaming with Connerat, he repeated, winning back-to-back national USTA Grand Slams in 1995 and 1996. The feat was beyond incredible. Ratcliffe, in fact, has won a USTA special achievement award for his "unparalleled success as a senior player."

At age seventy-eight—lean and mean at 5'8" and a fraction, and 138 pounds—Ratcliffe beat former Wimbledon champion Gardnar Mulloy in the national grass courts championships in Hartford, Connecticut. After the final stroke, he leaped over the net and told the former king, "Better luck next time."

Until a year ago, you could find Ratcliffe playing four or five times a week at Atlanta's Bitsy Grant Tennis Center, where he's both a legend and an institution. These days, if you want to catch him in action, you have to get to the tennis center on Tuesdays at 1 P.M. The rest of the week he's home caring for his ailing wife, who suffers from heart disease and high blood pressure. Ratcliffe washes the clothes and does all the cleaning and cooking. For some twenty years, up until a year ago, he delivered Meals on Wheels to the bedridden in Hapeville.

Ratcliffe didn't grow up in meager circumstances—he grew up in poverty. Born in Atlanta on January 7, 1910, he was raised on a farm off the old Bankhead Highway and in a three-bedroom house on English Avenue, in the Bellwood section of the city. Both homes were on the old streetcar lines but on the wrong side of the tracks. They had no indoor plumbing, no electricity, no telephone. Bathing was in a washbasin.

Bellwood was a tough neighborhood, so to survive Ratcliffe early on learned to compete. As a kid, he was a pretty good fighter, but on the streets of Bellwood, not in a boxing ring. Ratcliffe's father worked as a flagman and switchman for the old Atlanta, Birmingham, and Nashville Railroad. He barely made ends meet.

At age twelve, the younger Ratcliffe began delivering ice off a horse-drawn wagon to homes in the neighborhood and then threw two paper routes for the

Atlanta Journal. Between the two jobs, he earned about $8 a week, which he gave to his father to help on the rent.

Saturdays were spent at the old Peachtree Arcade, Atlanta's first enclosed shopping mall, which stood where the Five Points MARTA Station is today. Ratcliffe sold newspapers there for two cents apiece, earning a penny per sale. Some days he made as much as two dollars, a veritable fortune for the strapped family.

After graduating from O'Keefe Junior High School at age fourteen, Ratcliffe gave up the ice delivery job, but he kept throwing newspapers through his three years at old Commercial High. College was no option. There simply wasn't enough money, so the young graduate took a job with Southern Wax Paper Company, which eventually became part of St. Regis Paper. Ratcliffe spent his first year wrapping candy, bread, dinner rolls, and other food items. It was 1928, the year before the stock market crashed. He recalls:

> There were no labor laws in those days. Or if there were, they weren't enforced. I worked seven days and eighty hours a week. There were no machines. Everything was done by hand. I was the fastest wrapper in the plant. My pay was thirty dollars a week, or about 37.5 cents an hour.
>
> But I didn't realize how well I was paid until I got promoted. I had learned bookkeeping at Commercial High, so after a year in the plant, I was made a bookkeeper. My pay went from thirty dollars a week to fifteen dollars. I said I wanted to go back to the plant, but my boss said they needed me in the office.

When St. Regis took over Southern Wax, Ratcliffe became a sales coordinator, taking orders over the telephone. "I did that job for forty-one years, and when I retired, I was making $1,200 a month. To the college graduates who were outside salesmen at St. Regis, my salary was a mere pittance. But to me, it was a small fortune."

In 1936, Ratcliffe met and married Nell Edwards of Atlanta. "We met at a dance at the West End Woman's Club. It was love at first sight. It was also the height of the Depression, but we didn't care. That poverty-stricken marriage has lasted over sixty-three years." For the past fifty years, Bubba and Nell have lived in the same three-bedroom, two-bath house in Hapeville.

Along the way, Bubba sang in the choir for twenty years at the Hapeville Baptist Church and played amateur softball for thirty-five years, until age sixty-one. He also played amateur baseball. Once his Hapeville team faced a Fulton team led by Luke Appling, who became a member of baseball's Hall of Fame.

"I take nothing away from Luke, but he hit his last home run in an old-timers game at age seventy-five," says Ratcliffe. "In tennis, I'm still hitting the equivalent of home runs at age ninety."

At sixty-nine, Bubba took up golf, but riding around in a golf cart was not his idea of exercise. So, at seventy, he found his way to the Bitsy Grant Tennis Center and has been a fixture there ever since. "Everybody loves him," says seventy-year-old Phil Slotin, a longtime Bitsy Grant regular. "He makes us all feel young."

In his first year at Bitsy Grant, Ratcliffe was a whipping boy for former city champion Hank Crawford and the immortal Grant himself. Only a year later, at age seventy-one, he and a pickup partner won the city doubles tournament. At age seventy-eight, he and Harold Wiese won the seventy-and-over national grass courts doubles championship.

Ratcliffe has been blessed with good health. His medical chart shows only a tonsillectomy, hernia, and knee surgery. How much longer will he play competitive tennis? "As long as my health permits, even if I live to be 100," he said. "Or until my wife's illness keeps me home twenty-four hours a day. I will not put her in a nursing home. I love the game, and I love all the guys I play with, even those who cheat. It's a big thrill for me to see these old codgers like me playing like a bunch of kids."

Bubba has five children, thirteen grandchildren, and eleven great-grandchildren. Plus a lot of great memories.

BILLIE CHENEY SPEED
The First Woman Sports Writer

Billie Cheney Speed, the first woman sportswriter in America, is dying from liver and lung cancer, but you would never know it by talking with her. She's the same enthusiastic, warm, upbeat person she was when she joined the *Atlanta Journal* sports staff as a twenty-year-old cub reporter back in 1947.

"Why not?" she says cheerfully. "I'm blessed with a wealth of friends, many of whom I've had for fifty years or more. I have classmates from high school and college who stay in contact with me. I hear regularly from former co-workers, and I have my own cheering section at the Timothy United Methodist Church in Stone Mountain. Life is wonderful."

So are the memories.

She was the first woman admitted to the press box at Grant Field (Bobby Dodd Stadium). She was the first woman ever to sit in the old Atlanta Crackers dugout. She interviewed former world heavyweight boxing champion Gene Tunney. She wrote feature articles on the immortal Bobby Jones and former national women's amateur golf champions Louise Suggs and Dot Kirby.

Times were different back then.

"I never thought of going into any team's dressing room to interview players or coaches," she says. "It never entered my mind. After the games, I was able to get all the quotes I needed while the players and coaches were still on the field. I never saw the necessity of entering a locker room then, and I don't today."

2000

While she served as religion editor of the *Atlanta Journal* from 1965 to 1989, she was honored by ministers, rabbis and priests alike. She became a close friend of Billy Graham.

"I'm not afraid of dying," she says. "I thank God day and night for all that has come to me." Last April, Billie elected to stop her chemotherapy treatments. "It's the quality of life that counts," she says, "not the length."

She lives in a four-bedroom ranch house on Rays Road in Stone Mountain. One of her daughters, Donna Adams, lives with her. She has two other daughters, Kathleen Windham and Melanie Wright. As this article was written, she was able to dress and feed herself, drive her car and cook her own meals. "I'm up at 6 A.M.," she says. "In the old days, when you worked for an afternoon newspaper, you had to be in the office at 7 A.M. I'm used to getting up early, and as long as I have the strength, I see no reason to change." As the day wears on, Billie tires and goes to bed. Hospice comes in twice a week.

For most of her life, Billie has been a bundle of perpetual motion. While attending West End High School in her native Birmingham, Alabama, she held a full-time job with the *Birmingham News*, the city's afternoon daily. Ironically, her dad worked as a linotype operator for the rival morning newspaper, the *Birmingham Age-Herald*, as did his father before him.

Billie fondly recalls:

> It was 1944, and World War II was going full speed. The military draft had taken two of the News' sportswriters, and replacements were hard to come by. So, Zipp Newman, the sports editor, sent letters out to the four high schools in Birmingham asking for recommendations. Because I had been editor of our school newspaper, my English teacher recommended me.
>
> When Mr. Newman got the written recommendation for a Billie Cheney, I think he thought I was a boy. To say he was surprised when this longhaired, freckled-face redhead came in for the interview would be a masterpiece of understatement. Whoever heard of a female sports reporter? No one. But he liked what I said and the samples of my writing I brought him, so he gave me the job.
>
> I covered bowling and swimming. I was seventeen years old and not a licensed automobile driver. So whenever I covered any events, I took the old street cars.
>
> At the office, I answered the telephone and took results of high school football and basketball games. I don't remember how much I was paid, but I do know that if Mr. Newman had asked me, I would have worked for nothing.

Billie went to West Georgia College. When she graduated in 1947, her dad accepted a job with the *Atlanta Journal*. So the family moved to Atlanta, and Newman sent a letter of recommendation to his friend George Biggers, who was president and publisher of the *Atlanta Journal*. On her way to Biggers' office, she walked through the newsroom, wearing high heels, a light blue sweater, and a navy skirt. The red hair flowed. The crackling of the typewriter keys stopped, and eyes focused on the young woman.

When she opened the door to Biggers' office, the stunned publisher asked incredulously, "Are you the sportswriter?"

"Yes," replied Cheney. Biggers picked up the telephone and dialed the number of Edward Friend Danforth, his gifted and highly respected sports editor.

"Danforth," the publisher bellowed, "I have a new sportswriter for you. And it's a girl!"

The *Journal* billed her as "the first woman sportswriter on a major daily newspaper in the United States," but as far as anyone can tell, she was the first female sportswriter for any newspaper or any magazine in the country.

For the *Journal*'s sports desk, Billie did it all. She wrote headlines, edited copy, wrote feature stories, went to the Krystal and got hamburgers and coffee for her staff mates, picked up out-of-town photos from the airport, and had her own sports show on WSB Radio, where she predicted scores of high school and college football and basketball games. Fellow sports staff members adored Billie. They liked her smile and her excitement in tackling any assignment, be it a girls basketball game or a professional wrestling match. In her spare time, she obtained the birthdays of staff members and baked them cakes.

"I think I had the respect of every staff member," she says. "But I also think I was looked upon as every staff member's baby sister."

Being one of a kind, she was sought after by touchdown and other sports boosters clubs around the state. She spoke everywhere from Blairsville to Homerville. "Most of the time, I spent the night at the homes of club members," she recalls. "They didn't think it was right to put up a young woman in a hotel."

For six years (1947–53), Billie was "Ms. Versatility" of the sports staff. She then spent ten years as assistant promotion director to Pat Noot LaHatte. In promotion, she met and married Thomas Speed Jr. In 1965, she was offered and accepted the job of religion editor, which she held for twenty-two years, until her retirement.

"I never wanted to do anything but work for a newspaper," she says. "When I was four years old, my daddy taught me to read by reading me the newspaper every day. With him and my granddad in the business, I never knew there was anything else."

In the spring of 1994, Billie was struck with uterine cancer. She had surgery and chemotherapy. The cancer went into remission. Three years later, it reappeared in the lungs and liver. There was more surgery. Then a lung collapsed. In March 1999, she went back on chemotherapy and suffered a mini-stroke. She recovered. She continued the chemotherapy—one treatment a week.

Her oncologist, Dr. Edward Weiser, said the chemo was not helping much and gave Billie the option of continuing or stopping treatment. Continuously sick and without energy, she stopped. That was last April. She knows the cancer is terminal. Facing death is not new for Billie Cheney Speed. She lost a grandson when he was only eighteen years old. Her twenty-eight-year marriage to Tom Speed Jr. ended two years ago when he was killed in an automobile accident.

Without the chemo, she knows she can live life almost as actively as she used to, at least for a while. She paraphrases the Bible, "This is the day the Lord hath made, and I will rejoice and be glad in it."

"The world is beautiful," she says. "I have resumed my duties as president of my Sunday School class and president of the church senior citizens group. My faith in God has not wavered. I will keep on keeping on."

Today, most major daily newspapers have at least one and often two women writers on the sports staff. All the TV networks have at least one. It's been a long time coming. Billie Cheney Speed was years ahead of her time. Today she's listed in Who's Who in America. I've known her for fifty-one years. If they had such things, she would be listed in All-American Human Beings.

PEPPER RODGERS
"Mr. Spice"

Mention Franklin Cullen Rodgers Jr. and folks might be puzzled. Say "Pepper Rodgers" and most everyone recognizes one of Georgia's most colorful coaches and personalities. He was funny and irrepressible, sometimes to his own detriment in the athletic arena.

Says the sixty-eight-year-old Rodgers:

> The toughest obstacle I have had to overcome in my life is getting people to take me seriously,". "People remember me for doing cartwheels as I led my football teams on the field on game days, for going into the stands during pregame warm-ups and talking to the students, for hopping out of a casket on my television show and hollering, "We're not dead yet."
>
> What they don't remember is that I am a professional. I was an Air Force pilot. I quarterbacked championship football teams in college and high school. I had successful coaching careers in college and professionally. I have contributed to my community.
>
> I have always believed in having fun. I have my own little subculture. I am not so much of a maverick that I disregard every rule in the book. But on the big things—how I think, what I value—I don't let society determine that for me.

James A. "Jim" Schultz, director of public relations for the Atlanta Braves, was sports information director at Georgia Tech in 1974 when Pepper reported for his first day as head coach. "He was wearing a shoulder bag," recalls Schultz. "He rode into the coaches' parking lot on his Harley and sporting a new perm, not entirely the Tech image. But I will tell you this about Pepper: He was a caring individual. He treated the janitor as well as he did some of the old alumni at the Capital City Club. In his eyes, every human being was the same."

I've known Pepper since 1949, when he quarterbacked Brown High School in Atlanta's west end to the state Class AAA football championship, and I've never known him to be unhappy. Not even when he was on a fishing trip in Florida and the engine exploded and he was blown into the water literally on fire. He was taken to a Gainesville hospital with burns over most of his body. "I am blessed. I'm alive, and I feel great," Pepper told a visitor the next day. "All we need in this room is a little music."

Today Pepper lives in Memphis, in good health and happily married. He will be going to Washington, DC, this month to do consulting, public relations, and marketing for Federal Express and the new Fed Ex Stadium, home of the Washington Redskins. He is writing his fourth book—*Fast Backs, Big Linemen, Beautiful Women and Good Music.* Rodgers was in Atlanta in June for his fiftieth Brown High School Reunion and to play in the annual Bobby Dodd Charity Golf Tournament.

One of the big mysteries is why Rodgers has not been admitted to the Georgia Sports Hall of Fame. Maybe he did put on a wig and show up for a Tech football practice in disguise. Maybe he did insert taped interviews with Bob Hope, Ronald Reagan, and other celebrities into his Sunday TV football show. Maybe he did sue Georgia Tech for $331,000 for perks (fringe benefits) when he was unceremoniously fired by the Tech athletic board in Atlanta while he was dining at the White House with Jimmy Carter. But what has all that got to do with his qualifications for the Georgia Hall of Fame? Truth be known, aside from a very few Hall of Fame members, nobody is more deserving to be in the 280-member organization than Rodgers, and if he's not admitted next year, there ought to be some kind of state investigation.

Consider this: At the University of Kansas (1967–70), he was twice named Big Eight Coach of the Year and once was runner-up for NCAA Coach of the Year. At UCLA (1971–73), he was twice named Pacific Coast Coach of the Year. At his alma mater, Georgia Tech (1974–79), he was twice Southern Independent Coach of the Year. His overall college coaching record was 73-65-2, and he was 34-31-2 at Tech.

Not to mention, of course, his glittering credentials as a player. In the 1952 Orange Bowl, he kicked a field goal in the final two minutes to give Georgia Tech a 17-14 victory over Baylor. In the 1953 Sugar Bowl, he kicked a field goal and three extra points and threw a touchdown pass to lead his Yellow Jackets to a 24-7 victory over Ole Miss. In 1954, he was voted Most Valuable Player in the Sugar Bowl after passing for three touchdowns and kicking four extra points and a field goal in a 42-19 rout of West Virginia.

Now, if that won't get you into the Georgia Hall, what would?

During his three years on the Georgia Tech varsity, the Jackets went 32-2-2. His thirty-nine extra points in 1952 established a Tech single-season record that stood alone for thirty-eight years until Scott Sisson tied it in 1990. His sixty-eight career extra points rank fifth on Tech's all-time list. While a player at Tech, Rodgers shrugged off a complaint by his head coach, the late, legendary Bobby Dodd, that he was missing too many placekicks in practice. "Put 40,000 fans in the stands and then see how many I miss," he replied.

Besides what he accomplished as a college coach and player, Rodgers has made major contributions to his community wherever he's been. In Memphis, where he had coached the Memphis Showboats of the now defunct US Football League and the Memphis Mad Dogs of the Canadian Football League, he spearheaded a drive to land the NFL's Houston Oilers. The Oilers eventually went to Nashville and became the Tennessee Titans, but Rogers did promote four preseason NFL games that raised hundreds of thousands of dollars for Junior Achievement, Saint Jude's Hospital, and Big Brothers and Big Sisters. As Tech coach, he raised funds for the American Cancer Society, the Colitis Foundation, Heart Disease Foundation, Hodgkins Disease Foundation and the Georgia Mental Health Society.

Even his wife, Janet Livingston Rodgers, got into the act. In 1978, when Rodgers' Yellow Jackets were to play the Purdue Boilermakers in the Peach Bowl, the demand for tickets was less than awesome. In fact, it looked as if the Peach Bowl, which had struggled for years, was on its last legs. Two weeks before the game, Livingston (as Rodgers calls her) paid visits to the heads of Atlanta's major corporations and convinced them that supporting the game was a matter of civic pride. Tech lost but thanks to Livingston, the house was almost filled and the Peach Bowl survived.

Reliable sources say some of Dodd's former players are keeping him out of the Hall of Fame, possibly because Rodgers preferred to hang out with his neighborhood crowd and not the country club set. Or maybe because after he was fired, Rodgers filed the unprecedented lawsuit over his lost perks—Cadillac, country club membership, and loss of income from radio/TV shows, summer youth football camps, and promotional appearances. (Tech had agreed to pay Rodgers for the two remaining years of his contract and eventually settled for $100,000 of his $331,000 perks lawsuit.)

It's not that he doesn't have support for the Hall of Fame. Rodgers has been recommended by Tech Athletic Director David T. Braine, former *Atlanta Constitution* sports editor Jesse Outlar, and retired *Journal-Constitution* executive editor James E. Minter. But to this point, the Hall of Fame selection committee seemingly has cared more about Rodgers' style than his accomplishments.

His roots in Georgia are deep. The son of the late Franklin Cullen and Louise Rodgers was born in Atlanta's Crawford Long Hospital on October 8, 1931. His grandfather was an ardent fan of the Saint Louis Cardinals Gas House Gang, especially outfielder Pepper Martin. He immediately hung the nickname on his grandson.

Pepper's father was a perennial candidate for political office but his only victory was election to Atlanta's school board. Meanwhile, he sold real estate and served as an auctioneer. Pepper's mother was a teller at Peoples Bank at Five Points. The income was sufficient to put a roof over their heads on Stewart Avenue SW and food on the table, plus have enough left over to send Pepper to the Jack Rand School of Dance.

In an omen of what was to come, little Pepper at age six burst on the local entertainment scene. Dressed in a red, white, and blue Uncle Sam outfit, complete with top hat, he sang and danced his way across the stages in Atlanta's neighborhood theaters. He even performed at the storied Loew's Grand, site of the "Gone With The Wind" premiere, tapping and singing "Ding Dong Daddy From Dumas" in the city's annual Kiddie Review. Later, at Brown Junior High School he took up the clarinet and was third soloist in the school orchestra. The biggest fear he ever had, he says, was at the school's annual orchestra concert when the first two clarinet players failed to show.

In 1947, Brown became a high school and Pepper became a three-star athlete deluxe. In guiding the 1949 Brown team to the state football championship, he won All-State honors. He had already won All-State honors in basketball and baseball.

Rodgers entered Georgia Tech in the fall of 1950, continuing a love affair that began at age twelve, when he served as a Boy Scout usher at Grant Field on game days. "All I ever wanted to do at Tech was make my parents proud of me," he says. That he did, helping lead Tech to three Bowl games and earning a degree in industrial management. While at Tech, he married his high school sweetheart, Judy Ragsdale. The marriage lasted twenty years and produced four children—Rick (forty-six), Terri (forty-five), Kyle (forty), and Kelly (thirty-five). Pepper has two stepchildren, Jana (forty) and Paige (thirty-five) and six grandchildren. He and Livingston have now been married for twenty-five years. "Next to my parents, Livingston is the best friend I ever had."

Pepper stories at Tech are legendary. A favorite involves a hotly contested game during his senior season when he made two successive miscues at quarterback. Coach Dodd brought Pepper to the sidelines and told him to get on the phone with offensive chief Frank Broyles, who was calling plays from the press box. Pepper put on the earphones. Broyles, thinking Pepper was still in the game, screamed into the phone, "Get that [expletive, expletive] Rodgers out of there." Pepper calmly handed the earphones to Dodd and said, "Coach, I think this is for you."

Pepper Rodgers is a member of the Georgia Tech Sports Hall of Fame. And his induction into the Georgia Sports Hall of Fame is long overdue.

A TRIP THROUGH TIME

Over the past four and one-half years, I've had the pleasure of writing about fifty of Georgia's legendary figures, of one stripe or another. Many were athletes. Some were longtime public officials. All contributed, often in dramatic ways, to this state's success. A few showed great courage in the face of impending death.

To celebrate this fifteenth anniversary issue, here's a brief update on some of the remarkable people who have come our way.

ELLIOTT H. LEVITAS, FORMER US CONGRESSMAN AND ONE of Atlanta's leading attorneys for the past sixteen years, may have won the biggest case of his life recently, arising from a historic class action lawsuit (*Cobell v. Babbitt*) in federal district court in Washington, DC. Levitas and other lawyers, representing over 300,000 Native Americans, sued the federal government for the loss of billions in trust fund money.

The court's decision found that the government had committed "serious, long-time breaches of trust" against the Indians, dating back to the 1880s. The judge said the decision rectifies "the injustice, mistreatment, and mismanagement by the government." A second part of the case, expected to be tried this fall, involves the restatement and correction of trust fund ledgers to reflect the true amount of money that should be held in trust for beneficiaries.

A senior partner in the international law firm of Kilpatrick Stockton, Levitas represented Georgia's 4th Congressional District from 1975 to 1985.

LEGENDS GENE ASHER 2000

Beyond working on the mammoth case, Levitas serves on the boards of the National Building Museum and the Southern Center for Environmental Studies. He has represented the US in international political forums in the Republic of Georgia, Turkey, Mongolia, and Germany. A bundle of perpetual motion, Levitas is a guest instructor at the Emory University Law School, plays tennis and spends time with his grandchildren.

Elected to the Georgia House in 1965, Levitas logged five consecutive terms in the General Assembly, where he was considered one of its most effective members. At age sixty-nine, he's physically fit and has no plans to retire.

HUSBAND-WIFE TEAM MAKE HISTORY. THERE NEVER HAS been a husband-wife combo as dominant as William L. and Jeanne Daprano. Husband Bill has won more than 100 Masters Track awards. He helped set world records as a member of the US 4 x 200 and 4 x 400 relay teams. He has captured three national titles in the 200 and 400 meters, a national pentathlon (five events), and raced on two 4 x 400 national championship relay teams.

This past May, he broke the world record for age seventy-three in the pentathlon with 3,254 points, snapping a thirteen-year-old record by sixty-four points. In August 1999, in Gateshead, England, he won gold medals in the 4 x 100 and 4 x 400 relays. But his most important win at Gateshead was the heart of Jeanne Hoagland, a woman he met at a Masters dinner and married four months later. Jeanne doesn't take a backseat to her husband, matching him almost medal for medal. She holds US women's age records for the 400 meters, 800 meters and 1,500 meters. Two years ago in South Africa, she won three gold medals in the World Games. Last June, running with a group of 100 women, she broke the world record for her age group in the mile. At sixty-two, she was the oldest woman in the meet.

The Dapranos live in a three-story home in Riverdale. When not competing in world events from Finland to Australia, they work out at Lakewood Stadium or Landmark Christian School.

Bill was a track star at old Atlanta Tech High School and the University of Georgia. He coached football at the former Saint Joseph's High School in Atlanta in the 1960s, where his teams won three region championships. After a ten-year coaching career and a 59-31 record, Daprano turned to homebuilding and became a millionaire. At age seventy-three, he's looking forward to his next national championship competition in October in Eugene, Oregon. His running mate—and wife—will compete in the women's races.

HARRY L. JOHNSON JR., A TWO-TIME MR. AMERICA IN THE 1950s, was a recent guest of honor at New York's prestigious Downtown Athletic Club, the recipient of a lifetime achievement award for bodybuilding. In presenting the award, Vic Bobb, president of the International Association of Oldtime Barbell and Strongmen, said that "for more than four decades, Johnson has represented the true ideals of physical culture. He is one of the truly greats in iron game history."

At age seventy-six, Johnson still pumps iron daily and looks as fit as he did at thirty-six, when he became the oldest man ever to win the Mr. America contest. A native of Atlanta, he was one of the most popular students ever to attend old Atlanta Tech High School. There he twice won the state prep light heavyweight boxing championship, was an All-State guard on the football team and entertained his fellow students between classes by playing a mean harmonica. Johnson and his wife, Joyce, live in Auburn, Georgia, about thirty-five miles north of Atlanta.

THREE BLOCKED ARTERIES AND A LIVER AILMENT HAVE failed to slow down ninety-year-old tennis wizard Herman Lee "Bubba" Ratcliffe of Hapeville. Playing in ninety-degree heat, he and former Atlantan Vince Connerat last June won the Super Seniors Hardcourt Doubles Championship at Palm Desert, Calif. It was his twenty-second senior national championship.

With one hour's rest, he entered and reached the finals of the singles tourney before the humidity and chest pains sidelined him. Chest pains brought him to his knees over the recent Fourth of July weekend at Atlanta's Bitsy Grant Tennis Center. The next day he underwent an arteriogram, which revealed three blocked arteries.

Dr. Mark Silverman, a noted cardiologist, said he would probably need surgery if he was going to play tennis again. Bubba has been meeting with Dr. James Kauten, a cardiac surgeon, to determine if he is fit for the procedure. The verdict was still out at press time.

Said Bubba, "No matter what he says, I'm going to play tennis again. If I die on the tennis court, that will be a perfect way for me to go."

GENERAL RAYMOND G. DAVIS (RET.), WHO EARNED THE Congressional Medal of Honor in Korea, is now eighty-five years old. No matter. He's busier that ever, traveling the fifty states urging veterans organizations, civic clubs, chambers of commerce, and the news media to support a strong national defense.

Gen. Davis was the driving force behind the erection of the Korean War Memorial in Washington, DC He serves as national chairman of the US-Korea 2000 Foundation, commemorating the fiftieth anniversary of the Korean War. Whenever he slows down, a rare occurrence, he spends time with his wife, Knox, in their Stockbridge home.

The general remains the Corps' most decorated Marine. In addition to the Medal of Honor, he has been awarded the Navy Cross, two Distinguished Service Medals, two Silver Stars, two Legions of Merit, five Bronze Stars, and a Purple Heart. In more than three decades of active service in World War II, Korea, and Vietnam, he filled every possible staff and command assignment.

THE NATIONAL BESTSELLER *FLAGS OF OUR FATHERS* by James Bradley, the story of the Marines on Iwo Jima, brings back proud and painful memories for retired architect and noted Marine James H. "Bill" Finch.

Finch, who retired from the Marine Corps Reserve as a colonel, was a major and executive officer of the Second Battalion, 28th Marine Regiment on Iwo Jima. It was his battalion that stormed Mount Suribachi. Finch's personal runner, Ray Gagnon, was one of the Marines who raised the Stars and Stripes over Suribachi, captured in one of World War II's—and the twentieth century's—most famous pictures. Finch's battalion landed on Iwo Jima with 2,000 Marines. When the battle was over, only 177 were left.

"Many received decorations and many didn't," he says. "But every Marine who landed and fought on that island was a bona fide hero."

Finch retired from a distinguished architectural career twenty years ago. He designed the old Atlanta-Fulton County Stadium and twenty-nine other professional and college sports stadiums around the country. Today, Finch is eighty-six and physically fit. He works out with weights seven days a week and walks five miles daily. The rest of his day is spent working on his fifteen-acre farm in Alpharetta, shoveling manure, mowing, pruning, chipping, shredding and feeding more than 100 animals, not including his four house cats.

"I am doing nothing constructive," he says, "and loving every minute of it."

GEORGE R. PENDLEY, WHO PLAYED COMPETITIVE TENNIS for five years while suffering from bone cancer, died on July 13, 1998. "He was a medical miracle," recalls his radiation oncologist, Dr. Fred Schwaibold. "Only his moral strength to persevere, his indomitable spirit and his faith in God kept him alive and playing tennis."

A veritable tennis machine, Pendley was one of Georgia's all-time great senior amateur players. From age forty-five to sixty-five, he was ranked No. 1 in his age division in both singles and doubles. Over a thirty-year period, in state, regional, and national competition, he won 200 tournaments with thirty different partners in age groups from forty-five to seventy. All told, he captured fifty singles championships.

Pendley grew up in Atlanta, attended Boys High School, and graduated from the University of Georgia. He was seventy-three when he died.

BILLIE CHENEY SPEED, THE FIRST WOMAN SPORTSWRITER in America, died in July at age seventy-three from liver and lung cancer. She was the first woman admitted to the press box at Grant Field (Bobby Dodd Stadium) and the first woman to sit in the old Atlanta Crackers dugout. She started writing sports as a teenager for the *Birmingham News* and joined the *Atlanta Journal* sports staff after graduating from West Georgia College in 1948. In 1965, she became the paper's religion editor, and during her twenty-two years on the job was honored by ministers, rabbis, and priests alike.

FURMAN BISHER'S UNTOLD STORY

In 1962, I walked into the office of my boss, Furman Bisher, and told him I was resigning to enter the life insurance business. "If I make it," I added, "I can thank two people—you and my Marine Corps drill instructor."

The words were spoken with gratitude and respect because Bisher and Sgt. Bamford gave me the discipline never to give up. As sports editor of the *Atlanta Constitution* (1950–57) and then the *Atlanta Journal*, Bisher was demanding, tough, and unyielding. He expected you to get all the facts right—the first time.

In the 1950s and 1960s, the *Journal* and the *Constitution* were separate. If there was a scoop to be had, Bisher expected you to get it. No excuses. There was no such thing as overtime. Sgt. Bamford said your time belonged to the Marine Corps. Bisher said your time belonged to the sports department.

On the *Journal*, if you came in at 7 A.M. to help get out the first edition, it had no bearing on the rest of your day—or night. I was prep sports editor. After the final edition came out about noon, I spent the afternoon at some high school and perhaps at a football or basketball game that evening. And then it was back on the sports desk early the next morning. So it went.

Today, there are between fifty and sixty *Journal-Constitution* sportswriters. Under Bisher's leadership, we got three editions out every day with nine people. And what's become of those people who worked with me under Bisher's guidance? It's an impressive roster: Edwin Pope—sports editor of the *Miami Herald* and like Bisher, one of the top columnists in the country; Jesse Outlar—retired sports editor of the *Atlanta Constitution*; Lee Walburn—editor of *Atlanta* magazine; Jim Minter—retired editor of the *Journal-Constitution*; Gregory Favre—corporate editor of the *McClatchy New Chain*, former editor of the *Sacramento Bee* and former president of the Society of Newspaper Editors; Terry Kay—noted author of fiction and nonfiction; John Logue, former editor of Oxmoor House Publications; Larry Fox—former baseball writer for the *New York Daily News*; Bob Christian—former vice president of Eastern Air Lines; Gerry Chatham—public relations executive; the late Bill McGrotha—sports editor, the *Tallahassee Democrat*; and the late Lewis Grizzard—nationally syndicated columnist and author.

Bisher may have been a perfectionist but he got results. As a Marine, if I were going into combat tomorrow, Bisher is the type of guy I would want on my flanks. He never let you down. But there's another side of Bisher. He is kind, thoughtful, generous, caring, loyal and supportive.

In 1952, when I went to Korea as a rifle platoon leader with the First Marine Division, Bisher had a copy of the *Sporting News* airmailed to me every week. Whether our company was on line in combat or in reserve, the *Sporting News* always was there.

In the fall of 1950, I began my senior year at the University of Georgia, and Bisher named me his Athens sports correspondent. It was my job to get the sports news out of Athens, and to wire in feature articles when there wasn't any news. I remember doing a poll during the 1950 football season in which UGA team members picked the best player at each position. Some of those named were seeing a lot of action in scrimmages but little on game day. The article irritated the head coach, who complained to Bisher, who reminded him that I worked for the *Constitution*, not the University of Georgia, and that I was free to write whatever I thought was news.

After my Marine Corps duty and a move to Daytona Beach, I returned to Atlanta in 1957. Ed Danforth, the venerable sports editor of the *Journal*, had retired, and Bisher, by then one of the premier sports columnists in America, was named to replace him. Bisher hired me as his prep editor and director of sports promotions.

One promotion was the *Journal*-sponsored North-South High School All-Star Football Game. One of the starting players for the North squad was Atlanta's Larry Lafkowitz, the Joe Lieberman of his day.

Was Bisher supportive? During the ten days of practice, I wrote about Lafkowitz four days running. On the fourth day, Bisher called me into his office and gently admonished me. "Don't you think you're overdoing it a bit on Lafkowitz?" he asked. "No," I replied. "He's the best-looking running back on either squad."

"Well, Ash, maybe you're right," he said. "If you don't write about Lafkowitz, we don't have anyone else who will." In the All-Star game, Lafkowitz gained more than 100 yards, scored the only touchdown, led his team in tackles and set an All-Star punting record with a 48.5-yard average. He was a unanimous choice for game MVP. Bisher loved it.

Supportive? One day I received a telephone call at the sports desk from a theater promoter. He told me Pete Rademacher, who had been on the US Olympic boxing team, was going to make his professional debut against Floyd Patterson, the reigning heavyweight champion of the world. I told Bisher about the phone call. "It not only sounds ridiculous, it sounds impossible, but if you want to write it, go ahead and write it," he said. I did. The title fight came off, and Patterson won by a knockout.

In 1958, Bob Christian, the *Journal* baseball writer, wrote a story alleging several baseball players around the Southern League were consorting with gamblers. Charlie Hurth, then president of the Southern League, threatened to sue Christian and the *Atlanta Journal*. But Christian had his facts. He also had Bisher. Bisher phoned Hurth and told him he had verified Christian's facts, and that if he didn't stop his threats, there would be other articles. Hurth dropped the matter.

Loyal? In the early 1950s, when Bisher was at the *Constitution*, an executive in the front office wanted to fire Edwin Pope because he didn't like the lead paragraph on an article. Bisher confronted the executive eyeball to eyeball and said, "If Pope goes, I go, too."

Generous? Bisher has given over $500,000 to Furman University (no kin but one of his alma maters) to set up scholarship funds and help construct a building for the Journalism Department. Says Pope of Bisher, "In some sixty years in this business, he's the only real mentor I ever had. I've never known a better sportswriter or a stronger man, and I've never had a better friend."

Says Christian, "When Bisher came to the *Constitution*, the first thing he did was get me a pay raise. It was the first one I'd had in five years."

Today, at age eighty-two, James Furman Bisher has no plans to retire. This fall, he plans to cover the National League baseball playoffs, the World Series, Tech-Georgia football, the Falcons, at least two college bowl games, and the Super Bowl. "Bisher is indefatigable and finds his greatest enjoyment in writing," says Pope.

And what writing! Bisher has been named National Sports Writer of the Year more times than anyone can remember. His articles have been honored eighteen times by the Associated Press and twice by the Florida Breeders Association. More than once, he has been named by *Time* magazine as one of the nation's five best columnists. He has written more that 1,000 stories for such magazines as the *Saturday Evening Post, Golf Digest* and *Sports Illustrated.*

As he celebrates his fiftieth year with the *AJC*, he can look back on a career in which he covered every major sports event in the world. Each year he has attended the four golf majors, the World Series, the Super Bowl, the NBA championships, and the Kentucky Derby. He's been to the Masters golf tournament and the Kentucky Derby fifty times each. He was in the press box when the US hockey team upset the Soviet Union and went on to win the gold medal in the 1980 Olympics. He covered the first NASCAR race on a dirt track outside Charlotte in 1940.

Bisher was born in Denton, North Carolina, one of four children of Chisholm and Mamie Bisher. By age ten, he was a walking baseball encyclopedia and rules book, so much so that local umpires sometimes turned to Bisher before making a decision. "I loved baseball more that anything," he says. "We had a good team in Denton. At age thirteen, I worked as the team statistician. From that point on, all I ever wanted to do was be a sportswriter. I wanted to ride the trains, see the sights, talk to the players." After high school, Bisher enrolled at Furman University, then transferred to the University of North Carolina after his sophomore year because Furman had no journalism school and UNC did.

Bisher could have left Atlanta years ago for better pay and a larger audience. He was offered lead columnist positions in New York, Chicago, San Francisco, and Washington, DC. Lucky for Atlanta, he turned them all down. Why? He loved Atlanta. It was Bisher who was the driving force to get Atlanta-Fulton County Stadium built as well as to bring major league baseball and professional football to town. You can also thank Bisher for the Peach Bowl, for he was the key person in convincing the NCAA to grant Atlanta the bowl game.

First and foremost, though, he's a writer. "No one can put more quality words on paper than Bisher," says Jim Minter, former editor of the *Journal-Constitution*. Bisher himself says he tries to avoid "careless" writing. But Pope adds that "there's more to it than that. He loves the language and absolutely refuses to abuse it. He is just as good now as he was fifty years ago."

Bisher is a member of the Georgia Sports Hall of Fame and the UNC Journalism Hall of Fame. The Dogwood Invitational Golf Tournament's annual amateur-amateur was named in his honor this year, and the Atlanta Sports Council honored Bisher with a luncheon this past summer at the All-Star baseball game. He has been recognized nationally for "long and meritorious contributions to the art of sportswriting."

Bisher lives with his wife, the former Lynda Landon, in a ten-room lakefront home off Lester Road in Fayetteville. It's his base of operations. He writes most of his columns there and modems them to the *AJC*. He rises at 7 A.M. daily, works out for thirty minutes, writes his column, and does the yard work on his ten acres.

Bisher has two sons by a previous marriage—Jamie, forty-three, who works in logistics with Northrup-Grumman in Baltimore, and Monty, thirty-eight, who works with Dell Computers in Austin. A third son, Roger, forty-four, died earlier this year. Roger had been named Small Businessman of the Year by the US Small Business Administration.

Calling on his fifty years' worth of lore, Bisher offers short takes on various subjects:

- No. 1 thrill? "The Atlanta Crackers winning the Southern Association pennant in 1954 and going on to capture the Dixie Series when manager Whitlow Wyatt, on a hunch, pulled his league-leading homerun hitter, Bob Montag, for pinch hitter Jim Solt. The Crackers were trailing by one run. With one man aboard in the ninth inning, Solt hit the first pitch out of the ball park."
- The athlete most fun to interview? "Race car driver Richard Petty, a country boy from North Carolina, just like me."

- The best athletes? "Ted Williams, by far the best baseball player. No one was close to him." Others: Warren Spahn (best baseball pitcher), Jack Nicklaus (golf), Walter Payton (football, Chicago Bears), Jackie Parker (football, Mississippi State), Charlie "Choo Choo" Justice (football, North Carolina), Pete Sampras (tennis), Elgin Baylor and Jerry West (professional basketball), and Pete Maravich (college basketball).
- Easiest coach to interview? "The Falcons' Dan Reeves. He is the most down-to-earth coach in the NFL." College coaches? "Wally Butts (Georgia), Bobby Dodd (Georgia Tech), and Gen. Bob Neyland (Tennessee)."
- How will golf superstar Tiger Woods compare with Bobby Jones? "We'll see when he has to get up at 2 A.M. to feed a baby."
- The happiest days of his life? "The day I married Lynda, the day Roger Bisher, my first son, was born, and the day I became the first sportswriter voted into the UNC Hall of Fame."

I love Furman Bisher. The work habits I learned from him enabled me to become a lifetime member of the Million Dollar Round Table in the insurance business and a member of the New England Life Hall of Fame. Besides, no one but Furman ever gave me two tickets to an earthquake—the 1989 World Series in San Francisco.

JOHNNY RAUCH

A Dawg For The Ages

Johnny Rauch, told by his high school team physician that he never could play football, became an All-American quarterback at the University of Georgia (1948). What's more, he became the first and only quarterback in Bulldog history to start every game four consecutive years and lead UGA to four consecutive Bowl bids. Three times he was named to the All-Southeastern Conference team.

Today, at age seventy-three, Rauch is an All-American human being living in Oldsmar, Florida. Instead of giving on the athletic field, he gives to his fellow citizens. Two days a week, he volunteers at the county hospital. One day a week, he volunteers at the Medical Arts Building, carrying blood samples from the outpatient clinic to the medical laboratory. Another day he drives a tram, ferrying patients from the parking lot to the main hospital area. Whenever he's asked, he speaks to high school student bodies within a fifty-mile area.

That schedule does not leave much time for golf, but it is Rauch's way of thanking God for all that has come to him—legendary status as a Georgia Bulldog, coaching the Oakland Raiders to the Super Bowl, a happy marriage of fifty-three years and two healthy children.

After his brilliant career at the University of Georgia, Rauch played professionally for the Detroit Lions and Philadelphia Eagles of the NFL and with the New York Yankees and New York Bulldogs of the old All-America Conference.

Rauch began his college coaching career at Saint Bonaventure as backfield coach, and later served as assistant coach at Florida, Tulane, UGA, and the US Military Academy at West Point.

In 1963, he joined the professional coaching ranks as an assistant to Raiders head coach Al Davis. When Davis became team owner in 1966, he turned over head coaching duties to Rauch. A year later, Rauch led the Raiders to the American Football League championship and the Super Bowl, earning Coach of the Year honors along the way. In three seasons at Oakland, Rauch teams posted a 33-8-1 record. Perhaps more impressively, two of the assistant coaches he developed were John Madden and Bill Walsh, who became Super Bowl legends for Oakland and San Francisco.

Ego never was a problem for Rauch. After his professional head-coaching career (he was at Buffalo in 1969), he served as an assistant in Philadelphia, Atlanta, and Tampa Bay. When he gave up professional coaching, he took on the job of coaching a prep school, Admiral Farragut Academy in Saint Petersburg, Florida.

In the annals of sport, there have been few stories more incredible than that of Johnny Rauch. As a freshman at Yeadon High School in Pennsylvania, Rauch was told by the team physician that he could never play football because of a heart defect. So Rauch sat out his freshman and sophomore seasons.

At the start of his junior year, he convinced the head football coach to get a second medical opinion. So Rauch was taken to a cardiologist, who diagnosed his heart problems as a "functional murmur." He saw no danger in Rauch playing football or any other sport.

Rauch quickly made up for lost time. He played football, basketball, and baseball and earned All-County honors in each sport. In baseball, he hit .500 his junior season and .450 his senior year. In basketball, he led the county in scoring two consecutive years and in 1944 set a state record by scoring forty-seven points in one game. In that era, most teams didn't score forty-seven points, much less a single player.

As the tailback on a losing football team, he attracted little attention from college scouts. The only offers he received were a basketball scholarship from Temple University and a combination football-basketball-baseball scholarship from Villanova.

Rauch turned them both down. He paid his way to Knoxville to try out as a single-wing tailback at Tennessee. Coach Bob Neyland looked him over and sent him back to Yeadon. but a friend of Georgia coach Wallace Butts ran the Yeadon Coca-Cola bottling plant. He recommended Rauch to UGA and paid his train fare to Athens. What Coach Neyland didn't see in Rauch, Coach Butts did—a 6'1", 180-pound, gifted passer who could throw accurately for more than fifty yards. Neyland was looking for a runner in his single wing; Butts was looking for a passer for his T-formation.

It was 1945. Due to the war, freshmen were eligible to play. Rauch played both offense and defense, averaging fifty-eight minutes a game for four consecutive years. Productive minutes they were. From 1945 to 1948, Rauch quarterbacked the Bulldogs to a 36-8-1 record, two SEC championships (1946 and 1948) and victories over Tulsa in the 1946 Oil Bowl and North Carolina (20-10) in the 1947 Sugar Bowl. He guided the 'Dogs to a 20-20 tie with Maryland in the 1948 Gator Bowl, and his passing put two touchdowns on the board in a 1949 Orange Bowl loss (41-28) to Texas.

As a freshman in 1945, Rauch's pinpoint passing enabled end Reid Moseley to lead the nation in pass receiving. In 1946, his passing and Charley Trippi's running enabled the 'Dogs to finish the season as the nation's only undefeated, untied team. In the 1947 Sugar Bowl against Charlie "Choo Choo" Justice–led North Carolina, he scored two touchdowns in the victory. In 1948, he was named SEC Player of the Year after leading the conference in passing and total offense.

Fifty-four years after the feat, Rauch still shares the Georgia record for most touchdown passes in one game (four against Clemson in 1946). He ranks second among Bulldog passing leaders in most career touchdown passes (thirty-three), average yards per attempt over a career (8.37), average yards per attempt in a season (9.27), and average yards per completion in a season (18.41).

Credit Rauch, as a professional coach, with effectively extending the length of the playing field. His two quarterbacks, Darryl Lamonica (Notre Dame) and George Blanda (Kentucky), frequently threw seventy-yard touchdown bombs to such receivers as Cliff Branch, Clement Daniel, and Fred Biletnikoff.

As good as Rauch was on the collegiate gridiron, he may have been even better at basketball. But Coach Butts did not want his quarterback traveling except with the football team, so no one will ever know how good Rauch may have been in basketball. Those who saw him score fifty-eight points in a semi-pro game at the old Atlanta Sports Arena after his senior football season can only imagine what he would have done in college.

John Rauch was born in Yeadon, a suburb of Philadelphia, in 1927, the son of Walter Rauch, a butcher, and Lillian Rauch, a homemaker. He was one of four children. His two brothers weren't athletes but his younger sister played hockey and basketball. Told his freshman year in high school that he couldn't play athletics, he became the equipment manager of the football team. When not carrying the water bucket or issuing equipment, he threw the football to a schoolmate or drew up plays in his notebook.

The young Rauch spent equal time eyeing one of the Yeadon High cheerleaders, Jane Livingston. After football practice, they would walk home together, and they have been walking together ever since. They started dating when he was fifteen and she was fourteen. Four years later, they married in New Orleans, after Rauch led the Bulldogs to victory in the Sugar Bowl.

Rauch has a tremendous sense of loyalty to the late Coach Butts. "He gave me an opportunity when no one else would," he says today. "He saw something in me that I couldn't see in myself. The greatest satisfaction I've had in life was being at the Waldorf-Astoria Hotel in New York when Coach Butts was posthumously inducted into the NCAA Hall of Fame."

Rauch is writing a book "about Wally [Coach Butts] and his boys." Of All-American halfback Charley Trippi, he writes, "He was the finest football player I ever saw, college or pro. He could run, pass, punt, and play defense, and he did them all at Georgia and with the old Chicago Cardinals of the NFL. Everyone raved about Trippi being a triple-threat. I particularly remember Trippi and that glorious season of 1946. Whenever we needed a first down, Trippi would bark in the huddle, 'Give me the ball, John, I'll get it for us,' and he always did." In his book, Rauch writes of his biggest football thrill—beating Georgia Tech in 1946 in a game in which he threw a touchdown pass to Trippi, and Trippi threw one to him.

Except for the annual Georgia-Florida matchup, Rauch rarely gets to a football game these days. He spends his Saturdays at home in his den, where three televisions and a radio go full blast.

For a boy who wasn't supposed to play, Rauch did all right: All-American; a starter in every game over four years at Georgia, averaging fifty-eight minutes per game; coaching a team to the Super Bowl; and membership in the Georgia Sports Hall of Fame.

Johnny Rauch a legend? What do you think?

VALDOSTA
Titletown USA

The year was 1989, and my sister and I were at the opening game of the World Series at Candlestick Park in San Francisco. Just before the game began, a tremor shook the stadium.

My sister grabbed me. "What was that?" she screamed.

"Probably fans stomping their feet."

"Seemed a lot more than that."

Almost automatically I replied, "That's because you've never been to a football game at Valdosta High School."

The San Francisco earthquake registered 8.1 on the Richter scale, but it was nothing compared to the foot-stomping on the metal bleachers at Bazemore-Hyder Stadium/Cleveland Field in Valdosta. Think it's wild for night games at Tiger Stadium in Baton Rouge? Believe they flip out at the Auburn-Alabama Iron Bowl? Think over 80,000 Georgia Bulldog fans barking "How 'bout them Dawgs?" is tumultuous? To quote the late Al Jolson, "You ain't heard nothin' yet."

2000

If you want to hear ear-splitting roars from the opening kickoff to the final whistle, go to a Valdosta football game on a Friday night. You'll hear not only 11,000 fans stomping their feet and screaming their lungs out for their beloved Wildcats, but also ninety cheerleaders rhythmically yelling "Go Cats" into megaphones, plus 220 musicians playing the Valdosta fight song.

Football is not a game in Valdosta, it's a way of life. Almost from the time a boy can walk, he carries a football and dreams of the day he will become a Valdosta Wildcat. And why not? His daddy played for the Wildcats, as did his granddaddy and likely his great-granddaddy before him. Beyond the love of sport, why do they play? One word: tradition.

It all starts with a feeder system. Youth league teams in Valdosta run Wildcat plays and employ Wildcat defenses. By the time players reach high school, they know exactly what to do. All they need to attain perfection is practice, practice, and still more practice, plus high levels of motivation. Through the years, such coaches as Buck Thomas, Bobby Hooks, Wright Bazemore, and Nick Hyder have provided both—in spades.

Behind the effort is unmatched community support. The Valdosta Touchdown Club is over 2,000 members strong, and they have much to cheer. Perhaps no other city in the United States, and maybe the world, can match Valdosta's gridiron record. Wildcat football teams have won twenty-three state championships and six national titles. In Georgia, the Wildcats have dominated every classification from Class B in the old days to AAAA today. Valdosta is Titletown USA.

Exaggeration? Wildcat teams have notched consecutive win streaks of forty, thirty-eight, thirty-seven, thirty, twenty-seven, and twenty-six games, plus enough All-State players to fill two of the Cats' 100-man rosters.

The winning tradition is infectious. It has spread to neighboring Lowndes County High School and to Valdosta State University. Lowndes County has a few football records of its own, including two AAAA state championships. Valdosta State, led by passing wizard Dusty Bonner, was vying for a NCAA Division II playoff berth this fall. The former Kentucky quarterback had completed 70 percent of his passes for 2,415 yards, both school records, with three games to go.

But back to Valdosta High. I'll never forget seeing the Wildcats play Columbus High in 1961. The two best teams on the field that night were Valdosta's first and second teams. The game wasn't fair. Every time a Columbus player carried the ball, a pack of Valdosta players would smother him. When a Wildcat carried, maybe one or two Columbus players would hit him. No, the Wildcats weren't perfect. They didn't score every time they had the ball. They failed once. Valdosta won 42-0—its eighteenth consecutive win—en route to a second straight Class AAA championship.

After the game, I talked with two scouts from future opponents. The pair agreed that the only way their teams could keep from getting beat by Valdosta was to cancel the games.

The coach of that 1961 Valdosta team was the immortal Wright Bazemore, who died in 1998. He compiled a 268-15-7 record at Valdosta, winning fourteen state and three national titles. Two players on that 1961 championship team, Billy Schroer and Bruce Bennett, went on to earn All-Southeastern Conference honors at Georgia Tech and the University of Florida, respectively.

Schroer says the secret to Bazemore's success was two-fold: "First, he convinced us that we could be better than we were, that no matter how well we played in our last game, we could play better in our next one. Coach had us reaching for new peaks every week. Second, he told us daily that with the effort comes the reward."

After Bazemore, nothing much changed. The Wildcats kept winning. His successor, Charlie Greene, ran up a 17-3-0 record over two seasons, before Nick Hyder came on to nearly rival Bazemore. Hyder posted a 249-36-2 record, adding seven state titles and three national championships to the trophy case. When Hyder died suddenly in 1996, assistant coach Mike O'Brien took over, and the beat went on. Two years later, O'Brien's team won a state championship.

The many Friday night victories, mostly routs, did not come without a price. The Wildcats usually scrimmaged Monday, Tuesday, and Wednesday and worked out in pads on Thursday. Four-on-one drills, which put Georgia Tech coach George O'Leary in hot water this fall, were commonplace at Valdosta. Workouts started in the early afternoon and did not end until dark.

John Lastinger Jr. was a Hyder product. "We worked so hard during the week that we looked forward to Friday night combat," he recalls. "Compared to our scrimmages and head-knocking, regular season games often were child's play." Lastinger went on to play for the University of Georgia, quarterbacking the Bulldogs in 1982 and 1983. A journalism major, he worked a stint at a Macon TV station and for the past eight years has been a successful stockbroker in Valdosta. His father played for Valdosta. So did his granddad. His brother Brad was a team manager. In other words, the usual order of things in Valdosta.

Schroer loved Bazemore, but not his practices:

> They were brutal and long. We'd go to a summer football camp before school started. We practiced three times a day—before breakfast, after breakfast, and again after lunch. The after-lunch practice lasted until it was so dark we couldn't see the football.
>
> Compared to Valdosta, practice at Georgia Tech was a cake-walk. Under Coach [Bobby] Dodd, once the season started, there were no scrimmages. At Valdosta, we scrimmaged three times a week throughout the season and during the playoffs. But we knew we were going to win on Friday night.
>
> Coach Bazemore was a disciplinarian. He believed in preparation. What we went through at Valdosta not only prepared us for winning football games, it prepared us for winning in life.

Schroer, an All-State tackle at Valdosta High and honorable mention All-American tackle at Georgia Tech, has been a top stockbroker in Atlanta for ten years. Over the past two decades, he's been an SEC and prep football official. In addition, he's on the board of the Atlanta Christian School, and is a board member and past chairman of Raintree Village Children's Home in Valdosta. Schroer has earned as much respect officiating as he did playing. He was the first SEC official to work a Rose Bowl game, and he has officiated in the Outback, Independence, Gator, Cotton, and Sugar bowls. So far, he's worked three SEC title games.

When Valdosta quarterbacks are mentioned, the exploits of Lamar Bruce Bennett and Buck Belue inevitably come up. Now fifty-six, Bennett quarterbacked the Wildcats from 1958 to 1961, winning state titles his last two years. His senior year, Bennett punctured Columbus High's vaunted pass defense with touchdown passes of seventy-two, fifty-nine, and fourteen yards. He completed ten of twelve passes, scored two touchdowns and compiled 248 yards in total offense.

Bennett was no less impressive at the University of Florida, where he was a two-year starter at safety. Georgia Bulldog fans may recall him. In 1963, he dashed Bulldog hopes by intercepting three passes, returning one for fifty-six yards and a Gator touchdown. The Bennett-led Gators won, 21-14. Upon graduating from Florida, Bennett played seven years in the Canadian Football League and led Saskatchewan to one CFL title.

Belue quarterbacked the 1980 Georgia Bulldogs to the national championship.

No Valdosta name carries more weight than Bazemore's. "He was way ahead of his time," says Bennett, who today is head football coach at Forsyth Central High School in Cumming. "Coach Bazemore was using spread formations long before the pros were. Mostly, though, he taught me the meaning of commitment—in sports and in life. He expected us to be good students, and if we weren't, we could sit on the bench."

Lessons learned on the Valdosta gridiron have carried over into many corners of Georgia. Consider the contributions of two former Wildcats—longtime Georgia State University President Dr. Noah Langdale and attorney Barry Phillips.

Phillips played for the Valdosta Wildcats at age fourteen and was an All-State tackle at sixteen. He attended the University of Georgia on a football scholarship and became a Phi Beta Kappa graduate. At age seventy-two, he's a senior partner in the prestigious international law firm of Kilpatrick Stockton. Phillips is a former chairman of the state Board of Regents, a former trustee of the University of Georgia Foundation and a former president of the Georgia Law School Council, among his many civic undertakings. One honor he treasures as much as any is a spot in the Valdosta-Lowndes County Sports Hall of Fame.

"Going out for the football team, the band or the cheerleading team was the thing to do," he says. "If you didn't participate in some phase of the football program, you really weren't with it."

The erudite Langdale played tackle for Valdosta and was captain of the 1936 squad, after which he was sought by colleges across the country, for his academic as well as his athletic talents. Langdale became a starting tackle at the University of Alabama and earned Phi Beta Kappa classroom honors before going on to graduate with honors from Harvard Law School.

Langdale became president of Valdosta State, but he's best known as the man who turned a parking garage into Georgia State University. Among his many honors was being selected to *Sports Illustrated* magazine's Silver Anniversary college football All-Star team and membership in the Valdosta-Lowndes Sports Hall of Fame. At age eighty, he's retired and living in Buckhead.

Valdosta's success has carried over to Lowndes County High School and to Valdosta State University. The Lowndes Vikings, under the guidance of Milt Miller, are defending state AAAA champions. Perhaps more importantly to them, they've beaten Valdosta three out of the last four years. Martin Stadium can match Bazemore-Hyder Stadium in seating capacity and sellouts.

Owen Prince, director of technology for the Lowndes County School System and a past president of the Lowndes Touchdown Club, says the school did not emphasize football until 1976 but produced a winning record the next season. Four years later, the Vikings won a state title.

Among recent Lowndes graduates are Jay Ratliff, a tight end for the Auburn Tigers; Michael Woods, a linebacker for Middle Tennessee State; and Vincent Burns, a defensive end at Western Arizona. At Lowndes, the baseball team doesn't take a back seat to football. It, too, has won a pair of state championships and is the current state AAAA titleholder.

For a one-time women's college, Valdosta State has done wonders, consistently fielding winning teams on the male side in football, basketball, baseball, golf and tennis, and on the female side in volleyball, softball, basketball, and tennis.

The men's basketball team won the Georgia Intercollegiate Athletic Conference championship eleven times and reached the quarterfinals of the NAIA national tournament twice. Distaff cagers have won their conference crown twice and once reached the Final Four of the NCAA tournament.

Under Coach Tommy Thomas—the winningest Division II collegiate baseball coach in the country with 1,089 victories—Valdosta State has been a perennial conference champion. In 1979, it captured the NCAA Division II title.

The baseball program first took off under the late Billy Grant, for whom the local diamond is named. Grant, all five feet and eight inches of him, was a huge presence when he quarterbacked the Valdosta Wildcats. Later he quarterbacked the Georgia Bulldogs to one of their greatest victories ever, a stunning 27-7 upset over top-ranked Maryland in 1950.

Led by Coach Chris Hatcher, the Valdosta State football team was contending for the Gulf Coast title this fall, a prize it captured in 1996 under Coach Hal Mumme, now at Kentucky.

No one is prouder of Valdosta sports than the trio of Mayor Jimmy Rainwater; Ken Garren, director of the Valdosta-Lowndes Industrial Authority; and Johnny B. Lastinger, president of Valdosta magazine.

"We have a population of 50,000, and about 45 percent of those people are involved with sports, either as players, band members, cheerleaders, Touchdown

Club members or just plain old fans," says Rainwater. "Wherever I go on city business, I find people have heard about Valdosta, Lowndes County or Valdosta State. People don't want to talk about politics or city government but how we are able to win year after year. They can't believe that almost every year the region football championship is decided by two teams from the same county. We're just as proud of Lowndes as we are of Valdosta High and Valdosta State."

The city's national sports reputation has helped it attract business and industry from across the Southeast, according to Garren. "It's not just football," he says. "Valdosta has attracted new businesses because of our high school bands. Almost every year, either the Valdosta band, the Lowndes County band, or both are invited to some major college bowl games."

Lastinger terms it all "a case of civic pride."

"What we have here cannot be measured in wins and losses," he says. "Thanks to sports, we have a united community. Our athletic program has touched the lives of thousands and put our city on the map in every part of the universe."

Be warned, though, that the map is inaccurate. The name of the city actually begins with a T.

2001

PETE BROWN
The Greatest Blocker

It was the summer of 1961. As prep sports editor of the *Atlanta Journal,* it was my duty to promote the annual North-South Georgia high school All-Star football game held at Georgia Tech's Grant Field.

I was sitting at my desk rereading the promotion piece on the game I'd written the day before. I'd researched the history of the contest and discovered that twelve players had come out of the game and had gone on to All-American collegiate honors. We played the article to the hilt. It was the lead story in the sports section.

Mentally, I was patting myself on the back for producing this masterpiece when I felt a tap on my shoulder. I turned around and this 6'2", 200-pound gentleman looked me in the eye and politely asked, "Aren't you Gene Asher?" I admitted I was.

"Well," he said softly, "you hurt someone's feelings very badly with that All-American, All-Star article you wrote yesterday."

"I did?" I said quizzically. "How did I do that?"

"You left out one of the All-Americans who played in the game," he said.

"I don't think so," I replied. "Who on earth could I have omitted?"

"You left out Pete Brown," he said, almost in a whisper, "and Pete was really hurt by it."

"I have the paper right here," I said. "I was just rereading the article, and we can check it. But I'm certain I included Pete Brown."

Together, we picked up the paper and reread the article. There were the names—Fran Tarkenton, Leon Hardeman, Ray Beck, etc., but no Pete Brown.

My head dropped to my knees. My face turned red. "I don't believe I did that," I said. "I feel terrible."

My visitor put his arm around my shoulder.

"Don't worry," he said. "I know the kind of guy Brown is, and he'll get over it. He's downcast now, but he'll be joyful in the morning. Forget it. I know Pete will."

My visitor turned around, walked out of the sports department. Seconds later, the bell in my brain went off.

I jumped out of my chair, raced toward the elevator and barely caught him as the door opened.

"You wouldn't happen to be Pete Brown, would you?" I asked with a smile.

My visitor burst out laughing.

Thus was my introduction to Samuel Morris "Pete" Brown, a graduate of the *Journal* All-Star Football Classic, an All-American at Georgia Tech, a one-time starting center for the San Francisco '49ers, and a member of both the Georgia Tech Sports Hall of Fame and the Georgia Sports Hall of Fame. Nearly a half-century after he played, Brown is still considered the greatest downfield blocker in Georgia Tech football history.

Off the field, Brown was a fun-loving, easy-going guy who never took himself or anyone else too seriously. On the field, he was a veritable terror, flattening any opposing player in sight.

Edwin Pope, then an *Atlanta Constitution* sports scribe and now sports editor of the *Miami Herald*, recalls Brown: "Pete came to Georgia Tech as a punter and fullback, but after a glorious freshman year—in which he averaged forty-five yards per kick and eight yards per carry—he neither punted nor played fullback again. Instead, he became an offensive center. It seemed on every snap, he knocked down the defender playing on his nose and then raced downfield, decking sidebacks and safety men. He was the greatest blocker I ever saw."

The years were 1951 and 1952, and Brown's unselfishness and flaming competitive spirit led Coach Bobby Dodd's Yellow Jackets to two undefeated seasons and one co-national championship (1952). In the four years Brown played at Tech, the Jackets never lost to the Georgia Bulldogs. In his junior season of 1951, he was All-Southeastern Conference, and Tech defeated Baylor in the Orange Bowl. His senior year, Brown was one of six Tech players named All-American, and the Yellow Jackets went on to trounce Ole Miss in the Sugar Bowl.

Said Coach Dodd, "As a downfield blocker, Tech never had seen anything like him and likely never will. Pete Brown paved the way for our running backs who were legends in their own right—[Leon] Hardeman, [Billy] Teas, [Glenn] Turner, and [Johnny] Hicks."

Today, at age seventy, Brown is still battling—and this time he's in the contest of his life, undergoing radiation and chemotherapy to fight an inoperable, malignant brain tumor. Although he has his depressed moments, Brown still shows flashes of that wonderful sense of humor. I paid a recent visit to him at his ranch-style Doraville home and heard him recall a conversation he had long ago with a Syracuse sportswriter. Brown was being interviewed before playing in the old College All-Star game against the NFL champion Detroit Lions.

"Where are you from?" the Syracuse writer asked Brown.

"Rossville, Georgia," Brown proudly replied.

"I don't think I ever heard of that," said the writer.

"That's all right," Pete answered. "I doubt if anyone in Rossville ever heard of Syracuse."

In his illness, some of Brown's old Tech teammates have rallied to his cause, taking him to football games, out to dinner, and out on the town. Others have telephoned regularly, visited him at home and taken him for car rides. (Pete cannot drive.) Among those giving rock-like support have been Darrell Crawford, who quarterbacked those unbeaten 1951 and 1952 teams; All-American halfback Leon Hardeman; All-American linebackers George and Larry Morris; defensive end Sid Williams, the founder and president of Life University; and one-time National Football League All-Pro Bill Paschal.

Pete Brown is remembered not just for being Tech's best-ever downfield blocker but also as one of the most beloved athletes ever to wear the White and Gold. Says Crawford:

> Here was this big fullback, one of the top ground-gainers in Georgia prep football, coming to Tech and looking forward to becoming a top runner in the league. But we had a gaping hole at center and no solid player to fill it. Not until Pete stepped forward and told Coach Dodd he wanted the job. It took only one scrimmage—in which Pete unerringly snapped the football and blocked one player after another—for Coach Dodd and our line coach, Ray Graves, to know they had their man. Brown never again got a chance to score a touchdown for Georgia Tech, but his blocking helped put many points on the scoreboard. I don't think any of us ever will forget that.

Samuel Morris Brown—nicknamed "Pete" by one of his brothers—was born in Oak Ridge, Tennessee, but grew up across the state line in Rossville, where he became a legend. He earned sixteen athletic letters, four each in football, basketball, baseball, and track. His Rossville sports sweater had so many award stripes, it looked like a zebra. Brown didn't just earn letters, he earned All-State honors in each of the four major sports.

Brown was highly sought after by the University of Tennessee, Georgia Tech, and the University of Georgia. But the only Bulldog he wanted to be was a Rossville Bulldog. Growing up in the 1940s, Brown's hero was a hometown boy from Oak Ridge who was a wingback on Coach Bob Neyland's 1946 Tennessee Volunteers team. Bob Lund's running and blocking helped put the Vols in the

1947 Orange Bowl. Brown wanted to emulate his hero, but at Georgia Tech, not Tennessee.

"Once I met Coach Dodd, I knew there was no place for me but Tech," says Brown. "I would have run through a brick wall for him." Dodd signed the strapping 200-pounder on the recommendation of his recruiters but did not actually see him play until the 1949 state high school All-Star game. That contest was jammed with college prospects. In addition to Brown, there were Marist's Bobby Jo Anglin; Lauren Hargrove, the Fabulous Phantom of Fitzgerald; "Fiddlin' John" Carson of Roosevelt High; Gainesville's Jackie Roberts; Marietta's Bob West; and Richmond Academy's Derwent Langley, all headed for Georgia. Marist's Chappel Rhino was bound for All-SEC honors at Georgia Tech; quarterback Jack Langford of Griffin was destined for stardom at Auburn.

Langford later became a Fulton County Superior Court judge. Rhino, a teammate of Brown's at Tech, made honorable mention All-American, while Carson was a bona fide All-American at Georgia and later an All-Pro with the Washington Redskins.

There was no mistaking one of the game's heroes. Brown's slashing running at fullback set up two North touchdowns in a 19-0 victory.

Being the team man that he was, Brown's biggest thrill at Tech was not being named All-American or receiving "greatest ever" accolades from his head coach and line coach. It was "never losing to Georgia in four years" and "our team winning the Orange and Sugar Bowls."

After the national co-champion season of 1952, Brown, with an industrial management degree in hand, went into the Air Force as a second lieutenant. He had received his commission at graduation, having completed Tech's advanced Air Force ROTC program.

Although he flew airplanes at Shaw Air Force Base, Brown spent his Saturdays on the gridiron, continuing flawlessly to snap the football at center and racking up most any defender who got in his way, plus some who did not. He was named to both the All-Air Force and All-Armed Services All-Star teams. Following his service, Brown had brief stints with the San Francisco '49ers and Vancouver of the Canadian Football League.

Shoulder injuries hampered him with both teams. So Brown came home and went to work with his former All-American teammate Leon Hardeman at Owens-Illinois Glass Company. Brown was a salesman for the company and stayed for twenty-seven years. Since his retirement, Brown has coached girls' softball and played basketball with the Peerless Mills team in Rossville.

In 1977, Brown was the organizing force behind the Atlanta NFL Alumni Club, and served as its president three times. Ironically, he put together the NFL Alumni Golf Tournament, which benefits children with cancer. Among the legends he has brought here to participate have been New York Giants Charlie Connerly and Sam Huff, Chicago Bear running back Gayle Sayers, and Charley Trippi, the Georgia star who made All-Pro with the old Chicago Cardinals. The tournament has raised millions of dollars for cancer patients.

It was only fitting that a few years ago the city of Rossville staged a Pete Brown Day. There was a parade over a mile long, with ten bands and eighteen floats. Each float represented a chapter in Brown's life. Chattanooga also joined in the festivities, the only time the two cities have combined to honor anyone. More than 600 Georgians and Tennesseeans attended a banquet to pay tribute to Brown.

Brown is married to the former Janet Dickinson, and they have one son, Jason, age thirty-four. Tim, forty-six, is his son from a previous marriage.

For the record, I did leave Brown's name out of that promotion piece back in 1961. But give me credit. When I goof, it's in a big way. I could not have left out any player more vital to Georgia Tech's great success in the Roaring 1950s.

Ten years ago, Brown and his wife attended Georgia Tech's 100th birthday celebration. Brown recalls the moment. "I turned to her and said, 'Can you believe I was part of all this, that I went to a school where President Jimmy Carter, Bobby Jones, Sam Nunn, and two astronauts [John Young and Richard Truly] went?"

Samuel Morris "Pete" Brown belongs in the same company.

CHARLEY LOUIS TRIPPI
Did It All . . . and Then Some

Charley Louis Trippi was the best all-around football player the University of Georgia has ever known, maybe the best the world has ever known.

"That's an incredible statement," you might say. "What about Frank Sinkwich and Herschel Walker at Georgia? What about Red Grange, Jim Thorpe, Sid Luckman, Don Hutson, and Jim Brown?"

What about them? They all were great, but how many of them ran, passed, caught, kicked, intercepted, and hiked the ball—and blocked and tackled with devastation? How many of them averaged fifty-eight minutes of playing time a game?

Trippi, who played at Georgia in 1941, 1942, 1945, and 1946 (he was in the Air Force in 1943 and 1944), is comfortably retired following a successful career in real estate, and living in a brick ranch home in Athens with his lovely wife, Peggy.

He weighs 198, a mere ten pounds over his playing weight when he was the rage of the nation, first for the Georgia Bulldogs and then for seven years with the old Chicago Cardinals of the National Football League, where he was All-Pro four times.

Now about those accolades. Don't take them from me, take them from the writers and coaches who saw him play regularly.

In 1946, Trippi led Georgia to an undefeated, untied season (11-0-0), to the Southeastern Conference championship and to a 21-10 victory over North Carolina in the Sugar Bowl. The late Ed Danforth, then sports editor of the *Atlanta Journal*, covered the 1946 Tech-Georgia game, which Georgia won 35-7. Excerpts from his account:

"Charley Trippi took a good Georgia Tech football team apart Saturday. Playing his final game on home turf, he dominated the game from start to finish."

"His 66-yard touchdown run in the final quarter was pure gridiron magic."

"The man was seven furies and a holocaust. When he made his move to the goal line, he could not be stopped. He ran for two touchdowns, passed for a third and caught a pass for a fourth touchdown. He also intercepted two passes."

After the 1946 Georgia-Alabama game, which Georgia won, 14-0, the late Fred Russell, sports editor of the *Nashville Banner*, wrote:

> Pass the pedestals please and save the tallest of the lot for Charley Trippi, the greatest one-man band in the history of Southern football.
>
> Playing 58 minutes, all Trippi did was throw a nine-yard touchdown pass, race weavingly and brilliantly 46 yards for a second touchdown, carry the ball 16 times for 104 yards, and average 40.7 yards punting. On defense, he never missed a tackle and never allowed a pass to be completed in his zone of coverage.

After Trippi led Georgia to a 41-0 win over Auburn in 1946, Auburn coach Carl Voyles called Trippi "the greatest halfback in America, pro or college."

In the 1946 Oil Bowl, in which Georgia defeated Tulsa, 20-6, Frank Godsoe of the *Houston Press* described Trippi's sixty-yard touchdown run like this: "Eleven brutes from Tulsa each took about three shots at Trippi and grabbed nothing but lint from his uniform and the breeze as he passed by."

Trippi was voted Co-Most Valuable Player with teammate Johnny Rauch in the 1947 Sugar Bowl, a game in which victory did not come easily. Georgia trailed, 10-0, at halftime. Trippi, captain of the team, asked Coach Wally Butts and his assistants to leave the dressing room.

With the coaches gone, Trippi slowly walked around the room, stopping, and looking each player in the eye. Then he climbed a bench, and admonished his teammates in clear, unmistakable tones. "We have waited all year for an undefeated, untied season. We are not going to blow it all now. Those of you who do not want to give 100 percent, take off your uniform and get in the shower now. Those who want to give it everything they've got, let's go get 'em and go out like champions."

The team nearly broke down the dressing room door. Led by Trippi and Rauch, the Bulldogs scored twenty-one points in the second half and held North Carolina scoreless. After the game, the jubilant Bulldogs went out on Bourbon Street to celebrate, all except Trippi, who returned to his hotel room to be with his first wife, Ginny, and their one-year-old daughter.

Trippi was named captain of the 1946 All-SEC team. He was a unanimous choice on every All-America team—Associated Press, United Press, International News Service, *Collier's*, the *Saturday Evening Post*, *Look*, *Football Digest*, and *Paramount News*. The All-America Football Board named him captain of its All-America team.

Trippi also won the coveted Maxwell Trophy, given by the Philadelphia Touchdown Club to the nation's outstanding collegiate football player. After receiving the Maxwell Trophy, Trippi was honored by his hometown of Pittston, Pennsylvania. Over 1,000 of the town's 20,000 residents attended a testimonial dinner in which Trippi was lauded by sportswriters, sportscasters, and coaches from across America. When it was his turn to speak, Trippi told his admirers, "I just want to be a good example for the next generation. If I can inspire them, it will mean more to me than any honor I ever could receive."

Today Trippi is a member of the College Football Hall of Fame, the Pro Football Hall of Fame, the Rose Bowl Hall of Fame (as a sophomore, he was MVP in Georgia's 9-0 Rose Bowl win over UCLA), the Pennsylvania Hall of Fame, the Georgia Sports Hall of Fame, the Blue-Gray Game Hall of Fame, and the Italian Hall of Fame. He's Hall of Fame, Inc.

In a 1950 front-page column for the *Atlanta Constitution*, the great Ralph McGill, a former sportswriter, wrote, "He was the best the modern game of football ever produced. I have never seen anyone in his class."

For the want of a pair of football shoes, Trippi's fabulous career may never have come about.

At Pittston High School, there was never enough money in the budget for football shoes, so each player had to buy his own. Trippi, a 160-pound sophomore, went to his dad for the money.

"Football shoes?" barked his father, an anthracite coal miner. "We got no money for football shoes. You got no business playing football. You'll get your leg broke. And when you do, I'll break the other one."

There was no chance of either leg being broken because Trippi couldn't play without shoes. So he missed his sophomore season. The next spring, during a school recess, Trippi borrowed a football from a classmate, went out to the practice field in street shoes and began punting. The ball kept going farther and farther—"Thirty, thirty-five, forty yards," Trippi recalls.

Pittston coach Paul Shelby happened by and noticed the booming punts.

"Why don't you come out for football?" he asked.

"Because I have no shoes," Trippi replied.

"We'll find you a pair," Shelby said. "You're going to be our punter."

The next fall, Trippi was Pittston's No. 1 punter. He also played center but not for long. In the third game, back to punt, he literally fumbled his way into gridiron glory. Trippi dropped a low pass from center, picked the ball up and zig-zagged eighty yards for a touchdown. Pittston had a new back and went on to become conference champion.

As a senior, Trippi ran, passed, and punted Pittston to a second consecutive title and attracted the attention of Harold Wayne Ketron, who owned the Coca-Cola Bottling Company in nearby Wilkes-Barre. Ketron was a former UGA football player and assistant coach.

Ketron told the 6'0", 158-pound Trippi that he needed to beef up and gain more experience in a tougher league than Pittston's Class C circuit if he ever wanted to play major college football. He told Trippi to play one year at a prep school (LaSalle Academy on Long Island) and that he would not only guarantee him a scholarship to LaSalle but also to UGA. Trippi had done nothing in life but shovel coal, so it was an unbeatable offer. A year later, after running and passing LaSalle to a conference championship, Trippi, now 175 pounds, enrolled at Georgia.

Said Papa Trippi, "I no believe they are going to pay your college expenses so people can jump on you and break your leg."

Jump on him? They rarely laid a hand on him. In his four years at Georgia, the Bulldogs never lost to Tech. In his first season of varsity football in 1942, with a bid to the Rose Bowl at stake, he and Sinkwich led a 34-0 rout of the previously unbeaten and untied Yellow Jackets. In the Rose Bowl, Trippi outgained the whole UCLA team. In 1943 and 1944, he played football with the Third Air Force and was named to the Military Service All-American team both years.

Trippi was the No. 1 choice in the pro football draft. When he signed with the Chicago Cardinals, Charles Einstein, sports editor of the International News Service, wrote, "Charley Trippi, the triple-threat magician of the gridiron, spun his wizardry into gold by signing a four-year contract with the Chicago Cardinals for $100,000.

"Signing the six-figure contract produced one of the most dramatic moments in sports history, as the most sought-after athlete in the world wrote himself into a record-breaking salary figure."

As it turned out, Trippi ended up with $110,000, for he signed a one-year baseball contract with the old Atlanta Crackers, playing in 1947 for $10,000.

The investments paid quick dividends for Cardinals owner Charles Bidwell and Crackers owner Earl Mann. In his first pro season, Trippi led the Cardinals to the NFL championship and scored two touchdowns in the title game. He hit a team-high .335 in his only season with the Crackers.

To list all the honors won by Trippi would require more space than allotted, so let's move on to the Trippi of today, who lifts weights, walks two miles daily and plays golf about three times a week. At seventy-nine he still looks fit enough to play football.

Trippi has a message for Georgia's new head football coach, Mark Richt:

Be your own man. Don't let anyone tell you how to run your program. Benefit from Coach [Jim] Donnan's mistakes. If you are going to have a call-in radio show, let the boo birds have their say. Remember, you catch more flies with sugar than vinegar. Some of those call-in fans may be big alumni contributors.

And never, ever glamorize your team before the start of the season. When Coach Donnan told the Atlanta Bulldog Club he had waited fifty-five years to coach a team like this, it was the kiss of death.

Most importantly, you gotta beat the big boys—Auburn, Florida, Tennessee and especially Georgia Tech.

The biggest thrill Trippi ever had, college or pro, was playing in the Rose Bowl. "Can you imagine what it was like coming from a town of 20,000 and playing in a stadium before 90,000-plus screaming fans?" he says. "It wasn't so much winning the MVP Award, it was just being there."

The late Coach Wally Butts described Trippi as "the finest human being and greatest athlete it has been my privilege to coach. He was a team player. Everything he did was with one thought in mind—winning."

Trippi may not have been a one-man team, but at the end of Georgia's 1946 championship season, William Tucker, Southeastern sports editor for United Press, picked the following All-SEC football team:

"Left end, Trippi; left tackle, Trippi; left guard, Trippi; center, Trippi; right guard, Trippi; right tackle, Trippi; right end, Trippi; quarterback, Trippi; left halfback, Trippi; right halfback, Trippi; fullback, Trippi."

Any questions?

ELLIOTT GALLOWAY
A Miracle Man

Legends? If there's a greater one than John Elliott Galloway, I've yet to meet him. Talk about cockamamie ideas. Here is a man who thought two-year-olds would sit at a table and read, four-year-olds could operate a calculator, and students of all ages would spend the day studying or just plain sitting under a tree, twiddling their thumbs.

Here is a man who in 1965 left a secure position at highly regimented, highly respected Westminster School in Atlanta to start his own school, one with no classrooms, no students, no faculty, and no money.

"When Elliott first told me of the idea, I thought he was ready for Peachtree-Parkwood Mental Hospital," recalls Emmett W. Wright Jr., then headmaster of the Westminster Boys School. "It sounded preposterous. Most of our teachers thought it was an April Fool joke. But those who knew Elliott's track record realized it was no joke. With his faith, understanding, patience, and persistence, they knew he could make miracles happen."

Which is precisely what he did. With the help of Ross Arnold, an attorney and father of one of Westminster's star football players, Galloway obtained a school charter and a dilapidated old folks home in Atlanta's Chastain Park that had been condemned by the city. Buoyed by a $6,000 loan from a banker friend in his native Moultrie, Georgia, and with manual labor from a handful of prospective students and teachers, Galloway completely refurbished the building.

2001

Among the handful of refurbishers and true believers was Dr. G. Hugh Russell, at the time a management professor at Georgia State University and a consultant to businesses across the country. Russell was smitten by Galloway's concept that different students progress at different speeds and should not be held back when they are capable of doing advanced work. So in his off hours, Russell installed windows and shelving in the new Galloway School, and his son Paul became one of the first to enroll.

With another loan, this one for $5,000, Galloway, a retired naval officer, went to the US Government Surplus Office and purchased tables, chairs, and bookcases.

Few prospective students or teachers applied at first, but that didn't last long. Eventually, about 1,000 youngsters applied, but Galloway accepted only 375. Of the 800 who sought faculty positions—educators from most every private school and some public schools in Atlanta—he picked twenty-nine. On September 3, 1969, the Galloway School opened in that single building. Galloway says it was the happiest day of his life.

Today there are 735 students and 100 faculty members at the Chastain Park school, which encompasses three buildings on an eight-acre campus. And what students they are. Nearly all Galloway graduates go on to college, and 98 percent of these earn a degree. Graduates have included the children of Dr. Martin Luther King Jr., Hank Aaron, and Hugh Russell. Galloway graduates become doctors, ministers, educators, attorneys, business executives, and entrepreneurs. They owe much of their success to one man and his dream.

Just reading about a typical Galloway day when he was putting his school together can be exhausting. Reveille was at 6 A.M., followed by a one-hour run, shower, light breakfast, and reading two newspapers. Then off to work, to interview prospective students and faculty, assemble a board of directors that eventually read like a Who's Who of Atlanta, and attend an Atlanta Chamber of Commerce function, followed by a Boy Scout troop committee meeting. Then back to his modest home on Mt. Paran Road for dinner, before going to a board meeting of the Atlanta Track Club, a meeting of the Cobb County Library Board or an organizational meeting for Little League baseball. Bedtime? Who sleeps—and sometimes he didn't—when there is so much to be done?

Today, at age eighty, the man remains indefatigable. Galloway ran in the first Peachtree Road Race in 1973, which his son Jeff won, and he has run in every Peachtree since. In his seventies, he ran four Boston Marathons, two New York City Marathons, and three Marine Corps Marathons. He still coaches Little League baseball, serves as a director of the Atlanta Track Club, is involved in UNICEF activities in the Atlanta community, and runs an hour every day—and don't forget that Sunday school class at Log Cabin Community Church near Vinings, which he has taught for the past forty-seven years.

Make no mistake about it, besides his school, running is Galloway's top priority. "I want to die running up Lake Forrest Road to Powers Ferry Road," he says. Running runs in the Galloway family. Both of his sons—Jeff, now fifty-five, and Charlie, now fifty-two—were champions. Jeff was on the 1972 US Olympic team and set a national record for the 10,000 meters. At Wesleyan College in Connecticut, he was named All-American in both track and cross country. Charlie won three state championships while attending Westminster School and was captain of the track team at Florida State University, where he set a school record in the triple jump. The three women in the Galloway family, mama Kitty (Katherine Warren Galloway) and twin daughters Kay and Fran, now forty-eight, have been cheerleaders for the boys.

"God has blessed me," Elliott says. "He has given me everything I have needed—Kitty, my twin girls, and the boys. He helped me become what I wanted to be—a teacher, a naval officer (commander) and an ordained minister. He gave me a dream and helped me make it come true. My dream was a school where children could take from three months to three years to advance to the next grade, a school where they could advance at their own pace."

Ken Kiesler, who taught at Westminster when Galloway was principal of the Westminster Lower School, remembers one student who knew more about math than his teacher. "Elliott took the youngster under his wing. By the ninth grade, he was taking advanced calculus. He made a perfect score on the final exam and an incredible 1600 on the college boards. By the time the student was a senior, Elliott had left Westminster. But when he was named Westminster's STAR student, he picked Elliott as his STAR teacher, not a teacher from Westminster."

Kiesler, who later became principal of the Lovett School, recalls another student. Lovett was going to dismiss her because she didn't write well. "I sent her to Elliott," he says. "She not only tested well, but under his guidance, she became an honor graduate."

The Galloway philosophy is that children learn best when they are drawn rather than pushed to learning. He believes students should be comfortable, respected, and challenged. Galloway students are not asked to do things until they are ready, but neither are they held back when they can move ahead.

Students sit around tables, not at desks. The grading system reads like a Navy/Marine Corps officer's fitness report. There are no As, Bs or Cs. Students are graded "outstanding," "excellent," "above average," "average," or "below average." Like officers up for promotion, top students can readily move ahead, while the "below average" may spend a year or more in the same course. The system works, as evidenced by the high number of graduates who enter Harvard, Princeton, Yale, Brown, and other Ivy League colleges.

"We have two requirements," says Galloway. "Students must try, and they must behave." The system makes students responsible for their performance. The lazy don't advance. In fact, they don't last long.

On sports, Galloway paraphrases the late Vince Lombardi's adage, "Winning isn't everything; it's the only thing." In Galloway's view, "Winning isn't everything; wanting to win is." The Galloway School competes in Region 6-A in boys' and girls' basketball, track and cross country.

"Any student can try out for a team and no one is cut," he says. "The kids that stick it out know they are going to play. We use every player on the squad. This season we lost a basketball game by one point. We could have won it had we stuck with our starting lineup, but we believe it's more important to get every squad member in the game than it is to win."

Galloway is a winner, make no mistake about that. In its fourth decade, the school is flourishing. Galloway is now graduating his second generation of students, and many members of the faculty and staff have been at their jobs for twenty-five years or more. Walking the halls gives you a warm, fuzzy feeling. Smiling students greet you, and it all seems genuine. The walls are covered with bright watercolors done by students ages two on up. Students give the impression they are exactly where they want to be.

Galloway began his own odyssey in Wilson, North Carolina, where he was born on November 30, 1920, the son of Ben Galloway, a tobacco demonstrator and farmer, and Elizabeth Knox Galloway, a housewife. When Elliott was eight, the family moved to Moultrie and class began to tell. The boy was up at daybreak, picking cotton on his daddy's farm before going to Moultrie Elementary School, then back to pick more cotton.

At Moultrie High School, Galloway was president of the student body, the best football and baseball player, and the best cotton-picker in town. He played guard on the Moultrie football team for Coach Grant Gillis, who had been an All-American legend at Alabama. Galloway was chosen to play in Georgia's first annual North-South prep all-star football game. His South team, coached by Georgia Tech immortals Bill Alexander and Bobby Dodd, whipped the North. After the game, there was a mad rush by college recruiters to sign this scrappy 170-pound guard to a football scholarship. Galloway was intent on becoming an ordained minister, so he picked Wake Forest, the Baptist school in his old home state of North Carolina.

At Wake Forest, an injury cut short his football career, but Galloway continued to excel elsewhere. He captained the track team and was president of the student body. For him, the best part of Wake Forest was the women, that is, one woman—Elizabeth "Kitty" Warren. They were married in 1942, just before Elliott was commissioned an ensign in the US Navy, then heading into action in World War II.

After the war, he returned to Wake Forest before going on to Columbia University, Union Theological Seminary, Emory University and Georgia State University for graduate degrees. When the Korean War broke out in 1950, Galloway was recalled to active duty. He was assigned as director of the Naval Training Command in San Diego, and there was spawned the idea of the Galloway School.

"One of our missions was to prepare non-high school graduates for the General Educational Development Test (GED), which would get them a high school diploma," he says. "We had sailors from vastly different backgrounds, with vastly different interests and aspirations. So we let them advance at their own pace. If someone could absorb the material faster than the general group, he could take the test early and get his diploma. It was a tremendous motivator.

"If it works here," he reasoned, "why won't it work back home?"

By then, "back home" was Atlanta, where Galloway first taught at West Fulton High School and then Westminster. He spent four years as headmaster at Holy Innocents Episcopal School before opening the Galloway School. Today, Galloway is headmaster emeritus, but Monday through Friday will find him roaming the halls or visiting with students and faculty from 9 A.M. to 5 P.M. You can spot him running up Lake Forrest Road from five to six, some days A.M., some days P.M.

Galloway makes time to speak to civic clubs and high school graduation classes all over the state as well as counsel dreamers on how they can put together a Galloway-type school of their own. Then there are conferences with the Atlanta Association of Independent Schools, the Georgia Independent School Association, the Mid-South Association of Independent Schools, the Southern Association of Independent Schools, the Southern Headmasters Association, the Atlanta Mental Health Association, the Atlanta Track Club, the March of Dimes, ad infinitum.

Had enough?

Although he's hardly ready for the geriatric center, Wesley Woods honored him as a "legend whose vigorous and long productive life has enriched our world."

GEORGE MORRIS
One for the Ages

If you did not see George Augustus Morris Jr. play football at Georgia Tech, then you missed seeing "the greatest football player" the late, legendary Bobby Dodd said he ever coached. Morris, the 6'2", 195-pound center and linebacker out of Vicksburg, Mississippi, was the defensive master of Tech's undefeated, once-tied 1951 and unbeaten and untied 1952 co-national championship teams.

Dodd told me shortly after he retired in 1966:

> I coached twenty-one All-Americans in my thirty-five years at Tech, and they all were great. But George Morris was something special. He was not only a great center and a devastating linebacker but also a coach on the field.
>
> With all due respect to our regular defensive coaches—and we had some of the best—George could and did diagnose enemy offenses better than anyone on our staff. I was always telling Ray Graves, our defensive line coach, that I would rather have George calling defensive signals than him. He was uncanny in sensing plays.

In the 1953 Sugar Bowl, Tech whipped Ole Miss, 24-7. "We had a defensive scheme set up, but it wasn't working," said Dodd. "Ole Miss was moving the ball on us. George took it upon himself to change to a defense (6-4) that we had not used in three years. We never even discussed using it in the game. And he never asked any of our coaches, he just changed it on the field. Of course, we still had to make the tackles, but his alignment change was what stopped Ole Miss."

After the 1952 Georgia Tech-SMU game, which Tech won, 20-7, the *Atlanta Constitution*'s Furman Bisher wrote, "Twice [Morris] intercepted passes, not ordinary interceptions, but one-handers, like an outfielder making a grandstand catch. He could only get one hand on the interceptions, but where the other fellows used that hand to bat the ball down, Morris reeled them in for himself. Later, he dived and stole the ball from an unfortunate SMU back. It was so slick a maneuver that statisticians tried to credit Morris with another interception." Oh yes, he also made sixteen solo tackles.

The next day the Dallas sports pages appeared with cartoons of Morris wearing a black mask and toting a six-shooter. "George Morris was everything a great linebacker could possibly be," wrote columnist Blackie Sherrod.

When the season ended, Morris was chosen on everybody's All-American team—*Look* magazine, *Collier's* magazine, Associated Press, United Press, and International News Service. He made academic All-American and was chosen Southeastern Conference Defensive Player of the Year by the Atlanta and Birmingham touchdown clubs.

At the *Look* football banquet, legendary sports writer Grantland Rice said, "In thirty years of picking All-Americans, I've seen great linebackers, like Bulldog Turner [of the Chicago Bears], but George Morris is the greatest of them all."

Tim Cohane, the magazine's sports editor, said, "In college football, success goes to the team with the best linebacker, and in George Morris, Georgia Tech has the best of them all."

Morris finished the season with 114 solo tackles, a Tech record.

Following the banquet, his hometown held a George Morris Appreciation Day. He was the first All-American ever to come out of Vicksburg. There was a parade from the outskirts of town to City Hall, where the mayor gave him the keys to the city. More than 2,000 fans attended.

At a George Morris luncheon, Coach Dodd told the crowd, "Morris was the difference between being a good ball club and a great ball club. He was an inspiration to the whole team. He is the best defensive player in America."

Chosen to play linebacker in the College All-Star game against the NFL champion Detroit Lions, Morris pushed off blockers and consistently made tackles. Even though his team lost, 24-10, he was runner-up for Most Valuable Player.

If you think the all-American boy of the 1950s has let up in the new millennium, think again. At age seventy, living in Buckhead with his high school sweetheart and wife of forty-nine years, the former Polly Wren, Morris runs a thriving marketing business, is president of the Bobby Dodd Coach of the Year Foundation and co-chairs the Bobby Dodd Memorial Golf Tournament. He has helped raise hundreds of thousands of dollars for Hospice Atlanta and the Metropolitan Atlanta Boys and Girls Clubs.

It's been a fascinating journey. Morris was born on March 19, 1931, in Vicksburg, the first of five children of George A. Morris Sr., a supervisor with the US Army Corps of Engineers and a brigadier general in the US Army Reserves, and Mildred Morris, a housewife. At Vicksburg's Carr Central High School, the Morris family earned thirty-five letters. George and twin brothers Jimmy and Johnny played all sports, while sister Grace played girls basketball and was a football cheerleader.

It was a Huckleberry Finn youth. As a teenager, Morris spent many a summer night on sandbars in the Mississippi River, shooting fish with his .22 rifle. When World War II broke out, Daddy Morris left for active duty and the European Theater. Dee Jamieson, baseball coach at the Vicksburg American Legion Post, took the boys under his wing and kept them busy in athletics until their dad returned in 1945. By then, George was well on his way to stardom and brother Jimmy was not far behind.

George was an A student at Carr Central, where he did everything but the school laundry. In football, he played wherever he was needed—end, guard, tackle, center, fullback, and linebacker. On the track team, he threw the shot put, discus, and javelin and ran the relays. He played center on the basketball team and outfield on the baseball team. He was president of his freshman, sophomore, junior, and senior classes and president of the student council. He sang in the glee club and acted in the school play. Otherwise, he was a complete nobody.

In the first game of his senior year, Morris tore the muscle and ligaments in his left knee. Considering he played on only one good leg, it's nothing short of a miracle that he played college football at all. But his size, determination, and leadership ability attracted the attention of most every college scout in America, despite the fact that he hobbled through the last nine games of the season.

"Nobody called him The Gimp because he led us to an undefeated season," said Carr Central coach Raymond Ray. "George led the team in tackles, pass interceptions, and rushing. I was wide open about the injury. I told college coaches that in no way did it reduce the way this kid played. He was all heart. College coaches would watch films of George and wouldn't believe he had a bad knee. He never missed a step in getting to ball carriers. You can't coach that sixth sense. You either have it or you don't. George had it."

The late great Notre Dame coach Frank Leahy paid a visit to Vicksburg and said, "Morris plays better on one leg than most anyone else I've seen plays on two." So in 1948, Notre Dame, Alabama, West Point, Tennessee, Georgia, UCLA, Southern Cal, Georgia Tech, and other gridiron giants had their top recruiters camping on the banks of the Mississippi.

Two Tech alumni, Brooks Pearson and Jack Rushin, had seen Morris play and convinced Coach Dodd that even though he had one of the nation's best recruiters in Dick Jones, he had better come down himself if he wanted to sign the finest football player ever to play in Mississippi. That was good enough for Dodd.

"Dad had come home from the Army," recalls Morris. "He had been promoted to brigadier general. He and Coach Dodd, who had played for another general, Robert S. Neyland at Tennessee, spoke the same language. Coach Dodd convinced my dad and me that I would have a tremendous opportunity for academic growth as well as growth on the football field. I think that sealed the deal, although what really sealed it was when my dad and Coach Dodd first shook hands."

After receiving All-State, All-Southern, and honorable mention All-American prep honors, Morris entered Tech in 1949 with top billing. He far exceeded expectations. As a member of the Tech freshman team, he was a starter at center and linebacker. His coach, Lew Woodruff, called him "the best freshman center I've ever seen." As a sophomore in 1950, his perfect snaps from center and fierce tackling at linebacker earned him equal playing time on the varsity with senior and two-year starter Bob Bossons.

Remembers line coach Ray Graves, later head coach at Florida, "Day after day in practice, we watched George hobble back for an opponent's pass, jump up on one leg and haul down the football. Having to run on one leg had the power of suggestion. George would make interceptions with one hand."

By his junior season, Morris was in charge at center and linebacker. His was a constant name on the Associated Press' SEC Team of the Week. He was chosen Most Valuable Player by his teammates and was a unanimous choice on the AP's All-SEC first team. After his spectacular, senior season in 1952, when he captained the (12-0-0) Sugar Bowl champions and then the College All-Stars, Morris went into the Army Corps of Engineers. Wouldn't you know it, he played football. And wouldn't you know it, he was chosen All-Army. He also served a tour of duty in Korea as a combat engineer.

Released from active duty in 1956, Morris reported to the San Francisco '49ers, where he suffered still another blow to his damaged knee. This one ended his playing days, but pain and all, he served as a football official in the SEC for the next thirty years. During his officiating career, which ended ten years ago in the Fiesta Bowl, he worked every major bowl game except the Rose Bowl. All told, he officiated fourteen bowl games, twenty All-Star (Senior Bowl) contests, and two national championship games.

Morris briefly considered a coaching career but decided against it. "I didn't want to be wondering what a nineteen-year-old kid was doing on a Saturday night, plus I didn't want to subject my family to possibly moving ten or fifteen times," he says. What Morris did was go to work as an engineer for Georgia Power in Atlanta (1957–62) and then moved to Columbus, where he spent twelve years as a vice president with Royal Crown Cola.

George Morris and Associates opened in 1974. "I wanted to move back to Atlanta, be my own boss, work my own hours, and have the opportunity to earn as much money as I was worth," he says. His advertising specialty business of pens, plaques, calendars, and sports items may not sound like much, but last year's gross sales were almost $1 million. Clients include Coca-Cola and the Miller Brewing Company.

Except for a broken heart the last two years, with the death of his mother and then his brother Jimmy (an All-SEC center at Tech), Morris is doing fine, thank you. He's the same happy, unpretentious, unselfish person he was when he used to float down the Mississippi. In typical Morris fashion, he says of his many honors, "I had a strong supporting cast. I played with twelve All-Americans, two of whom [Larry Morris and Ray Beck] are in the National College Football Hall of Fame. I played with eighteen All-SEC players and was tutored by three coaches—Dodd, Graves, and Frank Broyles—who are in the National College Football Hall of Fame."

Morris served six years on the Georgia Tech Athletic Board. "We had several alumni who thought just because they had played varsity football, they had a license to run the Tech football program," he says. "We had to set these people straight. If you accept a free education for four years, football player or not, you need to repay your college with long and dedicated service, not criticism."

Morris is a member of the Georgia Tech, Georgia, Mississippi, and National Collegiate Sports Halls of Fame. He is a member of Georgia Tech's All-Time football team, little wonder in that he was called by his coach "the finest of the finest."

George and Polly Morris have one son, George Morris III, and four daughters: Sherilyn, Suanne, Thames, and Thea. George, or "Gus," was an All-State football player at Atlanta's Marist School and an All-Conference fullback on the Millsaps College football team. He is in the Millsaps Sports Hall of Fame. The four girls were all high school cheerleaders.

Talk about good breeding.

WHY NOT DOOLEY FIELD?

Georgia Tech has Bobby Dodd Stadium/Grant Field. Why isn't it Sanford Stadium/Vince Dooley Field at the University of Georgia? Why not indeed?

Besides Vince Dooley, what other Georgia Bulldog football coach won a national championship and six Southeastern Conference championships? Who else took twenty teams to bowl contests, won 201 games and had only one losing season in twenty-five years? Name another coach in Georgia gridiron history to be named SEC Coach of the Year seven times and National Collegiate Coach of the Year twice.

The answer, dear readers, is that there is none.

So, at the start of the next football season, when a new era begins under Coach Mark Richt, what better time could there be to rename the place Vince Dooley Field at Sanford Stadium?

By no stretch of the imagination would this detract from the memory of Dr. Steadman Vincent Sanford, the University of Georgia president who raised the money to build the stadium in 1929. "Sanford Stadium" would stay in place. If anything, attaching "Dooley Field" would add luster to an already illustrious name.

Fact is, no one has been a bigger credit to his university than Dooley, a past president of the National Association of Collegiate Athletic Directors; past president of the American Football Coaches Association; and past chairman of the NCAA football rules committee. Plus, he's in the National Collegiate Football

2001

Hall of Fame, the Georgia Sports Hall of Fame and the Mobile and Alabama Sports Halls of Fame. Only ten Division I football coaches ever won 200 games.

A credit to his university? Dooley has been a perennial giver of his time, money, and leadership to heart fund, multiple sclerosis, juvenile diabetes, Boy Scout, homeless, and Salvation Army causes. For twenty-eight years, he's been chairman of the Georgia Easter Seals Society. He and his wife, Barbara, co-chair a fundraising campaign to establish a Catholic high school in Northeast Georgia. Dooley was instrumental in raising big bucks for the recruitment of non-athletic students; for an expansion of the university's chemistry building; and for an addition to UGA's performing and visual arts center. With a personal gift of $100,000, he initiated the Vincent J. Dooley Library Endowment Fund, which he has added to time and again.

"Vince Dooley's generosity to all facets of the university and to the Athens community has been above and beyond the call," says Scott Sikes, UGA's director of development. Others agree. The Northeast Georgia Boy Scouts, for instance, has recognized Vince as Man of the Year and Barbara as Woman of the Year.

Football swings the most weight in college athletics, of course, but under Dooley, UGA has built one of the top all-around athletic programs in the nation. Since 1979, when he became athletic director, UGA teams have won sixteen national championships and sixty-four SEC titles. More than 100 Georgia student-athletes have been named first-team Academic All-American, and over thirty have received NCAA post-graduate scholarships. Bulldog sports teams have generated over $200,000 for the university's general scholarship fund.

There are those in the Bulldog Nation who say any tribute to Dooley should be made at his retirement in 2003. Others, including UGA President Dr. Michael Adams, oppose making any change in the stadium name. Still others, like former longtime regent Barry Phillips, say the state board historically does not name a facility for a living person.

To all that, I say, hogwash! Dooley is sixty-eight years old. Although in good health, he's nearing his biblical three score and ten. Make it Sanford Stadium-Dooley Field now, while he can still smell the roses. As for not naming a facility for someone still living, the regents made an exception in the case of Tech's legendary Dodd, so why not for Georgia's legendary Dooley?

"I'm not much on hyphenated names," says Dr. Adams. "I'd be in favor of finding something of significance to honor Coach Dooley. He's a living legend. But I would not be in favor of diminishing the Sanford name."

Diminish the name? How on earth would adding "Dooley Field" diminish anything? Dooley spearheaded six stadium expansions, and Georgia teams justified every expansion. Sanford Stadium, which seats 86,250 today, is now the fifth largest stadium in America. Not like hyphenated names, my eye. It should be, "Thank you, Mr. Dooley."

"I think the world of Vince Dooley," says Phillips. "As a coach, administrator and student, [Dooley earned a master's degree in history while athletic director] and citizen, he has been a perfect role model for athletes and non-athletes alike."

It wasn't easy in the early years, even for a budding role model. Consider, if you will, what Dooley stepped into when he was named head football coach at the end of the 1963 season. The previous three Georgia teams had losing records, posting an overall 10-16-4 mark. The Bulldog Nation was in turmoil. The late Wallace Butts had been unceremoniously "retired" as coach, and his longtime loyalists were not exactly supportive of his replacement, Johnny Griffith.

And, there was "The Story of a College Football Fix"—which appeared in The Saturday Evening Post magazine, alleging that then–Athletic Director Butts had given Georgia's game plan to Coach Paul "Bear" Bryant of Alabama before the 1962 Georgia-Alabama game. Alabama won, 35-0. Nasty lawsuits were brought against the magazine. The Butts trial, held in federal court in Atlanta, included conflicting testimony that further divided the Bulldog Nation. (Butts won a judgment, and Bryant settled out of court.)

What Rome experienced under Nero was akin to what Dooley inherited when he replaced Griffith. To put out the fire and reunite loyalists was a job for a big-name coach, like a Dodd from Tech, a Frank Broyles (Arkansas) or a Bud Wilkinson (Oklahoma). It certainly was not a job for a virtually unknown freshman football coach at Auburn University. Vince Who?

While only thirty-one years old, Dooley was a former Marine Corps officer, a disciplinarian who demanded the best from his troops and got it, a man who had a knack for developing loyalty in coaches and players alike. Dooley had the situation well in hand long before anyone ever dreamed he would. His first team posted a 7-3-1 record and earned a bid to the Sun Bowl, where it defeated Texas Tech, 7-0. Two years later, Georgia won the SEC title. What Dooley accomplished in three years was downright remarkable.

"I remember the day he arrived," says eighty-six-year-old Bill Hartman, an assistant coach under both Butts and Dooley. An All-American fullback at Georgia in 1937, Hartman was later elected to the College Football Hall of Fame. He describes the day:

> It was December 1963, and we were having a snowstorm in Athens. Boy, was that prophetic. Vince impressed me as very much the introvert, but he had a well-written plan on what he was going to do and how he was going to do it.
> He took charge immediately. He hired a staff, interviewed his players, and held meeting after meeting in preparation for his first spring practice. Frankly, I didn't see much hope for that first season. But I never had seen more dogged tenacity in anyone. He not only had a carefully put together plan, he had drive, determination and a competitive spirit, which he instilled in his players.

Pat Hodgson played on Dooley's first two teams and later served under him for nine years as an assistant coach. "He was a great organizer. He was meticulous. He paid great attention to detail. Nothing was left to chance; he prepared for every possibility. That's why we won so many games in the fourth quarter."

Dooley didn't resist delegating authority, says Hodgson. "He surrounded himself with good assistants and let them do their jobs. He was a tireless worker and expected you to be the same. We had coaches meetings before practice, after practice, and again after dinner. It was detail, detail, detail."

Howard "Doc" Ayers, who had been head football coach at Cedartown High School, was one of the first coaches Dooley named to his staff. "It all was so well-organized," says Ayers. "He kept a log on every practice, what went right, what went wrong, and how we were going to fix it. All the assistant coaches had input. We knew who was boss, but we were like one, big, happy family."

Dooley's first assistants included Erskine "Erk" Russell, from Atlanta's Grady High School, who would go on to carve out a legend of his own, both at the University of Georgia and later at Georgia Southern University; Ken Cooper of Tifton High School; John Donaldson of Jesup High School; Frank Inman from Richmond Academy in Augusta; Jim Pyburn from Auburn University; Sterling Dupree from the University of Florida; Hootie Ingram, an import from Virginia Tech; and brother Bill Dooley from Mississippi State. Hartman, who had retired from coaching in 1956, returned to serve as kicking coach. The late Mike Castonis (Georgia) was freshman coach; Dick Copas (Auburn) served as trainer.

Dooley provided the leadership. Few coaches were better at inspiring players to win. "He could tear you down when you goofed up, but he could build you back up so high that you thought you could whip the world," says Leman L. "Buzzy" Rosenberg Jr., an All-SEC defensive back in 1970.

"I remember the first game that season," he says. "We were playing Tulane in New Orleans. He had me so fired up I couldn't wait to get the ball. I was playing safety. The first time Tulane punted, as the ball was in the air, I thought, 'It's our first possession, and Coach Dooley wants me to run it back for a touchdown.' I did—about sixty yards."

Then there was the Auburn game, when the Bulldogs went up against Heisman Trophy-winning quarterback Pat Sullivan and his All-American receiver, Terry Beasley.

"We were twenty-eight-point underdogs," says Rosenberg. "All week long we drilled on fundamentals and rehearsed our game plan. He kept telling us we could be better than we were. He kept saying, 'We'll beat Auburn.' And we did, 31-17."

Dooley's finest hour came in the 12-0-0 national championship season of 1980, capped by a victory over Notre Dame in the Sugar Bowl. The Bulldogs had but a single question mark going into the first game—running back. Then a freshman from Wrightsville, Georgia, showed what he could do. Did Dooley think Herschel Walker was the answer to his problems? "Not until the first game, when he ran smack over the Tennessee safety on that touchdown run," says Dooley today. "Herschel was the key, but we had a total team—a great kicking game, solid defense, ball control, team unity, tremendous spirit."

Dooley's championship season triggered a four-year run that ranks among the best stretches in collegiate football history. In three years with the Heisman-winning Walker and one without him, Dooley's teams went 43-4-1, won three

SEC titles and Sugar Bowl and Cotton Bowl championships. For four consecutive years, Dooley's 'Dogs were unbeaten against Georgia Tech, Florida, and Tennessee.

Like his scrappy Junkyard Dawg defenses, Dooley was a born fighter. He grew up near the docks in Mobile, Alabama, and spent several years in his youth as a member of a gang of toughs. When he got to McGill High School, the football/basketball coach, Ray Dicharey, convinced him there was another way to compete—on the athletic field. Dooley listened and the advice changed his life. He went out for football and basketball, made All-State in both sports and had dual scholarship offers from most colleges in the Southeast. Not bad for a 5'9", 150-pounder.

Dooley chose Auburn, where he was an All-SEC quarterback on Coach Ralph "Shug" Jordan's football team and a starting guard on Coach Joel Eaves' basketball team. He earned a degree in business management while also participating in Navy ROTC. Upon graduation in 1953, Dooley served two years in the US Marine Corps. He loved the discipline and considered a career as a Leatherneck. When Coach Jordan called for an assistant, though, the Marine Corps lost one of its brightest young officers.

Jordan wanted him to be varsity quarterback coach, but Dooley pleaded and got the freshman team's head job instead. He wanted the responsibility for a whole team. "When I told my daddy I had turned down a job on the varsity for the freshman post, he said I was going backward in my career," recalls Dooley. "But I wanted the whole coaching experience and to be held accountable for an entire squad's record. I coached the freshman team for five years. I had five winning seasons. Equally important, I had five years on the road scouting future opponents with Coach Joel Eaves. He was an astute teacher. And he must have thought something got through to me, because when Georgia picked him as its athletic director, he picked me as head coach. The first thing I did when I got to Georgia was to pay my respects to Coach Butts. I think he always appreciated that."

Today, as athletic director, Dooley starts his day at 5:30 A.M., and frequently does not stop until near midnight. After a morning workout on his stationary bicycle and treadmill, he's at his office in the Butts-Mehre Building by 9 A.M. The day is usually filled with meetings, telephone calls, planning sessions, and consultations with student athletes and non-athletes alike. He's home for dinner at 7 P.M. but usually back in his office at 9 P.M. "I get more work accomplished when most everyone else has gone," he says. Then there are the speaking engagements, fund-raising events and travel. The calendar is full. No room for golf.

What he does make time for is study—the Civil War, American and European history, political science, art, and gardening. The outside of the Dooleys' colonial home is a showplace, so much so that it was featured a year ago on the Home and Garden cable TV network. Over 1,000 varieties of flowers and shrubs have bloomed in Dooley's one-acre garden.

Dooley's wife (the former Barbara Meshad of Birmingham) is a celebrity herself who also is extensively involved in civic and community affairs. The Dooleys have four children: Deanna Cook, an Athens housewife; Daniel, a financial planner in Athens; Denise Mitchell, an Atlanta housewife; and Derek, an assistant football coach at Louisiana State University. Nine grandchildren add to the crew.

There have been so many thrills in Dooley's life that he's unable to pinpoint the biggest. "The thrills have been in having the privilege of being at this university for thirty-seven years; being a part of the growth; seeing our teams in all sports compete at the highest level; watching football, baseball, swimming, gymnastic, and tennis teams win national championships; seeing our women's teams attain national prominence; and even appreciating the agony of defeat."

The toughest obstacle Dooley ever faced? "People not understanding a series of defeats," he says. Always criticized for his ball-control, run-oriented offenses, Dooley faced a tough stretch in 1969–70, when he went 5-5-1 and 5-5, but few remembered that when his 1971 team went 11-1 and defeated North Carolina in the Gator Bowl. His teams were 201-77-10 in twenty-five seasons. Dooley won seventy-one more games than Butts, who is second in career victories.

Says Dooley:

> You have to keep faith in yourself, rise above what people may say about you, analyze criticism, and make adjustments when they're justified. Sports stir great passion in people, and they may say unkind things when they may not really mean them.
>
> I've had an exciting life, and I've never felt like I've been at work. I've enjoyed everything I've ever done associated with athletics. I enjoy players and fellow coaches, and seeing former players come back as successful businessmen and citizens, contributing to their communities. It's been a lifetime of thrills.

Regent Don Leebern was a Georgia Bulldog standout in the 1950s. "Coach Dooley elevated the sights not only of his players but of all who came in contact with him," he says. Former Coach Hodgson says "there is no one more deserving of having the Sanford Stadium field named after him than Vince Dooley. He took Georgia from the pits to the penthouse." Says Bulldog historian Dan Magill: "Dr. Sanford would be proud to have Vince's name alongside his."

To quote Hillel, the ancient Rabbi: "If not now, when?"

KING OF THE FLATS

Biblical advice from one of Georgia Tech's greatest quarterbacks, Donald Kimbrough "Kim" King: "This is the day the Lord hath made, rejoice and be glad in it." King, who broke thirteen individual records at the Flats and led the Yellow Jackets to two bowl games, is battling multiple myeloma, one of the more deadly forms of cancer. He does not take one day at a time, he takes one moment at a time.

After two years of chemotherapy, the cancer is in remission. Meanwhile, King performs his daily duties, developing real estate throughout Metro Atlanta, doing color commentary on Tech radio football broadcasts, spending time with his family, and giving to his alma mater and community. Who wants to be a billionaire?

As a child who grew up on Atlanta's southwest side, King did. He wanted all the luxuries his family did not have—the big car, the three-story home, the oceanfront villa, the hundred-plus acre farm. Now he has them all, but what matters most to him are the things money cannot buy: good health and good friends. He's working on the good health, and the friends he has in abundance.

Few people have given more of themselves than King. He served on the Scottish Rite Football Committee, which promoted the old Tech-Georgia freshman football game, which netted hundreds of thousands of dollars for the former Scottish Rite Hospital. He was a director of the Georgia Amateur Athletic Association, a trustee of the Georgia Tech Foundation, a member of the Georgia Tech presidential search committee, chairman of the Georgia Tech Success Center

2001

project, a director of the Georgia Tech School of Management, chairman of the board of Georgia Public Broadcasting, and a board member of the Cobb-Marietta Coliseum. That's a bare pittance of his contributions of time and money to his community. For instance, he will be incoming board chairman of the Bobby Dodd Foundation, which benefits Atlanta Hospice, Boys and Girls Clubs, and children with mental disabilities.

Cancer struck two years ago. This can't be, he told himself. "From the day I was a kid playing on the sandlots, I exercised vigorously. I always got my eight hours of sleep, I ate nutritious foods. I thought it must be some mistake, but believe me, it was no mistake."

It was May 1999. King was on a golfing trip to Myrtle Beach, South Carolina. The first day out, he felt pain every time he swung a club. The second day, he picked up his driver and felt an excruciating pain in his back. A tumor had crushed his vertebrae. He had a broken back.

A friend flew him to Atlanta in his private jet. His internist, Dr. Thorne Winter, took him to Saint Joseph's Hospital for tests. King had multiple myeloma. In June, oncologist Dr. Ken Braunstein confirmed he had one of the rarest forms of cancer. Soon King was at the Sam Walton Clinic/University of Arkansas Medical Center to begin the first of a two-year treatment program that he finished last month. "Every second is precious to me now because you may not have another," he says. "I feel good again. God has blessed me."

Although not moving at the same speed as before, King still lives a whirlwind life. He's up at 5 A.M.; in his home gym at six, lifting weights, stretching and doing a punishing array of calisthenics. At seven, it's a three-mile neighborhood walk. By nine, he's in his Vinings office. "I like to have fifteen things going at once," he says. "There are deals to make, board meetings to plan, property to inspect and meetings with politicians." King was finance chairman of Roy Barnes' 1998 race for governor. He's chaired some twenty boards, ranging from the Atlanta Touchdown Club to the Piedmont Driving Club

Some things never change. King was busy from the day he climbed out of his crib at his parents' West End home. A natural athlete, at age ten he led his Gra-Y football team to an undefeated season and the basketball team to a league championship. He hurled three shutouts in baseball. So what he accomplished at Joe Brown High School was no surprise—twice All-City and All-State in football, basketball, and baseball. By the time he was a junior, he had attracted the attention of football and basketball coaches from all over the country and three professional baseball scouts.

As a 6'1", 180-pound junior quarterback, he rewrote the passing records for city of Atlanta schools, then rewrote his own records as a senior. In 1961, he threw for 1,204 yards and nineteen touchdowns. In 1962, he completed eighty-five passes for 1,233 yards and twenty touchdowns. Wrote the late Charlie Roberts, then dean of Georgia prep sportswriters, "King is the finest long-throwing left-hander ever produced in Georgia."

In two years, King rushed and passed for over 3,000 yards. He captained the 1962 Class AAA All-State football team, captained the North Georgia All-Star football squad, and was MVP of the All-Star game. He was the Atlanta TD Club's Back of the Year.

In his senior baseball season, he pitched a no-hitter, and in his senior basketball season he hit 68 percent of his field goal attempts to lead his team in scoring and to a region championship.

Talk about Jack Armstrong, the all-American boy. King was president of his Brown High senior class, and a straight A student. He was co-captain of the prep All-American football team. "You'd love to have him for a son," said his Brown coach, Joe O'Malley. "He was not only a great athlete but a gentleman who had a smile and a kind word for teachers and students alike."

For college, King had his choice of which sport to play and where to play it, but there was never any doubt. It would be Tech football for Coach Bobby Dodd. Although recruiters came with promises of a starting quarterback job as a sophomore (freshmen were ineligible for varsity), King politely said no to everyone from southern Florida to South Bend, Indiana, to Southern California.

From the time he was ten and a Gra-Y sensation, King had worn the No. 11 of his hero, Georgia Tech All-American quarterback Wade Mitchell, and dreamed of playing for the Yellow Jackets. There would be no turning back. When he was a junior at Brown High, the University of Florida recruited his older brother, Buddy, who had also had a distinguished career at Brown High, and Buddy's high school teammate, Charles Casey, an All-American pass receiver.

Florida coach Ray Graves sent his assistant, Pepper Rodgers, to Atlanta to stress to Kim the close-knit relationship he would have playing with two of his former prep teammates and for a coach who himself had once quarterbacked Brown to the state title.

"When Coach Dodd heard about Coach Rodgers' visit, he came to my house to reassure me I was going to be the next great Tech quarterback," recalls King. "I told him that my father and grandfather had been Tech fans ever since I could remember, but that they were no bigger fans than I was. The first day it was legal, I signed with Tech."

True to Dodd's words, King did become Tech's next great quarterback. Held out for seasoning after his freshman season, he broke into the starting lineup as a sophomore, shattering eight Tech offensive records in leading the Jackets to a 7-3-1 record, including a 31-21 win over Texas Christian in the Gator Bowl.

No one ever had a more auspicious rookie season. King broke two records held by Tech Hall of Famer Billy Lothridge, smashing his single-game pass completion record by hitting twenty-one of thirty for 319 yards in a 42-19 victory over Virginia. Then he erased Lothridge's season pass completion mark of eighty-three with 112. King also eclipsed Tech Hall of Famer Darrell Crawford's season passing yardage record of 1,153 yards, with 1,331. Crawford's mark had stood for fourteen years.

"As a sophomore, King probably became the greatest quarterback Tech has ever seen," wrote *Atlanta Journal* columnist Furman Bisher. Tech was 2-1-1 and a big underdog when it hosted Auburn before the largest crowd ever to see a game at Grant Field. King completed the first nine passes he threw, passed for one touchdown and ran thirty-one yards for another in a stunning 23-14 Tech win. Auburn coach Ralph "Shug" Jordan, who had seen many a Tech quarterback in his twenty-eight years of playing or coaching against the Jackets, called King "the most complete quarterback I've ever seen in a Tech uniform." Wrote *Atlanta Journal* football analyst and former University of Georgia and Ole Miss football coach Harry Mehre, "In all my years of playing, coaching and watching football games, I never have seen one football player dominate as King did." When he entered the dressing room after the game, his teammates stood and cheered.

As a junior in 1966, King, for the most part, was unstoppable. Despite a broken right arm, the lefthander led the Jackets to a 9-2 season and a berth in the Orange Bowl, where they lost to Florida, 27-12. One win was a 42-0 rout of Vanderbilt, after which Coach Dodd said, "He is one of the best quarterbacks in the country, even with a broken arm." Others agreed. King was named honorable mention on two All-American teams.

Coach Dodd retired in 1966 and was replaced by Bud Carson. In Carson's home debut against TCU, before a record-breaking crowd of 55,299, King welcomed the new coach by unloading an eighty-yard touchdown bomb that shocked the Horned Frogs and sent Tech surging to a 24-7 victory. It was the longest pass and the longest touchdown pass in Tech football history.

Despite playing on bad ankles most of the season, King finished with career records of most yards passing (2,763) and most total yards running and passing (3,269). Tech suffered through a 4-6 season, but assistant coach Dick Bestwick said, "A healthy Kim King would have put us in a bowl game." He was chosen to play in the college All-American game and was drafted by the Pittsburgh Steelers.

The NFL was not to be. Coach Dodd told him that with his friends, fans, and work ethic, he should go into business. That is exactly what King did, first with Adams-Cates in the mortgage loan department, then with Kim King Associates Inc., a real estate development company he started from ground zero and turned into one of the largest companies of its kind in America.

King's love and loyalty to his alma mater are unsurpassed. He was one of the founders of the Yellow Jacket Club, which raises money for the Tech athletic program. He has served on the athletic board for eight years. The "young lefthander"—as he has been known since that sensational sophomore season in 1965—has been the Georgia Tech radio color commentator for twenty-seven years.

King goes after things with the same fierce determination he showed on the gridiron. For instance, when he hit a stone wall in trying to get Tech's Arthur B. Edge Athletic Center started, he went to another Tech graduate, then-President Jimmy Carter. Thanks to Carter, the program got up and running. The $7.5 million complex today is one of the finest in the nation.

Why such drive? "My mother challenged me to set difficult but attainable goals, and that once I reached them, to set higher ones. She was an intense competitor, and she encouraged me to be the same." His mother played basketball and tennis and ran track at old Atlanta Girls High. "She used to take me out on the front lawn and pitch me the football," says King. "I was three or four. She took me to watch my dad play semi-pro baseball. She would tell me what the pitcher was throwing and why the coaches kept scratching their arms and touching their caps. And she never missed a game of mine, not at Gra-Y, not at Brown, not at Tech. She even came to some Tech practices. Coach Dodd would call her 'Coach.'"

Even greater than King's love for Tech is his love for his late mother, and his wife, the former Gail McLennan. They have been married for thirty-two years. "Gail has been the love of my life, my strength. She has been beside me through good days and bad. Her support and optimism has been a major help in my cancer recovery. I don't know what I would have done without her. I love her every bit as much today as I did the day we married."

The Kings have three children: Angela, twenty-nine; Beau, twenty-eight; and Abby, twenty-two. Angela is married to Pano Karatassos Jr., son of the president of the Buckhead Life Restaurant chain. Beau recently joined his father in Kim King Associates. Abby is a senior at the University of Miami. Angela ran track at The Lovett School in Atlanta; Beau was a varsity wrestler at Washington & Lee University.

"I've much to be thankful for," says King. "At age twenty-five, I started my own company. It has put together some of the largest business centers in Georgia. But that's a distant third to my loving wife and children."

The thirteen records he set were accomplished in three years, while most who broke them did so in four. King was on the Dean's List at Tech. He's in the Tech Hall of Fame and the Georgia Sports Hall of Fame. In the coaching era of Bud Carson, Bill Fulcher, and Pepper Rodgers (1967–79), King was named Tech's No. 1 quarterback. He was picked as one of Tech's greatest athletes of the twentieth century. King's biggest disappointment? "In my three years of varsity football at Tech, we never beat the University of Georgia."

Whether the fifty-six-year-old King lives another moment or another fifty years, he'll be remembered not only as a great player but as one whose life was dedicated to serving others.

WILLIAM COLEMAN "BILL"HARTMAN

A Back of All Trades

William Coleman "Bill" Hartman, the eighty-six-year-old legendary Georgia Bulldog, was not only a jack-of-all-trades, he was a "back" of all trades: All-American football player, record-breaking punter, famed kicking coach, civic leader, multi-million dollar salesman, twice president of his university's alumni society, US Army intelligence officer in World War II. Name it and Hartman has done it, everything from jerking sodas to co-chairing the old Tech-Georgia Development Fund.

But if Harry Mehre, Hartman's football coach at UGA, were alive today, he would rave mostly about Hartman's versatility on the gridiron. In Mehre's old Notre Dame box formation, Hartman played all four positions—quarterback, tailback, wingback, and fullback. He also backed up the line on defense and, when needed, played sideback and safety. Talk about your Sinkwiches, Trippis, and Walkers—this man did everything but carry the water bucket.

Talk about a shining example to your children. Consider the words of his son, Bill III, the WSB-TV sportscaster:

> Whenever I think of my dad, I think of unselfishness, character, and integrity. He not only preached loyalty, charity, truthfulness and honesty, he practiced it. As a child in the early 1950s, I remember poor people—black

and white alike—coming to the door and asking for money. Dad didn't have much back then, but to my knowledge, he never turned anyone away.

Nor did I ever hear him use one word of profanity or raise his voice in anger. My dad was bigger than life. He knew everyone from the mayor to the janitor, and he gave them all the same warm greeting. In his eyes, all human beings were kin. That's his legacy for my two sisters and myself.

As important as football was in Hartman's life, service to his community and alma mater were equally important. He served as president of the Athens Jaycees, the Athens Chamber of Commerce and the Athens Community Chest. He served three years on the Athens City Council and one year as mayor pro tem. He served on the board of trustees of the University of Georgia Foundation. He was the perennial (nonpaid) chairman of the Georgia Student Educational Fund.

All this, mind you, while he was coaching football and maintaining one of the largest one-man life insurance practices in America. Marathon man? What else? There's been nothing to come along like Hartman, and it's unlikely anything will after him.

Today, Hartman lives with his wife of two years—former college classmate Mary Brazell Hartman—in a modest home on Lucy Lane in Athens. His first wife, also a college classmate, the former Ruth Landers, died five years ago. They were married for fifty years.

Before he retired seven years ago, Hartman had served fifteen years as a paid backfield coach for the late Wallace Butts and twenty years as a volunteer, non-paid kicking coach for Vince Dooley and Ray Goff. He refused to accept pay from either. During his fifteen years as backfield coach, he tutored three All-Americans—halfbacks Frank Sinkwich and Charley Trippi and quarterback Johnny Rauch. He also tutored halfbacks Joe Geri and Floyd "Breezy" Reid. Geri was an All-Southeastern Conference choice at Georgia, an All-Pro with the Pittsburgh Steelers and winner of the old Dapper Dan Award, given to the outstanding athlete in the city of Pittsburgh. Reid was an All-Pro with the Green Bay Packers.

As kicking coach, Hartman tutored All-Americans Allan Levitt, Rex Robinson, and Kevin Butler. Butler recently was elected to the College Football Hall of Fame (the first full-time kicker to be so honored) and was named Kicker of the Century by *Sports Illustrated* magazine.

"Hartman would have been a great head coach," says the legendary Trippi, who not only played for Hartman but also served with him on Coach Butts' staff. "He was admired and respected by his fellow coaches as well as his players, and I never knew any coach who was sounder in the fundamentals."

Hartman had offers from more than one college, but he turned them all down. He simply did not want to leave Athens, where his gridiron feats put him in the College Football Hall of Fame, the Georgia Sports Hall of Fame, *Sports Illustrated*'s Silver Anniversary All-American Team, and UGA's coveted Circle of Honor.

Although Athens has been his home for sixty-seven years, he was born in Thomaston and grew up in Madison. A natural leader who instilled confidence in teammates, Hartman was captain of his football team at Madison High School, Georgia Military College, and UGA. At Madison High, where he ran, passed, and punted his team to four championships in four years, Hartman attracted the attention of scouts from Tech, Georgia, and Auburn. But the head coach at Georgia Military College convinced him to play two seasons of football for his GMC Bulldogs. The coach was James Wallace Butts.

As a rookie in 1932, Hartman led Butts' GMC Bulldogs to an undefeated season and followed it up in 1933 by running and passing the 'Dogs to the Southern prep championship. Talk about a one-man show. Hartman scored all thirty-five points in a 35-0 rout of Gordon Military in the title game.

Once a Bulldog, always a Bulldog. Hartman opted to play college football at UGA, despite strong overtures from Auburn and Georgia Tech. The Georgia Bulldogs were not as successful as the GMC Bulldogs but Hartman was. Playing every backfield position for Coach Mehre, he was a standout.

In his sophomore season, against Furman University, he set up the first score by running the opening kickoff back eighty yards. Wrote Ralph McGill of the *Atlanta Constitution*, "Furman made the mistake of kicking to the bone-crushing Hartman. He returned the ball like a Spanish bull sighting a flag of red. He was traveling ninety miles per hour when he struck the Furmans and splattered them all over the landscape. The difference in the game was Hartman. He battered the Furman line into a state of dizziness."

Hartman was a legitimate 185-pounder, but his voracious appetite was fast pushing him toward the 200-pound mark. "I was getting so big I was afraid Coach Mehre was going to move me to the line, so I cut down to two meals a day," he recalls. "It worked. I got back to 185 pounds, and Coach Mehre never said a word." Weight loss or not, it was unlikely Mehre would ever have said a word. In his senior season in 1937, Hartman was voted team captain by his teammates and drew raves from all over the country.

At South Carolina, he set up the winning touchdown with a booming sixty-seven-yard punt that went out of bounds at the Gamecock five-yard line. Against Mercer, he led a Bulldog shutout victory by keeping the Bears bottled up all day with sixty-yard punts. Despite a 7-6 loss in Boston against Holy Cross, Hartman's running and punting kept the Bulldogs in the game. Wrote Edwin Camp of the *Atlanta Journal*, "When Hartman left the game in the final minute, the locals gave him the most tremendous applause I ever heard."

Hartman saved his best for last against Tulane, Auburn, Georgia Tech, and the Orange Bowl dedication game against the University of Miami. He played sixty minutes against each team, all but Miami heavily favored to win. Against Tulane, he boomed a forty-four-yarder that went out of bounds on Tulane's two-yard line. Tulane could not dig out of the hole and punted, and Georgia's Vassa Cate returned it for the winning touchdown. Any hopes of a Tulane rally were erased with two more coffin-corner punts by Hartman, one for seventy-four yards, the other a record-breaking eighty-two yards, which set a UGA standard that stood for thirty years.

In a scoreless tie with Auburn, the Tigers' much-heralded punt-returner, Billy Hitchcock, later a baseball manager for the Atlanta Braves, never had a chance. Hartman punted fourteen times, and the brilliant Hitchcock could get his hands on only two, which he returned for a total of ten yards.

Hartman's *piece de résistance* came against the much-hated Jackets. Georgia made only one first down in the first half. Hartman took the second-half kickoff at his seven-yard line, fumbled the ball, calmly picked it up as he was being surrounded by Tech players, bolted up the middle, and raced ninety-three yards for a game-tying touchdown. Hartman did not stop running until he passed through the goal posts and ran over a wire fence in the Grant Field end zone. Georgia made only one more first down, but Hartman's punting again foiled the opposition.

Finishing with a 5-3-2 record, the Bulldogs were invited to play the Miami Hurricanes in the Orange Bowl dedication game. It was a banner day for Hartman in more ways than one. While the rest of the team went to Miami on the train, Coach Mehre granted Hartman permission to fly down with his wife-to-be, Ruth Landers. She had been named Miss University of Georgia and was to participate in the opening Orange Bowl ceremonies. Hartman expressed his appreciation by running for one touchdown, passing for another and setting up a third with a punt to the Miami 1. The Bulldogs won, 26-0. After the game, Hartman wired his mother, "Delightful trip. Disregard all marriage rumors. Love, Bill."

"Hartman is one of the greatest players in America," said Mehre. "He was the perfect team captain. He was an inspiration to his teammates. He is the finest kicker I have ever seen, and he is just as good at blocking, tackling, running and passing."

After graduation with a business degree in 1938, Hartman married his sweetheart, then joined the NFL's Washington Redskins. In his first game, he threw a league-record seventy-five-yard touchdown pass. Filling in for the immortal Sammy Baugh, who was injured, Hartman completed 55 percent of his passes, once completing thirteen in a row against the old Brooklyn Dodgers.

Hartman was primed for a second season when fate stepped in. Joel Hunt, who had replaced Mehre as Bulldogs coach after the 1937 season, was fired after a single season. James Wallace Butts was named to replace him, the same Butts whose GMC team had won the Southern prep championship in 1933, thanks mainly to Hartman. Hartman was the first man Butts hired. "It was a wise move," recalls Bulldog historian Dan Magill. "No other assistant coach ever had more to do with the success of a Georgia football team than Coach Hartman."

With Hartman tutoring such backs as Sinkwich, Trippi, and Heyward Allen (captain of the 1941 team), the Bulldogs were nearly unbeatable. They went to the Orange Bowl, where they whipped Texas Christian University, 40-26 in 1942, and the Rose Bowl, where they blanked UCLA 9-0 in 1943.

After the Rose Bowl, Hartman joined the US Army and served four years. He was discharged as a lieutenant colonel. Returning to Athens as backfield coach in time for the 1946 season, he sharpened the passing and running games of Trippi, Rauch, and Geri in what was to be Georgia's first unbeaten season (11-0) and second SEC championship.

Hartman retired from coaching in 1956, but it was only temporary. Coach Dooley lured him back as voluntary kicking coach in 1974, and he stayed on for twenty years. Hartman even returned to the classroom so that he could qualify as a graduate assistant coach. He was seventy-seven years old.

He coached for the love of the game. He certainly did not need the money. From the time Hartman began selling life insurance out of his Athens office in 1946 until he retired fifty years later, he was one of the top salesmen in America. He was even president of his company's (National Life of Vermont) president's club.

The list of Hartman-trained kickers is almost endless. Besides Leavitt, Robinson, and Butler, he turned out Bucky Dilts, who made it with the Denver Broncos and Baltimore Colts, and Chip Andrews, who holds the UGA record for season punting average (45.4 yards in 1984). The names include Mike Garrett, Dax Langley, Scot Armstrong, Jim Broadway, and Cris Carpenter, besides Trippi, Rauch and Geri.

Although retired, Hartman's pace has slowed little. He still rises at 6:30 A.M., chairs the Georgia Student Educational Fund and serves as an emeritus member of the University of Georgia Foundation. He's in good health, swimming three times a week and walking daily in his neighborhood. But at 250 pounds, he would have difficulty getting into his old varsity uniform. Hartman makes no secret about it—he loves to eat.

Retired or not, he still has some surprises up his sleeve. Pound for pound, who was the finest player he ever coached or played with? No, not Walker, Sinkwich, or Trippi. It was Alex Ashford, an end on Coach Mehre's 1935 team. "He put a hit on me I've never forgotten. I felt like I was run over by a speeding train. He weighed 134 pounds."

Surprise No. 2: Of all the teams he coached, which was the best, the unbeaten 1946 and 1980 teams or the 1942 Rose Bowl team? "Neither," he says. "The 1941 team was the best. Sinkwich played most of the season with a broken jaw for which we had a special cast. We finished the year 9-1-1, then went up to New York and beat a great Columbia team led by All-American Paul Governali. That season we whipped a solid Auburn team and whitewashed Coach [Bill] Alexander's Tech team, 21-0."

Hartman has these words for new Georgia head coach Mark Richt: "You are not going to get the same type of player as you did at FSU. You are going to have to recruit a more intelligent athlete, one who not only can get in Georgia but can stay in."

Besides his son, Hartman has two daughters: Barbara Howell, fifty, an administrator with the Bulldog Club in the UGA athletic office, and Laura Ciucevich, fifty-five, a staff member in the UGA School of Social Studies.

Although right on most matters, the man is human. Some time ago we were standing in a New Orleans hotel lobby discussing who is the better football player, Charley Trippi or Frank Sinkwich. A distinguished-looking gentleman standing nearby approached us. He was immaculately dressed in a hand-tailored silk suit.

"I couldn't help but overhear," he told us. "I'm a longtime Bulldog fan myself, and I know about those players." He went on to introduce himself as the secretary of the New Orleans Racing Commission.

"I like the Bulldogs so much that I'm going to see that you take some extra money home with you," he said. "There's a horse in the fourth race at the Fairgrounds today that can't miss. It's going off at 10-1, so if you gentlemen give me $20 each, I'll see that you'll have $200 in your mailbox tonight." Since the horse couldn't miss, Bill and I readily gave the nice gentleman $20. As he departed, he said, "Look in your mail boxes tonight, and Go Dawgs!"

Imagine our excitement that afternoon when the *Times-Picayune* reported that our horse had indeed gone off at 10-1 and won, paying 200 smackeroos, just as our Bulldog friend had said. It was a wonderful day indeed.

Only one part of the story was not so wonderful: There was nothing in our mailboxes either that night or the next morning. We never saw the gentleman again or our $200.

SHEA AND O'MALLEY
Peas in a Pod

Once they left the University of Georgia, two National Collegiate Hall of Fame football players earned their highest marks—but on the hardwood, not the gridiron.

They were a pair of smiling Irishmen—Joseph Patrick O'Malley and Donald Patrick Shea. Both were All-Southeastern Conference and honorable mention All-American. After graduation, O'Malley won further honors as a basketball coach, as did Shea as a basketball referee and later judge of basketball officials in the SEC and NBA.

Famed Georgia coach Wally Butts called O'Malley, captain of the 1954 team, "one of the best defensive ends I have ever seen." Butts described Shea, alternate captain of the 1955 squad, as "one of the best interior linemen we have ever had."

Both were highly sought after by the pros—O'Malley by the Pittsburgh Steelers and Chicago Bears of the National Football League and the Dallas Texans of the old American Football League, and Shea by the Washington Redskins of the NFL. Each played one pro season, O'Malley with the Steelers and Shea with the Redskins. Injuries cut short both pro careers, although the Texans thought enough of O'Malley to offer him a contract after he had been out of football for two years.

Ever the cool one, never taking himself too seriously, O'Malley reported to Atlanta's Joe Brown High School in the spring of 1958 to be the assistant football coach. He couldn't wait to begin. That first season, he helped coach the team to a 7-3 record, a region championship and a berth in the Milk Bowl, the city's title game. At season's end, O'Malley had planned a two-week rest before sitting down with head coach Jack Peek to set goals for spring football practice.

Meanwhile, the basketball season was beginning to crank up. In Roy Rowlett, Brown boasted one of the top coaches in Georgia, high school or college. The Cage Master, as he was known, had guided Brown to a state Class AA championship in 1952 and had his team in state title contention every year since.

But before the opening tipoff of the 1958–59 season, Rowlett resigned to enter chiropractic school. The man picked to fill his giant-sized shoes was an assistant football coach, Joseph Patrick O'Malley. In typical O'Malley fashion, he was unfazed about succeeding a legend in prep basketball circles. "Hey," he said, "in the great scheme of things, this is no big deal. I played on my high school basketball team [he was twice All-County], and I know how to coach. We'll get the job done."

Get the job done? Not even the most cockeyed optimist could have foreseen what the former football star would produce. In his first season, O'Malley won a state championship in the highest classification in Georgia—AAA. In the finals, Brown whipped LaGrange High, the pre-tournament favorite, by ten points. LaGrange was led by two future All-ACC selections, Randy and Donnie Mahaffey. The Grangers had averaged forty-eight points but were held to a mere twenty-five.

O'Malley was chosen state Class AAA Coach of The Year and head coach of the North Georgia All-Stars in their annual summer classic against the South Georgia All-Stars.

O'Malley's teams followed up the state championship with two region titles. In seven seasons, his squads won 163 games and lost only thirty-nine. His teams won two city championships and qualified for the state tournament six out of seven years. When head football coach Peek resigned in 1965, Brown High again turned to O'Malley. Although his teams won no championships, they posted a 35-16-2 mark over five seasons.

In 1970, O'Malley resigned and joined his former Georgia Bulldog teammate Bill Young, who owned General Wholesale Company, an alcoholic beverage distributing company. He spent twenty-four years with General Wholesale, first as a salesman and then as a sales supervisor. He retired in 1994.

Today, at age sixty-nine, O'Malley is about twenty pounds beyond his 215-pound playing weight for the Bulldogs and Steelers. He lives with his wife of forty-one years, the former Joyce Ervin, in a four-bedroom home in Conyers, in the Atlanta suburbs. Joyce is a one-time Teacher of the Year at Heritage High School. It's a simple life. O'Malley rises at 8 A.M., has a light breakfast, takes a two-mile walk, and lifts weights. He likes to read, visit his three children—Karen Laplatney, Joseph II, and Mike—and play with his four grandchildren. Mike is the head pro at Athens Country Club.

Life wasn't always simple for O'Malley. He grew up in Scranton, Pennsylvania, in the coal mining region, one of seven children who worked every honest job he could find to help his parents put food on the table. He shined shoes, delivered papers, cut grass, and was a busboy at the Scranton Hotel.

In high school, he turned to athletics. As a freshman, he made varsity in football, basketball, and track. As a sophomore, he was a starter in football (end) and basketball (center), and as a junior and senior he was All-County in both sports. The *Scranton Tribune* called him the "greatest athlete ever to come out of Scranton Tech High School." He's a member of the *Scranton Tribune* Sports Hall of Fame.

O'Malley captained the football and basketball teams and was the leading scorer and rebounder in the county. He set the single-game county scoring record with forty-five points, and led the basketball team to the county championship. The *Scranton Daily Times* called him "not only a great athlete but a scholar and a gentleman." Twice he was selected to the county All-Scholastic team.

O'Malley was the most highly publicized athlete in the region since Charley Trippi, the UGA football great who played a decade before him. Duquesne and Seton Hall, two Eastern powerhouses, aggressively recruited O'Malley for basketball. Georgia, Miami, and Maryland wanted him for football. It was 1950 and Maryland was at the top of its game.

Georgia had a roster packed with Ohioans and Pennsylvanians. A man with a fighting heart, O'Malley had heard about Georgia's "smash-mouth football" and wanted to be in the middle of it. Not long after O'Malley reported in 1951, Bulldog end coach Perron Shoemaker called him "the most rugged football player I ever coached."

As a sophomore, in a 21-16 victory over Tulane, *Atlanta Constitution* sports editor Furman Bisher wrote, "O'Malley put on the finest defensive performance the Sugar Bowl Stadium has ever seen." O'Malley wrecked Tulane's split-T options and set up the winning touchdown by intercepting a pass and returning it forty-six yards. After the scoreless 1954 Georgia-Alabama game, *Atlanta Journal* sports editor Ed Danforth wrote, "O'Malley was flawless. Every time Alabama tried to run his flank, he murdered them." Although the Georgia team had a 6-3-1 season the year O'Malley was captain (1954), it lost a heroic effort against heavily favored Georgia Tech, 7-3. "Tech won mainly because it stayed away from O'Malley," said Butts afterward. "We lost the game, but in O'Malley we had the finest player on the field."

SEC coaches named O'Malley the top defensive end in the conference in 1954. He was chosen to play in the North-South and Blue-Gray All-Star games. As good as O'Malley was, he was no better than his friend and teammate, Donald Patrick Shea. Like O'Malley, Shea came out of Pennsylvania, was All-everything on the prep football circuit, and was highly recruited by most colleges on the Eastern Seaboard.

Shea had a love affair with the US Naval Academy. He had twice been Navy's guest at the annual Army-Navy game, and he had the leadership qualities and brainpower to gain entrance. After one season at Annapolis, though, he discovered Navy life was not for him. He was a hero on Saturday afternoons, but the only person he outranked the other six days was the Navy Goat.

Notre Dame had courted Shea since his sophomore season at Saint James High School, where he was the rage of the Metropolitan Philadelphia Catholic prep league. When legendary Irish coach Frank Leahy learned Shea was not going to return to the Naval Academy, he paid a personal call on the Sheas at their Collingsdale, Pennsylvania, home. The only problem was that Notre Dame had a rule forbidding transfers from four-year colleges. As powerful as Leahy was—his teams were perennial national championship contenders—he was unable to get the university president to waive the rule. So Leahy, an old friend of Butts, telephoned the Georgia coach and said, "The best guard I have ever seen is available."

Butts dispatched Harry Wright, his top recruiter and a former Notre Dame guard, to the Shea household. Wright did such a sales job that when he flew back to Athens, Shea was with him. At Georgia, the 230-pound Shea more than justified Leahy's recommendation. He became one of the school's all-time great interior lineman and today is in the UGA Football Hall of Fame.

Like O'Malley, Shea played in Dixie's post-season All-Star games and was named to Collier's "Unsung All-American" team. But Shea says his greatest feat at Georgia was not playing football but meeting and marrying his campus sweetheart and now wife of forty-five years, the former Joyce Lathem. They live in Atlanta, just east of Roswell Road. Don and Joyce have one child, Donna, age thirty-two, and one grandson, Charlie, age two, a budding UGA guard.

After one season with the NFL's Washington Redskins, Shea turned to coaching, both basketball and football at Newton County High School in Covington for two years, and then at Atlanta's Marist School as head football coach for twelve years. It was a whirlwind pace at Marist. When not coaching football, Shea was officiating high school basketball—in the Metro Atlanta area during the regular season and everywhere from Atlanta to Tybee Light once the playoffs started.

The pace quickened when he left Marist to join Nationwide Paper Company. Shea sold paper by day and officiated at night, first for the small colleges, then the SEC, where he refereed for twenty-seven years. Some weeks he officiated six nights a week, calling games at every college in the conference except Georgia. (Officials cannot referee their alma mater's games.) He accumulated enough frequent-flier points to fly around the world.

The only thing that slowed Shea was a heart attack and five-artery bypass surgery in 1994. His nights of running up and down basketball courts were finished, but his contributions to the game were not. SEC coaches had consistently ranked Shea among the top three officials in the league, so it was fitting that SEC basketball commissioner John Guthrie named Shea to be the chief judge of conference officials. It was Shea who proposed that the conference use three game officials, not two, and his proposal was unanimously adopted by the coaches. The three-referee system became so popular that it was adopted by colleges and high schools across the country.

The National Basketball Association got wind of Shea's supervisory success and hired him to do the same job.

At age seventy, this marathon man, who's five pounds under his playing weight, sees 100 games a year between the SEC and NBA. He is retired from his day job at Nationwide Paper, where he worked for twenty-seven years, ranking No. 1 in sales more years than not. Where does his energy come from? "Whatever I've accomplished, I credit Coach Butts," says Shea. "He taught me discipline. He taught me never to give up."

Despite his love for Butts, the record shows Shea had the drive and determination long before he played for Georgia. How else do you explain that he flourished in a home of thirteen children and gutted it out as a fourteen-year-old freshman varsity football player at Saint James High School, where he started as an offensive guard and middle linebacker and was selected to the All-County and Greater Philadelphia All-Catholic teams four consecutive years?

Shea and O'Malley. Two peas in a pod.

ACKERMAN EXTENDS
A HELPING HAND

Never mind that Oliver Perry "Sonny" Ackerman won three American and three Canadian National Senior Amputee Golf Championships. Never mind that his Atlanta Athletic Club Hall of Fame plaque hangs alongside those of Bobby Jones, Charlie Yates, and Alexis Sterling. What matters most is the care and concern this native Atlantan shows for his fellow human beings.

Why else would he give up a successful real estate business to help the physically challenged get back on the golf course? Why else would he work so diligently with single-, double-, and triple-amputees; the wheelchair-bound; and the victims of stroke, multiple sclerosis, brain tumor, and heart attack? Maybe Ackerman will not produce the likes of Tiger Woods, but he gives the greatest gift of all—hope—to those whose dreams have been shattered.

No Ackerman student is too young and none too old. Sonny has taught a four-year-old girl who could barely maintain her balance. She has one leg and can hit a golf ball twenty-five yards. Then there's the ninety-three-year-old nursing home resident in Alexandria, Louisiana. Her memory is failing, but she knows where the cup is once she gets on the green.

One of Ackerman's pupils was Jimmy Southard, former star quarterback at Decatur High School who went on to play for Georgia Tech in 1947–49 and is now in the Georgia Tech Sports Hall of Fame. Two years ago, Southard suffered a stroke to both sides of the brain. He had been a pretty fair country club golfer, but the future outlook for golf looked bleak—that is, until Southard's wife, Bettylou, noticed a poster at the Emory Rehabilitation Clinic promoting Sonny Ackerman's "Adaptive Golf."

Four months into Ackerman's program, Southard was driving balls 200 yards down the driving range. Last April, less than two years after his stroke, he was playing in a foursome in a club tournament—driving, chipping, and putting for eighteen holes. Southard's foursome won.

"Without Sonny's constant encouragement, without him adjusting my positions, I never could have made nine holes, much less eighteen," says Southard.

Ackerman, whose base is the River Pines Golf Club in Alpharetta, conducts his Adaptive Golf clinics all over the United States. What is Adaptive Golf anyway? Besides tutoring the physically challenged in how to hold and swing a golf club, the program teaches that instructional art to clinical therapists. Therapists learn how to hit a golf ball standing on one leg, with one arm, and sitting in a wheelchair. Patients aren't charged, and club owners like Roger Miers of River Pines not only waive greens fees but provide golf balls and use of club facilities. Financial support from the J. E. Hanger Company of Atlanta, which makes artificial limbs, and from such participating hospitals as Emory University Hospital help offset the cost of the clinics. Participating nurse practitioners and therapists earn continuing education credits.

Ackerman's Adaptive Golf workshops have shown the medical community that when it comes to playing golf, being confined to a wheelchair or losing the use of an arm or a leg is nothing more than a sand trap or a bad lie. It's an obstacle that can be overcome. "The program gives everyone hope, a new outlook on life," says Ackerman. "The challenged find they can do something anyone can do. Even pupils bound to a wheelchair find a way to hit the golf ball straight down the fairway."

Who is Ackerman? Who is this man who not only founded the program but helped golf club manufacturer Mizuno produce longer clubs with special grips for the physically challenged, as well as modify golf carts so that they can be driven on greens without damaging them?

I first met Ackerman in 1949, so long ago that Avondale High School was playing six-man, not eleven-man, football. I was covering prep football for the *Atlanta Constitution*, and Ackerman was one of the finest—if not the finest—passer in Metro Atlanta. He was so quick at getting the ball away and on target (he completed 70 percent of his passes) that he was offered several scholarships to play eleven-man college football. He chose Mississippi State but played only one year. Homesick, he returned to Atlanta.

The next time I saw him, Ackerman was at the U.S. Marine Corps Recruit Depot at Parris Island, South Carolina, assigned to my company. At 6'1" and 180 pounds, he looked like the poster Marine—crew-cut, trim, and completely squared away. Out of 225 recruits, he might have been the best, but the Parris Island football coach pulled him from my ranks to quarterback the base's football team. My loss was the team's gain. Ackerman led our Marines to a winning season, and in intraservice competition, he outshone the likes of All-Americans Bill Wade and John Mazur.

When his two-year Marine Corps tour ended in 1955, he returned to Atlanta, selling real estate by day and attending Georgia State University at night. Faster than he could throw a football, he turned the Royal-Ackerman Company into one of the hottest real estate firms in DeKalb County. He made the Million Dollar Club and earned his college degree. The good times rolled for thirty years—booming business, big home, and membership in a country club. Then Ackerman's world turned in 1984 when a severe ice storm hit Atlanta. A tree, resembling the leaning tower of Pisa, hung perilously close to his home. Taking a six-foot stepladder, Ackerman started to cut off the limbs. But when he reached the top of the ladder, he slipped and fell, suffering a compound fracture of his left leg.

Over the next five years, Ackerman underwent twenty-four operations. He developed a staph infection. He went to the Mayo Clinic, where doctors told him they would have to amputate. "I was scared to death," Ackerman recalls. "I loved golf from the time I first picked up a club, and I asked myself how I was going to play with one leg. I thought my whole world was coming to an end."

In many ways, though, life was just beginning. Ackerman was fitted with an artificial leg and was soon back on the golf course. He attacked the game with the same maniacal passion that he had showed in football. He spent long hours on the driving range and putting green. He studied films of golf greats and worked out in the gym to increase his strength and stamina. By 1994, he was five strokes better than he had been before his surgery. He became a prominent fixture on the amputee golf tournament circuit, winning eleven tournament championships.

Ackerman credits his comeback to the encouragement he received from his wife and high school sweetheart, the former Jane Powell; his two children, LuAnn Budd and Dusty Ackerman; and his longtime golfing friends, Tom Faulkner and Joe Rogers. "I was hospitalized for five months, and Rogers never missed a day visiting or telephoning me," he says.

It's not so much what Ackerman has accomplished as a player but what he has given to others. He has conducted clinics for Atlanta's Scottish Rite Children's Healthcare Center, the Georgia Nurses Association, Shepherd Spinal Clinic, and the Arthritis Foundation. He has taught more than 12,000 physically challenged people and over 4,000 rehabilitation therapists. Students have included the likes of Mike Reeder of Forsyth County, who lost both legs above the knee, and Cleve McLary of Pauleys Island, South Carolina, who is missing an arm and an eye.

"Maybe 50 percent of my students will never play a round of golf," says Ackerman. "But at least they are out doing something and regaining their strength and balance. Golf teaches hand-eye coordination as well as balance. It not only builds strength in your arms and legs, but equally important, it gets you out in the fresh air."

On the fourth Thursday of each month, about forty patients join Ackerman for a clinic at River Pines, as they have for the past eight years. Says host Roger

Miers, "We have physically challenged people who come from all over the state. At each clinic, we have to make people take time out to rest. They just don't want to stop hitting golf balls."

Oliver Perry "Sonny" Ackerman was born on June 15, 1932, in Preston, Georgia, about nine miles from Plains. His down-the-road neighbor was a fourth cousin named Jimmy Carter. "If I had known he was going to become president," says Ackerman, "I would have spent more time in Plains."

When he was nine years old, the Ackerman family moved to Decatur, and Sonny began playing football, basketball, and baseball at Winnona Elementary School. At Avondale High, he was good enough to earn All-State honors in all three sports. Summers were spent in the construction business. One employer, B. H. Cherry, gave him this advice: "If you want to succeed, you have to learn how to play golf. Most business is conducted on the golf course, not in a prospect's office."

"Thank goodness for Mr. Cherry," says Ackerman.

When Ackerman left for the Marines in 1953, DeKalb County was a mere dot on the Metro Atlanta map. When he returned two years later, he found the beginnings of sprawl. His old high school had gone from six-man to eleven-man football and had jumped from Class B to Class AA in size. New residential areas were opening in Tucker and southwest DeKalb. It was about that time that Ackerman met Jack Royal, and Royal-Ackerman would soon become a household name in DeKalb County.

Today, the sixty-nine-year-old Ackerman and Jane live in a four-bedroom home in Rivermore Park in Suwanee. He also has a home on Lake Burton. Ackerman rises at 6 A.M., eats a light breakfast, and then goes to the Atlanta Athletic Club, where he works out on Nautilus machines. After that, he hits balls for an hour on the driving range. Then it's off to River Pines or to Louisville, Dallas, or most any city in the US to conduct his golf clinics, which are endorsed by the Professional Golfers Association.

It's been a memorable life. Five months after he was fitted for his new leg, he danced with Barbara Mandrell at Chastain Park. He has driven the pace car at the Daytona 500. He has played golf with Patricia Neal, the former movie star who herself was a stroke victim, and the late Harold "Pee Wee" Reese, a member of baseball's Hall of Fame. Nothing, though, compares to the thrill he gets when he sees a physically challenged pupil hit a ball as well as a healthy golfer.

Sonny Ackerman may be remembered by some as a national amputee golf champion. To his pupils, he'll always be the man who extended a helping hand to those in need.

THE DURHAMS
Sportscasting Family

It is not easy being the son of a living legend. If you doubt that, just ask Wes Durham, Georgia Tech's Director of Sports Broadcasting and the school's football and basketball voice. Wes is the son of Woody Lombardi Durham, himself voice of the University of North Carolina Tar Heels for the past thirty-one years. Before Wes was born, Woody had been recognized by the National Sportscasters and Sportswriters Association as the North Carolina Sportscaster of the Year, an honor he has earned nine times more.

"He has been my hero, my tutor, my inspiration," Wes said, "but it was awfully tough growing up in North Carolina and being known as Woody Durham's son, not Wes Durham. No matter where we went in the state—to the beach, a dinner meeting, a restaurant, a movie, a ball game. It was always, 'There goes Woody Durham and his son—or his sons.'" (Wes has a younger brother, Taylor, also in broadcasting.) "Not having my own identity was the toughest obstacle I had to overcome," Wes said. "On the other hand, being Woody Durham's son opened doors."

Wes has his own identity now. He is in his seventh season of doing Georgia Tech football and basketball, and last year he was named Georgia Sportscaster of the Year. At age thirty-five, he is riding a rocket. He is employed by Georgia Tech, the first Atlantic Coast Conference broadcaster to be employed by a college rather than a radio station. He has broadcast 403 games at Georgia Tech and 207 before he got to Tech—at Vanderbilt and Marshall. Wes' career is remarkable for the fact that he reached Division I-A level announcing while he was still in his twenties.

Ironically, Georgia Tech Athletic Director Emeritus Homer Rice hired both Wes and his dad. Rice was AD at UNC when Woody was selected as voice of the Tar Heels in 1970 and was AD at Georgia Tech when he named Wes to succeed the late Al Ciraldo as the voice of the Yellow Jackets in 1994.

"The first time I got to do a game with dad," Wes said, "was October 14, 1995, a date I never will forget. Dad was in the next booth to me. I was having an anxiety attack from the moment I got to the press box. I mean it was nerve racking. Even though I knew he was going to be busy on the Tar Heel Network, I kept thinking 'Daddy is watching me and listening to what I am saying.' It was like a challenger going up against the champion in a boxing ring. You are plenty nervous until the first blow is landed. Once the game started I was fine."

Says Woody, "All I remember is how proud I was of my son being in the next broadcasting booth. I knew he was going to do a great job. And I do remember we lost the game, 27-25. That year was a series sweep for Wes. His Jackets not only won the football game but they beat us twice in basketball as well. You cannot imagine the pride I felt that first year, not only in what Wes was doing but in the fact I was the guy he came to for advice on how to position himself and how to prepare for the games. To know that the way I taught him, based on the way I was doing it…seeing him get great results tells me that I am doing it the right way. It was something special."

Asked how he benefited from his father's tutoring, Wes answered:

> Preparation. Woody prepares for a game better than anyone I know. Preparation is his trademark. I learned from him to allot at least twenty hours before the game, studying what defenses and offenses the opposition might use, the names and numbers of the players on the first two opposing squads, the height and weight statistics, the average yards per carry of the leading enemy ball carriers, the pass completion percentage and number of touchdown passes thrown by the top two opposing quarterbacks, the average yards per punt of the opposing kicker, the home town of each player, whether a player had a daddy or brother playing at one time. What I learned from Woody was preparation, preparation, and more preparation.
>
> When Woody comes to town for the Carolina-Tech game or I go to Chapel Hill, I always search his coat pockets as he does mine. I find a copy of Tech's two-deep lineup and team specialists in his pocket and he finds a copy of Carolina's in mine.

Says Woody Durham of his son, "He is awfully good because he has worked hard and has refused to rest on his laurels. He knows he has to get better with each game. I may have been around longer than Wes, but in Atlanta my only identity is being Wes Durham's dad."

Woody Durham was born August 8, 1941, in Mebane, North Carolina, in the Piedmont section of the state, halfway between Durham and Burlington and about twenty miles from Chapel Hill, home of Carolina Blue. His dad worked in a textile mill in Albemarle, where he moved the family when Woody started school. His dad was a Carolina football fan and took Woody to all the home games. Before he got out of elementary school, Woody was wearing a Carolina blue football jersey with a big number 22 on the back. That was the number worn by the legendary Charlie "Choo Choo" Justice, who led the Tar Heels to the Sugar Bowl in 1946, and later became a member of the National Collegiate Football Hall of Fame.

He was still in elementary school when he decided to be a sports broadcaster. He began by making believe he was Justice, Art Weiner, Hosea Rodgers, or one of the other UNC greats of the 1940s, and announced to himself every move they made as he played sandlot football games.

When Woody was fifteen, Carolina's basketball team went 32-0 and won triple overtime games in the semifinals and finals of the NCAA championship tournament. Woody announced the action in his own basketball games, recalling what each player did as he dribbled, feinted, picked, and blocked every shot of the game. "Today," Woody says, "I am a close friend of Justice and a close friend of everyone on that 1957 basketball team."

Durham got his first radio job before his sixteenth birthday. The manager of an Albemarle radio station judged an oratorical contest in which Woody competed. He won the contest and a job announcing on the weekends. He was on his way. After his high school graduation he enrolled at the University of North Carolina and became director of WUNC-TV, the college's own TV Station. After graduation and stops at WBTW-VTV in Florence , South Carolina, and WPF-TV in Raleigh, North Carolina, his alma mater called and offered him the play-by-play job. It was a dream come true.

"When I go on the air, for football or basketball, the best way to describe what I do is 'partial objectivity.' I am partial but I am objective about what I say because if the team is not playing well or is playing well, it is my job to say so. I give a Carolina perspective on the game but if we stink it is my duty to say so."

Wes grew up in Greensboro and Cary, a suburb of Raleigh. When he decided on a broadcasting career, he started the same way his father did—in the land of make-believe. He would stand on the pitcher's mound announcing Sandy Koufax winding up and firing a ninety-eight-mile-per-hour fastball. In high school he played football, basketball, and baseball but he knew he wanted ultimately to broadcast games, not play them. At age fourteen, he became a "go-fer" for his dad's broadcast crew at Carolina football and basketball games.

"There was a night when the crew had no one to cover the visiting dressing room," he said. "Someone handed me a tape recorder and sent me down to interview the coach. It was Bobby Cremins in his first season at Georgia Tech. Boy, what a thrill for me. I asked him three questions and from then on I was hooked," Wes said.

Unlike his dad, Wes had no interest in attending UNC; he attended Elon College in North Carolina. "I became the color commentator on Elon's football and basketball games and eventually became the play-by-play man. By the time I graduated I had worked 150 football and basketball games. One summer I

2001

interned at Capitol Broadcasting in Raleigh and learned the sales end of the business. I learned nothing happens unless you sell something. And you cannot have a radio program without a sponsor," Wes said.

When he graduated from Elon, he went to work as basketball play-by-play announcer at Radford College in Virginia, where he met his wife Lynn, who was working on the school's public relations staff. Then it was two seasons at Marshall and three at Vanderbilt before Homer Rice picked him to replace the retiring Al Ciraldo.

Wes works seventy to eighty hours a week during football season, spending his time in the press box or his Tech office and emceeing charitable or civic functions. He is on the Board of Directors of the Children's Healthcare Hospital and the Lymphoma and Leukemia Society.

What advice does he have for those who aspire to be sports announcers? "Listen to Larry Munson of Georgia, Jim Phillips of Clemson, and John Ward of Tennessee. And especially listen to my dad."

For a combined total of forty-eight years, the Durhams have painted pictures over the airwaves in ways that have made the games as exciting for the listener as for the fans in the stands. At sixty, Woody is only five years from "normal" retirement age. Wes is in the second year of a two-year contract. The obvious question: Will Wes ever succeed his father at UNC and become the second-generation "Voice of the Tar Heels"?

Says Woody, "I am blessed with good health. I certainly would not want to retire before age sixty-five. On the other hand, I don't want the audience telling me it is time to quit. As far as a second generation of Durhams on the Carolina network, that would be up to Wes and UNC."

Wes says, "I am happy at Georgia Tech. Everyone here has made me feel like family. For me to go anywhere else, well, it would have to be an incredible opportunity. Of course, following my dad at the microphone would be an emotional experience and a signal honor."

There's no getting around the fact that the Durhams look alike and sound alike. They like to tell the story of a former N.C. State basketball coach who was listening to one of Woody's Carolina game broadcasts while he was driving in South Carolina. As he crossed the state line, static interfered with his radio reception, and he began turning the dials. He thought he had found another station on the UNC network and drove several more miles before it dawned on him that what he was hearing was not Woody Durham but Wes Durham broadcasting a play-by-play of a Tech game.

Like father, like son.

THE MOOSE IS LOOSE

If you think Ronald Reagan portraying Notre Dame immortal George Gipp in the movie classic "Knute Rockne, All-American" was something, then you never saw a video of Atlanta's Frank "Moose" Miller's run in the 1948 Cornell-Harvard game.

Twisting, turning, reversing his field three times, he shook off or eluded fifteen would-be tacklers (some opponents had two shots at him) who had a hand on him but could not bring him down. After the game, Jerry Nason of the Boston Globe wrote, "You had to see it to believe it. Miller zigzagged back and forth across the field, squirming out of the clutches of anyone who had a grip on him. It was the run of the century. He only got credit for 37 yards but he ran at least 137."

Moose Miller gave up a promising football career at Georgia Tech to attend Cornell, avoided a soft Army life to jump out of airplanes with the 82nd Airborne, and left a secure job as an insurance salesman to chart new waters selling life insurance and mutual funds. In business, Miller, now seventy-one, was a generation ahead of his time. When he left Home Life of New York in 1963, the life insurance industry was strongly opposed to any of its agents selling equity products. Today almost every life company in the industry requires dual-selling. Moose Miller, John Keeble, and David Vaughan put Financial Service Corporation on the map.

Miller was a trailblazer in the football business as well as in the financial services industry. A native of Decatur, he rewrote all the scoring records at Decatur

2001

High School and in the North Georgia Interscholastic Conference (NGIC). He was the first Georgian to head east to play his collegiate football. In the East, he darn near *was* college football.

Of the 1948 Cornell-Columbia game, Jack Hand, sports editor of the Associated Press, wrote, "On a 37-yard touchdown run that clinched Cornell's victory, Miller was trapped three times but he changed direction twice and then bulled his way into the end zone carrying three Columbia defenders with him." Miller did this as a sophomore, averaging seven yards per carry, leading Cornell to its first of two consecutive Ivy League championships.

The Big Red, as Cornell was known, won eight of nine games, thrashing national power Penn and losing only to nationally ranked Army. In the Ivy League title game with Dartmouth, Miller averaged twelve yards per carry and scored two touchdowns, leading his team to a 27-26 victory. Jesse Abramson of The New York Herald-Tribune wrote, "Miller didn't lead the Cornell team, he was the Cornell team."

Miller was not only the rage of Ivy League football, he was the rage of the East. As a much-heralded junior, "Mr. Cornell" put the finishing touches on a second Ivy League crown by bolting twenty-five yards late in the final quarter and sending Princeton down to a 14-12 defeat.

Miller was plagued with knee and ankle injuries his senior season and saw little action, but his backfield coach, Lou Conti, told me, "If Moose had stayed healthy, he would have been a bona fide Heisman candidate. I'm not saying he would have won it but I will tell you this: In thirty years of coaching football, I never saw a more gifted runner. He had it all—balance, maneuverability, power, and speed to burn."

Who is this Moose Miller, the greatest halfback ever to come out of Decatur High School and one of the greatest ever produced in the state of Georgia? He grew up on the Decatur sandlots, an only child whose parents divorced when he was five. While his mother worked as a secretary, he played football, basketball, and baseball at Ponce de Leon Elementary School. He ran everywhere—to school, on the schoolyard, and back to his home. By the time he got to Decatur High, he was the fastest man in town—and, boy, could he play football. As a freshman he was a starting halfback. As a sophomore, junior, and senior he led the entire North Georgia Intercollegiate Conference in scoring. He scored 120 points as a junior and 129 as a senior. These were the days of the eight-game schedule. That means he averaged better than fifteen points per game. Five times he had touchdown runs of more than sixty yards. Once he caught a punt on his goal line and returned it 100 yards. Said his coach, Lew Woodruff, "He was unstoppable. I used to have to take him out of the games just to hold the score down."

Miller did not save his best for the most important games, he gave his best in every game. But it just so happened that when the big chips were on the table, Miller collected them. For instance, in the state high school All-Star game, he led the North to a two-touchdown victory. He had touchdown runs of sixty-five and twenty-five yards and averaged an incredible twelve yards per carry. It's like making a first down every time you touch the ball. Of his sixty-yard touchdown gallop, John Bradberry, then sports editor of the *Atlanta Constitution*, wrote, "He could have run to Five Points [downtown Atlanta] because there was no one on the field who could catch him."

When it was time to decide on college, Miller had his pick—anywhere. Although he had been sought after by colleges all over the country, he was only interested in two—Cornell and Georgia Tech. From the start, he preferred Cornell but because his dad went to Tech and his Decatur High quarterback Jimmy Southard was going to Tech, Miller signed a grant-in-aid with Tech. It was not a match made in heaven. At the end of his freshman season, he told Coach Dodd he was leaving school. He did not like engineering. He wanted to study Business Administration and he wanted to do it at Cornell.

When Miller looks back at his decision to leave Tech, he says, "I have no regrets. Four years at an engineering school for me would have been a waste. I made a big mistake signing with Tech and I wanted to correct it as quickly as possible. I thought the best way to do that was to tell Coach Dodd and just go."

Today Miller lives in Sandy Springs with his wife Jerrie, who was his elementary school sweetheart. They have two children and a granddaughter. Moose looks twenty years younger than his age. At 5'10", he weighs 165 pounds—the same as he did when he played for Cornell. He is a voracious reader who is in the office by ten each morning, running his one-person financial planning company called Planning Concepts of Georgia. Don't let the name fool you—he has clients all over the globe.

Just as it took a great deal of courage to quit Tech, it took an equal amount to walk out of the Atlanta Jim Dudley agency of the Home Life Insurance Company of New York in 1963. Miller was at the top of his game, having become a qualifying and Life member of the insurance industry's Million Dollar Round Table. However, he wanted to offer his clients investments as well as insurance, which he has done most successfully for the past thirty-eight years.

Miller says his mother and Jimmy Southard have been the biggest influences of his life. "My mother not only worked but she took in a boarder so that I could stay out for all the sports. Southard, at an early age, talked to me about honesty, loyalty, dedication, and service to others. He gave me a value system, one which he lived. He was the big brother I never had."

The Moose has no retirement plans. The Moose is loose.

Miller has been one of my heroes, not because he was a football star but because he was a risk taker and because he always had a warm, friendly greeting for the man who ran the corner grocery store as well as the mayor. He made no distinctions. The day I decided to enter the life insurance business was the day I discovered Moose Miller and Jack Jordan, a guard on my favorite Tech football team, were in the business.

One final note: Because of the terrorist attack on America, this has been a difficult article for me to write. I take solace in the display of patriotism I see everywhere. In my sixty-seven years of attending High Holy Days services at The Temple on Peachtree Street, for the first time I hear not only hymns, but an overflowing congregation standing and singing "God Bless America." I see Sen. Max Cleland being wheeled to the front of the pulpit, where he delivered a stirring, patriotic speech and received a standing ovation that must have lasted as long as his five-minute address.

As it says in the Good Book, good comes out of evil. I see American flags on shirts and blouses and red, white, and blue ribbons worn by men and women alike. I see people no longer taking our freedom for granted but treasuring it as a precious gift.

And now it is Saturday. I turn on the television to watch the Michigan State-Notre Dame football game and 80,000 spectators are waving 80,000 flags. The Fighting Irish may not be back, but patriotism is.

MARIST'S DRIVING FORCE

Talk about irony. When Marist School was located in downtown Atlanta on Ivy Street, it was known as Marist College. It had one classroom building, no gymnasium, no baseball diamond, no track, and no football stadium. It did have a football practice field but it was covered with rocks, pebbles, and assorted other obstacles.

Except for the basketball team, which used the neighboring Sacred Heart Gymnasium, there was no such thing as a sports "home and home" series. The Ivy Street Cadets played all their games "away," at such places as Ponce de Leon Park (home of the old Atlanta Crackers), Griffin, Rossville, and Kingsport, Tennessee.

A college? The Marist campus would have compared favorably to very few high schools in Georgia. I know because back in the 1950s, I covered so many Marist athletic events the guys on the Atlanta Constitution sports desk used to call me "Father O'Asher." That was okay with me even though the only confirmation I ever had was at the reform Jewish synagogue called The Temple.

Today Marist School, now located on a sprawling fifty-seven-acre campus on Ashford-Dunwoody Road, looks more like a college than a high school. There are three classroom buildings, a library, theater, science and computer centers, and athletic facilities that rival many of the finest colleges in Georgia. The football and baseball stadiums are both lighted. The swimming pool is Olympic size. There is a new track, plus three gymnasiums and individual athletic offices for

2001

both boys' and girls' varsity coaches, a weight room, training room, and a fulltime athletic trainer.

The school has a long history of athletic success, having won state championships in football, baseball, basketball, boxing, wrestling, golf, tennis, track, swimming, girls' soccer, cross country, and volleyball.

The new facility was the result of a concerted effort by Marist alumni, but make no mistake about it, the leader of the drive and the one who made sure every brick was in place, was Father James Leo Hartnett, S.M., who retired as Marist President this past June. He retired on the heels of one of his most successful projects, a $25,000,000 alumni fundraising drive.

In his forty-six-year Marist career, Father Hartnett served at every post— teacher, treasurer, principal, president, and fundraiser deluxe. For ten years he taught world history, English, and Latin to eighth and ninth graders and economics and religion to twelfth graders. He organized the alumni association. He has officiated at weddings and funerals. He has baptized children. He has served as a pastoral counselor. He has literally done it all—everything but conduct bar mitzvahs, and he could probably do that. According to Marist historian Richard J. Reynolds III, one of Marist's most distinguished graduates, he was the first president to hire Jewish faculty members, Sergio and Stefanie Stradler. Sergio's girls' volleyball and soccer teams have been perennial state champions.

When Father Hartnett was principal, he made some tough decisions, among them eliminating mandatory ROTC and accepting female students. Marist had long been recognized for its military program and took great pride in its military honors day, but in 1974 Father Hartnett made the ROTC program optional and five years later, when it could no longer keep up the required number of students in the program, ROTC was off the campus. Since its inception in 1901, Marist had been an all-male school. In 1976, under Father Hartnett's guidance, Marist became co-educational.

"Although there were a few grads against co-ed, the majority of our students and alumni were in favor of it. If we were going to continue to grow and become a school for all children, we needed to act," Father Hartnett said. Once the change was made, enrollment soared—from just under 700 to more than 1,000.

Father Hartnett believes strongly that Marist should be a school for children of all faiths. Although 74 percent of the student body is Catholic, 26 percent are of other faiths. Two of the greatest athletes in Marist history are Jewish: the late Joe Wasser, who won a football scholarship to Notre Dame in 1940, and Paul Muldawer, who excelled in football, basketball, and baseball.

Under Father Hartnett, Marist was named a National School of Excellence by the US Department of Education and received an award for Academic Excellence from the College Board for Advanced Placement Studies Program. Marist graduates include a Rhodes scholar, Pulitzer Prize winner, and nationally known personalities in science, medicine, business, literature, law, education, religion, architecture, military, sports, entertainment, and the diplomatic service.

One of Father Hartnett's proudest moments came several days after the September 11 terrorist attack when Notre Dame was playing Michigan State. At halftime, with 65,000 on-lookers in the stadium and millions more watching on television, Marist graduate Jim Carroll, president of the Notre Dame National Alumni Association, was presented the American flag at midfield. Carroll was an All-American football player at Notre Dame.

Among Marist's most famous sports families are the Rhinos—Chappell, Randy, and Kelley. Grandfather Chappell and his son Randy earned All-American recognition at Georgia Tech, and Randy's son Kelley is on his way to national honors as the Georgia Tech punt return specialist.

Father Hartnett was born October 12, 1926, and grew up in the suburbs of north Philadelphia. He had three siblings, none of whom opted for the priesthood. His dad was first a machinist, then a produce man selling fruits and vegetables door to door. To help his family, the young Father Hartnett worked in a pawnshop and unloaded luggage at the local Greyhound Bus terminal. He walked to school, three miles each way. At the age of seventeen, he was graduated from Roman Catholic High School and promptly joined the Navy. We were in the midst of World War II. "I did not want to be drafted," he said. "I couldn't imagine myself an Army grunt dying in some ditch. If I was going to die, I wanted it to be in nice, clean water. That's why I joined the Navy."

He went through boot camp and radio school. He was on a troop ship headed for the South Pacific when the Japanese surrendered. "I think that was the day I surrendered to God," he said. "As I look back on my life, there is nothing I would change. I wanted to be a sailor, teacher, and a priest."

After the war, he went to Marist College in Washington, DC to study theology. He was ordained a priest at Marist and then went on to earn M.A. degrees in philosophy and education at Catholic University and Duquesne University. He was assigned to Marist in Atlanta in 1955. When he was named principal in 1971, his first project was to organize an alumni association and hire a full-time alumni director. That was thirty years ago. Today the alumni association has 6,000 members who attend class reunions and golf outings and, most importantly, contribute to capital fund drives. It is the capital fund drives which have made possible the construction of the Bishop Gunn Administration building, the Laird gymnasiums, the Woodruff Auditorium, music building, computer center, Alumni Development Building, girls' softball field, cross country track, Jerry Queen baseball stadium, Monsignor McDonough Courtyard, aquatic center, and the science and art classrooms.

Father Hartnett, now seventy-five, lives in the rectory on the Marist campus and plans to remain there until the day he dies. "My next move," he said, "will be to Westview Cemetery."

"He is a friendly presence to all who know him," said Father Richmond Egan, S.M., the new Marist president. "They consider him a man who lives his values, the embodiment of the best in what he has made Marist stand for. We could have no finer role model."

When I asked Father Hartnett who his heroes were, he did not hesitate:

First and foremost, Father John Edward Gunn, then Father Phillip Henry Dagneau, Father Vincent P. Brennan, and Father Valentine Becker. Father Gunn first," he said, "because he founded Marist. Few people believed he could have opened a Catholic high school in Atlanta in 1901. The climate was not entirely friendly.

Father Dagneau ran the Ivy Street school from 1927 to 1953. When he arrived the school was facing loss of accreditation by the Southern Association of Colleges and Secondary Schools. He put Marist on a sound basis and the loss of accreditation never happened. His job was scarcely completed when the Great Depression hit. He had little money and Marist families had even less. But he got us through with sound fiscal policies. He was a great believer in athletics. He founded the North Georgia Interscholastic Conference and later had Marist admitted to the Georgia Interscholastic Association.

Father Becker was president and Father Brennan was principal in 1962 when they raised the money for Marist to buy the fifty-seven-acre piece of property on Ashford-Dunwoody. They also convinced Cecil Alexander, a Marist graduate and one of the nation's premier architects, that he should do the design work.

The Very Rev. William F. Rowland of the Society of Mary said, "The sense of family you see on this campus is due largely to the leadership of Father Hartnett. The future of Marist to which he has devoted so much of his time, energy, and skill insures a bright future for our school for many years to come. He gave us a true esprit de corps."

2002

THE LIFE OF REILEY

Chuck who? He was not selected on any of the Georgia high school All-State football teams, and when college scholarship signing time came, there was no great demand for his services. Not from the Techs, not from the Georgias, not from the Alabamas, not even from the Vandys. Wake Forest, not exactly an Atlantic Coast Conference power, eventually signed him, to its good fortune, but the only other colleges with a smattering of interest in him were the Presbyterians, the Citadels, and the Elons, not exactly backbones of major league football.

He had wanted to play for Clemson. But Clemson did not want him. It was a decision Clemson would later regret.

Chuck who?

He was the prep football player no college gridiron giant wanted, even though he had directed his Decatur High School team to two consecutive 9-1 seasons in the late 1950s. They all said he was too short (5'10") and too light (155 pounds) and that the strength of his passing arm was questionable. If those college recruiters had dug a little deeper, they would have discovered it was not the size of his body that counted, it was the size of his heart. And Charles Edwin "Chuck" Reiley had enough heart for a whole football team.

Talk about Horatio Alger, talk about Frank Merriwell, talk about the Little Engine That Could—Reiley was all three wrapped in a bundle of burning desire. Even though coaches selected him as a quarterback in the 1958 Georgia North-South All-Star high school football game, they did not expect him to play. After all, the North had a quarterback, not just a quarterback but a genuine superstar in

LEGENDS GENE ASHER

2002

Stanley Gann, a triple threat who was one of the most sought-after prep players in America. So when the All-Stars went through their seven days of practice, Reiley spent most of his time as an observer, watching Gann run the option, pass, punt, and play defense.

The night before the All-Star game, Gann was stricken with mononucleosis and the day of the game he was too sick to play. Enter Reiley, a.k.a Frank Merriwell. A record crowd of 45,000 came to Georgia Tech's Grant Field (Bobby Dodd Stadium) expecting to see the much-heralded Gann work his magic for the North but what they saw was an unheralded Reiley work his own magic, passing on the run, concealing the ball on quarterback keepers, and directing his team on a flawlessly executed, game-winning, sixty-five-yard touchdown drive.

At Decatur High, Reiley was a bona fide three-sport star. Not only did he lead his football team to two ultra-successful seasons, he hit an incredible .500 for the Decatur baseball team and was the ball-handler deluxe and team leader of Decatur's state Class AAA Champion basketball team. He was selected for the Greater Atlanta All-Star baseball team as a junior and a senior and led his team in hitting both years. All this, mind you, while making straight A's in the classroom.

At Wake Forest, he was captain of the football team, a part of the finest 1-2 quarterback combination in the Atlantic Coast Conference, a defensive standout, and the second best punter in the league. He made the dean's list four consecutive years and was a member of the college honor council. A terror on the football field, he was the consummate gentleman off the field. He was always the same modest, unassuming, humble person he was when he was the quarterback nobody wanted.

Today, Reiley is sixty-three years old and looks not a day over forty. He weighs the same 155 pounds as he did at Decatur, five pounds less than his playing weight at Wake Forest. He works out at the Asheville, North Carolina, YMCA three days a week and plays golf twice a week. There is no cart. He walks the course carrying his own clubs.

He lives with his wife of thirty-nine years, the former Lucy Barnes, in Black Mountain, North Carolina. He has two children and two grandchildren. Reiley is retired after a thirty-eight-year career with BellSouth. During his career, he headed BellSouth operations in Charlotte, Raleigh, Morganton, and Asheville. When he retired two years ago he was regional director for all BellSouth operations in western North Carolina.

Reiley has been a 100 percent giver—not only on the athletics field and in his BellSouth career, but in his civic and community involvement as well. In Asheville, he has been board chairman of the YMCA, Children First, a group that raises money to support handicapped children, and United Way. He is District Governor of fifty-one Rotary Clubs in western North Carolina and a perennial elder in Asheville's Grace Covenant Presbyterian Church.

Chuck Reiley was born in Appleton, WI. His dad, a former football player at Purdue University, put a football in his crib. Once he could stand, there was not a night his dad was not pitching him a football. When he was four years old, his family moved to Avondale Estates. He began hearing about Larry Morris, a football and baseball star at Decatur who would go on to win All-America football honors at Georgia Tech and All-Pro honors with the Chicago Bears. Reiley wanted to be just like Morris. He wanted to play for Decatur High, just like Morris did. There was one problem. The Reileys lived in Avondale, not Decatur. His parents had to pay the Decatur city school system $100 per year for out-of-city tuition.

Reiley belongs in the Georgia Sports Hall of Fame with Decatur High graduates Larry Morris, Frank Broyles, and Jimmy Southard. His football career at Decatur High, although impressive, was vastly over-shadowed by Gann, who had led Atlanta's Northside to the state AAA finals one year and the state championship the next. It was no surprise when the coaches designated Reiley for that backup quarterback job.

"When they told me the day of the game that Gann was sick and I would start," Reiley recalls, "it was kind of scary. All eyes had been on Gann during our practice sessions. I had never played before more than 5,000 people, then suddenly I am the quarterback for 45,000 fans who came to see someone else. Then I thought, hey, wait a minute, this is a golden opportunity, even though I hate it comes as a result of someone's sickness."

When he arrived at Wake Forest, he ran into another "Gann," only this one was bigger—6'4", 215 pounds. His name was Norm Snead, a sophomore who was headed for All-American honors. He certainly did not expect to give up his job to a 5'10", 155-pound rookie. These were the days freshmen were ineligible to play on the varsity. But his freshman team won three of four games. Chuck threw for four touchdowns and ran for four more. He had a sensational sophomore year. Although he did not beat out Snead for the starting job, head coach Paul Amen frequently worked him in at quarterback in what he called his "double-barreled attack." In Wake Forest's game against Virginia Tech, with Wake Forest holding a slim lead, Reiley directed a forty-eight-yard touchdown drive in the last minute, which he capped by running up the middle on a nine-yard touchdown gallop.

If Reiley could not be the starting quarterback, he determined he would find a starting job somewhere else. He found and won the No.1 job at safety. Physically, at 5'10", he was no match for the opposition's 6-foot-plus pass receivers, but they were no match for him when it came to desire. He led the ACC in pass interceptions his sophomore and junior seasons, snaring seven enemy passes each year. His teammates were so impressed with his ability to leap high in the air to bat down or intercept passes they nicknamed him "The Frog."

I asked Reiley how a 5'10" guy intercepts so many passes. He said, "It is a matter of timing. You never let the receiver get behind you. You have to keep three to five yards behind him. Then out of one corner of your eye you focus on the passer so you know which way he is going to throw. You move into the front of the receiver at the time the ball gets there and if the need be, you high jump like you are a member of the track team."

When Snead graduated in 1961, Reiley took over the No. 1 quarterback job. It was not a good year for Wake Forest or Reiley. The team won only four games, but for Reiley one of those four was unforgettable. Captain Reiley fearlessly marched his team into Death Valley, home of the potent Clemson Tigers. With 50,000 fans rocking the stadium and Tiger paws everywhere, it was intimidating. The crowd noise was deafening—but not for Reiley. It was payback time for him. He directed touchdown drives of sixty-one and sixty-five yards, tossing the winning score himself in one of the year's biggest upsets. It would be the last time Wake Forest would beat Clemson for the next forty years.

Reiley, who spent two years on active duty in the US Army, credits his dad, Charles Edward Reiley, who died last October, with being the biggest influence in his life:

> He got me started in football and he was always offering words of encouragement. I don't think he ever missed a football, basketball, or baseball game I played in at Decatur. He attended so many practices and games at Wake Forest that the coaches made him an honorary letterman and awarded him a letterman's jacket.
>
> But the greatest thing my dad gave me was a sense of values. At an early age, he made it clear to me that what mattered mostly was being honest, unselfish, courageous and loyal. He also told me that with effort comes reward.

Chuck Reiley got the message. He never has forgotten it.

A BULLDOG ROLE MODEL

Members of the S. A. Roddenbery family have distinguished themselves in America for more than 200 years, but none more so than eighty-six-year old Dr. Seaborn Anderson "Andy" Roddenbery of Hamilton. A Georgia Bulldog immortal, not so much for what he did on the gridiron, but for the life he has led, he is a recipient of the Bill Hartman Award, which recognizes student athletes who distinguish themselves as alumni. Roddenbery has literally been a role model to Bulldogs and non-Bulldogs alike—a role model for the human race.

Reared in central and south Georgia in the late teens and early twenties of the twentieth century, he grew up in an era of racial intolerance, but by the time he finished medical school at Harvard University he had overcome his prejudices. After he established a surgical practice in Columbus, in his quiet, gentlemanly, and determined manner, he convinced his colleagues to accept a black physician on the staff of what had been an all-white hospital. In expressing his feelings about justice and equality, he told the medical society, "It's the right thing to do. White race, black race, we all are members of the human race. If the doctor is qualified, he should be admitted."

It was through Roddenbery's leadership that Dr. Delmar Edwards was admitted to the hospital staff during the Jim Crow days of the 1960s. The story is told in a book written by Roddenbery entitled *I Swear By Apollo*. The title is the opening phrase of the oath of Hippocrates, the historic document that establishes the ethical code of medicine.

2002

Last March, fifteen years after his retirement, the Muscogee County Medical Society presented Roddenbery with its "Lifetime Achievement Award." The award recognizes physicians who have demonstrated the principles of leadership in the Muscogee County area throughout their career and who reflect the highest honor on their profession. Roddenbery practiced general surgery in Columbus from 1950 through 1986. He was one of the first board certified specialists in the Columbus area and pioneered the use of endoscopy in Columbus. He was president of the Georgia Surgical Society.

Said Dr. Tommy Lawhorne, defensive team captain of Georgia's 1967 Cotton Bowl championship team, and a noted Columbus thoracic surgeon, "I have never met another human being with his courage, his sensitivity, and his determination. His vast knowledge, innate understanding of people and gentleness of manner endeared him to patients and friends alike. All those who know him have been blessed."

Three years ago, Roddenbery was honored by the University of Georgia with the coveted Lifetime Achievement Award for "long and meritorious service to his university, his community and to humankind."

It is little wonder that Roddenbery has been such a major player in the game of life. A distant cousin George Roddenbery, born in 1758, was a Revolutionary War hero, and Gene Roddenbery, another cousin, authored the Star Trek chronicles after a career as a combat pilot in World War II.

The first S. A. Roddenbery was the leading physician in Decatur County. He built a home on the Thomasville to Bainbridge stagecoach road. Later he and his sons opened a store in Cairo and began packing and shipping cane syrup and pickles, for which they became nationally famous. S. A. Roddenbery Jr., Andy's grandfather, was elected to the Georgia state legislature at age twenty-one, and in 1910 was elected to the US House of Representatives. John Roddenbery, Andy's father, sang the leading role in "Blossom Time," a smash Broadway musical. With those kind of inherited genes, how could Andy miss? He couldn't and he didn't.

He was born in Thomasville on August 6, 1915. At the age of ten his family moved to Macon, where he first began playing football on a neighborhood sandlot team. At Lanier, he played three years of varsity quarterback and, although he was no superstar, his blocking and leadership helped his team to a state championship. But where he really sparkled was in the classroom, maintaining a straight "A" average. He got to Georgia on an academic scholarship.

He played quarterback and halfback for Coach Harry Mehre's Bulldogs in 1935–37, not bad for a walk-on, non-athletic scholarship player. In his sophomore season in 1935, he made one of the longest runs in Georgia gridiron history, going ninety-two yards against Furman University before being pulled down at the two-yard line. His friend and fullback, Bill Hartman, bucked it over for the touchdown.

Edwin Camp of the *Atlanta Journal* wrote of him, "Roddenbery is not big (165), not fast, only a mediocre passer, a fair ball-carrier and not a punter at all. But he is as good a blocker for his size as any player in the Southeastern Conference and he is a battler to the last ditch."

If the NCAA had had an Academic All-American team, Roddenbery would have been team captain. At Georgia, he lettered as halfback for the 1934 freshman team, scoring a touchdown on a forty-five-yard run against Georgia Tech in the annual Bullpups-Baby Jackets Thanksgiving Day classic. He graduated summa cum laude, three months ahead of his class. He was Phi Beta Kappa and Phi Kappa Phi.

Neither his run against the Tech freshmen nor his ninety-two-yard sprint against Furman was his top Bulldog sports thrill. That came in the old Polo Grounds (where the old New York Giants baseball and football teams played) when Coach Mehre's Bulldogs held the vaunted Fordham Rams and their "seven blocks of granite" to a 7-7 tie. It knocked the Rams out of a Rose Bowl bid. A member of the mighty Fordham forewall was Vince Lombardi, who became a legend as coach of the Green Bay Packers.

Roddenbery was headed for a career in the family pickle business, but a fishing trip and subsequent emergency surgery that he performed made him think of medical school instead. He had been invited to fish with two of his Georgia assistant coaches, Ted Twomey and Rex Enright, who later carved a successful coaching career at the University of South Carolina. It seems that as Enright was casting his line he got the hook on his line stuck in his scalp. The task of removing it fell on Roddenbery.

"It was kitchen table surgery," he recalls. "It was pitch black dark. First we had a twenty-five-mile canoe trip to get back to camp. Back in camp, all I had to see by was candlelight. I was plenty scared. But Coach Twomey told me to get the fish hook out and that is what I did."

"Coach Twomey was so impressed with what I did he told me to forget about pickles, I was going to medical school. I had no money for medical school, especially the expensive ones. But Coach Twomey went to Harold Hirsch, a Georgia graduate who was the chief lawyer for the Coca-Cola Company. Mr. Hirsch and Mr. Harrison Jones, also of the Coca-Cola Company, arranged a loan for me so I not only got to medical school but Harvard Medical School, one of the finest in the country."

It was at Harvard that Roddenbery met his future wife, Grace George of Manchester, New Hampshire, a nurse who was assistant director of the operating room at the Robert Brigham Hospital at Harvard. He received his M.D. from Harvard in 1938 and his post-graduate surgical training at Roosevelt Hospital in New York, Emory University hospital in Atlanta, and Riverside Hospital in Jacksonville, Florida. When World War II broke out, he entered the Army Air Corps as a flight surgeon and attained the rank of major.

When the war ended, he and Dr. Abe Conger, a close friend, drove throughout the state of Georgia looking for a place to set up a joint surgical practice. "When we got to Columbus," Roddenbery recalls, "we saw this sign which said, 'Welcome to Columbus, Georgia's Most Progressive City.' We took the sign to be true so that is why we settled on Columbus to open our practice."

The Roddenbery-Conger medical practice attracted patients not just throughout Georgia but also throughout the southeast. Roddenbery became chief of surgery at the Columbus Medical Center and Saint Francis Hospital.

Three years ago, when his wife of fifty-five years died, he established a memorial scholarship fund in her name.

Roddenbery lives in Hamilton, about twenty miles north of Columbus, in a bungalow on 400 acres of land, where he looks after forty-five Black Angus cows and three dogs. One of his grandsons, Travis Alston, was a highly regarded pitcher in the Pittsburgh Pirates organization last year.

Roddenbery was a role model for other Bulldog football players who became physicians, including George Skipworth (1944), Clyde Harrison and Hurley Jones (1952), Tommy Lawhorne and Happy Dicks (1968), Rosie Gilliam (1977), Chuck Heard (1971), and Scott Rissmiller (1992).

In receiving the Bill Hartman Award, Roddenbery said, "This has special significance for me because Bill Hartman and I played in the same backfield for four years and were inseparable friends off the field. I have never met a finer human being."

MURPHEY PUT LADY BULLDOGS
on the National Map

Memo to the Georgia State Sports Hall of Fame: What is required to gain membership in your august body? How in heaven's name can you omit Elizabeth Dee Murphey, who put women's athletics at the University of Georgia on the national map? Not just on the national map but in the hallowed hall reserved for national champions?

In 1995, you honored Liz Murphey as Sports Administrator of the Year. But isn't that a little shabby for someone whose athletics program has been remarkable in every women's sport? For instance, Georgia's 1994 women's tennis team won the NCAA championship. Georgia's lady netters also had two NCAA singles champions and eleven All-Americans. In track, there were five NCAA champions, seventeen SEC champions, an SEC outdoor team championship, and a second place in the NCAA Indoor Championships. In addition to directing Georgia's entire women's sports programs, Murphey also coached golf, turning out six SEC championship teams, three NCAA champions and eleven Academic All-Americans.

The Lady Bulldogs basketball teams won five SEC championships, made four NCAA Final Four appearances and turned out sixteen All-Americans. How about gymnastics? What about three NCAA championships, seven SEC crowns, twelve straight "Top 10" national finishes, and more than fifty individual All-Americans?

Doesn't it seem odd that all of this happened under her guidance without her being tapped for Hall of Fame honors?

What about swimming? Would you believe that Georgia women's teams had thirteen "Top 20" finishes, more than fifty All-Americans, twenty-eight Academic All-Americans and seven NCAA post-graduate scholars? Her ladies had brains as well as brawn. And look carefully at Lady Bulldog volleyball teams—seven NCAA tournament appearances, six times ranked in the Top 20, twenty-five All-SEC performers and four Academic All-Americans.

All this, mind you, and Murphey started the women's program with no money, no budget, no scholarships, no nothing.

Not putting Liz Murphey in the Georgia Sports Hall of Fame is a gross error of omission by the selection committee. There are members of the Hall of Fame whose credentials would pale next to hers. Frankly, if her selection does not come forth promptly there should be a state legislative investigation. After all, the Hall of Fame receives money from the state of Georgia.

Said Vince Dooley, University of Georgia Athletics Director, "Liz Murphey was the pioneer in women's collegiate athletics, not just in the Southeastern Conference but throughout America. She was not only a great administrator but a great golf coach as well. The records of our women's sports teams are incredible. Liz's leadership was the foundation of that success." She is a charter member of the National Collegiate Golf Hall of Fame, a past winner of the women's NCAA Coach of the Year award, and last year was inducted into the University of Georgia's coveted Circle of Honor, the highest tribute paid to former Bulldog athletes or coaches.

Murphey retired six years ago, but at sixty-eight she has the energy of someone half her age. Today she lives in rural White County, where she is involved with the local League of Women Voters (she used to be president), and serves on the board of the recreation department. She is the driving force behind the Georgia Forest Watch, an organization dedicated to the preservation of trees. She is treasurer of the Mt. Yonah Homeowners Association. In her spare time, she leads high school children on hikes and coaches the White County High School girls' golf team.

Liz Murphey was born in Newnan, Georgia, but grew up in Springfield, Tennessee, about twenty miles north of Nashville. Her mother, Mattie Crowe Murphey, was a vocalist who sometimes sang with the Grand Ole Opry. She wanted her daughter to study music but Liz had other ideas. She dribbled a basketball from the time she could walk, getting her sports sense from her father, no doubt. George Murphey, a salesman for Purina Mills, was on the track team at UGA.

"My dad put up a goal in our back yard and from the time I was in elementary school every kid in the community would come over and play," says Murphey, who was a basketball player, cheerleader, and editor of the school's first yearbook at Springfield High, and spent summers as a lifeguard and director of a day camp for preteens.

She worked her way through Maryville College in Tennessee, washing dishes and waitressing in the school cafeteria, and cleaning the office of the college president. While earning her master's degree in physical education and recreation at the University of Tennessee, she worked with teenage patients at a local hospital. "The toughest task I ever faced was finding enough hours in the day," she says.

Her first full-time job was at Lynchburg College in Virginia, where she spent ten years, setting up the women's sports program and coaching tennis, golf, basketball, and lacrosse while directing the college intramural program. In 1967, when an opportunity came to do graduate work and be a student teacher in the UGA physical education department, she grabbed it. She so impressed her boss that she had a full-time position one year later. There were no women's intercollegiate teams as such. The women's program consisted of club sports. Coaches were faculty members of the P.E. department.

"Funding of those clubs was a major project," Murphey recalls. "There was not much enthusiasm from those who put together our budget. When we took the track club for an out-of-town meet, we traveled in borrowed vans, slept in tents, and roasted hot dogs over a campfire. There was no motel money so we set up tent camps. On a meet with West Georgia College in Carrollton, we had an overnight camp in the track infield. We had to break camp early in the morning so we could hold the track meet."

In 1973, Murphey became coordinator of women's athletics, moving from the P.E. department to the athletics department. She was charged with organizing the program. Initially, she received little support from her fellow coaches. One coach on the athletics staff flat-out said, "I don't think women should sweat." To fund eight sports programs Murphey had $15,000. Today the women's budget is more that $2,000,000.

"I remember one of the first basketball games we played on campus," she says. "We had no numbers on our jerseys. When the referee called a foul on us, he had no way to report who committed the foul. So, we went to the First Aid kit and taped numbers on our jerseys. That was fine except the players would sweat and the numbers would fall off. The NCAA refused to let the women have scholarships so there was no recruiting. We were so bad, every team in the conference wanted to play us."

Title IX changed all that, leveling the scholarship-money playing field between men and women and requiring full-time women's coaches.

Murphey credits Athletics Director Vince Dooley for easing her way. "While others had not been helpful, Vince Dooley went out of his way to help," she says. "He said to let him know what I needed and he would get it for me. And he did."

Murphey was responsible for the hiring of most of Georgia's women's coaches, including gymnastics coach Suzanne Yoculan and basketball coach Andy Landers, both of whom developed national powerhouses. When both coaches threatened to file a sex discrimination lawsuit based on inequitable salary for men's and women's coaches, Murphey worked behind the scenes to get them substantial pay raises. "The thing I respect mostly about Liz was the way she went about assisting each individual coach," says Landers. "She never bothered them.

She allowed each coach to develop his or her own technique. She was the spark-plug in increasing our budgets."

Murphey emphasized academic as much as athletic performance. Her athletes had a 90 percent graduation rate. What she did for the women's sports programs at UGA was tantamount to what Knute Rockne did for football at Notre Dame.

In more than forty years of coaching and administrating, her biggest thrill was getting Terri Moody, who had been offered more than 100 scholarships, to sign a grant-in-aid with the University of Georgia. Moody became the first Lady Bulldog to win a national golf championship, earn All-American honors, and win a place on the Curtis Cup team. Although she lives in the mountains, Murphey gets back to Athens for every home football game, women's basketball game, and the golf tournament named in her honor.

Liz Murphey is already a member of the Women's Golf Hall of Fame. Her admittance to the Georgia Sports Hall of Fame is long overdue.

TENNIS ACE LARRY SHIPPEY

He's a six-time US forty-five-and-over doubles champion who played with the late Bitsy Grant and holds more city titles than anyone can remember. Court jester, raconteur, rocking-chair philosopher—Atlanta's Lawrence M. "Larry" Shippey is all these. But that is only a part of who he is.

With Bitsy or without, Shippey was a king. He won a fistful of sterling silver trophies with Russell Bobbitt, Tom Bird, Crawford Henry, and the late, legendary Georgia Tech football coach, Bobby Dodd. Shippey and Bird captured the National Senior Clay Courts doubles championship in 1970. As early as the 1940s Shippey was making headlines. He and the late Alice Marble won the first mixed doubles tournament ever held in Atlanta. He is a member of the Georgia Tennis Hall of Fame.

Today, at age eighty-six, Shippey is not the player he was. The dynamic serve and the unhittable backhand are gone, but he still has enough left to whip opponents half his age. He rarely misses a day playing doubles at the Bitsy Grant Tennis Center. Not bad for a man who underwent surgery for a melanoma ten years ago and had thirty-five radiation treatments for prostate cancer two years ago.

Shippey is indefatigable. He is up at 5 A.M., walks three to five miles every day and then spends thirty minutes to an hour on his rowing machine. Then he is off to the tennis center where he holds court before taking on anyone from a pre-teenager to an octogenarian. He is having fun, just as he did when he was winning all those tournaments.

Says sixty-seven-year-old Sonny McAdoo, a mere pup compared to Shippey:

> When is he not playing a match, he is sitting on the Bitsy Grant club-house porch entertaining his buddies. We don't play 'Simon Says,' we play 'Shippey Says.' He will tell about how a young Pancho Gonzales upset top-ranked Jack Kramer in the old Georgia Tech Alexander Memorial Coliseum back in 1950, how he kept Kramer on the run, lobbing shots barely over the net and then slamming one deep into the corner of the back court.
>
> He will talk about how Frank Parker eliminated Pancho Segura in the semi-finals of the 1944 Nationals by rendering No. 1 seed Segura's polished weapons inadequate against his machine-like efficiency.
>
> We sit and listen spellbound as he relates one tennis tale after another. None of us were around then so we cannot dispute any thing he says. We just say if Shippey says something, it must be true because nobody can disprove it. I think we all believe the man is a walking tennis encyclopedia.

One of Shippey's greatest tennis days occurred when he and Coach Dodd put on one of the biggest snow jobs ever seen at Bitsy Grant Tennis Center. It was at the opening round of the Atlanta Invitational Tournament, and he and Dodd were scheduled to meet Whitney Reid and Gene Scott, two of the top doubles players in America.

As they began their warm-ups, Shippey and Dodd missed one shot after another. Dodd was indecisive at the net and Shippey's normally brilliant backhand was nowhere in sight. The classic display of ineptitude worked. Expecting little or no competition, Reid and Scott were supremely overconfident.

Once the match started, Dodd, the classic competitor, and the well-armed Shippey bore down with every shot in the book. They won the first six games with Shippey's immaculate drives and high-powered service and Dodd's playing the net as if he owned it.

The second set was a real shooting match, but Reid and Scott never gained control. Shippey's forehand and backhand stood up staunchly and Dodd never relinquished command of the net. The hundreds of spectators went wild as Shippey-Dodd swept the second set, 6-4. The visiting celebrities had been had.

Ralph Foster, who managed Bitsy Grant Tennis Center when it first opened, said, "I remember the first day Shippey came to the center. He was a perfect gentleman. He shook hands with everyone, introducing himself and flashing a warm, friendly smile. I was at the tennis center thirty-two years and I never heard anyone ever say an unkind word about Shippey."

Seventy-two-year-old Phil Slotin, a Bitsy Grant center regular, says there is another side of Shippey:

> When he is teaching, and he taught me, he is like a Marine Corps drill instructor at Parris Island. He expects you to pay attention. But he taught me how to play the game. And he taught me well. I had been trying to make a perfect serve, a perfect net shot and a perfect backhand. He taught me to relax. He told me there is no perfect shot, that all I had to do was to get the

ball over the net and let my opponent worry about making the perfect shot. He turned my game from a chore into a joy.

Larry Shippey was born in 1915 in Enigma (population 862) in Berrien County. When he was four years old, his family moved to Waycross where he saw his first baseball game and his first tennis match. As a sophomore at Waycross High School, he earned an outfield berth on the baseball team. In the field, he was so-so, but at bat he was something else. He could hit line drives to every field, and there was not a pitcher in the region who did not dread his coming to the plate. Unfortunately for the baseball team, when the season ended he became smitten with tennis.

I figured if I could hit a baseball with a skinny wooden bat, I sure as heck could hit a tennis ball with one of those fat racquets. It looked simple. But when I started playing competitively, I got my brains beat out. I kept working at it—the serve, the forehand, the backhand—and eventually it all fell into place. One of the top players at school thought I was a real patsy. One day after classes he dared me to play him. He brought his girlfriend out to show how good he was. Well, I upset him and from that point on I knew tennis was my "racquet."

The next year, at age eighteen, Shippey won the Waycross city singles championship. He played two years at Georgia Southern College in Statesboro but was ineligible to play when he transferred to the University of Georgia. He concentrated on his studies when he was not at the Athens city tennis court, whipping every pickup player in sight. He received his degree with a major in journalism, but turned down a newspaper job at the *Macon Telegraph* to join his father's Hudson automobile dealership in Waycross.

After the Hudson faded into oblivion, his dad, a first-class mechanic, opened a garage and young Shippey joined the Naval Air Corps in 1940. He completed flight training at Pensacola Naval Air Station. When he received his wings, he moved on to the Jacksonville NAS for advanced training and the resumption of his tennis career. He quickly became the No. 1 player on the air station's tennis team.

Shippey was as good at flying as he was playing tennis, so the Navy sent him to the NAS at Chamblee (now the DeKalb-Peachtree Airport) to become a flight instructor. The Piedmont Driving Club, which spawned Bitsy Grant and a host of other notables, had a special low-rate membership available for the military. When he was not instructing young pilots, Shippey was at the driving club taking on anyone looking for a game.

It was at the driving club that he met Anne Owens, a tennis player herself and the daughter of Frank Owens, perennial club champion and one of the leading real estate salesmen in Atlanta. In less than one year, Shippey and Owens were married. It was a match made in heaven—they recently celebrated their fifty-seventh wedding anniversary. They were nearly unbeatable playing together in club mixed-doubles tournaments.

When Shippey was discharged from the Navy at the end of World War II, he went into the building business and became quite successful. His business, though, seldom took precedence over his tennis. In singles, Shippey never could beat Bitsy Grant, but as a team they were in a class by themselves. He also was unbeatable playing with Russell Bobbitt. The Shippey-Bobbitt combo won the city championship three times and the state title twice.

Shippey credits Grant with much of his success. "He taught me to relax, to stay loose no matter how far behind I might be. He told me to stick to my game and not worry about my opponent."

Shippey no longer remembers how many championships he, Grant, Bobbit, and Dodd won, but he does remember how much money the championship trophies brought him when he sold them all in the 1980s during the height of the silver market. "I got $10,000 for the bunch of them," he said. "I don't need trophies. I know what I did."

One of the Shippeys' two sons, Bill, was the first player ever to win a tennis scholarship at the University of Georgia. He was Georgia's No. 1 singles player in 1967 and 1968 and finished his Bulldog playing career by winning the Southeastern Conference singles crown.

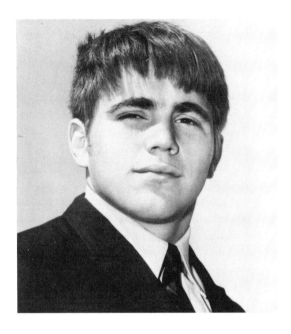

SEVEN "HALL-WORTHY" ATHLETES

Some first-rate Georgia sports figures are conspicuous by their absence from the state's Sports Hall of Fame It is time to break up the club.

Four years ago I wrote a column about how the Georgia Sports Hall of Fame had long excluded seven highly qualified candidates. In the years since, none of the seven, all five-star candidates, has been selected for membership.

The exclusion of Ron Blomberg, the late Erskine Mayer, Franklin C. "Pepper" Rodgers Jr.*, Dr. Noah Langdale Jr., Leman I. "Buzzy" Rosenberg, Natalie Cohen, and the late Jake Abel is a grave injustice. If it is not corrected, the Georgia legislature ought to withhold funds appropriated to the Hall until it is.

This is not to imply that the Hall is without 24-karat members. There are Charley Trippi, Herschel Walker, the Morrises—Larry and George—Furman Bisher, and many others of their ilk. But there are also members whose credentials pale compared to the unlucky seven who apparently do not fit the Hall mold.

If the Georgia Sports Hall of Fame is to be an authentic Sports Hall of Fame it needs to admit those seven athletes without delay. It should also admit the late Sammy Mayer, the late George Pendley, Bill and Jeanne Daprano, and Larry Shippey.

How, in heaven's name, can Erskine Mayer not be in the Georgia Sports Hall of Fame? All that Mayer, an All-Star pitcher, did was post back-to-back twenty-one-game-winning seasons for the Philadelphia Phillies and pitch the Phillies into

2002

the 1915 World Series. He was a native Atlantan, a graduate of Atlanta Boys' High School, and brother of Sammy Mayer.

I wish someone would explain to me why Blomberg is not in the Georgia Sports Hall of Fame. He may have been a New York Yankee but he is a native of Atlanta, a graduate of Druid Hills High School and maybe the best all-round (*Parade* All-American in football, basketball, and baseball) athlete this state ever produced. He could have gone to college anywhere in America to play basketball, but he was major league baseball's No. 1 draft pick and signed with the New York Yankees. Blomberg was baseball's first designated hitter. His bat is in the Hall of Fame at Cooperstown, New York.

Blomberg played eight seasons for the Yankees, was selected once to the American League All-Star team and played in three World Series. He had a lifetime batting average of .296. If all this cannot get you into the Georgia Sports Hall of Fame, what can?

As big a miscarriage of justice is keeping Pepper Rodgers out. Here is a guy who was in charge of football operations for the Washington Redskins. Here is a guy who coached football successfully at Georgia Tech, the University of Kansas, and UCLA. Here is a guy who was twice named "Coach of The Year" both in the Big Eight Conference and in the Pacific Coast Conference. Here is a guy who was once runner-up for the National Collegiate Athletic Association "Coach of The Year." Rodgers was twice named "Coach of The Year" of Southern Independent schools while coaching the Tech Yellow Jackets.

As a reminder to the selection committee, he did have glittering credentials as a player. In the 1952 Orange Bowl, he kicked a field goal in the final two minutes to give Tech a 17-14 victory over Baylor. In the 1953 Sugar Bowl, he kicked a field goal and three extra points and threw a touchdown pass to lead his Tech team to a 24-7 victory over Ole Miss. In the 1954 Sugar Bowl, Rodgers was named Most Valuable Player after passing for three touchdowns and kicking four extra points and a field goal in a 42-19 rout of West Virginia. His thirty-nine extra points in 1952 established a Tech single-season record that stood for thirty-eight years and his sixty-eight career extra points rank fifth on Tech's all-time list.

Dr. Noah Langdale was good enough to be selected to *Sports Illustrated*'s Silver Anniversary All-America college football team. Why isn't he good enough to be in the Georgia Sports Hall of Fame? Langdale served as state chairman of the National Football Hall of Fame and on the NCAA's Presidents Commission.

What should be most embarrassing to the Georgia Sports Hall of Fame is that in its second year of existence it asked Langdale to be its chairman. Isn't it strange that Langdale was good enough to help get the Hall of Fame off the ground but is not good enough for membership? You can check out Langdale's playing and coaching credentials. He was a starting tackle on the 1941 University of Alabama's football team that defeated Texas A & M, 29-21, in the Cotton Bowl and was line coach of the 1942 Alabama team that defeated Boston College, 37-21, in the Orange Bowl. As an aside, it was Dr. Langdale who turned a parking garage, then known as the Atlanta Division, University of Georgia, into Georgia State University.

How about Buzzy Rosenberg, fifty-one years old and a beverage company sales manager in Jacksonville? He played safety for the Georgia Bulldogs and twice was selected to the All-Southeastern Conference football team. Rosenberg is listed in the University of Georgia media guide ten times. He is first in average punt return yardage for one game—40.4—and first for most punt return yardage in one game—202. Both records still stand after thirty-one years. His Atlanta Northside High School coach, the late, legendary Wayman Creel, said of the 5'7" Rosenberg, "Inch for inch, he is the finest football player I ever saw, prep, college or pro."

I don't know how many accolades, trophies or championships it takes to impress the Sports Hall of Fame, but it appears that eighty-nine-year-old Natalie Cohen does not have enough. Her nomination apparently was deposited in file thirteen, despite an incredible tennis career which included thirteen consecutive Georgia State Women's Open Doubles Championships, thirteen consecutive Atlanta City Women's Open Doubles Championships, two Atlanta City Women's Open Singles championships, one Georgia State Women's Open Singles title, and one Atlanta City Mixed Doubles Title. For more than fifty years she has been a certified tennis official, serving as linesman, umpire, and referee for the city of Atlanta, state of Georgia, Southeastern regional, NCAA, and professional tournaments. Natalie Cohen is a native of Atlanta, a resident of Buckhead, and a graduate of old Atlanta Girls' High School and the University of California.

The late Jake Abel, a professional prizefighter, went the distance with Benny Leonard, considered the greatest world lightweight champion of all time. Although he was not born in Atlanta, Abel fought many of his fights at the old Atlanta City Auditorium.

The late Samuel Franklin Mayer never made it big in the big leagues of baseball, but he wrote his name indelibly into the old Atlanta Crackers history books. He did everything but sell peanuts. He played centerfield, and he served as team captain, team manager and part owner. He played professional baseball for twenty-two years, led the Crackers to a Southern Association championship, and was selected to the league All-Star team.

The late George Pendley was a native Atlantan and one of Georgia's all-time great senior amateur tennis players. Over a thirty-year period, in state, regional and national competition, he won 200 doubles tournaments and fifty singles tournaments. From age forty-five to sixty-five, he was ranked No. 1 in his age division in both singles and doubles. Pendley is in the Georgia Tennis and the Southern Tennis Halls of Fame, but not the Georgia Sports Hall of Fame.

In the annals of US Masters Track competition, there never has been a husband-wife combo as dominant as William L. and Jeanne Daprano. Bill has won more than 100 Masters Track awards and broken fourteen world records. At seventy-five, he is going faster than ever. He recently won his third consecutive National Pentathlon Championship in Baton Rouge, Louisiana. Jeanne, now sixty-five, set two world records (800 and 1500 meters) last year. She also set a mile Masters record and last year broke her own records. All told, she has won ninety-two pieces of gold.

Then there is a highly qualified Hall of Fame candidate in Larry Shippey. The man won seven Senior National Doubles Championships, six with the late Bitsy Grant and one with Tom Bird.

In a loud and clear call for fairness and legitimacy, I urge Executive Director Loran Smith and strong men George Morris, Howard "Doc" Ayers, and Charley Trippi to lead the way in opening the gates. Let's make the Georgia Sports Hall of Fame an organization that honors all deserving candidates.

*Rodgers was admitted to the Georgia Sports Hall of Fame in 2004.

2002

YELVINGTON
King of the Hill

Richard Joseph "Dick" Yelvington never made All-America at the University of Georgia, but he was King of the Hill.

Death Valley, The Swamp, Tiger Stadium…they were all child's play compared to what went on at Ag Hill, practice field—no, battleground—of Coach Wallace Butts' Bulldogs. It was smash-mouth football at its best, and only the fit survived. No one was more fit than Yelvington, a 6'1", 200-pound offensive tackle from Daytona Beach, Florida.

There was head-knocking from sunup to sundown; you could hear the leather popping from Lumpkin Street to Milledge Avenue. There were tackling and blocking drills of 2-on-1 and 3-on-2 and sometimes 3-on-1. Then it was game-type scrimmages where giving less than 100 percent meant you were on the next train home—Coach Butts, nicknamed the Little Round Man, would see to that.

Most players go through three spring practices. Yelvington, whose college career was interrupted by a stint in the military, had four such practices, plus a summer season, which the Southeastern Conference permitted in 1946 to allow returning veterans to adjust to a new environment.

The summer of 1946 found Yelvington, scarcely out of Daytona's Mainland High School, going head to head with twenty-two year-olds, most of whom already had a varsity football season or two under their belts. "Forget my games in

Sanford Stadium," Yelvington says today, "and even my games in Yankee Stadium [with the NFL New York Giants]. What I am most proud of is the years of spring, summer, and fall practices at Ag Hill and never once crying for help or needing first aid."

Yelvington did more than survive Ag Hill; he was a starter for three years (1949–51), a distinction that few Bulldogs in history can claim. He was chosen to play in the 1951 North-South College All-Star game where, according to his Bulldog and All-Star game teammate, halfback Zippy Morocco, his blocking opened holes big enough to drive a truck through. Morocco and other South running backs had a field day in a runaway victory.

Morocco says Yelvington never got the credit he deserved at Georgia. Yelvington claims he was nothing special, just another team player. However, Steve Owens, coach of the New York Giants, thought he was much more when he drafted Yelvington for the Giants. Owens was right: For six seasons, Yelvington was a starting right tackle for the Giants and it was his blocking that helped enable running back Frank Gifford to become a legend and the Giants to win a National Football League championship.

Yelvington is one of the few Bulldogs who wear what is tantamount to a Super Bowl ring. He is also one of the few Bulldogs who can talk about Chaucer, Schopenhauer, and Shakespeare. He may be the only Bulldog who stayed single until he was age sixty-five, when he married his childhood sweetheart. Today Yelvington lives with his wife of eight years, the former Peggy Sembler, in a three-bedroom, ranch home in Lake Charles, Louisiana. He is the same size he was when he played in the NFL championship game of 1956, in which his Giants erased the once-mighty Chicago Bears, 47-7.

He has been retired now for thirty years and no longer works out. He spends his days reading and doing odds and ends around the house. He suffered a brain hemorrhage at age forty-four but has had no major medical problem since. He still has a wonderful sense of humor.

He clearly recalls one of the many long scrimmages in 1950, the year he was alternate team captain. His team had made three consecutive long gains but after each one Coach Butts would scream, "Penalty, bring it back!" First it was "offsides," then it was "backfield in motion," then it was "holding." "Coach Butts was furious and believe me, when he was furious, he was furious. It was getting late in the day. It was almost dark. 'We're going to run that play until we get it right, even if we have to stay out here all night,' Coach Butts hollered."

On the next play, Yelvington blocked his man and then raced down field leading Morocco on an eighty-yard touchdown run. Coach Butts blew his whistle again, then screamed, "Illegal motion, bring it back!" Yelvington removed his helmet, threw it on the ground, threw his hands up in the air, and bellowed, "The whole world is against us!" Coach Butts, eighty yards up field, raced full speed down field to Yelvington, looked up at the towering tackle, and yelled, "If you ever open your mouth again I will run you out of here!" The Dogs got it right on the next play and the practice ended.

In his high school days, Yelvington attracted the attention of scouts from Florida and Georgia. He was actually a guest of the Gators when they met the Bulldogs in Jacksonville in 1945. The Bulldogs won the game, 34-0, and also the signature of Yelvington. He checked into Milledge Hall, resident football team dorm, in June 1946. As fodder for some 100 returning veterans, it was to be a summer he never would forget.

"I, along with other new high school graduates, was part of the 'hamburger' squad. We scrimmaged every day, the kids against the old men. The old men won. They were bigger—their line averaged about 230, ours about 190—and more experienced. It was like a daily blood bath."

Before the football season started—before Yelvington was even enrolled—he was drafted. He had no intention of returning to the Bulldog meat-grinder, but one of his teammates, Eddie Roberts of Decatur, sent Coach Butts a telegram that read, in part, "As soon as Yelvington and I complete our two-year tour, we shall return."

"When Roberts told me what he had done, I could have killed him. I had not planned to go back but I felt obligated and reasoned I had rather be a Bulldog in Athens, Georgia, than a dogface somewhere in Korea," Yelvington says.

After eighteen months in Korea, he returned to Athens just in time for…another football practice. The practices were just as rough as before, but now a much bigger (220) Yelvington was dishing out the punishment. A true freshman in 1948, he won a backup job behind All-Southeastern Conference tackle Porter Payne, father of Atlanta Olympic organizer Billy Payne.

Yelvington played in every game in what became a grand and glorious season of nine wins, two losses, and a bid to the Orange Bowl. Then the Bulldogs were trounced in the Bowl game, 41-28, by the Texas Longhorns, led by halfback Tom Landry. The game was a harbinger of bad times ahead. Despite a host of returning lettermen in 1949, including Yelvington, without its 1948 leaders Johnny Rauch and Joe Geri, the Bulldogs suffered through a 4-6-1 season. In 1950, the Bulldogs managed only six wins, and in Yelvington's senior year of 1951, the team struggled through a 5-5 season.

"We left a lot of our football on the practice field," Yelvington says. "We worked so hard during the week that by the time Saturday rolled around we were too pooped to pop. We were too tense. A lot of the guys, me included, were afraid of making a mistake, like missing a block or a tackle. We would be inviting the wrath of the Little Round Man. That's something nobody wanted to do."

Compared to Georgia's, Yelvington found New York Giants' practices a breeze:

> Once the season started, there was little contact. Most of the time we practiced in shorts, worked on timing and special situations like goal line stands and racing against the clock.
>
> We were expected to know our game assignments and we were expected to execute. There were no threats, no screaming by the coaches. They

expected us to perform like professionals. And those who did not were soon gone.

I have always felt that motivation comes from within. A stirring rah-rah speech may get you up for the moment but it does not last. You have to want to do the best. If you do not have the desire to excel, nobody can put it there.

After football, Yelvington was an undercover narcotics agent for the Treasury Department before illness forced him into early retirement. "I have no regrets," he says. "I was a three-year starter for the Bulldogs and a six-year starter for the Giants. And I have an NFL championship ring."

How many people have done all that?

"I feel blessed. I have a wonderful wife. I had a loving, caring, nurturing mother who was always there for me."

What does Yelvington think has been the biggest change in football since his playing days? "A no-brainer," he says. "It is size. Today we have 300-pound high school players. When I played we did not have 300-pound professional players. Today's players are not only far bigger but much stronger."

He has some advice for someone wanting to play football today. "Never give up. No matter how bleak the situation may look it can change. Convince yourself your time will come and when it does, be ready."

BUCK MARTIN
A Georgia Tech Immortal

Buck Martin, the 1952 Georgia Tech All-American end, is battling cancer, fighting for his life. But he became immortal fifty-one years ago, on a sunny October afternoon when he caught four touchdown passes from quarterback Darrell Crawford, a Georgia Tech single-game record and only the third time in Southeastern Conference history any end ever caught four in one game.

It happened on Grant Field, now Bobby Dodd Stadium, before a screaming crowd of 31,000. Tech was on its way to its first undefeated season, having beaten Southern Methodist, Florida, Kentucky, and LSU. But Tech assistant coaches who had scouted Auburn saw no way the Jackets could whip Coach Ralph "Shug" Jordan's first Auburn team.

Tech backfield coach Frank Broyles, now athletic director at Arkansas, recalls the Sunday before the game. "We had our regular scouting report meeting and I remember telling Coach Dodd, 'Our scouts all agree. We can't think of a single play that will work against Auburn.' Dodd turned to line Coach Ray Graves, who also had seen Auburn's mighty defense, and Graves said, 'Coach, there is no way. They are too strong up front.' And then Dodd spoke. 'We will win the game. We will beat Auburn with the Kingsport play, a play I designed in the dirt back when I played in the Kingsport sandlots.'"

Dodd had five practice sessions to install the play. His quarterback, Crawford, had run the play at Kingsport High School, and in Martin he had a 6-4 pass receiver with basket hands. The play was simple. Crawford would put the ball into the belly of halfback George Maloof and then quickly remove it as Maloof headed upfield. Meanwhile, Crawford would turn his back to the line of scrimmage, count to three, turn and fire the ball to Martin.

It was early in the game when Dodd first called the play. Crawford could have won an Academy Award as he faked the handoff to Maloof. Meanwhile, Martin decked an Auburn tackle, drifted into the secondary, and pulled in a fourteen-yard touchdown pass. Dodd called the play again in the second quarter, and this time it went for thirteen yards and another Martin touchdown. But the play that brought 31,000 fans to their feet came in the third quarter. With the game threatening to turn into three-yards-and-a-cloud-of-dust football, Martin took a Crawford pass at his own twenty-six-yard line. An Auburn defender by the name of Vince Dooley quickly put a lock tightly around Martin's legs. Martin twisted, turned, snapped the Dooley lock, and sprinted seventy-four yards for his third score of the game.

For his fourth touchdown, Martin made like a fullback. Covered by an Auburn defender in the end zone, he broke clear and ran to the five-yard line, caught another Crawford pass, pivoted, and then ran smack over the Auburn safety man at the goal line.

Wrote Furman Bisher, then sports editor of the *Atlanta Constitution*, "Crawford and Martin did their jobs so well you almost became oblivious to the other twenty men on the field." Says Sam Lyle, then Georgia Tech's end coach, now retired and living in Atlanta, "Buck had the best pair of hands of any pass receiver I ever saw—college or professional. He not only was a great pass receiver but he also was one of the best blockers I ever coached."

Although the Auburn game was his best, Martin was brilliant in many other contests. He had the most touchdown receptions for a career (fourteen) at Georgia Tech, a record that stood for thirty-two years. His name is listed in the Tech media guide again and again: most touchdowns in one season (fourth on the all-time list) with yearly reception records in 1951, with thirty-seven catches for 506 yards and eight touchdowns, and in 1952, with twenty-eight receptions, 396 yards and six touchdowns.

The Martin records are remarkable in that they were made during the years Georgia Tech was basically a running team with guys like Glenn Turner, Leon Hardeman, Billy Teas, Larry Ruffin, and George Maloof. Martin's ability to catch the ball and run either around or over a defensive back helped Tech to an undefeated season in 1951 and an undefeated and untied record in the national championship season of 1952.

He caught four passes in leading Georgia Tech to a 17-14 victory over Baylor in the 1952 Orange Bowl. Martin was selected to the 1951 All-Southeastern Conference team and the 1952 All-America team. He is a member of the Georgia

Sports Hall of Fame and the Georgia Tech Sports Hall of Fame and was selected to the Bobby Dodd era (1945–66) all-time Tech team.

Today Gerdis M. Martin, that 6'4", 220 pounds of athleticism, is seventy-two years old. He has inoperable lung and brain cancer. At this writing, he was living in an Atlanta rehabilitation facility after falling and breaking his hip. I did not interview him for this article. Instead, I spoke with his wife of fifty years, the former Carolyn Foster of Hapeville; some of his former teammates; and of course, Lyle, his end coach.

"I think he is one of the most loved human beings I ever knew," says Carolyn Martin, "not only by his family but by his teammates, fellow students, faculty, and coaches. He was just about the greatest thing that came out of his hometown [Haleyville, Alabama]."

Says Lyle, "I coached three years at Georgia Tech and I would say he was the most respected player Tech had. He could outrun any of our defensive backs. Nobody could catch him. In twenty years of coaching, I never saw one player dominate a game like he did against Auburn. Other than the four touchdown passes he caught, all our other plays netted only thirteen yards."

All-American George Morris calls Martin "the most unassuming guy I knew. All the players talked about how talented he was. No matter how much praise he got—from the coaches, players, or the media—he was always that good ole boy from Haleyville."

All-American Larry Morris says, "He taught me all the ropes. He was an inspiration not only to me but to the other young guys. When we had questions about blocking assignments or pass routes, everyone went to Buck. He was like a coach on the field."

Quarterback Darrell Crawford says, "Whenever we needed yardage, he was my go-to guy. It wasn't difficult to complete passes when you had a big target like Buck. He always wanted to get to practice about thirty or forty minutes early so we could sharpen our game. He could run his pass routes blindfolded and be exactly where the ball was thrown."

Martin was born November 4, 1928. His dad was an engineer and drove a train on the old Central of Alabama Railroad. His mother was a housewife. By the time Martin got to Haleyville High School he was already 6'4", 190 pounds, big enough to bring smiles to the face of football coach James S. Woods.

He earned all-conference honors three times. Auburn and Alabama competed fiercely for his signature on a grant-in-aid, but Martin narrowed his choices to Notre Dame and Georgia Tech. When he visited Tech, Coach Dodd convinced him to sign with the Yellow Jackets, via Notre Dame prep school in Chattanooga.

In the Tech classroom, he did well enough to make the Dean's List. He was president of the senior class. He met Carolyn at his Kappa Sigma fraternity house and they were married immediately after the 1952 Orange Bowl (which Tech won, 17-14, over Baylor University). Martin was used mostly as a decoy in the game but caught all four passes thrown to him, including one for a touchdown. Dodd said Tech could not have won without his downfield blocking, which made space for Tech's bevy of running backs.

In his three years of varsity football, Martin missed only four passes out of ninety-eight. *Collier's* picked Buck Martin as one of eleven players on its 1952 All-America team. After Tech, he turned down a professional football offer and entered the US Army.

Martin never was just a jock. Although he loved tennis and played on the ALTA teams, he also taught Sunday school at the Saint Matthew United Methodist Church in Vinings and at the First Presbyterian Church in Richmond when a job with Honeywell took him there. He was president of his children's school PTA. He and his wife have two children, Brad, forty-two, and Leslie Burrell, thirty-five.

DARRELL CRAWFORD
The Man with the Golden Arm

Georgia Tech has had its share of great quarterbacks—Billy Lothridge, Frank Broyles, Wade Mitchell, Kim King, and Joe Hamilton—but none was greater than Darrell Crawford out of Kingsport, Tennessee. In 1951 Crawford out-dueled the so-called "five finest passers in America." He became the first player in Southeastern Conference history to throw four touchdown passes in one game, and he quarterbacked the Yellow Jackets to their first undefeated season in the Bobby Dodd era.

Along the way to an 11-0-1 record, Crawford out-passed the much-heralded Billy Wade of Vanderbilt, Vito "Babe" Parilli of Kentucky, Heywood Sullivan of Florida, and Fred Benners of Southern Methodist University. Then he topped that in the Orange Bowl by out-performing All-American Larry Isbell of Baylor.

Crawford was the man with the golden arm. *Atlanta Journal* football analyst Coach Harry Mehre wrote of Crawford's performance against Louisiana State University, "Crawford personally carried the Yellow Jackets to an easy 25-7 victory over a good LSU team. Crawford is 'the' reason and the whole reason why the Jackets are unbeaten.

"His selection of plays is flawless. He is the best field general in the SEC. From where I sit, he is the best all-round back in America."

Of his out-shining Wade (sixteen completions to Wade's nine), *Atlanta Journal* sports editor Ed Danforth wrote, "Wade was supposed to be the man of the hour, but it was Crawford who kept the fans on their feet by ducking and dodging on-coming linemen and throwing for completion after completion. Crawford was not as good as Wade was advertised, he was better."

Wrote Jerry Bryan of the *Birmingham News*, "In eluding Vandy's aggressive pass rush, Crawford was an escape artist deluxe as he broke out of trap after trap. Six times he was engulfed by would-be tacklers and six times he broke clear and completed his pass. Crawford is not the key to the Georgia Tech attack, he is the Georgia Tech attack."

After Crawford threw three touchdown passes in a 27-7 win over Alabama, Crimson Tide coach Red Drew said, "The SEC never has seen a finer quarterback." In a game the University of Georgia never will forget, Crawford directed the Yellow Jackets to a 48-6 rout of the Bulldogs to clinch the 1951 SEC championship.

The Orange Bowl selection committee wasted no time in extending Tech a bid to play Baylor New Year's day. The game was another Crawford masterpiece. He was Harry Houdini as he faked handoffs to running backs Bill Teas, Leon Hardeman, and George Maloof and then completing passes to his downfield receivers. He passed for 107 yards and one touchdown and set up the game-winning field goal by Pepper Rodgers. He was named the game's most valuable player.

For the year, he completed eighty-three passes for 1,327 yards and thirteen touchdowns. The United Press picked him on its "All-Bowl" team and the nation's coaches selected him to play in the College All-Star game against the champions of the National Football League. He was a unanimous choice for the All-SEC team.

All this, mind you, from a kid who learned to play the game with the bladder of a hog. A gutsy kid who, in his first sandlot football game at age ten, received a gaping leg wound that required twenty-six stitches. The next afternoon, he was back on the gridiron.

Today, that courageous kid of ten is seventy-three years old. He looks as fit (5'11", 170 pounds) as he did during his playing days. Three days a week he works out at cardiac rehab. He suffered atrial fibulation one year ago but has kept it under control with exercise and medication. When he is not at his sales management job with Momar Industries, you can find him at Eastside Baptist Church, where he is an associate deacon, or at the home of his next-door neighbor, William A. "Bill" Paschal, who like Crawford is a football immortal.

Crawford was born to the game—his hometown, Kingsport, is the Valdosta of Tennessee football. Just as the Wildcats dominate in southern Georgia, Kingsport dominates in eastern Tennessee. Among its native sons are the legendary Bobby Dodd; Bob Cifers, an All-American at the University of Tennessee; Hal Miller, an All-American at Georgia Tech; and Darrell Crawford and his brother, Denver Crawford, an All-American tackle at UT.

Darrell was born in 1929, the youngest of eight children, six boys and two girls. "There was no money in our family for a football," Crawford recalls. "So my brother Denver improvised. He killed a hog, cut out the bladder, blew it up and tied it at one end. It looked more like a basketball than a football but to us it was the real thing."

From the hog bladder to the pigskin, Crawford was in a class by himself. He led his sandlot team to a city championship and his high school team (Kingsport Dobyns-Bennett) to two consecutive state championships. He attracted the attention of almost every college football scout from south Florida to South Bend.

What impressed Tech's Dodd and Tennessee's coach Bob Neyland was not only Crawford's athletic ability but his leadership and classroom work as well. He was a standout baseball and basketball player, an A student, and president of his junior and senior classes.

The pressure to sign with Tennessee or Kentucky was enormous. After all, Dodd and Cifers were Tennessee legends. Brother Denver was captain of the 1947 UT team. Coach Neyland personally invited Darrell to every home game, housed him in the UT football dorm, and fed him at the UT team training table.

Even the legendary Notre Dame coach, Frank Leahy, sent him books on Notre Dame's glorious football history and its all-time great quarterback, Johnny Lujack. But the greatest pressure came from another legend—Paul (Bear) Bryant, then head coach at Kentucky. The persuasiveness of Coach Dodd, coupled with the fact that two of Crawford's Kingsport teammates, Jack Patterson and Harry Wright, were going to Tech, had led Crawford to sign a letter of intent with the Jackets. That did not faze Bryant. He made a trip to Kingsport and urged Crawford to telephone Dodd and ask for a release. He assured Crawford that he would be the starting Kentucky quarterback as a sophomore, even ahead of the great Parilli.

Bryant left Kingsport without Crawford, but he wasn't through yet. He dispatched his head recruiter, George Balitsaris, who played with Darrell's brother at Tennessee, for one more shot. "I was really feeling the heat," Crawford recalls. "I telephoned Coach Dodd and told him I was wavering, that Kentucky had promised me everything from a starting job to box seats at the Kentucky Derby. Coach Dodd said he already had my game jersey ready for me and that I was going to be Tech's next great quarterback. He erased any doubts I was beginning to have."

In Crawford's four years at Tech, the Jackets never lost to Georgia. But of all the highlights of Crawford's distinguished Tech career—the unbeaten season, the SEC record-setting four touchdown passes he threw to Buck Martin to stun Auburn in 1951, the four-game sweep against the Bulldogs—none compares to facing the mighty Vols as a sophomore.

Of the 15,000 citizens of Kingsport, almost every one was among the 45,000 who jammed Knoxville's Shields-Watkins Stadium to see the native son return. The screaming Kingsport throng came to cheer him, but the other Vols came to see him go down in defeat. They were disappointed. Crawford mystified the UT defense all afternoon, placing the football in the bellies of his running backs and magically removing it in time to escape and complete passes, two for touchdowns and two others to set up touchdowns. The final score: Crawford-led Tech 30, Tennessee 13.

Crawford is a member of the Georgia Tech Sports Hall of Fame. He is listed in the Georgia Tech media guide five times for passing performances. He was named most valuable player on the 1951 team. He, though, would like to be remembered not for any of his athletic achievements, not for playing when he was injured which he often did, but for being a good family man, a good friend and a good human being. Those who know him will remember him for just that.

EMMET JOPLING BONDURANT II
The "Indispensable" Man

Talk about the all-American boy. Meet Emmet Jopling Bondurant II, nationally renowned attorney at law. He's Jack Armstrong, the miracle Mets, and the incredible Jets all rolled into one.

He beat The Coca-Cola Company in a lawsuit brought by Coca-Cola Bottlers and defeated Atlanta's most prestigious law firm, King and Spalding, in a sex discrimination suit. In 1960, he won a US Supreme Court decision ordering the state of Georgia to conform its congressional districts to the one-man, one vote rule (*Wesberry v. Sanders*). He successfully defended eight individuals and Wyle Laboratories, Inc. in a lawsuit filed against them by Avnet, Inc., the nation's largest electronics distributor.

It would not have taken a clairvoyant to predict what this man was going to achieve. At Athens High School, he played shortstop on the baseball team, headed the student council, and was president of his senior class. In the summers, when he was not attending the Athens YMCA camp, he was loading and unloading trucks at his father's lumber company.

You name it, at the University of Georgia Bondurant did it. He was captain of the swimming team, despite the fact that he only swam at home meets. He refused to travel to the away meets because he did not want to miss classes or time he could be spending in the law library.

He was chairman of the university student council, a member of Sphinx, chief justice of the Law School Honor Court, president of the law school advisory council, and assistant editor-in-chief of the student editorial board of the *Georgia State Bar Journal*. He was in Phi Beta Kappa, Phi Kappa Phi, and Phi Eta Sigma, and the top man in his law school class three consecutive years.

He is a cum laude graduate of the University of Georgia and a magna cum laude graduate of the University of Georgia Law School. He received an LLM from Harvard Law School.

2002

He has run the Boston Marathon, the New York Marathon and more Atlanta marathons and Peachtree Road Races than he can remember. Last year he was named one of the "Top Ten Lawyers in America" by the National Law Journal.

Today Bondurant, sixty-five, has no retirement plans. He lives in Atlanta with his wife, Jane Fahey, a former attorney herself and now minister at the Trinity Presbyterian Church in Buckhead. The Bondurants' home, also in Buckhead, is a sprawling contemporary on two acres of wooded lot. They have five grown children.

Typical of Bondurant's courage and commitment is the way we conducted the telephone interview for this column. He had just arrived home from Piedmont Hospital after undergoing six hours of back surgery. I suggested we postpone the interview. He said, "Why? I am up to it if you are." So, for his first two hours at home, he answered questions. Pain or no pain, Bondurant knows only one way—full speed ahead.

A man of service? His contributions are enormous. Some of the more notable positions he has held are counsel and trustee to the Atlanta Commission on Crime and Juvenile Delinquency, vice president and director of Good Government Atlanta, member of the Board of Management of the Northside YMCA, director and president of the Atlanta Legal Aid Society, chairman of the Atlanta City Charter Commission, co-chairman of the committee for Sensible Rapid Transit, director of Research Atlanta, president of the University of Georgia Law School Association, and member of the UGA Law School Board of Visitors.

The city of Atlanta had been without a charter for 100 years when Bondurant took on the chairmanship of the Atlanta Charter Commission. Recalls Charles Wittenstein, who was executive director of the commission, "We never would have got the job done without Emmet. His dedication in time, his encouragement of all commission members, his commitment, his sheer enthusiasm was an inspiration to all of us. The man was indispensable."

Bondurant is the senior partner of the litigation firm of Bondurant, Mixson and Elmore. What started out as a seven-man firm has grown to a twenty-five-man firm. He often represents smaller companies against larger ones, individuals against corporations, corporate challengers against industry leaders. "If you are afraid to represent underdogs in litigation, you do not belong in the legal profession," Bondurant says. "We think even the rich and arrogant deserved to be sued."

He was a mere lad of twenty-seven when he did something most lawyers only dream of: he won a landmark case before the US Supreme Court. That was *Wesberry v. Sanders*, which forced the state of Georgia to redraw its congressional district lines to accurately reflect the state's population in keeping with the then novel "one person, one vote" legal principle. The verdict drastically shifted the balance of political power in Georgia from rural areas to the state's emerging urban centers.

Says his office manager Marjorie Stansel, who assists him on some of his cases, "He never works on a case unless he knows everything about it. He reads the documents, takes the depositions, and researches every aspect of the case.

During a trial he is always respectful of the court, even when the judge rules against him. It is always 'If the court please' and 'Thank you, your honor.' Opposing counsel often objects to his smiling and thanking the judge but the jury only remembers a gracious gentleman, calm, cool, and well-prepared."

Bondurant learned his manners and his bulldog tenacity from his parents, the late John and Mary Bondurant. He also learned the meaning of hard work. "According to the effort is the reward," his dad used to say. He got the message early. Recalls his older sister, Mary Warren, "Daddy had a deal with Emmet. If Emmet earned an A in school, dad rewarded him with a $5 bill. Emmet earned so many A's that dad had to put in overtime at the office."

Scholastics always came first and sports second, but it was on the advice of one of his swimming coaches, Irwin "Yutch" Stolz, a future Georgia Court of Appeals judge, that Bondurant entered law school. Three times he led his Bulldog swimming team to a second place finish in the Southeastern Conference championships, but that paled in comparison to what he did in law school.

He was the top graduate in law school and the first UGA student to be offered a Court of Appeals clerkship with Judge Clement Haynsworth on the US Court of Appeals for the fourth circuit in Greenville, South Carolina. The year was 1960. The civil rights movement was about to burst upon a reluctant South. It was in this crucible that Bondurant's social conscience was shaped. He made a firm decision that representing the underdog was to be his way of life.

Haynsworth was so impressed with Bondurant's commitment and attention to detail that he helped Bondurant land a scholarship to Harvard. It was at Harvard that he earned his master's degree in constitutional law and wrote a timely thesis addressing the issue of mounting a constitutional attack on the Georgia county unit system that would lay the groundwork for his first appearance before the US Supreme Court. When Bondurant returned to Atlanta, he worked as an associate for what was then called Kilpatrick, Cody, one of the city's largest firms. He earned $500 a month. Today that might buy you one hour of his time.

Bondurant has been uncompromising in his belief that every human being is entitled to fair treatment, regardless of his stature. The only private club he belongs to is the Commerce Club, which is nondiscriminatory. For 150 years the Bondurant family has stuck to a moral code of the highest integrity and no one has adhered more to that code than Emmet Jopling Bondurant II.

WILLIAM ALEXANDER "BILL" CURRY
Classy Coach, Classy Guy

LEGENDS GENE ASHER

2002

In the annals of college football, many coaches have better won-lost records than William Alexander "Bill" Curry, but none was more respected or more interested in the welfare of his players. Go as far back as Stagg, Rockne, Heisman, or as recent as Dodd, Dooley, or Jordan and you will find no one who preached that the human soul was worth much more than winning football games.

One of his former players, Delandual Conwell, said it best. "I was recruited by every college in the PAC-10, the Big Ten, and the SEC. But none of the coaches came across as straightforward, as honest, as empathetic as Curry did. When a tumor ended my playing career and kept me hospitalized, Curry, despite all his coaching and administrative duties, was right there for me. I never met a finer human being."

This is not to say that Curry was a nice guy who finished last. He didn't. When Curry was named head football coach at Georgia Tech in 1980, the football program was flat on its back. "We were at ground zero," Athletics Director Homer Rice said. "Curry restored it to national prominence."

In seven seasons at Tech, he had only a 31-43-4 record, but in his first season, with his team 1-7-0, he entertained undefeated Notre Dame, the No.1-ranked team in America and stunned the Fighting Irish, 3-3. Explained Notre Dame coach Dan Devine, "I was out-coached. Tech was more motivated and better prepared."

The next Saturday Notre Dame was to play Alabama. On the Monday before the game, Curry got the thrill of his life. His secretary came into his office and said, "Coach Bryant is on the line."

"I thought she was kidding me," Curry says. "But Coach Bear Bryant got on the phone and said, 'What can you tell me about Notre Dame?' He was asking me, a rookie coach, for advice. I nearly fell out of my chair."

Five years later, Tech finished 9-2-1, was second in the Atlantic Coast Conference and Curry was the unanimous pick for ACC "Coach of The Year."

Not a bad start for a native son who came back to his alma mater where he had captained the 1960 team and was selected to the All-America team at center. Not a bad start for a coach who insisted his players attend class and pass their work. His players had an 85 percent graduation rate.

In writing about Bill Curry, three words come to mind—dignity, class, and integrity. When he left Georgia Tech in 1987 and agreed to coach the University of Alabama football team, he did so only after a clear understanding with Alabama President Dr. Joab Thomas. If Curry had reason to kick the star player or any other player off the team, no matter how much pressure would be exerted by alumni, President Thomas would back him 100 percent. The agreement was sealed with a handshake.

In Curry's third season he led Alabama to the Southeastern Conference championship and its first Sugar Bowl berth since 1980. He did it by playing by the rules, and there was not the slightest sign of scandal. In his three years at Alabama, he led the Tide to a 26-10 record and three bowl appearances.

He was presented the 1989 "Bobby Dodd Coach of The Year" award, a national honor, "in recognition of a higher and more noble aspect of college coaching; a creed that emphasizes something more than winning; a belief that the game of football should be kept in perspective with college life in general."

Bill Curry is a renaissance man if ever there was one. When he was ten years old, he announced to his father that he was going to marry his elementary school sweetheart, Carolyn Newton. This year they will celebrate their fortieth wedding anniversary. He was an All-State football player at College Park High School. He played on four Super Bowl teams, two for Vince Lombardi at Green Bay and two for Don Shula at Baltimore. He was named twice to the All-Pro football team. He was president of the National Football League Players Association.

He is a member of the Georgia Sports Hall of Fame. He was a member of the American Football Coaches Association Ethics Committee. He co-authored a book with George Plimpton on professional football. He served on the Board of Directors of Scottish Rite Hospital. Twice he chaired campaigns in eastern Alabama to benefit cancer patients. You might say he has done everything but play in the band—except that he did that, too. He played the baritone in the College Park High School band three years before he made the varsity football team.

Today Curry is a respected football analyst for ESPN. He recently signed a new four-year contract. The Currys live during the weekdays in a Buckhead condominium; they also have a mountain home, near Murphy, North Carolina. "From our windows we can see three states," Bill says.

If you think the Currys have led a charmed life, think again. In the past thirty-seven years, with his playing and coaching, they moved thirty-one times. Despite his success, what they endured from zealous Alabama fans was a horrible nightmare.

What happened at Alabama the Currys will forgive but never forget. When Ray Perkins, one of Bear Bryant's former players, gave up the head coaching job in 1987 to become coach of the Tampa Bay Buccaneers, the most likely candidates to succeed him were Bobby Bowden, Howard Schnellenberger, and Danny Ford, all of whom had won NCAA national championships and had ties to Alabama or its late, legendary coach, Bear Bryant. The man President Dr. Joab Thomas picked was Bill Curry.

Curry bled gold and white and probably could have had a lifetime job at Georgia Tech. But his ego got the best of him. "Carolyn and I discussed it," he explains, "and she agreed that I ought to seize the opportunity of coaching a team which was a perennial national contender."

In making the announcement of Curry's selection, Thomas said, "He not only is a good football coach but he never has cheated, has no intention of cheating, and can use the word 'study' and 'hall' in the same sentence. He is not only free of any scandal but has been an outspoken critic of coaches whose teams have been placed on probation. He can win and he can improve the academic performance of our athletes."

To say that some Tide fans and Bryant disciples were less than enthusiastic about President Thomas' choice would be an understatement. They were downright livid. Before Curry even arrived on campus, he, his wife, Carolyn, and President Thomas all received death threats. There was a backlash from some of Bryant's former players.

Once Curry and his family settled into a home, the hostility increased. Rocks and assorted missiles were thrown through his office window. The unflappable Curry took it in stride. "In dealing with criticism, I studied a lot of people like Abe Lincoln, Helen Keller, Jackie Robinson. When they were criticized they just kept going. What I have gone through is a Sunday picnic compared to what they endured."

In his first Tide football season, when his team was expected to be an also-ran, he came within one game of winning the SEC. In his second season, he took his team to the Sun Bowl. Still the harassment continued. Some members of the media called for his resignation.

Furman Bisher, as always straight as an arrow, wrote, in part, "Winning does not impress the Crimson Tide. The problem is Curry is not one of them. The crazies want another Bear Bryant and comparing Bryant to Curry would be like comparing W. C. Fields to Dr. Norman Vincent Peale."

In his third season, Curry accomplished more than his predecessor did in four seasons. Even Bryant could not match Curry in his last three years—getting Alabama to the Sugar Bowl. Curry's three-year record of 26-10-0 and three straight bowls was as good as that of any coach in Alabama history.

After winning the SEC crown in 1989 he resigned to become the head football coach at Kentucky. He left Alabama with the same class with which he arrived. "Those rabble-rousers, those hangers-on, they are riff-raff who will turn on you in a minute." Curry didn't say it, Bear Bryant did.

Curry spent seven seasons at Kentucky. When his contract was not renewed, a columnist for the Lexington Leader, wrote, in part, "Curry is a good and decent man who told his players that if they were going to play football, they were going to classes.

"He gave them a model of gentlemanly conduct. He was an example of dignity in the face of shameful and unfair attacks. He had grace under fire. His departure is Kentucky's loss."

WILLIAM JERRY CHAPPELL
More Than Winning Games

Furman Bisher said it best: "Coaches like Bill Chappell have kept more kids out of jail, off the street, shown them the right track than any public official ever did."

William Jerry Chappell deserves to be called legendary. The former Dalton head football coach—the second winningest coach in the history of Georgia high school football, who two years ago was admitted to the Georgia Sports Hall of Fame and last year was selected to the Georgia Athletic Coaches Hall of Fame—never had one losing season.

Chappell's kids won 317 games, lost a mere seventy-four, and tied a paltry nine. In thirty-three seasons, his teams won one state championship, reached the state finals five other times, captured sixteen regional championships, and made the state playoffs twenty-seven times.

But if anyone ever understood that football is more than winning games, it is Bill Chappell. While demanding the best of his players, he gave the best of himself. While driving himself and his players on the field, he drove himself in civic activities. He served as president of the Dalton Exchange Club and never missed a Dalton Rotary Club meeting. He was a member of the Elks Club, a director of the Fidelity Savings Bank, a member of the city of Dalton Recreation Committee, and founder of the Dalton Quarterback Club.

As he was piling up victory after victory, larger prep schools in the state came calling, as did several colleges. Chappell, ever loyal and true to his adopted hometown, would not even consider a move. "I never was on an ego trip. Dalton gave me what I wanted—financial and moral support, a place in the community and the opportunity to work with young boys. Looking for something bigger never was my style. Why go chasing rainbows when you already have them?"

Chappell was twelve years old when he decided he wanted to be a football coach. His father wanted him to be a lawyer. "We had our first argument about that," he says. "After I got out of college [the University of Georgia], I landed an assistant's job at Perry High School. I was living with my parents. When I received my first paycheck and showed it to my dad, he said, 'And you went to college for that?'"

Chappell, now sixty-nine, was born in LaGrange and grew up in Hapeville. Although he was no star, he lettered three consecutive years in football, baseball, and track at Hapeville High School. What Chappell did not achieve as a player, he over-achieved as a coach. Chappell's 317 victories at Dalton is exceeded in the history of Georgia football only by Dan Pitts' 346 wins at Mary Persons High School and Larry Campbell's 346 victories at Lincoln County.

His accolades are too many to mention, though some of the more notable are: head coach of the Georgia North-South All-Star prep football classic; head coach of the Georgia team in the Georgia-Florida All-Star Football classic; honorable mention for National Prep Coach of the Year; Winner of the Dwight Keith award for coaching excellence; and winner of the Atlanta Touchdown Club Coach of The Year Award.

When Chappell was named head football coach in Dalton in 1964, he did not come on like gangbusters; he came on like the Marines attacking Mount Suribachi. In his first season, he gave Dalton its first regional championship. In three of his first four years at Dalton his teams competed for the state championship. In his third season he brought home the coveted state title trophy.

His strong leadership, his demand for academic success, and his teaching of respect and individual responsibility turned his boys into men. His gridsters have gone on to become medical doctors, attorneys, bankers, and some of Dalton's top business and civic leaders.

Chappell credits much of his success to his wife, the former Bennieta Andrew of Perry, Georgia:

> While I was out coaching football, watching game films, scouting future opponents, meeting with my coaches, attending civic clubs' board meetings, she was home raising the children [Andrea and William Jr.]. She cooked their breakfast, washed and ironed their clothes, got them to school on time, and fixed their dinner. One day I realized I knew everybody's kids but my own.
>
> On another day I had a massive chest pain. I ended up in the hospital emergency room for triple bypass surgery. The next year the man I succeeded as coach at Dalton in 1964, Alf Anderson [an old Atlanta Crackers

shortstop], died. Five years ago I was a pallbearer at the funeral of one of my closest friends, Gainesville High head coach Bobby Gruhn. I began hearing voices saying "back off, back off." I knew then it was time to quit.

Today, Chappell makes time to spend with his children and two grandchildren. "I missed my kids growing up. I am trying to make up for that with time with my grandchildren," he says. He is up every morning by six, eats a light breakfast, goes to the wellness center for a daily workout, plays a round of golf, and then goes to his son's home to play with his grandchildren.

But he retains his memories. "Looking back on it, it was humorous but at that time it was kind of tough to swallow," he says, remembering an almost-losing season. "In my first eight seasons, our team made the playoffs seven times. But in the ninth year, we missed, finishing with a 5-4-1 record. After we lost our third consecutive game, the talk around town was 'Chappell is getting too old for the job. The game has passed him by. Maybe we ought to start looking for a younger coach.'"

The next season Chappell's Dalton Catamounts finished 9-5 and the team was runner-up for the state championship. The Monday-morning quarterbacks suddenly disappeared. The next seven seasons Chappell's Catamounts won regional championships.

One of the most outstanding examples of Chappell's ability to draw the best from assistant coaches and players came during the 1967 season. The team was heavily favored in the Friday-night opener but lost to Rome, 7-6. After the game Chappell called his team together and, in his quiet voice, said, "We will practice tomorrow, we will practice all day tomorrow."

The next day, from morning to dark, the Catamounts blocked and tackled, blocked and tackled, blocked and tackled. The next week, Dalton won, 33-0, and then ran the table to reach the state finals.

"I can honestly say that I loved it," says Chappell of his thirty-three-year career. "You learn from the losses. There were games in which we were outclassed but we were never outfought. "How many people look forward to going to work every day? I did. I was blessed to work at a job I loved so much."

Honors came frequently but Chappell never accepted one as totally his own. He always gave his assistants and players the credit, admitting that if it had not been for them the accolades would have been impossible.

What did Chappell look for in his players? "Attitude, desire, and dedication," he says. "The last things I looked for were talent and size. You can take a 300-pounder—and we had some of those—with speed, quickness, and agility but it doesn't matter without commitment. I used some 140-pounders who had giant-sized hearts. What some players lack in physical assets they more than make up with 100 percent effort."

Along those lines, he offers some advice for aspiring football coaches. "If you can live without it, don't go into coaching," he says. "It is no nine-to-five job. You need to genuinely love kids and understand they are kids, not adults, and they are

LEGENDS GENE ASHER

2002

x

290

going to make mistakes. Above all, you must push yourself harder than you do your players. Don't expect your players to give 100 percent if you don't."

Chappell has been named "Coach of The Year" by the *Atlanta Journal-Constitution* and the *Chattanooga Times*. He has been recognized by the American Football Coaches Association, the Georgia Athletic Coaches Association, the National Education Association, and the Georgia Education Association.

About the only honor still missing is, inexplicably, election to the Dalton Education Foundation Hall of Fame. Surely the citizens of Dalton will do the right thing and encourage Chappell's admission at the foundation's very next meeting. It is an honor well deserved for this truly legendary coach.

SPECIAL-TEAM HUDDLE

It has been fifty-six years since Atlanta Tech High had a football team, but its spirit lives with the Fourth Quarter Club.

In the 1930s and 1940s, Tech High and its neighbor, Atlanta Boys' High, dominated prep football in Georgia. Tech High's unbeaten 1937 team won the mythical national championship and its unbeaten 1946 team, with only a tie to mar its record, claimed the Southern crown.

In a reorganization of the Atlanta City School System in 1947, Tech High and Boys' High were merged into Grady High School, but nothing could erase the memory of Tech High football and its Fightin' Smithy spirit. Bill Paschal, Preston West, Bob Greer, Lee Burge, and John Williams, all Tech High football greats, met in the fall of 1985 to form a club to preserve the school's memory and honor its last football coach, the late Sidney Scarborough. The club was called the "Fourth Quarter" because all members are in the fourth quarter of their lives.

There are twelve members, all former Tech High football players, and each hosts a luncheon meeting for each month of the year. So, on the second Tuesday of every month you can spot a group of twelve, mostly youthful-looking old-timers having lunch at either the Druid Hills Golf Club, Atlanta Athletic Club, or Fernbank museum. Charter members include Ray Barnes and Phil Timberlake. Charter members who have died are LaMar Sheats, Wayne Watson, Sam Lyons, Gus Cullins, Tommy Tucker, Coach Scarborough, and John Williams. Members who have replaced the deceased are this writer, Ben Rainey, Ray Chaney, Jim Hale, Jimmy Morrison, and Sid E. Williams.

Although having played football at Tech High is the only requirement for membership, Greer, Paschal, West, and Williams were named on All-Southern teams and were selected along with Burge, Childrey, and Watson on the All-Time Tech High Team, covering a span of thirty-five years. Few people ever miss a meeting.

There is no agenda at the Fourth Quarter meetings. The guys just sit around and talk, mostly about memories of bygone days: "Who was it who scored the winning touchdown in the 1942 Milk Bowl?" Greer might ask. Someone across the table will yell, "Donnie King!" And then Paschal will recall how the 1937 Tech High team took the train to Erie, Pennsylvania, and beat the socks off the unbeaten Pennsylvanians.

Chaney was the man of the hour in his senior year (1942) at Tech High when he blocked a punt and carried it fifteen yards to set up the winning touchdown in a 15-7 victory over Boys' High. During World War II, he served with the Army's 88th division in Italy, where he was wounded and received a Purple Heart. He is a retired union contractor. He and his wife, Betty, live in Peachtree City.

Garland Childrey played football, baseball, and basketball at Tech High. He served in the Pacific during World War II. After the war he opened and operated Garland's Dry Cleaners in Buckhead for twenty-seven years. He and his wife, Gerry, live in Grayson. He will be eighty-four years old this month but does not look a day over fifty.

William Lee Burge could put Horatio Alger to shame. He scaled every corporate rung in a fifty-two-year career at Equifax that culminated in his selection as chairman of the board. He was named one of the shapers of Atlanta in 1976 and twenty years later he was continuing to shape Atlanta. He spearheaded the Summerhill project, solving neighborhood economic and housing problems. At Tech High he was named the "most outstanding" student in school. Burge is another who does not look his age (eighty-four). He lives in Buckhead.

In his Tech High senior year of 1946, Greer was named Lineman of the Year by the Atlanta Touchdown Club. He was a starting guard and devastating blocker for the 1947 University of Georgia freshman team, but a knee injury during his sophomore season cut short his Bulldog career. He had an impressive coaching career at Atlanta Southwest High School and then spent twenty-seven years in the construction business pouring sidewalks for the cities of Atlanta, Decatur, and Hapeville.

A favorite Fourth Quarter topic is the four passes, including two one-handed catches, Jim Hale made in the 1944 Tech High-Boys' High game. No discussion of Hale would be complete without his one-hand push shot and one-hand jump shot, which revolutionized prep basketball in the state of Georgia. Hale was named the best athlete in the Tech High National Athletic Scholarship Society. He went to Georgia Tech and graduated in three years. Retired after a forty-year career with the British Oxygen Company, he is now in a second career as a travel agent. He and his wife, Martha, live in Dunwoody.

At age seventy-two, James A. "Jimmy" Morrison is the youngest member of the Fourth Quarter. He was a one-man wrecking crew on the 1944 and 1945 teams, each of which lost only one of ten games. He served in the Marine Corps during World War II and spent forty years as a regional sales manager with Westinghouse. Morrison and his wife, Louise, live in Smyrna.

William A. "Bill" Paschal was the greatest all-round back Tech High ever had, punting, passing, and running his team to an unbeaten season. He played professional football for the New York Giants and led the National Football League in rushing for two consecutive years. He was named Rookie of the Year in the NFL in 1943. Today his bonus would be somewhere around $2,500,000. When Paschal retired from professional football in 1949, he took over the family sheet metal business and operated it for forty years. Retired, he and his wife, Carolyn, live in Terrell Mill Estates in Marietta.

Eighty-six-year-old Phil Timberlake is a regular luncheon attendee. "I don't know how much longer I will be able to make the meetings," he says, "but as long as the breath of life is in me I am going to try." Timberlake was the founder and operator of Timberlake Toyota in Decatur before moving to Buford and starting Timberlake Oldsmobile-Buick, which he operated for forty years.

Ben Rainey was a three-sports star at Tech High. During World War II, he landed on D-Day with the Army's Second Ranger Battalion. Ben and his wife, Marsha, live in Buckhead.

Like other members, Ray Barnes, a four-letterman, comes to the Fourth Quarter meeting for the camaraderie, to hear about Paschal's ninety-nine-yard run or the way Greer punished those Boys' High guards in 1945. "For me," he says, "a Fourth Quarter luncheon is one of life's blessings."

Although Preston West was a superstar at Tech High, he was a bigger star at Georgia Tech, where he was an All-Southeastern Conference tackle. The legendary sportscaster, Ted Husing, called West's performance against unbeaten Notre Dame in 1942 "maybe the best single game performance I have ever seen." West played the entire game in a 13-7 upset victory over the Irish, making sixteen tackles on defense and knocking down two and sometimes three opposing defenders on offense. West joined the Navy after the 1942 Tech season. He served in the South Pacific in a PT boat squadron with future president John F. Kennedy.

Fourth Quarter member Dr. Sid Williams was president of Tech High, cadet colonel of the ROTC, and winner of most every other superlative the school had. He played end at Georgia Tech, where Coach Bobby Dodd called him, "pound for pound the finest football player I ever coached." Williams is founder, and he and his wife, Nell, are co-presidents emeritus, of Life University.

What makes these men come back month after month for the luncheon? They all feel as I do, that Tech High gave them more than they could ever repay and that as long as they live so will the memory of Tech High.

2003

EDDIE LEE
True Gridiron Grit

He grew up in poverty. He never knew his father. He was raised by his mother and grandmother, both of whom were on welfare. Knee and ankle injuries almost ruined his football career. A drug and alcohol problem almost ruined his life. Most mortals would have quit under such adversity, but Eddie Lee Ivery overcame every obstacle in becoming one of the greatest football players ever produced in Georgia and one of the true role models in the Greater Atlanta community.

At Thomson High School, about thirty-five miles west of Augusta, Ivery was the most sought-after running back in America. In his senior season of 1974, he gained a record-breaking 1,710 yards. He averaged 10.2 yards per carry—first-down yardage every time he touched the ball. He had ninety scholarship offers from colleges as far west as Southern Cal and as far south as Miami. He committed to the University of Georgia before Coach Dick Bestwick, then a Yellow Jacket and now a Bulldog, convinced Ivery he belonged at Georgia Tech.

At Tech, the 6'0", 200-pound Ivery scored twenty-two touchdowns for 158 points. He set an NCAA single-game rushing record of 356 yards and a single-season rushing record of 1,562 yards. In his Tech career, he rushed for 3,517 yards, the third-highest total in Tech history. He had 4,325 all-purpose yards, also third-best in Jacket history. He broke seven Tech rushing records and was selected

2003

to the Associated Press and United Press International All-American Football teams.

Ivery's most memorable game came in 1978 when Tech visited the Air Force Academy. In a blinding storm, with a wind-chill factor of zero and an accumulation of three inches of snow that made it difficult to walk, much less run, Ivery set his NCAA single-game record. With the stadium turf a frozen tundra, the game should have been cancelled. Instead Ivery slogged his way through for touchdown runs of eighty, seventy-three, and fifty-seven yards.

Franklin C. "Pepper" Rodgers, who coached Ivery from 1976 to 1978 at Tech, said, "Eddie Lee is the greatest football player I ever coached. He was a complete player, a gifted runner; he blocked, caught passes, returned punts and kick-offs, and passed the ball. Although he was probably the greatest football player in America in his senior season, he practiced every day like he was trying to make the team."

Russell Charles, who coached Tech running backs during the Ivery era, said, "He was the only football player I ever saw who could do it all. He could run around you or over you. He could make the best tacklers in our conference miss. He could fake you out of your drawers."

Ivery is a member of the Georgia Tech Athletics Hall of Fame and the all-time Tech football team during the Carson-Fulcher-Rodgers era. He was a first-round draft pick of the Green Bay Packers in the National Football League, where he played nine seasons and twice led the team in rushing.

Today, at age forty-five and still in playing condition, Ivery is back at the Flats as assistant director of player development. A strength and conditioning coach, he works in the weight room with the swimming team and cheerleaders as well as the football team. Relaxing in his weight-room office underneath the Wardlaw Building at the south end of Bobby Dodd Stadium, Ivery answered questions about everything from growing up in poverty to his bout with booze.

He was raised in Thomson by his mother and grandmother; his father left home when he was a baby. Ivery says:

> The only time I saw him was at his funeral. Thank goodness for food stamps. Neither my mother nor my grandmother worked. My mother was determined that when I grew up I wouldn't be on welfare. She was a first-grade dropout. Never went back. She used to come in my room in the morning and say, 'Boy, you better get your butt out of bed, get dressed, and go to school.' Those words still ring in my ears.
>
> She had my clothes laid out, firewood in the stove, and a hot biscuit on the table. And then she pushed me out the door. She and my grandmother were special. I have often looked back and drawn strength from what they endured. It helped me overcome some of my problems.

For Ivery, there were no problems at Thomson High School. With encouragement from his family, he played football, basketball, and baseball and ran track. In his senior football season, he gained 1,710 yards, averaging 9.4 yards per carry. He was named to All-State, All-Southern and prep All-America teams. When football scholarship offers came pouring in, his mother sat him down and told him how blessed he was to have an opportunity to get a college education.

"She reminded me that when she and her brothers were growing up there was no chance for blacks to have an opportunity like this. She told me that whichever college I attended, not to let football be my first priority, that the reason for attending college was to get an education and that she expected me to get one and a college degree."

Ivery had been looking forward to playing college football ever since he was a tot. His uncle, Jimmy Lee Ivery, a halfback for the local black high school, always brought his uniform when he came over to visit. "I used to put on his jersey and dream of the day I would be playing football," Ivery recalls.

Ivery narrowed his choices to Tech and Georgia. He had his heart set on Tech, but Thomson was Bulldog country and its citizens were making visits to the Ivery household night and day. Ivery committed to Georgia.

"When Coach Bestwick came to Thomson to recruit me for Tech, I knew I had made a mistake. I was trying to please the people around town, not myself. I thought about my visit to Tech and how impressed I was with Coach Rodgers and the players I met. I hugged Coach Bestwick and signed a Tech grant-in-aid."

Thirteen years after he finished his Tech playing career, he returned to the campus and earned his degree in Industrial Management. The same determination that made him successful on the football field brought him back to the classroom.

There were those who said the Packers' No. 1 draft pick in 1979 would never make it. No one questioned his heart; they questioned his ability to recover from injury. On the third play of his professional debut, he tore the ligaments in his left knee. His rookie season was finished before it ever got started.

"I accepted it," Ivery says of the injury, "and I was willing to pay any price to rehabilitate it." He underwent surgery, physical therapy, workouts with weights. When the 1980 season started he was ready, mentally and physically. He not only dislodged Terrell Middleton, who had been a three-year regular, from the starting running back job, but led the team in rushing and was second in pass receiving. He led the team in rushing again in 1981.

Ivery was on a professional high, but it was not the only high he was on. Drugs and alcohol almost did him in. "I got into the fast lane," he says, "drinking, using, and smoking. I wasn't being a father to my two children or a husband to my wife. I was selfish and self-centered. I thought I was the center of the universe and that everything revolved around me."

The fast lane cost him his marriage, which was enough to get him back on track. With the same determination he has exhibited throughout his life, he checked himself in to a long-term recovery center. "It gave me an opportunity to reflect on how I was living my life. I learned I was only one cell in a vast network of human cells. I made the effort to conquer the self-life."

Ivery played six more seasons with the Packers, going to player meetings and practices during the day and AA meetings at night. Back home in Atlanta, he has been clean and sober for five years. When he is not in the Tech weight room, he is speaking to elementary schools, middle schools, and high schools throughout metropolitan Atlanta. "I share my experiences," he says, "in hopes they will not go down the same path I did."

Eddie Lee Ivery not only had the courage to change but the unselfishness to help his fellow human beings as well.

GEORGE BERNARD MALOOF
Hometown Hero

Of all the greats who have come out of Georgia, the one the Atlanta Touchdown Club picked for its inaugural Legends of the Game honor was George Bernard Maloof. The TD Club could not have made a better choice. Maloof not only excelled as a player at Marist School, Georgia Tech and in the US Air Force but as a coach at Saint Pius X High School for twenty-six years. He is held in such high esteem that Saint Pius named its football field after him and Marist dedicated a special game in his honor. It may be the only time a school honored a former coach of its archrival institution.

Maloof is a special guy, make no mistake about that. When asked who had the biggest influence on his life, Bobby Dodd, the legendary coach at Georgia Tech, or R. L. "Shorty" Doyal, the immortal Marist coach, he says, "Neither. The biggest influence of my life was a nun, Sister Mary Kevin, who taught me in the fifth grade." Maloof named one of his sons Kevin, after her, and says, "If my first born had been a girl instead of a boy I would have named her Kevin, too."

Maloof will live forever in the hearts of Georgia Tech football fans and he will be forever No. 1 on the hate list of ardent Bulldog fans. In 1951, he scored four touchdowns in leading Tech to a 48-6 rout of the Bulldogs, an unbeaten season (11-0-1) and to the Southeastern Conference championship. No Jacket before or since ever put twenty-four points on the scoreboard against the Dogs.

Maloof was born in Atlanta at the old Piedmont Hospital, now a parking lot, where Atlanta-Fulton County Stadium used to be. He grew up in the Grant Park area and attended Immaculate Conception Elementary School, where he came under the influence of Sister Mary Kevin.

"I was ten years old," Maloof recalls. "She taught me how to read and how to speak. She taught me right from wrong and above all she taught me to stretch my thinking. She told me to keep reaching for higher goals, that there was nothing I could not accomplish if I thought I could."

Maloof believed. Two years later when he entered Marist, then an all-boys' military school located downtown, he set out to be the best all-round student in school, a goal he far exceeded. He was president of his freshman, sophomore, junior, and senior classes. He was business manager, military editor, and sports editor of the *Blue and Gold*, Marist's weekly newspaper. He was a colonel, the highest-ranking officer in the Cadet Corps. He was twice named the Corps' outstanding cadet.

He lettered four years in football, making All-State, All-Southern, and prep All-American teams. He lettered four times in baseball, making the All-Greater Atlanta and All-State teams and picked up two more monograms for basketball. He played in the Georgia High School All-Star Game and was named the outstanding player on the North team.

Enough, already? How about sharpshooter on the rifle team and an officer in the Society of the Blessed Mother? Talk about the all-American boy: The Atlanta Touchdown Club named him the most valuable prep lineman in Georgia.

At Georgia Tech, besides leading his team to an SEC crown, he played third base on Joe Pittard's baseball team and twice was named to the all-conference team. When Maloof graduated from Tech in 1952, he went into the US Air Force as a second lieutenant. He was picked to play on the Fort Bragg All-Star football team and was chosen most valuable player in the 9th Air Force.

Coming home to Atlanta after a two-year Air Force stint, he joined his prep alma mater, Marist, as assistant football coach. His stay was short-lived. Two years later, in 1958, Saint Pius X Catholic High School opened in Atlanta and the man it sought for the head coaching job was George Bernard Maloof. It was a wise choice.

Maloof kept going full speed for twenty-six years, posting a 168-85-12 record. His was the first Catholic school to win a state championship (1968). He whipped his prep alma mater and he was twice named Georgia Class AA Coach of The Year.

Pride and enthusiasm are the heart of Maloof's coaching philosophy. "It might sound corny," he says, "but if you have pride in your work and the enthusiasm to challenge anybody there is nothing you cannot accomplish. Above all, you must be fair, honest with your players. They need to feel they are being cared for whether they are being chewed out or not."

And how did the Pi Hi players feel about their coach? Chris Eck, a member of Maloof's 1984 team, says, "He gave so much of himself to others. I feel he really cared for me and all the other team members. It never seemed to matter whether we won or lost on the scoreboard because when you know the man as a coach and father figure, you know you were a better person for having come under his influence. He was tough, demanding. He asked for 100 percent and he got it. We felt he genuinely loved us and wanted us to become as good as we could be."

Maloof received a special John Paul II medal, for his achievements in education. It is one of the highest honors conferred by the Catholic Church.

His life has not been a bed of roses. His first wife of twenty-one years, two daughters, and two stepsons all died prematurely. Maloof had prostate cancer in 1988, which he says he has overcome. He has been fighting lung cancer for two years, which he says now is in remission. If that was not enough to put Maloof down, he was in a serious auto accident three years ago in which he suffered a broken hip and a leg fractured in five places. But except for the cane he needs to walk, Maloof is unchanged. The smile and the sparkling personality he had as a kid are still evident today.

Today, Maloof is retired and living in Chamblee. His greatest enjoyment comes when he and Anita, his wife of twenty-five years, plan holiday dinners for children and grandchildren. He fishes, plays golf and works around the house. His schedule is a far cry from the one he used to keep when he was football coach at Saint Pius, athletic director, assistant to the school principal, head of boys' discipline, and teacher of math and mechanical drawing. He brought game films home in the evening and watched them in his den, "so the kids would know they had a daddy."

Maloof had a chance to become an assistant college football coach at his alma mater in 1967 under head coach Bud Carson, but his love of family convinced him to turn it down. "I was away from home enough as it was," he says, "and going into college coaching would have kept me away much more. The college assistant is always on the road, with recruiting, scouting, speaking engagements. It would have been nice going back to Tech but not at the expense of family time."

Aside from his four-TD romp against the Bulldogs, Maloof's biggest thrill was September 15, 1995, at halftime of the Saint Pius–Chamblee game. A tent was erected in the Pius end zone and many of his former players and cheerleaders came for the dedication of George B. Maloof Field. "There is no way I can describe the elation I felt," he says. "I was brought to tears but they were tears of happiness."

Maloof's two sons, Kevin and Keith, are following in their dad's coaching footsteps. Kevin has won more than 100 games in twelve years, two at Meadow Creek and ten at Dacula. Keith, at Tucker for three years and Norcross for ten, has had his teams consistently in region playoffs.

Says Keith of his dad, "He instilled in me the ability to communicate with kids. When no one else believed in me, he gave me the vision and the strength to do things I never thought I could do."

Says Kevin, "He taught me what work ethic was all about. He taught me to do the best I could do with the talent God gave me."

For the Maloof boys, life with father has been pretty darn good.

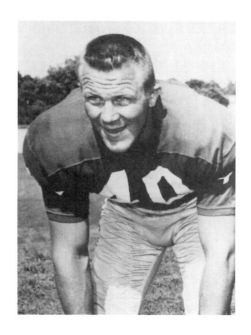

THERON COLEMAN SAPP
The Man who Broke the Drought

November 30, 1957 was a sub-freezing but delightful afternoon for Bulldog fans at Grant Field. A stiff wind was blowing out of the northeast as some 40,000 fans—mostly Tech partisans—came to see if Tech could make it nine consecutive victories over Georgia or if the Dogs would find a way to break the drought. They did, thanks to Theron Coleman Sapp, a mighty fullback out of Lanier High School in Macon.

The Bulldogs were suffering through a third consecutive losing season and had not scored a touchdown against Tech in four long years. But this was another day. After a scoreless first half, Sapp recovered a fumble at midfield. On third and 12 at the Tech thirty-nine, quarterback Charlie Britt hit Jimmy Orr with a thirteen-yard pass for a first down at the Tech twenty-six. From then on it was all Sapp…Sapp…Sapp.

He crashed into the Tech forewall on six consecutive plays, down to the Tech one-yard line. On fourth down Britt again handed off to Sapp, who powered his way into the right side of the Tech line for the Dogs' first touchdown against Tech since 1953 and the only touchdown of the game. Ken Cooper converted the extra point, giving Georgia a 7-0 victory. Sapp only crossed the goal line six times in his Georgia career but he did as much for Georgia pride with one touchdown as anyone in Bulldog history, including Frankie Sinkwich, Charley Trippi, or Herschel Walker.

The late, legendary Georgia Tech coach Bobby Dodd said of Sapp, "Walker won the national championship for Georgia (1980) and was awarded the Heisman trophy (1982) but to older Bulldogs who suffered through the 1950s, Sapp's breaking the drought was greater. He silenced eight years of bragging from Tech students and alumni. Breaking the drought was a remarkable achievement."

Sapp's number 40 was retired two months after the 1958 Tech game. His jersey, along with Sinkwich's, Trippi's, and Walker's, hangs in the lobby of the Butts-Mehre Building at the University of Georgia. Sinkwich gained 2,271 yards and scored thirty touchdowns, Trippi 1,669 yards and 32 touchdowns and Walker 5,259 yards and fifty-two touchdowns. Sapp rushed for just 1,269 yards, but he ripped the Jackets' line to shreds in breaking the drought.

Says the Drought-Breaker, "I never dreamed my jersey would be retired."

Sapp was named to All-Southeastern Conference teams in 1957 and 1958. He led the Bulldogs to a second win over Tech in 1958, 16-3. He was named most valuable player in the Tech game in 1957 and 1958.

Sapp was named Georgia's Back of the Decade (1950–59). His coach, Wally Butts, called him "the best offensive fullback I ever had." Sapp went to Georgia with a broken neck and finished an eight-season professional football career with a broken leg. In between, he was captain of the 1958 Bulldogs, named most valuable player in the North-South and Blue-Gray College All-Star games, and helped lead the Philadelphia Eagles to an NFL championship.

Today, the sixty-seven-year-old Sapp lives with his wife of thirty-seven years, Kay, in a two-story, five-bedroom house on twelve acres in Evans, Georgia, about fifteen miles north of Augusta. At 6'0", he weighs the same as he did when he played pro ball, 210, only ten pounds over his playing weight at Georgia. He works out three times a week, walking, riding his bicycle, and playing racquetball. He owned and operated four Maryland Fried Chicken stores in Augusta for twenty years. Now he is down to one store and in two years hopes to be completely retired. Then he and Kay can spend more time with their four children, nine cats, three dogs, two horses, and two billy goats.

Meanwhile, Sapp is up at 7 A.M. five days a week. He works on his yard, checks his animals, and heads for his fried chicken store where he does everything from cooking to greeting the customers. When the lunch crowd is gone, he supervises the cleaning up, talks with his employees, checks the books, and heads for home. He and Kay rarely miss dinner together.

He has not attended a Bulldogs football game in four years but he has never missed one on TV. "It is nice," he says, "to be able to avoid the traffic to and from Athens and to walk only a few steps from my den to the kitchen and have my own fried chicken."

What does he remember about breaking the drought? "On the bus trip from Athens to Grant Field, I remember telling Coach Butts that we were going to win the game. I told him I didn't sleep a wink last night, that all I could think about was that we were going to break the drought."

Sapp was born June 15, 1935, in Dublin, Georgia, the youngest of ten children. When he was three years old his father accidentally shot himself. His mother moved the family to Macon where she supported the children by working as a riveter at Robins Air Force Base, down the road in Warner Robins.

As he would be at Georgia, Sapp was a sixty-minute man on the Lanier High School football team. He played offensive fullback, backed up on the line on defense, kicked off, and returned punts and kickoffs. He led Lanier to the State Class AA championship and was picked on the All-State and All-Southern football team. He was recruited heavily by Auburn and South Carolina but had been listening to Georgia football on the radio since his preteen days. He signed a grant-in-aid with Georgia.

In the state's annual North-South High School All-Star football practice, his world came crashing down. In his first scrimmage, he drove into the defensive team's thickest part of the middle and was knocked head over heels in a major pileup, suffering three cracked vertebrae in his neck. His surgeon told him he should never play football again, that even a slight blow to the wrong place could be fatal.

Coaches Butts and Quenton Lumpkin came to the hospital and told Sapp he had his scholarship no matter what. He spent his entire freshman year at Georgia in a head-to-pelvis body cast. Coach Butts told him he should not play football again but Sapp convinced his mentor otherwise. He spent his sophomore year on the B team and his junior and senior years on varsity, bulling his way up the middle 258 times, right smack in the thick of things.

The Drought-Breaker flirted with death but became one of the greatest heroes in the history of University of Georgia football. Sound like fiction? It is the true story of a legend.

RONALD MARK BLOMBERG
Baseball's First DH

This month marks the thirtieth anniversary of Atlanta's Ronald Mark Blomberg's debut as baseball's first designated hitter. The date was April 6, 1973, the season opener for the New York Yankees and the Boston Red Sox. The place: Boston's historic Fenway Park. The park was packed, despite a bone-chilling temperature of thirty degrees.

Blomberg recalls:

> And when the public address announcer said, "Ron Blomberg, DH!" I wasn't sure what the DH was. But I went up to home plate to hit against the ace of the Red Sox pitching staff, Luis Tiant. The bases were loaded. I didn't get a chance to hit. I drew a walk.
>
> When the inning was over, I was left at first base. I was going to stay there because normally that was my position. But Elston Howard, one of my coaches, yelled from the dugout, "Come on back to the bench. You aren't supposed to stay out there."
>
> I went back to the dugout and asked Howard, "What do I do next?"
>
> He said, "You just sit here with me!"

The Red Sox won the game, 15-5, but the man who made history was Blomberg, soon to become the pride of the Yankees.

After the game, reporters swarmed the Yankees dressing room to interview Blomberg. Meanwhile, Marty Appel, the Yankees' public relations director, grabbed Blomberg's bat, jersey, and ball and shipped it all to the Baseball Hall of Fame.

It was to be a banner year for Blomberg: He hit .329, belted twelve home runs and drove in fifty-seven runs, and boasted a slugging percentage of .495. Topps put out a baseball card to commemorate his DH role. In seven seasons for the Yankees as a first baseman-outfielder-DH, he had a lifetime batting average of .295. He was selected once to the American League All-Star team and played in three World Series.

However, the fact that Blomberg's bat is enshrined in baseball's Hall of Fame does not impress the Georgia Sports Hall of Fame. The Hall of Fame inducted six new members recently, but Blomberg was not among them. Ignoring Blomberg since he was first recommended for membership in 1989 by Jimmy Booth, one of Atlanta's most knowledgeable sports buffs, makes the Georgia Hall of Fame look like a Hall of Shame.

But it's not too late. Hall of Fame leaders Howard "Doc" Ayers, Johnny Griffith, and Loran Smith could lead the charge to get Blomberg into the hall, something that has been overdue for fourteen years.

The Yankees, the DH, the All-Star game selection, and the World Series rings aside, Blomberg is Hall of Fame material on his high-school record alone. No other athlete has been chosen to the Parade All-America teams in football, basketball, and baseball. Roger Couch, Blomberg's basketball coach at Druid Hills High School, says, "Blomberg is the finest basketball player I ever saw—high school or college." He was sought after by every major college basketball team in America and was ticketed to play for the legendary John Wooden at UCLA until major league baseball made him the No. 1 draft pick in 1967.

Blomberg, now fifty-four, was born in Atlanta, grew up in the northeast section of DeKalb County and now lives in Roswell. Semi-retired, he spends much of his time with his family (wife and two children) and sharpening his golf game on the links of Brookfield West. (Maybe playing golf with some of the Georgia Hall of Fame selectors would improve his chances.)

Blomberg got his baseball start in DeKalb's Kittredge Little League. He hit home runs beyond the fences, attracting the attention of every prep baseball coach in the county. He spent almost two years in the minor leagues before making his major league debut in 1969 with three hits in six at-bats late in the season.

The next year he batted .322 and slugged at .477—the second lowest slugging percentage of his major league career. He was not big for a Yankee (6'1", 205 pounds), but his prodigious home runs earned him the nickname of "Der Boomber." His photograph was on the cover of *Sports Illustrated* and countless other baseball publications.

New Yorkers had dreamed for years that a Jewish baseball player would someday play for the Yankees. Blomberg fit the bill. "I did every bagel, cream cheese, and lox commercial in the city of New York," he recalls. "I also was claimed to be a member of every New York synagogue from the Bronx to Staten Island." Although Blomberg did not publicly refuse to play on Yom Kippur, the highest holy day of the Jewish year, he did make it possible for every Yankee fan to get home before the start of the holiday in 1971. The Yankees were deadlocked in the ninth against the Cleveland Indians. The holiday began at sundown, and the sun was slowly sinking when Blomberg came to bat. He hit the first pitch into deep centerfield, scoring Jake Gibbs and getting all the Jewish fans home in time for the Kol Nidre service. The next day the *New York Times*, in a rare banner headline, proclaimed, "Sundown Single Wins For Yankees."

In the dressing room after the game, Blomberg said, "I not only got that hit for our fans but for me, too. I was going to synagogue, too, and if I had not ended the game with that single, I would have left the stadium anyway. There are some things more important than a baseball game."

As a result of Blomberg's hit, at least one New York rabbi changed his high holy day sermon to "Sundown Kid Hits Deadline Single."

Blomberg's career .295 batting average is remarkable because during his seven years with the Yankees and one with the Chicago White Sox, he was plagued with injuries. He underwent four knee and two shoulder operations and had more muscle pulls than a human should endure. He never played an entire season. There is no telling how good he might have been had he stayed healthy, but one home run gives a clue: Blomberg took one of his powerful rips against Hall of Fame pitcher Nolan Ryan and sent a monstrous blast toward deep right field. The outfielders never moved, the fans stood in awe and Blomberg gazed at the rapidly disappearing sphere. The ball crashed against the upper deck facade of old Yankee Stadium, a mere foot and a half from leaving the park altogether. Only Mickey Mantle had smashed a ball for such distance.

Blomberg twice was voted the most popular person in New York, edging out Joe Namath, the pride of the Jets. Blomberg says:

> My greatest wish today is that playing for the Yankees in a World Series and in an All-Star game might be an inspiration to some youngsters who are dreaming the dream I was fortunate enough to have lived.
>
> My biggest thrill was just being a small part of New York's baseball scene. I would walk down the street, even when I was injured, and fans would come up to me and say, "Hang in there, Ron, we're behind you." New York Yankees fans are one big family.

At the end of the 1977 season, Blomberg opted for free agency and signed with the Chicago White Sox. He spent his final season mostly on the bench, plagued by injuries, but his career is worthy of the highest recognition.

While the Georgia Sports Hall of Fame fixates on high school coaches, a true injustice is perpetuated: the exclusion of a major league All-Star, Ronald Mark Blomberg. Keeping Blomberg out of the hallowed hall only diminishes its own claims to greatness. If Blomberg's historic feat is good enough for Cooperstown, why isn't it good enough for the Georgia Sports Hall of Fame?

THE DAPRANOS
A Golden Couple

Unless you read the *Fayette Neighbor,* or attended the World Masters Games in Melbourne, Australia, last October, you never would know that Bill and Jeanne Daprano won four gold medals between them.

Bill won gold in the pentathlon (long jump, javelin, 200 meters, 1,500 meters and discus) plus silver in the 100 meters and javelin; Jeanne won gold in the 1,500 meters, 800 meters and 400 meters and bronze in the 200 meters. You might say the Dapranos have a corner on the gold market. Bill and Jeanne each have won more than 100 pieces of gold since they started competing in the Masters program more than twenty years ago.

The Dapranos not only own a host of state, regional, and national records, they hold seventeen world records. Bill, seventy-six, owns outdoor world marks in the pentathlon (age seventy-three), 4x200 relays (ages seventy to seventy-nine), 4x400 relays (ages sixty to sixty-nine), and pentathlon (age fifty-six). He also owns world indoor records in the 4x400 and 4x800 relays (ages seventy to seventy-nine).

Jeanne is the speed merchant of the family. She owns twelve world records, is sixty-six years old, and looks ten years younger. In women's competition from age groups sixty to sixty-five and sixty-five to seventy, Jeanne holds indoor and outdoor records in 800 and 1,500 meters, the mile run and 4x800 relays. Last year she was nominated for the Masters Hall of Fame and chosen female track athlete of the year.

Three years ago, at Gateshead, England, they each won gold—Bill three pieces and Jeanne four. But their biggest win came off the field. The couple met at Gateshead for the first time. Bill, a native Atlantan, was living in Riverdale, Georgia, and Jeanne, a native of Iowa, was living in Long Beach, California. "The best thing about running," Jeanne says, "is the people you meet. I met Bill and he is the nicest person I know. It is not the medals that count, it is the human relationships."

Bill recalls:

> The first time I laid eyes on her I knew she was the woman for me. We were in the cafeteria line and I spotted this good-looking, trim blonde about four people ahead of me. When she sat down at a table, I broke through the line to make darn sure I would get a seat next to her.
>
> That night, there was a get- acquainted dance for all the track competitors. I asked her if I could have the first dance. She said OK. For the remainder of the evening neither one of us danced with anyone else. I was smitten—but good.
>
> For the next twelve days, I had breakfast with her every morning and dinner with her every night. When we were not competing on the track we were taking walks or sitting on a bench holding hands.
>
> I finally found the one person I wanted to live with. On the last day of the meet, I told her, "I am going to marry you." She didn't say yes and she didn't say no. But she agreed to meet me in Saint Louis for a Masters Track Meet, only three weeks away. She said yes in Saint Louis and a month later we were honeymooning in Hawaii.

The Dapranos now live in Fayetteville, Georgia. They will have a busy spring and summer, with the Southeastern Senior Classic in Raleigh, North Carolina, this month, the National Masters Championships in Charlotte in June, and the World Games in Puerto Rico in July.

Bill is retired from coaching and homebuilding and Jeanne from teaching. As coach at Atlanta's old Saint Joseph's High School, Daprano won three region football championships, posted a twenty-five-game winning streak, and a ten-year record of fifty-nine wins, thirty-one losses, and four ties.

After fifteen years as a teacher and high-school coach he entered the insurance and real estate business. In his first year, he more than tripled his coaching income. At the age of forty-three, Daprano was on his way to becoming one of the most successful homebuilders in metropolitan Atlanta. But the success took its toll. He says:

> I could not build houses fast enough. I was on the job site six days a week, encouraging supervisors, giving a compliment here and a kick in the rear there. I was on a constant deadline. I put unbelievable pressure on myself. My blood pressure was out of sight. My doctor told me I could give up the torrid pace I was on and find something that would relax me or die a young man. I wanted to live.

Daprano gave up the business but not the torrid pace. He simply redirected his energy into something positive—running.

Daprano grew up on the south side of Atlanta near Grant Park. He attended old Atlanta Tech High School, the University of Georgia and Livingston State University in Alabama, where he played football and baseball and ran track. At 5'10", 165 pounds, he is the same weight as he was twenty years ago.

His biggest thrill came in the Masters age fifty-five to fifty-nine competition when he beat his old hero, former US Olympic champion Bob Richards, in the pentathlon. Richards' photograph used to be a fixture on Wheaties cereal boxes.

Daprano has three children by a previous marriage (his first wife, Judy, died at age fifty-one): Bill Jr., forty-five, Judy, thirty-six, and Christy, twenty-nine.

Jeanne Daprano grew up as an "Iowa farm girl." She was born in Massena, a town of 300 people, where her parents had a farm on which she milked cows, planted corn, and drove the tractor. "I admired what my parents did," she says, "but after working most of our 160 acres I learned at an early age that I did not want to marry a farmer." She left Iowa for the University of Nebraska where she received a B.A. in elementary education. She went on for a master's degree at the University of California in Long Beach and taught at a Long Beach parochial school.

Her first marriage lasted twenty-six years before her husband discovered he had lung cancer. Four months later he was dead. "It was the low point in my life," she says. One of her friends suggested she start running for therapy, nothing competitive, just running on the beach.

"I got out there and it felt like a million dollars. It wasn't long before I was getting out of my 'poor me' state. I started running competitively and winning and it made me feel good enough to start a track program for kids, especially those in a Long Beach Cambodian community. I got so much pleasure out of running, not just for the fitness but for my whole demeanor. It got me in shape, mentally and spiritually."

Then she met Bill:

I was not thinking about marriage. It was the furthest thing from my mind. Bill was such a gentleman, such an athlete, such a magnetic person. He and I liked the same things—running, swimming, walking, biking, children. I never had children of my own but I felt like I did when I worked with [children in] the Cambodian community.

Of all the gold we have won, what we won in England is the most memorable of all because it was the beginning of a long, loving relationship.

> Think about it: Here is a woman over the age of sixty-five and a man over the age of seventy-five and they probably can outrun 98 percent of all the high school students in the world. When they compete in the World Games in July, you can bet they will win more gold.

JOHN S. HUNSINGER
A Winner in All Fields

Athlete, musician, dancer, family man, champion of charitable causes, civic-minded citizen, successful business man, and host with the most on the ball. John S. Hunsinger, native Atlantan, is all of these.

He grew up in West End, in a one-bedroom house he shared with his mother, grandfather, and three uncles. Today, he lives in a four-bedroom, four-bath home on an acre on fashionable West Wesley Road. He is president of one of the largest real estate companies in Atlanta. When he started his firm in 1969, it grossed $1 million in sales. Last year it grossed $130 million.

When he was a preteen, it would have taken no genius to predict Hunsinger's success. In the morning before school, he had a newspaper route for the *Atlanta Constitution*. Before dinner and after school and games of football, basketball, or baseball, he delivered newspapers for the old *Atlanta Georgian*. In the evening he studied and took music lessons on the French horn and trumpet.

At Brown High School, he led the football team to the state championship and was named on the All-City, All-State, All-Southern and prep All-America teams. He was chosen Back of The Year for the state of Georgia by the Atlanta Touchdown Club. Talk about the all-round student: Hunsinger played baseball and basketball, as well as trumpet in the school band. He was a straight A student and class valedictorian. He was sought after by almost every college in the Southeast but he decided to follow in the footsteps of his great uncle, the late

George "Pup" Phillips, an All-America center at Georgia Tech in 1916, and his father, John K. Hunsinger, who played on the 1928 Tech Rose Bowl team.

At Tech, he played running back on offense and linebacker on defense. His freshman team was undefeated. During his sophomore season in 1952, his Yellow Jackets were not only undefeated but declared national champions by the International News Service. He played in three bowl games, twice in the Sugar Bowl and once in the Cotton Bowl. The Jackets won all three.

His studies never suffered: He was named to the Academic All-America football team and twice received the top academic award in the Industrial Engineering department.

Today Hunsinger is seventy-two years old and looks fifty. At 5'10", 179 pounds, he is fit enough to get into his old Tech uniform. He exercises daily, running three miles before he goes into his office at 8 A.M. No one has given more to the culture or charitable needs of Atlanta than John Hunsinger. He sings with the Atlanta Symphony and the Saint Anthony Church choir. He serves or has served on the boards of the Atlanta Union Mission, the Episcopal Church Foundation, Children's Health Care of Atlanta, Boys and Girls Clubs of Metropolitan Atlanta, Atlanta Fine Arts Guild, and Atlanta Urban League, among many others. His sports promotions raised more than $1 million for the old Scottish Rite Hospital.

Hunsinger has been married to the former Kathy Blalock for nineteen years. They have two sons, Jonathan, fifteen, and Matthew, ten. Both are athletes. Hunsinger has three children by a previous marriage: John Jr., forty-three, a teacher, painter, and circus performer; Hall, forty-two, an off-Broadway actor in New York; and Robbie Lynn, thirty-nine, who plays the oboe with the Atlanta and Chicago symphonies. No matter how big a real estate deal he may be involved in, no matter what social function or board meeting he has scheduled, nothing interferes with being there when his children are performing.

Ten times a year he gives a gala party in the lobby of his office building for approximately 100 of his agents, clients, tenants and friends. The Hunsinger building is located at 1627 Peachtree Street, two doors north of The Temple. Every year, for the Jewish High Holy Days, Hunsinger, an Episcopalian, reserves 90 percent of his parking lot for Temple congregants who are too late to find space in The Temple lot.

"We are all God's children," he says. "We are all brethren."

JIMMY HARPER
A Record-Breaking Official

Jimmy Harper, one of the great Georgia Bulldogs, can thank three Georgia Tech Yellow Jackets for his incredible success as a college football official and a businessman.

It was Ray Graves, a longtime assistant to Tech's Bobby Dodd before he became head coach at Florida, who was one of Harper's sponsors for membership in the Southeastern Conference Football Officials Association. It was Pete Ferris, a former Yellow Jackets end, who got Harper an interview with the brokerage firm of Merrill Lynch. Harper has made them exceedingly proud.

First, his official stats: He officiated more football bowl games (forty-five) and for more years (thirty-six) than anyone in the history of the National Collegiate Athletic Association. He has been referee of three NCAA championship games and was an official when Paul "Bear" Bryant won his 315th game, becoming, at the time, the winningest college football coach. Last year Harper was honored by the National Football Foundation and College Hall of Fame for "unprecedented service as a referee of the game." He retired as an active official in 1995 but continues to serve the SEC as an observer of officials.

Harper owes his start in college officiating to another Yellow Jacket, Joe DeLany. It was DeLany, a star halfback for Tech in the 1950s, who recommended Harper as an official of Georgia high school football when he came out of the service in 1960.

Harper was as respected as a stockbroker as he was as a referee. In forty years with Merrill Lynch, he has been a perennial leading producer. He is a senior vice president and has been a member of the firm's elite Chairman's Club for more than thirty years.

Today, Harper, sixty-eight, lives with his wife, Claire, in a home on two acres in Buckhead. They have been married forty-seven years and have one son, James K. Harper III, and two daughters, Claire Anderson and Beth Fortune. They have ten grandchildren.

Harper grew up in Thomasville, the son of a football coach, J. K. "Doc" Harper. Although he did not play for his dad, he made the town of Thomasville proud, earning All-State, All-Southern, and All-America prep honors at Thomasville High School. He played basketball and baseball, pitching the baseball team into the finals of the state tournament. He had eleven football scholarship offers but there was no question where he was headed. The whole Harper family had been Georgia Bulldogs.

He played quarterback for the late Coach Wally Butts, making the squad as a freshman and earning four varsity letters, (1952–56). He was twice named to the Academic All-America team. One of his team captains, Don Shea, says, "He had as much character and courage as anyone I ever saw. He called the plays in the huddle and no one ever questioned him. He gave 100 percent on every play."

In 1954, Harper's sophomore season, it was one-platoon football. Harper played 550 out of 600 minutes. Graduating in 1956 with a degree in accounting, Harper joined the US Air Force and spent four years piloting multi-engine airplanes. When he came back to Atlanta and started his officiating career, he rarely saw his Bulldogs play. An SEC rule prohibited referees from officiating games in which their alma mater plays.

In 1984 he refereed his "most exciting game," the Orange Bowl for the 1983 national championship. It was Miami vs. Nebraska, with Nebraska a two-touchdown favorite and considered the best college football team in history. In a stunning upset, Miami led until the last play of the game when Nebraska scored a touchdown to come within one point of a tie. The Cornhuskers went for two and missed, and the Hurricanes went out with a 31-30 victory and the national crown.

Although Harper was considered the No. 1 referee in America for many years, even he was not perfect. In 1972, during the Tulane-Miami game, he unwittingly gave Miami five downs. "On the fifth down," Harper recalls, "Miami scored a touchdown to win the game. Nobody knew about it until we got back to the hotel and heard it on the radio. We had a police escort to the airport."

ROGER ALLEN KAISER
Everybody's All-American

It is one thing to be the greatest college basketball player ever in the state of Georgia. It's another to be the most successful basketball coach. But it's downright remarkable to be both.

Roger Allen Kaiser is Georgia's only two-time basketball first-team All-American and the only basketball coach in Georgia history to win a national collegiate championship. Actually, Kaiser-coached teams won four national titles.

At the time of his graduation in 1961, Kaiser held eighteen of twenty-five Georgia Tech records involving field goals and free throws. His 85.8 percent career free throw mark is still tops, both for Tech and the Southeastern Conference. (Tech was in the SEC when Kaiser played.)

You could rename the Tech basketball media guide and call it the Kaiser media guide, because he is listed for records, near-records or honors won no less than forty-one times. He scored 1,628 points during his Tech career. That was before the three-point game; because many of his shots were from far back, there is no telling how many points he would have scored under the three-point rule. He led the SEC in scoring in 1960 and 1961.

If ever there was an all-American boy, it is Roger Kaiser. He married his former Dale High School sweetheart and cheerleader, Beverly Hevron. He made speeches to civic clubs and Little Leagues, and graciously gave autographs wherever he went. He was captain of the basketball team in his junior and senior

2003

seasons and captain and most valuable player in the SEC, which he led in hitting, for the Tech baseball team.

"He was the best player I ever had," said his late Tech basketball coach, John "Whack" Hyder, "but that is only part of it. Everything he did, he did well. He had the drive for perfection, not just in sports but in the way he dressed. His shoes sparkled, front and back, and the belt buckle on his military uniform glistened."

The legendary Bobby Dodd said of Kaiser, "He was the best all-round athlete in Georgia Tech history."

For an All-American who never wanted to coach, Georgia Tech's most famous cager has one of the most sensational coaching success stories in history. Taking up residence at West Georgia College in 1970, he secured the first national collegiate crown ever won by a Georgia team four years later. In twenty years at West Georgia, he turned out three All-Americans and six players who made it in the National Basketball Association.

Dr. Sid Williams convinced Kaiser to start an athletics program at Life College. Among the fifteen national championships Life College sports teams won, three were Kaiser-coached basketball teams. In ten years at Life, Kaiser produced twelve All-Americans. Eight times he was named conference Coach of The Year. In thirty years of college coaching, Kaiser was named Coach of The Year in Georgia eleven times, state of Georgia Sports Hall of Fame Coach of The Year three times and NAIA Coach of The Year twice.

Today, Kaiser is sixty-five years old. During the week he lives with his wife of forty-three years in a condo in Marietta. On the weekends, the couple retreats to their lakefront home in Carrollton.

With all the honors and success Kaiser has enjoyed, his life has not been a bed of roses. He lost a daughter, Jill, at age thirty-five, to breast cancer and he has had bouts with colon cancer and prostate cancer. He is doing fine now, and spends many of his retirement days with his two children and five grandchildren.

Of Kaiser's many flawless performances at the Tech Coliseum, none matched his game against mighty Kentucky. Wrote Furman Bisher, "Under watchdog pressure for a full 40 minutes, he responded with a forceful performance that kept Tech in the game and then with the full burden of the evening thrust upon him, in the last five seconds he dribbled to the corner and delivered the last-second, one-handed shot that felled the powerful Wildcats, 62-60. All this, mind you, with a fractured thumb on his shooting hand."

Lamented Kentucky coach Adolph Rupp, "Everyone in the place knew that Kaiser was going to take the last shot but what could we do about it? We had two guys hanging all over him and he still got the shot off. Amazing. Simply amazing."

JOHN PAUL HOLMES JR.
Fast Finish For A Late Starter

Athlete, public servant, successful businessman, musician, bouncer. You name it and John Paul Holmes Jr. has done it.

Here is a guy who had never played anything but the saxophone, who turns out to be one of the great linemen in the history of University of Georgia football. You might call him a late bloomer, but he was more a late starter. He did not go out for football until his senior year at Atlanta's Northside High School but when he did, he not only made the first team as a defensive end but was the main reason Coach Wayman Creel's Tigers held opponents to an average of less than two points per game. Thanks to Holmes' ability to protect the flank and turn foes' running games inside, Northside not only won the state championship but shut out its opponents in the city, northern Georgia, and state title games.

Yet the college scouts were unimpressed—all but Georgia's, who saw tremendous potential in the highly motivated, 6'5", 220-pounder. Georgia shifted him to tackle and held him out one year for seasoning. Holmes started every game his sophomore and junior seasons and for his sparkling senior season in 1962, he was named the Dogs' most valuable lineman.

Holmes was drafted by the Denver Broncos but signed with the Dallas Cowboys. He played a rookie exhibition season for Dallas but was unable to oust perennial All-Pro Bob Lilly for a starting job and returned to Atlanta.

Today, Holmes lives in Monticello, where his wife is mayor and he is vice chairman of the Life of the South Insurance Company, a company he helped start with his two partners, Butch Houston and Lloyd Shaw, in 1979. In their first year in business they did $3 million in premium income. Last year they did $350 million with sales in every state in the country.

A terror on the football field, Holmes is Mr. Nice Guy in everyday life. More than a dozen of his friends and acquaintances had nothing but words of praise for him. "He is always doing something for others," says Bill Dukes, a prep football standout who played against Holmes in high school. "The only time I ever saw him mad was on spring break in Daytona Beach, Florida, when we were both at UGA. He was working as a bouncer at the Safari Beach Hotel. Some student had too much to drink and was cursing and threatening everyone in sight. Paul asked him to stop and the guy wouldn't. So, with one punch, Paul decked him and there was no more trouble."

Holmes was born March 21, 1940, in Goldsboro, North Carolina. When he was in elementary school, he played the saxophone so well he was selected to play in the Goldsboro High School band. He was a musician, not an athlete, until his family moved to Atlanta and Coach Creel convinced him to come out for the Northside football team.

In 1965, Holmes became a dairy farmer and went on a public service and political roll that took him from his town of 3,000 to almost every county in the state. At the tender age of twenty-eight, he became Commissioner of Jasper County. He was chairman of the Republican Party in Jasper County, chairman of the Jasper County Cancer Society, a director of the old Bank South, state director of the Farmers Home Administration, and state director of the Agricultural Stabilization and Conservation Service. Now, at age sixty-three, Holmes is a director of the Professional Association of Georgia Educators, a director of the Georgia Public Policy Foundation, and vice chairman of governmental affairs for the Georgia Chamber of Commerce. He chairs the Development Authority of Jasper County and the board of Griffin Technical College, and he serves on the state indigent defense council, which assists those charged with crimes who have no money for attorneys.

Holmes and his wife live in a 100-year-old house two blocks from downtown Monticello. They have three children and eight grandchildren.

GENE CHANDLER
The Block of the Century

In the sixty years I have been watching prep football, I never have seen a lineman as good as Gene Chandler. He was fast, quick, agile, and a devastating tackler. He was so fast that when he snapped the ball on punts, he would beat the ball down field and patiently wait for the safety man to catch it. Then he would crash into him with such force that he would often cause a fumble.

To say Chandler was a "hitter" would be a masterpiece of understatement. His late coach, Wally Butts, expressed it best when Chandler was a freshman at the University of Georgia. At the opening of fall practice, Butts assembled his squad and said how tough practices were going to be. Then he added, "I'll tell you another thing. You better not be standing around [twiddling your thumbs] when Gene Chandler is on the field. He will make you wish you played your football somewhere else."

By far the most vivid memory I have of Chandler was in the 1949 Tech-Georgia game. Tech had punted to Georgia safety man Ken McCall deep in Bulldog territory. Tech speedster Bob McCoy managed to elude Bulldog blockers—all, that is, but Chandler. Just as McCoy was about to nail McCall, here came Chandler, all 195 pounds of him. He struck McCoy from the blind side and the hit was so potent that McCoy went skyward about ten feet. Meanwhile, McCall raced down field to set up Georgia's only touchdown.

2003

Chandler retired in 1988 after operating his own State Farm Insurance agency for thirty years. He lives alone in Stockbridge. His wife of fifty-eight years, Jean Schiemeyer Chandler, died nine years ago. Chandler also lost a son six years ago. He has one daughter, Sandra Key, age fifty-five.

Ernest Eugene "Big Gene" Chandler was born June 16, 1925. He spent his preteen years in Valdosta, which has spawned as many great football players as any city in America. His family moved to Atlanta when he was thirteen. He grew up in the Grant Park area and became a child star of the Grant Park Aces, a championship sandlot team.

As a freshman at Tech High School, he won a place at center and linebacker on the varsity and by the time he was a senior he won a place in prep football history. He was chosen on the All-City, All-State, and All-Southern teams. In 1943 the Atlanta Touchdown Club named him Lineman of the Year. He was inducted into the Georgia Prep Sports Hall of Fame. Throughout his Tech High career, he walked to and from school every day, a round trip of some six miles. In the summers he worked first as a bag boy at the old A&P grocery, then as a laborer for a construction company.

Chandler could have chosen to play college football anywhere in the Southeast but he had his heart set on Georgia, much to the regret of the Georgia Tech coaches. World War II was in full blast when Chandler graduated from Tech High in June 1944. He spent two years in the Navy before beginning his remarkable collegiate career.

With a bunch of newly discharged servicemen headed for Georgia, the Bulldogs were loaded. But no one could stop the freshman Chandler from earning a starting job. It was the two-platoon era and Chandler played two years as a linebacker and two years as a defensive end. He played on three consecutive bowl teams.

He was an awesome sight. Down low, head up, he was like a snake, coiled and ready to strike. He fought off or evaded the best blockers in the SEC and was named most valuable lineman on the 1949 Bulldog team.

I have one more memory of Chandler. As tough and rough as he was on the football field, he was always a gentleman off it. Walking down the Tech High hallways, he spoke to students and teachers alike, many of whom were dumbfounded that they got a warm, friendly greeting from Tech High's greatest football hero.

CONSPICUOUS GALLANTRY

Of all the structures on the University of Georgia campus, none is more touching than the War Memorial monument in front of the Student Athlete Academic Center. The handsome red and black monument, made of Georgia granite, honors twenty-one student athletes who died in wars.

The first Bulldog to die in World War II, Marine Corps Captain Henry T. Elrod of Thomasville, was posthumously awarded the Medal of Honor. Elrod, who lettered on the 1932 football team, single-handedly attacked a fleet of twenty-two enemy planes, shooting down two. Then he attacked a fleet of Japanese warships, sinking one, despite a hail of enemy anti-aircraft gunfire. When his plane was destroyed, he organized a handful of ground troops on Wake Island and set up a beach defense that repulsed an overwhelming number of Japanese marines. In the face of withering enemy machine gun and mortar fire, he led his vastly out-numbered Marines until he was killed. In his honor, the modern guided missile frigate the USS Elrod was commissioned, and one of the main streets on the Marine Corps Base in Quantico, Virginia, was named "Elrod Avenue."

First Lieutenant Lacy F. Mangleburg of Athens, a star prizefighter at Georgia, was posthumously awarded the Distinguished Flying Cross. The University of Georgia named its student American Legion Post for Elrod and Mangleburg. Elrod died December 23, 1941, sixteen days after the Japanese attack on Pearl Harbor and Mangleburg died a day later.

2003

Marine Corps First Lieutenant Howard W. "Smiley" Johnson was awarded the Silver Star for "conspicuous gallantry" during the Saipan operation and was posthumously awarded a Gold Star for actions during the Iwo Jima campaign, in which he was one of more than 6,000 Marines who lost their lives in battle. Johnson played fullback and guard (1937–39) for three different UGA coaches, Harry Mehre, Joel Hunt, and Wally Butts. The Peach Bowl annually presents the "Smiley Johnson Award" to the game's outstanding lineman.

It was fifty-nine years ago this month that Army Master Sergeant Walter "Chief" Ruark was leading a five-man patrol to locate and eliminate a German sniper position. In doing so he took a direct hit in his chest. He was awarded the Silver Star. He was a two-time All-Southeastern Conference guard in 1941 and 1942 and was one of the standouts in the 1942 team's Rose Bowl victory over UCLA.

Army Captain James Skipworth Jr., a native of Columbus and captain of the 1940 Georgia football team, was killed while leading his troops in General Douglas McArthur's triumphant return to the Philippines. He was awarded the Silver Star for gallantry.

Silver Star winner Jack Cox of Waynesboro, a lieutenant in the US Marines, played tackle on the 1959 Georgia football team. He was killed by a sniper in Viet Nam.

The list of all honorees and the wars in which they died and sports in which they participated are engraved on the monument.

2004

NATALIE COHEN
Atlanta's First Lady of Tennis

Ninety-one-year-old Natalie Cohen is one of a kind. She played competitive tennis for seventy-three years, winning thirteen Georgia State Women's Open Doubles Championships. At age forty-two, she won both the Atlanta City and Georgia State women's singles and doubles championships, equivalent to the state's Grand Slam.

She was the first woman to chair an NCAA men's tennis championship and the first Southern woman to chair a match at Forrest Hills in the US Tennis Championships. For more than fifty years she was a certified tennis official, serving as linesman, umpire, and referee for the city of Atlanta, state of Georgia, Southeastern regional, NCAA, and professional tournaments.

But one of Cohen's greatest feats had nothing to do with tennis. It had to do with firing up her alma mater's football team in its game against archrival Stanford. At age seventy-four, she burst into the locker room of her California Golden Bears at halftime and delivered a pep talk that would have rivaled one of Knute Rockne's. The Bears were so motivated that they raced back on the field, overcame an eight-point deficit and upset the heavily favored Stanford Indians, 17-11.

As a student at Cal, Cohen had changed the way women were treated at home football games. It was 1930 when she went to the opening game at Cal's Memorial Stadium. Cohen remembers:

I sat with my friends, a bunch of women in Section RR next to the men's rooting section, where women were not allowed. As soon as the Cal team came on to the field, I stood up and let go with a beautiful "Rebel yell." Immediately, a male student grabbed my arm, pulled me down in to my seat and said in a voice louder than somewhat, "Sit down and be quiet!"

Imagine the nerve of that guy! I asked why should I sit down and he said, "Women don't yell." This guy is telling me I am going to be here for four years and I am not going to be allowed to yell for my football team. I'm thinking, He does not know Natalie Cohen.

Well, for the rest of that first game, I did not stand up or yell again. But the next Saturday I arrived early at the stadium and brought a bunch of women with me. We sat in Row 30, Section RR, across the aisle from the men's section.

When the men yelled, we would yell, almost in perfect unison. More and more women began to yell with us and by the next season we had cheerleaders stationed on platforms in front of our section to lead us in cheers.

She may be the only woman to have a seat dedicated in her honor. Seven years ago, in section RR, at the Cal home opener, Seat 1 was named the "Natalie Cohen" seat.

How did Cohen get to California in the first place? She was born and raised in Atlanta, and attended Fraser Street and Inman elementary schools, Bass Junior High School and Girls' High School. "When I was eight years old," Cohen says, "my dad began taking me to football games at the University of Georgia, his alma mater. I got so enamored with the game I decided I wanted to attend a college that had a great football team and Cal had one of the greatest."

She began playing competitive tennis at age eight and when she stopped at age eighty-one she had more than earned the title of "Atlanta's First Lady of Tennis." Of her forty-three-year career as a tennis umpire, she said,

I liked to officiate in tournaments where there was a minimum of uptight players and prima donnas. I preferred to be around people who enjoyed the game.

I was giving a clinic one day to some young players and I asked them, "When was the last time any of you asked a friend to play just for the fun of it?" I got a blank stare from the entire group. We need to teach kids to enjoy the game first and understand that every time someone goes on the court one will win and one will lose. Lessons in how to accept loss should be as important as how to hit a backhand.

GEORGE HAMILTON BRODNAX III
"A One-Man Wrecking Crew"

The first time I saw George Hamilton Brodnax III play a football game, he was a 175-pound end for the old Atlanta Boys' High School. He was running across the pitcher's mound at Atlanta's Ponce de Leon Park, site of all the Tech High and Boys' High home games. With outstretched hands, his body leaning forward at a forty-five-degree angle, he raced over the mound, pulled in the ball with his fingertips, and carried it across the goal line to bring his team back from almost certain defeat to a 13-13-tie with archrival Tech High.

The 20,000 fans who saw that catch never will forget it. Brodnax should have stumbled over the pitcher's mound and landed on his face but he maintained his balance and composure, to the disbelief of eleven Tech High Smithies and an overflow crowd perched everywhere from the grandstands to the outfield signboards to the top of the freight train cars parked on the track behind the right-field fence.

The catch was a harbinger of things to come. At Georgia Tech Brodnax was lauded not only for his pass receiving but for his defensive end play as well. In the 1947 Tech-Duke game, Brodnax dove into midair and, with his body parallel to the ground, snagged a mud-covered ball over the goal line. It was the only touchdown of the game. Four weeks later, at Grant Field, Brodnax caught a seventeen-yard touchdown pass to give legendary coach Bobby Dodd his first victory over Georgia.

In 1948 Brodnax's defensive play against Duke eliminated the Blue Devils from the nationally ranked unbeaten list. Furman Bisher, who covered the game for the *Atlanta Constitution*, says, "Brodnax was a one-man wrecking crew. He made tackles all over the field, completely dissolving Duke's running game."

Another coaching legend, Wallace Butts of the University of Georgia, who was a member of the old Collier's All-America team selection committee and had looked at films of the great college ends in the country, was quoted in *Collier's* as saying, "Everything an end has to do, offensively and defensively, Brodnax can do better than any other end I saw. He is a great blocker and maybe the finest pass receiver I have ever seen."

In his three years (1946–48) as a starter for Tech, the Jackets posted a 26-6 won-lost record and went to two Bowl games. Brodnax was president of his freshman, sophomore, and junior classes, a four-year member of Student Council, president of the ANAK Honor Society, colonel in the Army ROTC, co-captain of the varsity football team, and a member of Grantland Rice's 1948 All-American team.

He served on the board of trustees of the Tech Alumni Association. He is a life member of the Tech Athletic Association board of trustees and a member of the Tech Athletic Hall of Fame and Georgia Sports Hall of Fame.

When the Atlanta Athletic Club was preparing to host the 1976 US Open and the 1981 PGA Championship, the man it placed in the top leadership job was George Brodnax. All this, while he was serving on the Emory University Board of Visitors and on the boards of directors of the old First Federal Savings & Loan Association, Georgia Freight Bureau, Community Chest, Travelers Aid Association, and Boy Scouts of America, and operating a million-dollar business.

Today, Brodnax is seventy-six years old and doing well, thank you. He is retired from the company he founded twenty-nine years ago, Tech Steel, a steel fabricating company. He lives with his wife of fifty-four years, Jo Dale Dewees, in north DeKalb County. The Brodnaxes have five children and ten grandchildren.

He grew up in Atlanta's West End, the son of Virginia and George H. Brodnax Jr., a senior vice president of the Georgia Power Company. He played football, basketball, and baseball at old Atlanta Boys' High School. In football he was All-City, All-State, All-Southern, and one of the most sought-after athletes in the South.

Brodnax not only had brain and brawn, he also had glamour. In 1948, he was picked on the third annual All-American "Glamour team." And he still wears the smile that helped put him there.

TOMMY NOBIS
A Star On and Off the Field

Tommy Nobis may be the only football player nearly recruited from outer space. In 1965, when he was drafted No. 1 in the NFL draft by the Atlanta Falcons and No. 1 in the old AFL draft by the Houston Oilers, Astronaut Frank Borman, command pilot of the Gemini 7 spacecraft, radioed word from space encouraging Nobis to sign with the Oilers. The message was relayed to Nobis, who opted to sign with the Falcons and became the finest football player in the franchise's history.

In his first season, 1966, Nobis was selected NFL "Rookie of The Year." In ten of eleven seasons with the Falcons, he led the team in tackles. He was selected to the Pro Bowl five times and chosen for the NFL's "All Decade Team" for the 1960s. When you attended a Falcons game in the 1960s, you could be certain that the team would be outclassed at every position but linebacker, where Nobis was in a class by himself. When his team was trailing by forty or more points, Nobis hit with as much devastation as if the game depended on it.

Injured or not, Nobis played with intensity. He underwent knee surgery in 1969 and again in 1971 but he came back from both surgeries to earn another Pro Bowl spot in 1972.

In one of the great miscarriages of justice, Nobis has not been selected to the Pro Football Hall of Fame. Says Nobis, "My record speaks for itself. But that is not important. What is important is the impact I have on my family and my

2004

community." Whether he makes the Hall of Fame or not, he will be remembered as one of the great players of all time. He'll also go down in the record books as someone who made life better for others. Over the years he has devoted countless hours to the Special Olympics; he also founded the Tommy Nobis Center, which has trained thousands of disabled Greater Atlantans to earn their way in the workplace.

Today, Nobis is Falcons vice president for corporate development. He lives with his wife of thirty-eight years, the former Lynn Edwards, in Sandy Springs. They have two sons, Tommy III and Kevin; a daughter, Devon; and two grandsons. A true family man, Nobis says his biggest thrill was not on the gridiron but being in the hospital delivery room when his children were born.

Thomas Henry Nobis Jr., was born in San Antonio on September 20, 1943. He was an All-State offensive guard and middle linebacker at Jefferson High School. At the University of Texas, where he also played both offense and defense, Coach Darrell Royal called him "the finest two-way player I have ever seen."

Nobis was an All-American his junior and senior seasons and winner of both the Outland Trophy (best lineman) and Maxwell Award (most valuable college football player). His picture was on the cover of *Sports Illustrated* and *Time* magazines. He was the leading blocker and leading tackler on Texas' 1963 national championship and 1964 Orange Bowl championship teams. He not only was voted into the NCAA Hall of Fame and to the Halls of Fame of Texas and Georgia, he was also named to *Sports Illustrated*'s NCAA "All-Century" team.

At the height of the Vietnam War, after he had just completed another All-Pro season for the Falcons, Nobis went to Vietnam—not to the rear areas but to the front—to express his gratitude to troops who were laying their lives on the line every day. "It was scary but I am glad I went," he says. "I learned to stop taking life for granted."

After decades of helping others, Nobis has a message for today's prep and college students: "Put as much emphasis in the classroom as you do on the athletic field; otherwise you will make the same mistake I did. Not taking advantage of the educational opportunities I had at the University of Texas has held me back. Writing a letter is difficult for me. I don't have the grammatical skills I need. Opportunities came my way which I could not qualify for simply because I did not have the educational skills."

At the Falcons' home opener next season, Nobis will be inducted into the Falcons' "Ring of Honor" based on his incredible gridiron achievements. There ought to be a special award for him for elevating the disabled, enhancing their self-esteem, and providing them with skills they can take to the bank.

CHARLIE YATES
Master of the Greenways

This being the month of the Masters, thoughts turn to ninety-year-old Charlie Yates, who attended sixty-eight consecutive tournaments, played in eleven, and was low amateur in five. He became secretary of the Augusta National Golf Club in 1950 and for years was host extraordinaire to the national and international media. Yates will not be attending this year's Masters. He is ill and pretty much confined to his home in northwest Atlanta.

Next to Bobby Jones, Yates is the most successful amateur golfer the city of Atlanta or the state of Georgia ever produced. In 1938, at the age of twenty-four, he won the British Amateur at Royal Troon, which was tantamount to the World Amateur Championship. He was captain of one Walker Cup team and honorary captain of another. He brought one Walker Cup trophy back to America.

He twice won the Georgia State Amateur, once won the Western Amateur, and played in nine US Amateur Championships. In 1980 he received golf's most prestigious award—the Bob Jones award for sportsmanship. As famous as he was for his golf game, he was equally well known for community involvement and charitable causes. Although he is a Methodist, he was a staunch supporter of the National Jewish Hospital and Asthma Center. He was president of the Atlanta Arts Alliance (now the Woodruff Arts Center), the Georgia Chamber of Commerce, the Atlanta Symphony, and the Rotary Club of Atlanta. He was southern regional chairman of the USO and vice general chairman of the United

2004

Appeal. Yates also was an officer of the old First National Bank and later became vice president of two railroads—the Atlantic Coast Line and the Louisville and Nashville.

Charles Richardson Yates was born on Fourth Street in northeast Atlanta. His family moved to East Lake, a few steps across the street from the East Lake Golf Club, when Charlie was a tot. He was literally raised on East Lake course No. 2 which is now a public course named in his honor—the Charlie Yates Course.

His dad, the late Presley Daniel Yates, gave him his first golf club, an inexpensive one that turned out to be extremely costly. Young Charlie would swing at a ball on his front lawn, miss, and gouge out a huge hunk of turf, leaving holes all over the lawn. The Yates family never did have any grass.

Charlie won his first cup at age eleven in the city junior tournament and at age twelve took the city junior championship. He attended old Atlanta Boys' High School and Georgia Tech. At Tech he won the national intercollegiate crown. When he won the city amateur at age seventeen, more than 400 kids, many of them caddies, took the day off to watch their hero play.

When he went to Scotland for the British Amateur, Bobby Jones gave Charlie his "lucky, red flannel, long john underwear." In the final round, using an old, rusty putter he bought from an Atlanta caddy for one dollar, he sank an eight-foot putt to win his thirty-six-hole match. The entire gallery of 7,000 unloaded a terrific shout, disregarded ropes and marshals, and mobbed the new champion. Yates simply stood there until police grabbed him, put him in a police car, and took him to the clubhouse. On his return to Atlanta, he was met at the old Terminal Station by Mayor William B. Hartsfield, Bobby Jones, and thousands of well-wishers.

Three years later, at the start of World War II, Yates enlisted in the Navy, served three years on a destroyer and participated in the major landings in Italy.

Before his dad died, he said of Charlie, "His character is as steady as his golf game. He is clean and fine and everything a son ought to be. He neither smokes nor drinks. As marvelous as his golf game is, I am more proud of his character."

George Sargent, his golf instructor at East Lake, said of Yates, "He was not only the ranking golfer of the world, he was the most popular player known in the game."

Charlie and his wife, the former Dorothy Malone, will celebrate their sixtieth wedding anniversary in May. The Yateses have four children, Dorothy, Charles Jr., Sarah and Comer.

Charlie's two brothers, Dan and Alan, were both fine golfers; Dan also was a state champion.

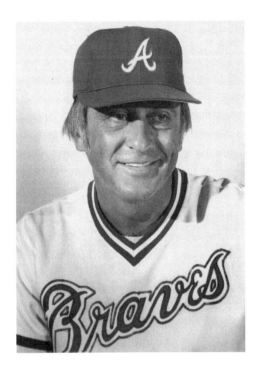

PHILIP HENRY NIEKRO
Knucksie

Nothing came easy for Philip Henry Niekro, better known as "Knucksie." At nineteen, he tried out for a pitching job with the Pittsburgh Pirates. He was turned down. That same year (1958) he was signed by the Milwaukee Braves but he did not see major league action for the next six years. His pitching days were spent in the minor league cities of Wellsville, New York, and McCook, Nebraska.

After he ended his career as one of the finest pitchers in the history of the game, it took him five years to be elected to baseball's Hall of Fame. Never mind that he was selected to the major league All-Star team five times, won five Golden Glove awards, and held almost every Atlanta Braves pitching record in the books. As former *Atlanta Journal-Constitution* Braves writer I. J. Rosenberg wrote, "It took Niekro as long to reach the Hall of Fame as it did for his famous knuckle ball to make it to home plate."

But the toughest obstacle Niekro ever had to overcome was being released by the Braves after the 1983 season. "Being let go by the team that I had won 268 games for was the biggest downer of my life. I thought it was not only the end of my career, but the end of my life. I was 45 years old. Joe [Manager Joe Torre] told me he was going with the younger guys. That was it. I felt like I could still win. Fortunately the New York Yankees did, too. They picked me up and I had back-to-back sixteen-game winning seasons." Knucksie then spent two mediocre seasons with Cleveland and one with Toronto before the Braves brought him back for one last hurrah.

It was September 27, 1987. The fans came early. They cheered Niekro when he walked to the bullpen. They cheered him when he walked to the pitcher's mound. They cheered him in his first at bat and again in the fourth inning when he was leaving the game with the bases loaded. Manager Chuck Tanner went to the mound to get him. He put his arm around Knucksie's shoulder and they stayed together as the matrix board came on with all fourteen of Niekro's records. Then they headed to the dugout as the fans stood and cheered for more than five minutes.

Then there was the unveiling of the statute of Knucksie gripping his knuckler, right beside the statues of Ty Cobb and Hank Aaron.

What a career! He had a total of fourteen consecutive years with twenty or more wins. Four times he pitched more than 300 innings in a season, with a career high of 342 innings in 1979. He led the National League in innings pitched four times. In 1973 he pitched a no-hitter to beat San Diego.

Niekro holds or shares fourteen Braves career pitching records, including most games pitched (689), most complete games (226), most innings pitched (4,533), most games won (268), most strikeouts (2,855) and most shutouts (43). He clinched the 1969 division title for the Braves with a victory over the Cincinnati Reds and in 1982 he shut out San Diego and hit a home run to spark the Braves to their second division flag. Most of his 268 victories came while pitching for some lousy Braves teams.

Phil and his wife Nancy now live in Flowery Branch, forty miles from Atlanta. Their home fronts on Lake Lanier. "It takes me ten seconds to get to my dock," he says, "and in less than one minute I can be in the boat fishing."

Niekro grew up in Lansing, Ohio, a coal-mining town. His dad had pitched in the sandlots, and after he came home from the mines he took young Phil and his sister, Phyllis, in the back yard and taught Phil how to grip and throw the knuckleball and Phyllis how to catch it. "When Braves scout Bill Maughn came out to our home and asked my dad how a $500 bonus sounded it was the biggest thrill of my life," Niekro said.

Today Niekro's biggest thrill is being with his family. At 191 pounds, he is only one pound over his pitching weight. Phil's brother, Joe, pitched twenty-two seasons in the major leagues. Together, the Niekros won 537 games, more than any other brother combination in major league history.

AARON COHN
The Goodness of His Deeds

There is a passage in the Jewish prayer book that reads, in part, "only by obedience to Thy commandments, by faithfulness to our duties, by the goodness of our deeds, can we make our worship acceptable to Thee." No one could live that passage more than eighty-eight-year-old Aaron Cohn, perhaps Columbus' most beloved citizen, the longest serving (forty years) juvenile court judge in America and one of the greatest Georgia Bulldogs of them all.

Judge Cohn, a competitive tennis player until age eighty-five and a former University of Georgia tennis team captain (1937), has given of himself to his city and his fellow human beings, not until it hurts, but until "it feels good." Last year the Chattahoochee Valley-Fort Benning chapter of the US Army Association selected Judge Cohn for the 2003 Cliff Livingston Citizen/Soldier of the Year Award. The honor is presented annually to a former member of the US military who has achieved success in other areas of life, especially in the community.

In World War II, as a lieutenant colonel in the US Cavalry, Cohn led his unit into the concentration camp at Ebensee, Austria. As a member of the Jewish faith, it gave him particular pleasure to liberate a death camp where thousands of Jews had been murdered. He was honored by the US Holocaust Commission for his role in the liberation.

Cohn served as Combat Operations Officer for General George Patton's Third Army in four major campaigns: Northern Europe, Central Europe, the

2004

Ardennes, and the Rhineland. He fought in the Battle of the Bulge. When the war ended he returned to his native Columbus, where he immediately joined an Army Reserve unit. After thirty years' service, he retired as a full colonel.

Eight years ago, Cohn received the Jim Woodruff Jr. Memorial Award from the Columbus Chamber of Commerce for his "continuous service to humankind." Former Columbus Mayor Frank Martin says, "Of all the lawyers and judges I know in Columbus, Judge Cohn is the most well-liked and most respected. He earned the respect because he has always been honest and upright."

Cohn is a former chairman of the Columbus March of Dimes who organized the polio foundation board. He coached Little League baseball and Pop Warner football for ten years and then served on the board of directors of both for another decade. He is an active member of the Columbus State University Athletics Board and rarely misses a home basketball game. Despite cardiac bypass surgery in 1983, he and his partner won a Georgia State Tennis doubles championship in 1984.

His actions have garnered much attention: He's been honored by the Georgia legislature (both the House and the Senate) for distinguished service to the state of Georgia; UGA presented him with the Distinguished Alumni Merit Award; and the American Criminal Justice Association honored him for outstanding contributions to the Juvenile Justice System.

Although he was widely respected for his contributions throughout the Columbus community, he did not neglect his synagogue. The only home Bulldog football games he misses are those that fall on a Jewish High Holy Day.

Cohn was born in Columbus to a Lithuanian mother and a Russian father. He literally grew up at the Columbus YMCA, for which he won a state featherweight wrestling championship, state table tennis title (he beat his lifelong friend, Dan Magill, in the finals) and helped win ten state volleyball crowns. He received a tennis scholarship to the University of Georgia but lost it when the football coach took it away and gave it to one of his gridders. Cohn remained on the tennis team and lettered three consecutive years (1935–37).

When Cohn was presented with the opportunity to become a Superior Court judge, he turned it down because he liked working with kids in the juvenile system. What words does he have for today's law students? "You must be caring about the people you represent and the community in which you live. Never take a client you don't believe in, and keep in mind that you do not have to be aggressive to be successful."

Judge Cohn is married to the former Janet Ann Lillenthal; this month they will be celebrating their sixty-third wedding anniversary. They have three children and seven grandchildren.

2004

GARLAND FOLSOM PINHOLSTER
Old-Fashioned "Gumption"

Maybe he didn't become president of the United States like Jimmy Carter of Plains, but for a boy born in Clyattville and raised in Ray City, Garland Folsom Pinholster did quite well for himself. For one thing, he let the word out loud and clear on what had been Atlanta's best-kept secret—Oglethorpe University. For another, after his coaching days at OU, he became one of Atlanta's most successful businessmen. When he entered politics, he became chairman of the minority caucus of the Georgia House of Representatives, and last year he was elected to the Georgia State Board of Transportation. He is a past Republican "Legislator of the Year." This past May he was awarded an honorary doctorate from Oglethorpe.

Talk about drive and discipline—that's what made him a champion in every venture he has undertaken. He's a past president of the Buckhead and Canton Rotary Clubs, a member of the Executive Board of Boy Scouts of America, a member of the Georgia State Board of Education, a board member of the Frank Heritage Center of Reinhardt College, and a chairman of the Governor's State Physical Fitness Commission. He was coach of the 1963 USA Pan American basketball team and has written five books, published in four different languages, on the art of defensive basketball. He is a member of three sports halls of fames: the

Valdosta-Lowndes County Hall, the Oglethorpe University Hall, and the Georgia State Hall. Although he rarely plays competitive tennis anymore, he was once ranked No. 4 by the Southern Lawn Tennis Association. Today, Pinholster, seventy-six, and his wife of twenty-six years, the former Darsa Hayes, live in Ball Ground in a log cabin on the Etowah River.

He was the youngest of twelve children. At Clyattville, he learned to play basketball on a dirt court. There was no gymnasium. The Pinholsters dominated the basketball team, holding three of the five positions. Pinholster admits to being a "mama's boy." "Whatever success I have had," he said, "I owe to my mama. She preached gumption day and night. 'Without gumption,' she said, 'you can't do anything. With gumption you can do whatever you want.'" And Pinholster has gumption. He had it when he earned twenty-five cents per hour as a sharecropper on a farm during his high school years; he had it selling fresh eggs on the street corner; and he had it working in a saw mill and driving a taxi in Valdosta.

He saved his money for tuition at North Georgia College, where he earned a bachelor's degree and a second lieutenant commission in the US Army. He coached the Fort Benning basketball team and taught physical fitness programs at the Fort Benning Infantry Center. Here he was, a mere lieutenant, teaching thirty-two generals—and the sons of Mark Clark and Dwight David Eisenhower.

His first civilian job was at Summerville High School where he won a state championship. In one season at Rockmart, he had a 16-4 record. He took two Southwest DeKalb teams to the state finals. When he took the Oglethorpe job, his friends said he was crazy. Oglethorpe Who? The college was a virtual unknown. But Pinholster remembered what his mother had said and couldn't wait to get started. His first team was a loser but the next year he was 18-6 with only six players. From then on it was Katie-bar-the-door. His team joined the Georgia Interscholastic Athletic Conference and never lost a game. He won the GIAC championship four straight years. Not only that but his team, the Stormy Petrels, was invited to the NCAA tournament in 1963, and reached the semifinals. Pinholster turned out the nation's best defensive basketball team, yielding a mere 42.5 points per game. But his greatest pride was having 100 percent of his players graduate and four of them eventually named to the Oglethorpe Board of Trustees. With no previous business experience, in 1972, Pinholster purchased a midtown supermarket that was scarcely making a profit. Did that take guts? "No," Pinholster said, "gumption." He turned it into a giant moneymaker and went on to open and operate four more stores, each of them a success.

MARION CAMPBELL
The Swamp Fox

There was so much talent on the 1950 University of Georgia football team it was nearly impossible for anyone to stand out. Nine Bulldogs made it in the pros and six of these became All-Pro: ends Bobby Walston, Harry Babcock, and John Carson; tackles Dick Yelvington and Marion Campbell; and center-linebacker Art DeCarlo. But if there was one superstar among them it was three-time All-Southeastern Conference, two-time All-American and one-time All-Pro Francis Marion Campbell, the "Swamp Fox" out of Chester, South Carolina. Campbell was big (6'2", 238 pounds), quick, and strong. He was a devastating blocker and such an immovable rock on defense that foes carefully avoided running plays his way. The late, legendary Coach Wally Butts flatly called him "the best tackle I ever had."

A sixty-minute man, Campbell was a two-way selection on almost everyone's All-America team. One All-America team selector, Stanley Woodward, said of Campbell, "When he gets his shoulder into a defensive lineman or linebacker and starts driving with his powerful legs there is no stopping him."

Ralph "Shug" Jordan, Campbell's line coach at UGA, said of him, "Not only was he the best defensive lineman I ever coached at UGA but he was a one-man wrecking crew against my first Auburn team." Georgia whipped Jordan's Tigers, 46-14, with Campbell carving out huge holes in the Auburn defense.

2004

As impressive as Campbell was as a college player, he was equally noteworthy as a professional, first as a player and then as an assistant coach. He was a linebacker and defensive tackle for the 1960 National Football League champion Philadelphia Eagles and was twice selected to the NFL Pro Bowl. As an assistant coach in charge of defense he built two of the most successful defensive units in NFL history—the L.A. Rams' "Fearsome Foursome" and the Minnesota Vikings' "Purple People Eaters." For the Eagles, he coached units that twice led the NFL in scoring defense during a stretch of four consecutive playoff appearances including a spot in the 1981 Super Bowl.

Said Dick Vermeil, Eagles head coach when Campbell tutored the defense, "There was no better football coach in America than Campbell. When we went to the Super Bowl, I got the credit because I was head man; but we never would have gotten there without Marion and his staff."

As a two-time Atlanta Falcons head coach, Campbell inherited and was stuck with a bunch of underachievers. In parts of three seasons (1974–76), his teams posted a 6-19 record, creditable considering the team's acute shortage of talent.

Said Claude Humphrey, the Falcons' All-Pro defensive end under Campbell, "Honesty is something you do not find in this game, but Campbell was always a straight shooter. He was above board with me and everyone else." Campbell had forty-four years with the pros, thirty-six as a coach and eight as a player.

Today Campbell is seventy-five years old and weighs no more than he did when he played for the Bulldogs. He lives in Saint Augustine, Florida, with his wife, the former June Roberts. The Campbells, childhood sweethearts, have two children—a daughter, Alicia Johnson, and a son, Scott, who attended the University of Georgia on a football scholarship and now works for a Yellow Jacket, Pepper Rodgers, as personnel director of the Washington Redskins.

Campbell grew up in Chester, a town of 6,500, about halfway between Columbia and Charlotte, North Carolina. At Chester High School, he is remembered as the only football player in the school's history twice named outstanding prep player in the state, twice selected for the S.C.-N.C. Shrine prep All-Star game and the only South Carolinian picked on the first Wigwam Wisemen All-America team.

Campbell was sought after by most every college football coach in the South but picked Georgia "because line coach J. B. Whitworth told me I would be a starter on the freshman team and a starter on the varsity as a sophomore." Campbell not only started as a sophomore, he was named to the All-SEC team. He was named Georgia's most outstanding lineman as a junior and senior and was top lineman in the College All-Star game, the Blue-Gray game, and the Senior Bowl.

Says Bulldog historian Dan Magill, "Regardless of position, Campbell was one of the greatest football players Georgia ever had."

GEORGE DOUGLAS SANDERS
Beat the Best

He beat Jack Nicklaus, Arnold Palmer, and Tom Weiskopf. He won back-to-back professional tournaments in four different years, and when Ben Hogan introduced the 1967 US Ryder Cup team as the "finest golfers in the world" he was among them. "He" is George Douglas Sanders, winner of twenty official PGA tournaments and, a native of Cedartown, Georgia, now living in Houston, Texas.

Doug Sanders was a swinger deluxe on the golf course and an even bigger swinger off the course. Asked if he ever stayed out all night and had a difficult time finding the first tee, Sanders replied, "There were a few days I had a hard time finding the golf course."

But that was then, not now. He has not had a drink in twelve years. He is a born again Christian and a regular attendee at Houston's First Baptist Church services. From 1956 through 1975, Sanders was golf's most flamboyant, colorful player. He was the PGA Tour's flashiest dresser. He wore shocking pink, lime green, and deep purple. His trademark was his wardrobe. At one time he had forty pairs of shoes and countless sweaters, shirts, and slacks of different hues. He even had colored golf tees to match the outfit he was wearing.

But don't get the idea Doug Sanders was just for Doug Sanders. He set up a scholarship fund for underprivileged boys. For twenty-one years he sponsored international golf tournaments for juniors. He was a major contributor to the United Negro College Fund and the Betty Ford Clinic.

Sanders has a story to tell and he is working on it in the form of a book. He came from a poor family in Cedartown. His father drove a truck and a taxi. Some days he never earned more than fifty cents. Doug said he was eight years old before he had his first pair of shoes.

He started out caddying at Cedartown's nine-hole course. He and several friends his age owned five clubs between them. When the club pro was out to lunch they sneaked onto the course to play a few fast holes. A non-descript at age sixteen, he entered and won the LaGrange, Georgia, Open. The next year he won the Southeastern Amateur.

The University of Florida awarded him a golf scholarship and as a freshman he responded by winning the National Amateur. As a sophomore he won the Florida State Amateur by eighteen strokes and as a junior captured the National Jaycees tournament. The city of Cedartown gave him a "Doug Sanders Day."

As a twenty-two-year-old amateur, he won the Canadian Open and then decorated the PGA tour for the next nineteen summers. He was second to Nicklaus in two British Opens, second to Gene Littler in the 1961 US Open, runner-up to Bob Rosburg in the 1959 PGA Championship and fourth in the 1966 Masters.

In 1970, he missed a twenty-eight-inch putt that would have given him the title at Saint Andrews. He lost to Nicklaus in a playoff. When asked if he still thinks about that putt, he said, "not more than every four or five minutes." In truth, he does not dwell on near misses; he prefers to count his blessings.

At age sixty he underwent surgery for "torticollis" an involuntary twitching of the neck. He spent ten days in a coma. "I am alive," he said. "I have dined with four US Presidents, kings from several foreign lands, and a host of Hollywood legends like Frank Sinatra, Jack Benny, and Sammy Davis Jr."

His biggest enjoyment came when he was playing a tournament and would take time to kid with the crowd and flash his almost ever-present smile. "Smiles make people feel good. I felt if I could make someone feel good, then I did some thing worthwhile."

In his nineteen years on the tour, he almost doubled his twenty championships. He finished second twenty-one times, third eighteen times.

Today Sanders is seventy-one years old. Although he is no longer on the circuit, he has made a business of organizing and playing in corporate golf outings, putting on clinics, presenting trophies, and telling his story.

Sanders lives in an 8,200 square-foot home on 2.3 acres, five miles from downtown Houston. He has one son, Brad, age fourteen.

"If I had it to do over again what would I change?

"I never would smoke, I would not party as much and I would make that twentieth-inch putt to win the British Open."

GEORGE MATHEWS
GWTW

George William Mathews Jr., one of the greatest and most successful Yellow Jackets of them all, wanted to attend the University of Georgia, not Georgia Tech.

When he was scoring touchdowns left and right for Columbus High School (1941–43), he was hailed by the Columbus media as "Another Frank Sinkwich." Sinkwich was Georgia's first Heisman Trophy winner, a unanimous All-America pick, and the man who, along with All-American Charley Trippi, drove the Bulldogs to the 1943 Rose Bowl and a victory over UCLA.

"Sinkwich and Trippi were my heroes," Mathews says, "but my dad made it clear that if I wanted his support, I would play for Tech, not Georgia." And boy, did Mathews play for Tech—as a freshman, sophomore, junior and senior. The 5'11", 155-pound wingback was a two-time All-Southeastern Conference choice and an honorable mention All-America. He was selected on the late, legendary Coach Bobby Dodd's all-time Tech team.

"Mathews could do it all and he did, " Dodd said. "He was a slashing runner, a brilliant pass defender, a great receiver, the best running passer I ever saw, and the smartest player on the field of any player I ever coached."

As a freshman in Tech's first victory ever in Georgia's Sanford Stadium (1944), Mathews led the 44-0 rout scoring three touchdowns, throwing a leaping pass for another and catching a dozen passes himself.

Wrote the immortal *Atlanta Constitution* Editor Ralph McGill, "Paul Revere's ride was dull as dishwater compared to the mad gallops of Mathews, who proved that fact was stranger than fiction."

2004

What longtime Tech fans most remember about Mathews is how he turned defeat into victory in the 1946 Navy game. Navy was leading, 20-14, and ready to score again with the ball on Tech's five-yard line and only three minutes left to play. Mathews caught a Navy fumble in midair, never broke stride and raced ninety-five yards for a Tech touchdown. Tech scored again and won the game, 28-20.

"When Mathews latched on to the ball," wrote Bill Tucker of the old United Press, "he was GWTW (Gone With The Wind). Nobody clocked him on his run because watches stopped along with 33,000 hearts in Grant Field."

The late, legendary Georgia coach Wally Butts said, "I'm not dumb. I knew Mathews was going to be a great one. When he was at Columbus High School, I spent most of my summers in Columbus trying to recruit him. He was good enough to play for any team in America."

On Coach Butts' recommendation, Mathews played and started for the College All-Stars his senior season at Tech and so impressed the New York Giants that they immediately offered a pro contract of $8,000, no small sum in the 1940s. Mathews declined the offer and the rest, as they say, is history.

After attending Harvard Graduate School, he joined the Bluebird Bus Company in Fort Valley and turned it into the largest maker of school buses in the world. He developed the charbroil grill. He took Columbus Iron Works and turned it into Columbus Foundries and then into Intermet, which did worldwide business.

You would think a guy whose companies were enormously successful and provided jobs for thousands and who had been a football hero at his alma mater might be a little bit stuck on himself. Not George Mathews.

When I visited his spacious office at Overlook in Vinings, I expected to see plaques and photos of Mathews adorning the walls. Instead, I saw photos of Bobby Dodd, W. A. Alexander, John Heisman, Tech's legendary coaches; Homer Rice, the Athletics Director who resurrected Tech's athletics program and CEOs and presidents of Intermet and it subsidiaries.

Mathews is retired. He maintains homes in Atlanta on the Chattahoochee River (Townsend Place), Big Canoe, and Sea Island. He has been married to the former Jan Kerr of Atlanta for forty-three years. They have two children, Kathleen Holstein and George III.

I wondered how many sixteen-year-olds would have gone to Tech to play football in 1944 when the team was stocked with seasoned personnel in the Navy's V12 and V-5 programs. Then I remembered what *Atlanta Journal* columnist, Morgan Blake, wrote: "Mathews can dish it out and take it. He is never so happy as he is when he is in the thick of battle. Although he is a kid on the team, he is an inspiration to the veterans."

Mathews has given more than his athletic talent to Tech. Among other things, he erected the George W. Mathews Heritage Center, which tells the story of Tech's sports history. It is open to Tech fans, alumni, and friends alike. The center is located on campus in the J. C. Shaw Sports Complex

ARTHUR ARNOLD DECARLO
Mr. Nice Guy

Meet "Mr. Nice Guy"—Arthur Arnold DeCarlo.

Never met a man he didn't like. Rarely saw him without a smile on his face. Extends a warm greeting and firm handshake to everyone he meets. Never been known to be unhappy.

At age seventy-three, if he had his life to live over again he would not change a thing. He would play college football for the University of Georgia and professional football for the old Baltimore Colts. He is still in love with the girl he met on a blind date forty-eight years ago and married three months later—Mary Kerr DeCarlo. The happiest time of his life is when he is playing golf with his wife.

If the Georgia football teams of 1950–52 had held popularity contests DeCarlo would have won by a landslide. If Bulldogs and Colts opponents had hit lists, DeCarlo would have been No. 1—no contest. He drove the opposition crazy by snapping the ball from center on one play and then catching a touchdown pass from his offensive end position on the next play. He backed up the line with authority on one series and then confounded the opposition by showing up as a sideback or safety. Wherever the action was DeCarlo was in it.

DeCarlo came out of Youngstown—a 1940s and 1950s hotbed on Bulldog talent. You can look it up, All-Americans Fireball Frankie Sinkwich and George Poschner, All-Southeastern Conference Al Bodine and All-SEC honorable mention Anthony Joseph "Zippy" Morocco, one of the most deceptive runners of them all.

It was Bodine who recommended DeCarlo to Georgia, but Coach Wally Butts was skeptical about offering him, at 6'3" and a mere 167 pounds, a scholarship. But Dick Barrett, DeCarlo's high school coach at Youngstown, told Butts, "Don't worry a minute about Art DeCarlo, his tremendous competitive spirit will more than make up for any weight shortage. He carries thirty pounds of character."

In his first four games at Georgia, he recovered eight fumbles, not bad for a sophomore who wasn't expected to play until his junior season. Four times he was picked on the Associated Press SEC "Team of The Week." By the time he was a senior, coach, Butts called him "one of the finest competitors ever to play for the Red and Black."

Said former Bulldogs backfield coach Bill Hartman, "In fifty years, I never saw a player with a better attitude than DeCarlo. Wherever we played him, he loved it. He had tremendous agility and quickness. Talk about versatility, he played everywhere. To my knowledge, he never criticized any player or any coach. He had tremendous team loyalty."

In his senior season he had grown to 195 pounds. He didn't lose a step from the extra weight. He caught eighteen passes, three for touchdowns, and continued to menace the opposition from his linebacking post.

He was twice named to the "All-SEC" team, twice received honorable mention on the All-American team and was selected to play in every post-season All-Star Classic, the Senior Bowl, the Blue-Gray game, and the coveted College All-Star game against the NFL champion Detroit Lions. He played in back-to-back NFL championship games, including the 1958 classic, the first sudden death overtime game in which the Colts whipped the New York Giants.

In 1966, DeCarlo received the post-graduate Achievement Award from the University of Georgia Chapter of the National Football Foundation Hall of Fame, given to former Bulldog athletes who have distinguished themselves in their chosen profession.

DeCarlo had six different careers, not all at the same time, and distinguished himself in all of them. He operated a fast food restaurant, worked for the National Security Agency, was National Sales Manager for a copying company, built houses, owned four putt-putt golf courses, and played seven pro seasons, five with the Colts and one each with the Steelers and Redskins. When he opened his fast food restaurant in Baltimore, he was so well liked by his former Colts teammates that almost all of them showed up for his grand opening.

Today, DeCarlo is completely retired and lives with his wife in a four-bedroom ranch house that he built in Ellicott, Maryland, a suburb of Baltimore. He maintains his playing weight by walking around his neighborhood fifteen minutes a day and around an eighteen-hole golf course two-three times a week.

He attends an occasional Ravens (nee, Colts) game and less frequently a Colts game in Indianapolis. But most of his leisure time is spent with his wife Mary and their five children, Art Jr. (forty-six), Tommy (forty-two), Linda (forty-two), Jimmy (forty) and Donna (thirty-eight).

WILLIAM DAVID (BILL) YOUNG
Gridiron Lessons Pay Off

If you think William David (Bill) Young succeeded in business by marrying the boss's daughter, think again. Young was a successful businessman in his own right long before he joined General Wholesale Co., one of Georgia's largest distributors of beer, liquor, and wine.

When Young's father-in-law, Earl Howard, died suddenly in 1965 at age sixty, Young vaulted from his insurance business into the liquor business without missing a beat. And he quickly began to prove that if you can succeed in one profession, you can succeed in another.

At the time Young took command, General Wholesale was operating quite profitably, profitable enough that Young could have spent his afternoons on the golf course. But that's not Young's style—not now, not then, not ever.

Check it out with Sam Hensley, Young's former teammate at Marietta High School fifty years ago and now a successful Cobb County builder. Or ask Joe O'Malley, co-captain of the football team when Young was wreaking havoc with opposing lineman as a tackle for the University of Georgia in the early 1950s.

Rest on his father-in-law's laurels? Never. As president, Young not only took General Wholesale to the next level, he took it to the next ten levels. Today, the business does well over $100 million in annual sales.

"I'm not surprised at what he accomplished. He may have been the most dependable player we had," says Hensley. "Whether it was making a key tackle

2004

when our backs were to the wall or opening a hole with a devastating block on a crucial, offensive play, you could always count on him. Whatever the assignment, Young was going to get the job done."

Says O'Malley, who played with Young at UGA and later became one of his sales supervisors at General Wholesale. "The same Bill Young I knew on the football field was the same Bill Young I knew at General Wholesale.

"Let me explain," the now-retired O'Malley adds. "As a tackle at Georgia, Young weighed between 185 and 190 pounds. He lined up against linemen 240 pounds or more. But he put so much effort into his execution that nine times out of ten he beat his man. He puts in the same kind of effort at General Wholesale."

And Young put in the same kind of effort as an insurance salesman—his first career after graduating from UGA and serving two years as an officer in the U.S. Air Force.

As a rookie insurance agent with Adair Realty and Leide Associates, he was one of Atlanta's leading general insurance (property and casualty, life and health) producers, and he held that distinction for ten years before he was called into the breech at General Wholesale in 1965.

Since 1965, here is what has happened at General Wholesale: Sales have grown 1000% and employee numbers have risen from 55 to over 300. Where warehousing once required only one building, it now requires three with 80,000 square feet of space. The business is growing so fast that Young is looking for another building with 120,000 square feet of space.

Young credits his drive to what he learned from his mother, now age ninety-seven and living in a nursing home, and from the late James Wallace ("Wally") Butts, Young's football coach at UGA.

Young's father died when he was three years old. His mother went to work at the old Bell Bomber plant in Marietta, now Lockheed, where she aided the World War II effort by re-designing and assembling aircraft tools.

"Mom taught me that if you work hard enough, you can realize your dreams. Her dream was to raise, feed, and clothe her family and to care for my adopted grandparents. She also taught me that if a task should be done, it should be done today."

"Now, about playing football at Georgia for Coach Butts. It was so grueling—two-on-one drills—and sometimes three-on-one—that many times I thought about quitting. But quitting was something I knew I never could do.

"Coach Butts said that the knocks in life were going to be a lot harder than the knocks on the football field, and that if you quit here you would quit in the business world. I never have forgotten what he said to me. He also taught me that it was better to act than to react."

Although he attends few games today, he and his lovely wife Jane are consummate TV watchers when the Bulldogs are on the tube.

The greatest thing that happened to me at UGA was meeting my wife, whom I married as soon as I graduated," he says. "We've had forty-five wonderful years together."

Says Jane of her husband, "Bill has to be the easiest person in the world to live with. When he walks in the door after work, I never can tell whether he had one of the best working days in his life or one of the worst. He is always the same—smiling, warm, comforting, and so understanding when I've had a bad day. No matter what is going on at business, it seems that whenever there is a home problem, Bill is there for me and the children."

Young grew up in a modest home in Cobb County. Today, he and Jane live in a Tara-like, six-bedroom home on Tuxedo Road. The beautiful well-coiffured grounds cover 3 acres. They are on the Greyline Tour route, just around the corner from the Governor's Mansion.

The Young children—there are three sons—no longer live at home. They all are married and have children of their own. But they are much involved in what goes on at General Wholesale.

Bill, Jr., age forty-three, heads the whiskey and wine division; Howard, forty, heads the beer division; and Steve, thirty-seven, directs operations at the offices in Spartanburg SC and Augusta GA. All are vice presidents.

So now that he's sixty-seven years old, why doesn't he retire and let the children run the business?

"For the most part," he says, "the boys run the business today. But I don't think Jane ever would let me retire completely. It's not because she's the boss (Jane is chairman of the board) but because she knows I love to be involved, and I love to have a hand in helping our business grow. I will be at some desk, I hope, for many years to come."

Although he does not work the twelve hours daily he once did, he continues to arrive at his office at 1271 Tacoma Drive, just east of Marietta Boulevard, at 7:30 A.M. He's on the go by 5:30 A.M., riding his bicycle for thirty minutes, followed by another thirty minutes of weight-lifting and calisthenics.

Maybe it is due to good genes or the exercise and a healthy diet that keeps Young looking young. But except for his graying hair, of which he has a full head, he looks more like the UGA football player he was in the 1950s than someone at retirement age. At 6'3", his weight is 190 pounds, scarcely 5 pounds more than his playing weight forty-five years ago.

Has success spoiled the kid who grew up two steps from poverty? In no way. He is the same modest, unassuming star I knew as a Georgia Bulldog. Six years ago, Young received the Terry Business School Alumni Award from his alma mater for outstanding contributions and achievements in the field of commerce.

Aside from business and weekend golf, Young has served the Georgia and Atlanta chambers of commerce, and has been a chairman and a member of the board of directors of the Georgia Beer Wholesalers Association and a member of the Rotary Club of Atlanta. He also is an elder of the Peachtree Presbyterian Church.

"We all need to make a contribution to humankind," he says. "If we take from society, it is only right we give something back."

EPILOGUE

The following LEGENDS have passed away since their stories were written:

PETE BROWN

GENERAL RAY DAVIS, USMC (Ret.)

JAMES H. (Bill) FINCH, COLONEL, USMCR (Ret.)

JOHNNY GRIFFITH

BEN GROSS

CHARLES HARRIS, CAPT., USMCR (Ret.)

BUCK MARTIN

BILL PASCHAL

GEORGE R. PENDLEY

BUBBA RATCLIFFE

JOHN ROUSAKIS

BILLY CHENEY SPEED

KIM KING

RAY BARNES

LARRY SHIPPEY

BEN RAINEY

PHIL ERICKSON